AF352448

BEAUTY IN THE CITY

BEAUTY IN THE CITY

THE ASHCAN SCHOOL

ROBERT A. SLAYTON

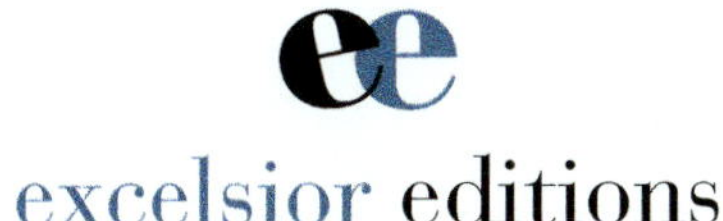

excelsior editions

Cover art: *Six O'clock, Winter,* by John Sloan, 1912, oil on canvas, 26^1/$_8$ × 32 in.,
acquired 1922, copyright Delaware Art Museum/Artists Rights Society, NY,
The Phillips Collection, Washington, DC. Used by permission.

Published by
State University of New York Press, Albany

© 2017 State University of New York

All rights reserved

Printed in the United States of America

No part of this book may be used or reproduced in any manner whatsoever
without written permission. No part of this book may be stored in a retrieval system
or transmitted in any form or by any means including electronic, electrostatic,
magnetic tape, mechanical, photocopying, recording, or otherwise
without the prior permission in writing of the publisher.

Excelsior Editions is an imprint of State University of New York Press
For information, contact
State University of New York Press, Albany, NY
www.sunypress.edu

Production, Laurie D. Searl
Marketing, Fran Keneston

Library of Congress Cataloging-in-Publication Data

Names: Slayton, Robert A., author.
Title: Beauty in the city : the Ashcan school / Robert A. Slayton.
Description: Albany : State University of New York Press, 2017. | Series:
    Excelsior editions | Includes bibliographical references and index.
Identifiers: LCCN 2016045129 (print) | LCCN 2016047726 (ebook) | ISBN
    9781438466415 (hardcover : alk. paper) | ISBN 9781438466439 (ebook)
Subjects: LCSH: Ashcan school of art. | Art and society—United States—
    History—19th century. | Art and society—United States—History—20th
    century. | City and town life—United States—History—19th century. |
    City and town life—United States—History—20th century.
Classification: LCC N6512.5.E4 S59 2017 (print) | LCC N6512.5.E4 (ebook) |
    DDC 701/.03—dc23
LC record available at https://lccn.loc.gov/2016045129

10   9   8   7   6   5   4   3   2   1

To the people of New York City
For the generations past, those at present,
and iterations yet to come

Contents

ILLUSTRATIONS

Acknowledgments

Daniele Struppa gave me more than gracious and emphatic support of this project, both of which he supplied in abundance. Because of his backing, despite the enormous scope of this project with its dozens of images, I was never worried about money. That's the most incredible gift; not just for me, but to any scholar. It was, and is, truly a remarkable thing. More than a thank-you, he has my immense gratitude and respect.

Wilkinson College and Dean Patrick Fuery also provided funding in the form of a Scholarly Grant. The Henry Salvatori Professorship at Chapman University enabled me to travel to show-ings of Ashcan art, which in turn allowed me to realize the greater significance of what these artists had achieved. Jennifer Keene, chair of the History Department, also provided crucial assistance.

Two colleagues made a world of difference in this project. Steve Ross read the entire manu-script and stepped in at a critical moment to reshape and save this project. Dominic Pacyga also endured every page and was a source of boundless faith throughout. My gratitude to these two friends is deep and vast, beyond mere words.

I also benefited from comments by Rebecca Zurier, James Tottis, and Richard Meyer. Amanda Lanne-Camilli at State University of New York Press was a font of wisdom and, even more, of patience. Members of the Los Angeles Social History Study Group read chapters and provided insights. My thanks go to: Hal Barron, Nancy Fitch, Frank Stricker, and Leila Zenderland. Wendy Salmond was a godsend, helping me decipher the art world. Melissa Goldstein at Bridgeman Images became the best partner anyone could have when it came to obtaining permissions and pictures. Charlotte Mitchell at Sotheby's obtained rights to a crucial artwork in private hands. Jonathan Spiro came through graciously with an important image. Special thanks go to Mrs. Barbara Palmer and Beverly Balger Sutley at the Palmer Museum of Art for their gracious support.

It was no easy task to manage a project of this size. My appreciation knows no bounds when it comes to Stacy Laird, administrator extraordinaire. This volume required over a hundred permissions and payments at an endless and changing list of institutions. It takes someone with remarkable abilities to handle a project like that, to keep track of it all and maintain order. Someone far, far better than me. Stacy Laird did it perfectly, never missing a beat, with grace and humor to boot. If this volume makes sense, if I am still (relatively) sane, you and I can thank Stacy Laird for that gift. Maci Reed also assisted with this formidable task. At Chapman University's Leatherby Libraries I thank, above all, Rand Boyd, archivist and friend. He never faltered, regardless of the magnitude or obscurity of the queries I sent his way. Kevin Ross and Carolyn Radcliff provided funding for crucial documents. Maria Yanez in the ILL Office did yeoman's work finding sources.

Two final citations are deeply personal. In the middle of this project I contracted transverse myelitis, a rare neurological disease, which paralyzed my left side. For a year I was at home performing administrative duties, learning about my new body, and, even more, my new life. Each and every week during that long sojourn, fellow Chapman historian Leland Estes picked up the books I had marked for Xeroxing and brought back the previous week's work; dropped off class papers for me to comment on, so I could remain active; and kept me up to date on news and gossip. I thanked him profusely, and all he ever replied was, "Bob, you'd do the same for me." He defines two words: friend and mensch.

And always there was Rita. Who just makes life worthwhile, as she has done for me for decades. I am still madly in love with her.

CHAPTER ONE

And Like That . . . They're Gone

The Ashcan artists drew a part of the city not previously the subject of great art, capturing the laundry lines, the crowded quarters, the smokestacks, and yes, the ashcans of the urban working class.

Befitting an analysis of such iconoclastic work, this study also takes a different approach. This is not a work of art history; there will be no attempt to analyze the aesthetics of the Ashcan painters, the brushstrokes they employed to tell their stories. Rather, this is explicitly a work of history—not art history—and should be understood within that discipline.

Instead, the vantage point will be that of a social historian; it is content that concerns us here. What did the Ashcan artists contribute to our understanding of the city during its boom era in American history? And what do these answers tell us about the development of American society when it was being transformed by the great forces of urbanization and industrialization? The answers to these powerful questions lie in the study of artists of ashcans.

Ashcan artists recognized that the city was the most exciting place to be in America at the start of a new century; their art has since lasted because that vision remains true amid the current vibrancy of places like New York City. By depicting the immense power and the allure of the metropolis, these artists captured an eternal truth. They created paintings of glorious yet gritty moments in time, construction sites and ferry boats, tenement apartments and newsboys and working women and men. They also bestowed on these urban players a respect that other artists had overlooked.

Another unique aspect of the Ashcan painters was their class perspective. Conventional artists at the time saw either the genteel upper bourgeois or the sad, despairing, downtrodden. The Ashcan school rejected both these impressions and instead focused on the broad middle, painting the working-class people that made up most of the city's population.

Ashcan artists understood that while city life was tough, it was also quite livable. You could find romance and a lover, join a neighborhood community, play games on the street, or watch illegal boxing matches. No artistic genre ever understood these features of city life with the same sensitivity and insight, one of the key points that made the Ashcan school unique.

By so doing, the Ashcan painters helped the rest of America understand these new places, these dense, novel, and frightening cities. This was at the height, the golden age, of the great American city and of the Progressive Era in art and literature and reform politics. Ashcan artists' unique renderings of this epic moment became a kind of guidebook for Americans in so many other kinds of locales, teaching them that decent people lived decent lives, even in Gotham. By instilling new, gritty subject matter with beauty, these painters made the urban scene part of the American experience.

The Ashcan artists painted the city as no school of art had ever done before. They understood the excitement of the metropolis and respected the working people who lived there, endowing these people with agency, the power to control the terms of their existence. Not surprisingly, art like this began in protest against the established order.

If you were a part of the American art scene as the clock struck in the new century on January 1, 1900, you knew exactly what the establishment was, and who presided over it. Bennard Perlman, who wrote several books on the art movements of this new era, summed up the status quo of that time: "Throughout the 19th and early 20th century the National Academy of Design dictated the course of American art, promoting the restrictive style that favored classical subjects and techniques." "Dictate" is a strong and tyrannical word, yet it seems chillingly accurate: "The annual juried exhibitions sponsored by the Academy were the artists' primary entrée to patrons and subsequent sales. Acceptance to the Academy's shows offered painters credibility and marketability; rejection could signal the opposite." This was immense power, the ability to make or starve a painter. Yet it was all in service to faded themes; Perlman reported, "Original subject matter or technique often guaranteed a painter that rejection."[1]

Not that everyone approved of this structure. Theodore Dreiser, in his critique of the art world, The "Genius," observed of the school his protagonist attended, "The class instructors must be of considerable significance in the American art world . . . or they were N.A.s, and that meant National Academicians. He little knew with what contempt this honor was received in some quarters, or he would not have attached so much significance to it."[2]

This rigid, outdated approach created problems, blocking new schools, new works. John Baur, in his study of modern American art, pointed out: "Aside from his art itself, the knottiest problem for the American modernist in the early years of the century was where to exhibit. The annual exhibitions of the National Academy of Design were still the principal medium; in how many biographies one reads sentences like Lloyd Goodrich's concerning Weber: 'He submitted work to a National Academy exhibition and was of course rejected, and never tried again.'" Many artists considered the Academy "the repository of an outworn and deadening system . . . an oversized, lumbering relic of the aesthetic age of dinosaurs, spiritually extinct but inexplicably still moving." John Sloan described it as "a place where you checked your brain at the door."[3]

Rebellion was inevitable. It began in 1906, when at their winter exhibition the Academy hung Sloan's submissions high above eye level, making them difficult to see and sure to be ignored. Robert Henri, the philosopher and leader of the Ashcan school, managed to include three of his own works, but William Glackens, George Luks, and Everett Shinn—other Ashcan artists—were completely excluded.[4]

Tempers flared the following year. Henri himself had been appointed to the jury for the 1907 show, but the honor was shallow. His recommendations were largely ignored: Sloan's submission went up high once again, and others were rejected entirely. Even more demeaning, Henri faced personal rejection; he had submitted three paintings, and on the first balloting, two of these received a rating of 1 (unanimous approval), the other only a 2 (approval by a majority required). On a second vote, one of the works in the first category was downgraded to a 2.[5]

Henri walked out, pulled his paintings, and contacted the press. Long known as a good source for a quote, Henri had reporters' ears. In quick time, the story, to use a modern term, went viral. The American Art News revealed, "Robert Henri's withdrawal . . . has caused a stir in art circles. At a meeting of the jury, of which Mr. Henri was a member, some spirited remarks were made by him . . . that . . . a majority of the judges were not inclined to yield to any innovations in art." The final denouement was a feature article in *Harper's Weekly*, which bemoaned the "penalization of originality."

Instead, it extolled the "school of Robert Henri," whose "painters convince us of their democratic outlook. They seek what is significant, what is real."[6]

The maître gathered his partners to revolt against the Art Establishment. "After dinner I went to a meeting at Henri's to talk over a possible exhibition of the 'crowd's' work next year," John Sloan wrote in his diary on April 4, 1907, "The spirit to push the thing through seems strong." Besides Henri and Sloan, other charter members included George Luks, Arthur Davies, William Glackens, and Ernest Lawson. Decades later, Everett Shinn, one of the first to join them, recalled, "Not one of us had a program . . . sure, we were against the monocle pictures at the Academy, but that was all."[7]

So they wanted to put on a show; now they had to find a hall. William Macbeth provided the venue. The entrepreneur landed in America in 1871, emigrating from his native Ireland; seeking employment, he obtained a position with the print sellers Frederick Keppel and Co., and within a decade he was a full partner.[8]

In 1892 he branched out on his own, opening a gallery at 237 Fifth Avenue, near Twenty-Seventh Street, not far from the Flatiron Building, by 1908 relocating to Fortieth Street and Fifth Avenue. What made this venture unique was that, bucking prevailing tastes for European art, Macbeth opened the first gallery in the city dedicated to American works. He told the marketplace, "The work of American artists has never received the full share of appreciation that it deserves and the time has come when an effort should be made to gain for it the favor of those who have hitherto purchased foreign pictures exclusively."[9]

Macbeth was an innovator in other ways as well, as he set out with passion to make his experiment work. New shows appeared regularly, often within a few weeks of each other, guaranteeing a steady stream of press notices. To reach out to buyers, he created his own periodical, *Art Notes*, part house organ and part commentary on the art world, and edited it personally until his death in 1917. As a result, according to one scholar, Macbeth soon "stood at the center of . . . contemporary American painting. He was at this time the most active, knowledgeable, and powerful dealer in American art.[10]

For the Ashcan artists, introductions were easy; Macbeth already knew most of the group. In 1902 he had hosted Henri's first one-man show in Gotham; the two had enjoyed a correspondence as early as 1899. The gallery owner soon worked with the others as well.

A deal was struck. Various accounts list Henri as the go-between, but all agree on the arrangements. Sloan visited Macbeth, who requested a guarantee of $500, later reduced to $400 (Sloan felt him, "a decent man if ever was one"), and paid in sums of $50 apiece by eight artists on May 2.[11]

Details began to solidify. Sloan organized specifics, handled funds, worked on the catalog, read proofs, and prepared mailing lists. One tricky decision involved whom to include. Of course, there were the Ashcan stalwarts—Robert Henri, John Sloan, George Luks, Everett Shinn, William Glackens. Boosting their numbers were Boston artist Maurice Prendergast, impressionist Ernest Lawson, and Arthur Davies. The group quickly dubbed itself "The Eight Independent Artists." Critics and later scholars shortened this to "The Eight" and immortalized them for this pioneering showcase; they would never exhibit together again. While the last three were not Ashcan artists by any stretch, others who worked in this style were turned down. According to one account, "Davies was the strangest member of the group in that his painting, in their subject and style, suggest no affinity whatsoever" with the others. Lawson, on the other hand, "seems to have been invited . . . simply because everyone liked him and accepted that he was a very gifted painter." Sloan later debated whether they should have dropped Shinn and instead added Jerome Myers (who was hurt by his exclusion). George Wesley Bellows, whom everyone recognized as a prodigy, was deemed to be too young. Each artist had twenty-five running feet of wall space, could choose which paintings to display and hang them himself. By December 19, 1907, a *New York Herald* article commented that "these painters believe they can reveal an art more forceful and individual" than any seen in New York.[12]

Opening day drew near. Publicity was assured; most of the artists had launched their careers by doing illustrations for the print media and so had plenty of contacts in the newspaper and magazine world. Two days prior to the event, the *Evening Post* crowed, "The principal art event of next week will be the opening . . . at the Macbeth galleries." Twenty-five hundred announcements were dropped in the mail, and papers started running announcements as early as two weeks before opening day. "The pictures left for Macbeth's in the morning," Sloan noted in his diary on February 1, 1908. "Now the time that we have all waited and worked for months past is here."[13]

February 3, 1908, was a cold New York day (*fig. 1.1*). Snow had fallen a week prior, and ice and slush lingered on the city's streets. The *Tribune's* weather page that morning recorded the previous day's high as twenty-five degrees, the trough at fifteen.[14]

No matter; as long as Macbeth's stayed open—from 9 am to 6 pm—the gallery would be packed. His upper space had two rooms, the paintings to be divided evenly between them. Visitors braved a small, crowded elevator to get there. Upon exiting, they moved to their right, exploring the works of Shinn, Lawson, Sloan, and Prendergast, then moved through an archway to view those by Luks, Henri, Glackens, and Davies. Every hour, three hundred people crammed into the small gallery, and Henri, who had feared a low turnout, gleefully told the press, "The show . . . is creating a sensation. It was packed like an Academy reception." Of course, not everybody approved; Macbeth's nephew claimed his uncle "received threatening letters, phone calls and visits, mostly to the effect that, 'if this is the kind of art you are going to sponsor, cross us off as clients.'"[15]

All the same, sales were solid, although only to a narrow group of customers. Three buyers purchased the seven paintings sold for $4,000, four of which went to Gertrude Vanderbilt Whitney. Macbeth estimated that if the effects of the Panic of 1907 had not lingered, it would have gone even better. Henri and Davies each sold two paintings, Shinn, Luks, and Lawson one apiece. Sloan recorded, "We've made a success. . . . Macbeth is 'pleased as Punch.'"[16]

Local press covered the exhibit, within limits. The *American* opened with: "Never at an art exhibition in this city has there been such an attendance as gathered to view the pictures shown by 'the eight.' . . . Only with the greatest of difficulty, by stretching of necks, crowding and other strenuous methods, were spectators enabled to see the paintings." The *Sun* spoke of "a group of eight painters who have been expressing their ideas of life as they see it in quite their own manner." Best of all, Charles De Kay, writing in the *Evening Post*, admonished readers to "join the throng that fills the elevator to the Macbethan sky parlors, and if you don't remain to pray, you will surely learn not to curse." Clearly not everyone approved of paintings of ashcans—or of art that was revolutionary.[17]

This is not to imply that the Eight changed the art world overnight or singlehandedly. Most of the press responded either by ignoring or condemning this new wave. Though the *Sun* had announced the show as early as the previous May, no mention was made on the day after, nor was there any coverage of the opening. The paper did find space, however, for such terribly important stories as "Y.W.C.A. Girl's Dress Afire," and how Newark's automobile club had selected a color scheme for their annual show.[18]

Even more telling was what failed to appear in the arts sections of various New York papers. In fact, there was frequently no mention of the show at the Macbeth whatsoever, although the *Tribune* did find space to run a more traditional piece entitled "Berthe Morisot: A Note on a Charming Figure in French Impressionism." An even better indication of how conservative

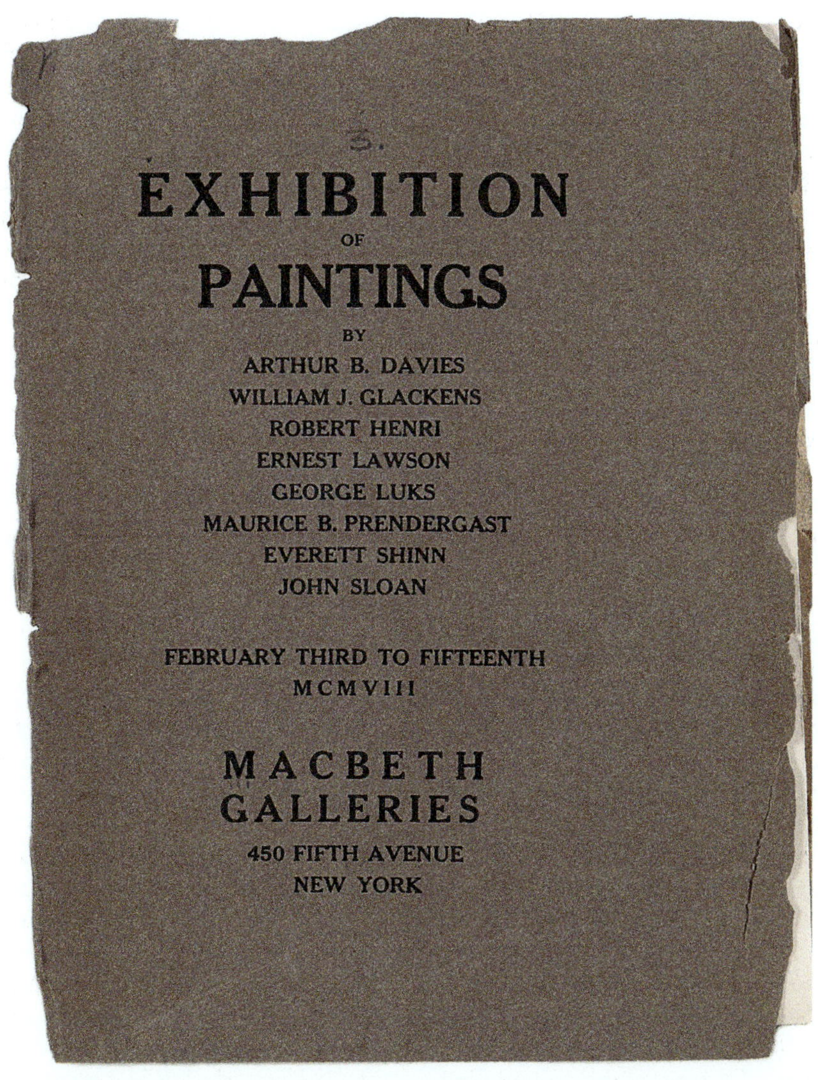

1.1 Front page of the exhibition catalog, *Exhibition of Paintings by Arthur B. Davies, William J. Glackens, Robert Henri, Ernest Lawson, George Luks, Maurice B. Prendergast, Everett Shinn, John Sloan,* February 3–15, 1908. Metropolitan Museum of Art, New York. Thomas J. Watson Library (118 R19). Image © The Metropolitan Museum of Art. Image source: Art Resource, New York.

the art world remained was the entire front cover of the magazine section in the *New York American,* which boldly proclaimed, "The Latest Fad in Portraiture," the most traditional of genres.[19]

Critics' responses eventually ran the gamut. The most important art critic in America at the time was James Huneker. Born in Philadelphia in 1857 to a cultured family—his father was an organist and composer—James took to the arts early in life and by 1875 was reviewing concerts for newspapers in the City of Brotherly Love. In December 1906, he moved north to become the art critic for the *New York Sun*, producing three to four articles a week.[20]

Unlike many critics of high repute, Huneker sought out young and unknown painters. He discovered Jerome Myers and gave John Sloan the painter's first positive review. Sloan felt that Huneker was "different from the average critic," folks "who usually think they are sent by God to shield mankind from what they don't care for themselves."[21]

Huneker began his review of the Ashcan exhibit with an intimate, positive tone: "At the exhibition of the Eight Painters at the Macbeth Galleries Henri's lifelike 'Laughing Child' faces you as you enter. It is superb paint. . . . Power is there." As for Glackens: "Here is mastery." Sloan "can see to the core of ugliness. His street scenes are full of rude animation. He is in a way a philosopher. . . . In the matter of pigment he grows every year." "These young men," the critic concluded, "have the courage to be natural with more or less success."[22]

Other journals sided with Huneker. In an unsigned article in the April 1908 issue of *Current Literature*, the author claimed that the Eight were "united in their impulse to escape mere 'prettiness' in art, and to express themselves in strong, individual, whole-hearted fashion"; indeed, all were "dominantly concerned with the portrayal of American life here and now." Sloan displayed "a phase of sordid existence painted with that sort of fine art which Rembrandt knew long years ago."[23]

Huncker's greatest competitor was Royal Cortissoz, an extreme conservative who had been the *New York Tribune*'s art critic since 1891.[24]

It was unlikely that Cortissoz would share Huneker's perspective. Two days after the opening, he described the works as "empty mannerisms . . . it is precisely the element of nature, of truth accurately seen and sensitively painted, that is lacking from this show." In a critique two years later, he claimed of the new art, "There is nothing . . . very startling about it . . . it has served no obviously fruitful purpose." "If this is the best that the Independent Artists can do," he declared, "we are quite well enough off as we are."[25]

Cortissoz' criticism was soft mush compared to what came next. No one had ever painted work sites or working-class people before, and to art critics these were ugly subjects, canvases filled with filth. Charles De Kay, writing in *Town Topics*, exclaimed, "Vulgarity smites one in the face at this exhibition, and I defy you to find anyone in a healthy frame of mind who" wants such paintings in his home, who will not "get disgusted two days later. Is it fine art to exhibit our sores—Bah!!" The *New York Commercial Advertiser*, a business paper, felt it had just seen a show "where joyousness never enters . . . and where unhealthiness prevails to an alarming extent." A recent scholar, in describing the clash, summed up the view of the National Academicians: "They knew very well what art was; art was beauty, and what Henri's friends were painting was just ugliness." Two days after the show opened, John Sloan wrote in his diary, "It is regrettable that these art writers, armed with little knowledge (which is granted a dangerous thing) can command attention in the newspapers. I'd rather have the opinion of a newsboy."[26]

Nevertheless, something had happened in the art world, something big. Ira Glackens, William's son, wrote that the show did not just live up to expectations, it "far outdid them." Walter Pach felt "they gave a show in 1908 that aroused New York as no other work by Americans had ever done." As one later scholar put it, "When the Eight closed their famous show at Macbeth's . . . they thought they had made a revolution."[27]

In terms of both its positives and its negatives, the Ashcan school had become the hot topic in American art and had risen to the forefront of what was then *en vogue*. They had introduced something new: a native art form that dealt powerfully with an America that was emerging, and the urban landscape and the working people who inhabited it.

The future only looked brighter. Yet, it was not to be. The heyday of this approach to art would last a bare five years and then be swept away even more suddenly and totally than it had just blown in.

The single most important art exhibit in American art history opened at the Sixty-Ninth Regiment Armory at Lexington Avenue and Twenty-Fifth Street on February 17, 1913. Nothing has been the same in the art world since.[28]

In December 1911, a few American painters—ironically, realists, it would turn out—got together to discuss "the possibilities of organizing a society for the purpose of exhibiting the works of progressive and live painters, both American and foreign; favoring such work usually neglected by current shows and especially interesting and instructive to the public." Among their numbers was Jerome Myers, an Ashcan stalwart.

In one sense, they were pursuing one of the broad aims of Henri and Sloan, to challenge the art world as it existed just then. According to Walt Kuhn, one of their leaders, "Two things produced the Armory Show: a burning desire . . . to be informed of the slightly known activities abroad and the need of breaking down the stifling and smug condition of the local art affairs." The result, however, took a different direction, more powerful than many had envisioned—one writer called it "an act of cultural sabotage"—and wound up reducing the Ashcan school to a subordinate position in the catalog of American art.[29]

On the fourteenth of that month the group formally organized as the American Association of American Painters and Sculptors (AAPS). In quick form they invited others to join, including Luks, Glackens, and Bellows, as well as a number of Academicians. The goal was more to introduce new modes of art, not to denigrate other forms. In his memoir, Kuhn noted how "at this time most of the younger American artists, especially the progressive ones, had no place to show their wares. No dealer's gallery was open to them, the press . . . was apathetic."[30]

Soon, however, their goal took on a different cast. Arthur Davies, one of the non-Ashcan artists in the earlier Macbeth show, was now president of the Association. With Walter Kuhn, he journeyed to Europe in search of artists they could potentially invite. Instead, the two returned overwhelmed by the modernist movement in art, and they determined to use their exhibition to introduce America to the new wave, while still highlighting local works. Davies told Myers, "You will weep when you see what we've brought over." The artist of the Lower East Side explained in his memoir, "And when I did see the pictures for the first time, my mind was more troubled than my eyes, for Davies had unlocked the door to foreign art and thrown the key away. Our land of opportunity was thrown wide open to foreign art, unrestricted and triumphant; more than ever before, our great country had become a colony; more than ever before, we had become provincials." Glackens remarked, "I am afraid that the American section of this exhibition will seem very tame beside the foreign section."[31]

Opening night became a big event in the New York artistic calendar. At 8:00 pm on February 17, the doors opened for a formal, invitation-only reception. Soon the large room filled with animated talk, while the music of Bayne's Sixty-Ninth Regiment Band played in the background.[32]

The next morning the public spectacle began; for an admission of $1 for adults and 25¢ for children, anyone could walk in between the hours of 10:00 am and 10:00 pm. Ushers helped move the crowds along, and a temporary post office by the entrance handled Armory Show postcards. Walt Kuhn told a friend, "Every afternoon Lexington Avenue and the side streets are jammed with private automobiles, old-fashioned horse equipages, taxi cabs and what not." In his memoir he simply concluded, "everybody came."[33]

What drew them was the novelty of the first show to introduce modern art, rather than the works of domestic painters, to an American audience on a large scale. In particular, cubism became a sensation, and the celebrity piece of the show emerged as Marcel Duchamp's *Nude Descending a Staircase*; at times the crowd became so thick a waiting line developed just to see this one painting (*fig. 1.2*). Newspapers carried jokes about this art and offered prizes to anyone who could actually find anything that looked like a nude in the painting. Even the *American*

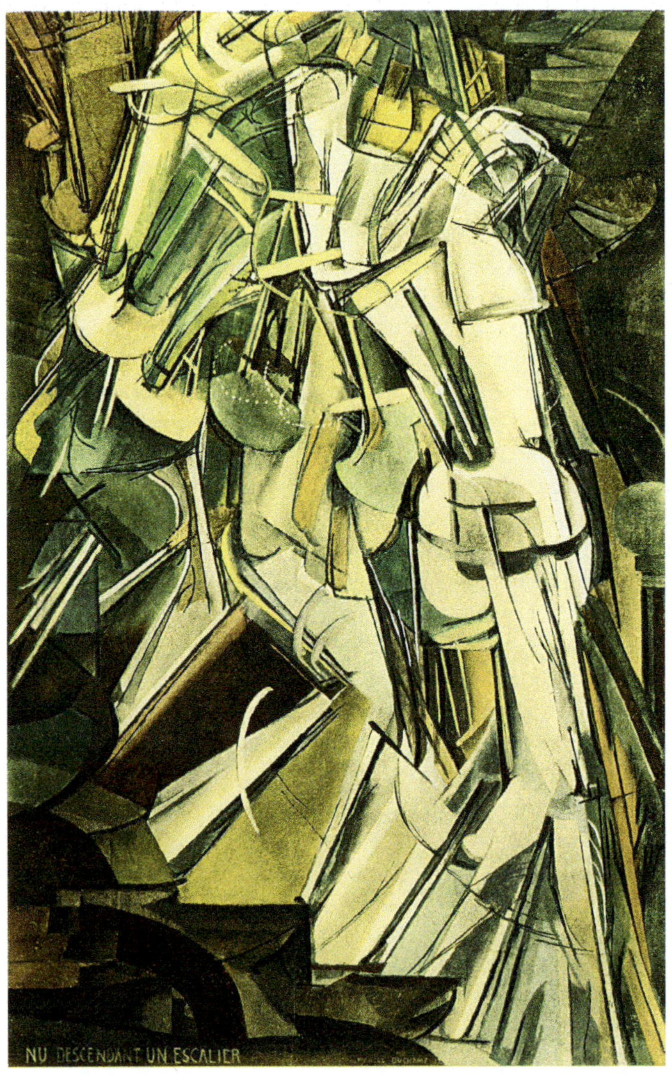

1.2 Marcel Duchamp (1887–1968), reproduction of *Nude Descending a Staircase*. Dated 1937. Collotype with hand additions, sheet: 13¼ × 7⅞ inches. Kay Sage Tanguy Bequest. (SC421.1974). The Museum of Modern Art, New York, New York. © 2016 Succession Marcel Duchamp/ADAGP, Paris/Artists Rights Society (ARS), New York. Digital image © The Museum of Modern Art/Licensed by SCALA/Art Resource, New York.

Art News offered $10 to anyone who could figure it out. When the show opened in the Windy City, a cartoonist for the *Chicago Evening Sun* rendered a satire entitled "The nude descending a staircase (Rush hour at the subway)."[34]

Modernism now became a national phenomenon, and scams both small and large followed. One of the most frequently asked question at the information desk was what was the most expensive picture at the show? Staffed by young artists, they would kindly escort the rich patrons to their own works and suggest a royal price that was, they claimed, a real bargain. Paris artists produced fakes for sale in New York, and an article in *The American Magazine of Art* later claimed "that a New York art student, impatient with his clay model, whacked it out of shape and exhibited it at a much talked of show."[35]

By any form of accounting the show broke records wide open. Estimates of attendance range from seventy-five thousand to a quarter million. Even more amazing, the art sold. Including the Chicago and Boston tours as well as the Lexington Avenue venue, 174 works were purchased, of which 51 were bought by Americans and 123 by foreigners. Dollar amounts totaled $44,148.75, which were broken down into $30,491.25 and $13,657.50, respectively, based on residency of buyer. One artist who made the first sale of his career was Edward Hopper. The Duchamp nude sold for $324 to Frederick C. Vorrey, an art dealer in San Francisco, and was later resold in 1927 to Walter Arnsberg. Recent research, including the discovery of the show's account books, "confirm," according to a *New York Times* report, "that American art was priced much higher than European art, but also show that . . . the majority of the sales were of European work." Much to the regret of the young hucksters, top financial return went to Cezanne's *Colline des pauvres*, sold to the Metropolitan Museum of Art for $6,700, the first work by that artist to become part of an American museum collection.[36]

While reactions to the show ran the gamut, most were of outrage. Given how novel this style of painting truly was, this came as no surprise. The *New York Sun* stood out as the leading defender among the dailies, declaring the show "sensational," that its creators had accomplished "something very like a miracle." Not so for the *New York Times*, which after identifying the dangers of these radical works asserted that the show would "disrupt, degrade, if not destroy, not only art but literature and society too." Royal Cortissoz rose to the bait, declaring of postimpressionism, "This is not a movement, it is unadulterated cheek," destined for "the rubbish heap." A New York group affiliated with the Academy put on an exhibition of fake European modernist paintings, then held it in the dining room of the Lighthouse for the Blind. When the show hit Chicago, one paper warned readers that the best way to prepare for a visit was to indulge in drugs ("smoke two pipefuls of 'hop' and sniff cocaine"). Even at the Art Institute, until Kuhn protested, teachers insisted on walking students through while denouncing the works on display. Maurice Prendergast, one of the Eight, felt that there was "too much Oh-my-God art here."[37]

The most famous commentator of the time was Teddy Roosevelt. Next to his cousin Franklin, the greatest showman in presidential history, he chose March 4, the day of Woodrow Wilson's inauguration, to attend. Escorted by Davies and Kuhn, he appeared "gracious, though noncommittal." In a follow-up article for *Outlook*, however, he was not nearly so polite. The second paragraph concluded with the observation that there were "thousands of people who will pay small sums to look at a faked mermaid; and now and then one of this kind with enough money will buy a Cubist picture, or a picture of a misshapen nude woman, repellent from every angle." He later declared, "In my bath-room is a really good Navajo rug, which . . . is a far more satisfactory and decorative picture."[38]

Roosevelt and the other critics were wrong about modernism and the Armory Show. Art historian Meyer Schapiro claimed that the exhibit "lifted people out of the narrowness of a complacent provincial taste and compelled them to judge American art by a world standard." Or as Walter Pach put it, "the lid was blown off of America's isolationism." A great deal changed, and in so many ways. While before American modernists found few galleries willing to accept their works, now the floodgates were opened. New magazines appeared to cover new art, and older publications began to publish critical reviews and discussions. Kuhn highlighted the decorative tumult that ensued, noting, "Drabness and awkwardness began to disappear from American life and color and grace stepped in. . . . The decorative side of Brancusi went into everything from milliners' dummies to streamliner trains. The exhibition affected every phase of American life." Modern art was now at the top of the art heap, the nouveau thing; realism was out.[39]

Compounding the damage, other new media forms had been stealing the Ashcan artists' originality. An American who wanted to visualize urban life could now go to the cinema. In 1911, two years before the Armory Show, audiences viewed *Martyr to His Cause*, the nation's first film made by a working-class organization.[40]

Even more, modernism created an entirely new mode for interpreting the city. Realism was out. Urban life would still be tackled, but with abstract images rather than straightforward depictions of the city. This shift would affect all forms of art, not only visual images but literature as well.

Thus, in a moment of deep irony, this new wave initiated the demise of the Ashcan school. Suddenly, the realists, last week's rebels, looked old-fashioned. Timing played a role, too; realistic urban art bloomed in a pre-WWI era of optimism, when progressivism was possible and a celebration of life—now extended to the kind on city streets—seemed relevant. One year after the Armory Show, a war to end all wars broke loose, and in its wake an era of cynicism and distrust of the human experience arose. By 1917 a writer in *Forum* stated bluntly, "Realism is dead, and so is subject painting." A 2007 review of an Ashcan exhibit in the *New York Times* carried this obituary: "In 1913 disaster struck the Ashcan School in the form of the Armory Show, which, by introducing European avant-gardists . . . to America, caused the near-total eclipse of native realism." On the evening after the Armory Show closed, organizers broke open champagne, amid celebratory calls. One of them, John Quinn, stood up and recited, "Don't you remember Captain John Philip of the *Texas?* When his guns sank a Spanish ship at Santiago, he said, 'Don't cheer, boys, the poor devils are dying!'" He might as well have been talking about the Ashcan school. The heyday of the urban artists had lasted a slim five years.[41]

The Ashcan artists did not do well with this shift. A critic who toured the gallery with George Wesley Bellows reported, "if Bellows' faith in himself could have been shaken it would have been shaken then." John Loughery, in an article on George Luks, commented how, "after the Armory Show, Luks and those urban realists . . . began to look increasingly old-fashioned to the younger generation and to more modernist-minded writers. To be viewed as radical one moment and old hat the next; this must have been difficult for Luks to accept, as it was for Henri and so many others."[42]

As the leader of a now-diminished school of art, Henri took it hardest. From the start, any attempts he made to influence the show were brusquely rebuffed. Davies ignored him altogether when setting up the show and went out of his way to let Henri know that the grand leader of the Ashcan school was being deliberately excluded in favor of the modernists. In a typical incident, Henri suggested shifting the height of one painting, but nothing happened. When he nostalgically told Walter Pach that he hoped for every European work sold that an American item would find a buyer too, Pach rattled back, "That isn't the proportion of merit," and he stalked off.[43]

Henri's leadership waned, not just over the Ashcan school, but in American art; as Mahonri Sharp Young put it in his classic study of the Eight, "his ascendency . . . over the fighting edge of American art was now broken." Stuart Davis, one of Henri's legion of former pupils, walked

away from the Armory Show and noted, "Talks with the other students about it left me with
the realization that the Henri school . . . this American free naturalism wasn't the answer, that
all kinds of new areas were opened up." After he heard about such remarks, Henri feebly told
Davis, "I didn't know you were interested in this type of thing." There are no diary entries from
Henri in 1913; scholars do not know if he decided against keeping one at that time, or if he
destroyed the pages chronicling that year.[44]

There are few major art genres whose time in the spotlight blazed for such a brief but epochal
moment. The Ashcan school stayed at the heights of artistic acclaim for a scant few years and
then fell from grace in critical and art history circles, evermore a curiosity, never a showstopper.
Yet its art and artists are still studied, perennially the subject of popular shows and scholarly
articles. The public came to see their works, but they were no longer progressive, no longer the
vanguard. Instead they became seen as old-fashioned and nostalgic.

This state of affairs raises a host of questions. Not just how, but *why* are the Ashcan artists
remembered? What makes them so compelling, even to present-day audiences? Why are they
still controversial? Art historians and critics debate whether they were foolishly sentimental,
if they just painted pretty pictures of the city, or if there was something more at work here.

They deserve better.

They deserve a new interpretation.

The Ashcan artists represented a revolution in subject matter, not in style. What they did was
change art from a subject for art critics and thrust it into one of the great social and industrial
narratives of the age, the rise of the city. The new, robust, city was their focus, with its powerful
machines and its issues of class, ethnicity, and gender. Ashcan art captured the power and the
players of a new era, the headline of a booming city and its industrial populations. As one writer
pointed out, their revolution was "social rather than artistic." Over time, their urban sensibility,
their unique understanding of and empathy for city life, remain their greatest contribution.[45]

This was unprecedented. Like many of their countrymen, these artists saw the metropolis
as a challenge, recognized that this was where modern America would begin. For a culture that
prided itself on its rural heritage, that realization was disturbing, since the dynamic force was
now the city.

But uniquely, these artists posed questions that no one, not even the great American
painters and the critics who wrote about them, had ever considered before. In this world of
turmoil, of reinvention, how were the city and its peoples—*all* of its peoples—thought about
and depicted visually? This had been a subject for elites and reformers alike, but both had failed,
both had missed the bulk of what Gotham was becoming. The Ashcan school instead offered
the unique belief that the working-class city was a fit subject for great art, without being either
condescending or pitying. They gloried in the drama of el trains and ferry boats, of all classes,
genders, and ethnicities. Above all, they understood that their subjects were complete, nuanced
human beings, not caricatures but men and women and children capable of deciding the terms
of and holding agency over their lives. In today's increasingly urban globe, these concepts still
merit our attention.

This approach was unique and differed in crucial ways from progressivism, the leading reform
movement of the era. True, they shared many qualities. Progressive reformers were trying to
interpret the new to middle-class America. They were living in the poorest of the poor sections,
and they were interested in the lives of urban residents.

Yet there were also crucial differences. Unlike these workers, Ashcan artists were not trying to
reform their subjects, instead celebrating urban, working-class life. Jane Addams, for example, one

of the greatest and best of the settlement house workers, often talked of giving the immigrants the gift of the ballot, handed down from above, or about how "the blessings which we associate with a life of refinement and cultivation can be made universal and must be made universal."[46] Ashcan practitioners were not didactic, nor did they aim to teach new values or change these sections.

Instead, they saw urban working-class life as sources of beauty, worthy of artistic treatment. In this they shared the vision of the best of the activists. Lillian Wald described a blazing hot night shortly after she arrived at the Henry Street Settlement. Sleepless from the heat, she looked out over the Lower East Side: "Life was in full course there. Some of the push-cart peddlers still sold their wares. Sitting on the curb directly under my window, with her feet in the gutter, was a woman, drooping from exhaustion, with a baby at her breast. The fire-escapes, considered the most desirable sleeping places, were crowded with the youngest and the oldest."[47] Life in the city could still command compelling interest.

It is time to enter the dawn of the metropolitan age in America, and to examine the prevailing art forms before the Ashcan artists challenged, and then overcame, these genres.

CHAPTER TWO

Top and Bottom

By the 1890s, Reverend Samuel Lane Loomis was at the top of his form. A born-and-bred New Englander, he had earned his Bachelor of Arts degree at Amherst College, then went to Andover Theological Seminary, topped off by postgraduate work in Berlin and London. By 1896 he was a lecturer in sociology, had authored several books and numerous articles, and had assumed the duties of pastor at the prestigious Union Congregational Church in Boston. Widely quoted, Reverend Loomis, who was a well-known figure in the America of his age, had arrived professionally and socially.

At the same time, the theologian remained a product of the era, so the critical subject of his work, his fascination, was the powerful, emerging city. To Loomis, the city was grandeur, magic, the greatest endeavor of the American. He introduced his major work, for instance, with the ringing declaration: "The city is the Gibraltar of civilizations . . . the great center of influence, both good and bad. It contains that which is fairest and foulest. . . . It is the mighty heart of the body politic, which sends its streams of life pulsating to the very finger-tips of the whole land."[1]

Numbers amply demonstrated what was so exciting. Between 1800 and the dawn of the twentieth century, the population of the United States increased fifteen times over, a robust, even startling figure. Yet the number of residents in incorporated cities and towns during that same hundred years multiplied by 150 times, an astronomical increase.[2]

These urban dwellers were different from past Americans, not only in the kind of places they inhabited but in their nationality and the kinds of work they did as well. By 1900, in the twelve largest urban centers, 60 percent of their people were either foreign born or of foreign parentage. With the Civil War about to erupt in 1860, the census recorded six million farm workers and four million nonfarm workers (e.g., urban and industrial laborers). Forty years later, the proportions were reversed, eleven million and eighteen million, respectively. The city had become the new America.[3]

Thus, as a new century broke open, there were two major, competing theories—impressions, really—in regard to the newly important city and its working-class residents. Although coming from wildly different sectors of the moral landscape, both were decidedly negative.

The first theory was the product of a very specific economic sector. This was the twilight of the Gilded Age, and America had produced an elite class that was unlike any that had come before it. Their lifestyle, which was drawn from the wealth of industrialization, was unprecedented. And they were not afraid to show it off, either, unlike past or future generations. Enormous mansions, gaudy jewels, and twelve-course meals, with each dish large enough to stuff a bison, were the order of the day. These were the people who ran the country, either from the political capital or from Wall Street, and hence dominated the nation's ideas and its art.

They created a new identity, in contrast to those with fewer resources, seeing themselves as natural leaders, biologically, socially, and culturally destined to be in charge of America. In New York and across the rest of the country, the rich declared their superiority, denigrating the city's working class and immigrants.

George Baer was a typical member of this group, and his moment of fame highlights many of these class issues. In 1902, replying to a letter from a minister, Baer proudly argued that "the rights and interests of the laboring man will be protected and cared for—not by the labor agitators, but by the Christian men to whom God in his infinite wisdom has given the control of the property interests of this country, and upon the successful management of which so much depends." Widely publicized, this statement has become an emblem of the insensitivity and crudeness of the industrial rich.[4]

Baer came by these views legitimately. A member of the country's elite, he had started, after law school, as a counselor for the powerful Philadelphia and Reading Railroad Company, where he later rose to become director, legal advisor to J. P. Morgan himself, and eventually president of the corporation. It was from this latest position that he uttered his infamous comment, adding in a statement about his firm's employees and their working conditions: "These men don't suffer. Why, hell, half of them don't even speak English." While the press dubbed him "Divine Right Baer," Clarence Darrow referred to "George the Last." His refusal to negotiate with labor earned him the wrath of President Theodore Roosevelt, who threatened to bring out the army to work the coal mines Baer also controlled and eventually forced a settlement. A stalwart believer in Social Darwinism, Baer served as president of Franklin and Marshall College, his alma mater, and saw himself as a custodian of the nation's culture.

By the turn of the century, Baer was hardly alone. As the historian Sven Beckert observed, "By the 1870s and 1880s . . . bourgeois New Yorkers articulated a consciousness of separate class identity," a belief that they were better than the human beings who often lived in cities and worked in mines, mills, and railroads. E. L. Godkin reported how "a large body of persons has arisen," all with the same economic, educational, and cultural background, "who firmly believe that they have reached in the manner of social, mental, and moral culture, all that is attainable or desirable by anybody."[5]

These were not just the snobbish utterances of a new class, either. Elites had a carefully thought-out philosophy to justify their beliefs, reasoned and articulated by some of the best minds of their time. The seminal idea was Social Darwinism, the concept that the survival of the fittest applied simplistically, and in a very short term, to the human struggle. Under this notion, the rich did not just enjoy more wealth; rather, they had achieved their position because they were biologically superior to lesser specimens.

Above all, this idea shaped how they perceived their economic inferiors, the workers and immigrants who filled the cities. First, and most important, if wealth and distinction were the result of superior genes, so too must poverty or diminished status derive from an inferior condition and an individual's shortcomings rather than from society's malefactors or from predatory actions. David Starr Jordan, a leading eugenicist and president at different times of Indiana and Stanford Universities, argued that "poverty, dirt and crime" were solely the product of a poor genetic background, and that "it is not the strength of the strong but the weakness of the weak which engenders exploitation and tyranny."[6]

The foremost popularizer of these ideas was Madison Grant, a remarkable individual and author of a remarkable book (*fig. 2.1*). Grant, a Scottish American who had descended from a Jacobite firebrand, was born into and remained a member of the elite. A lifelong New Yorker,

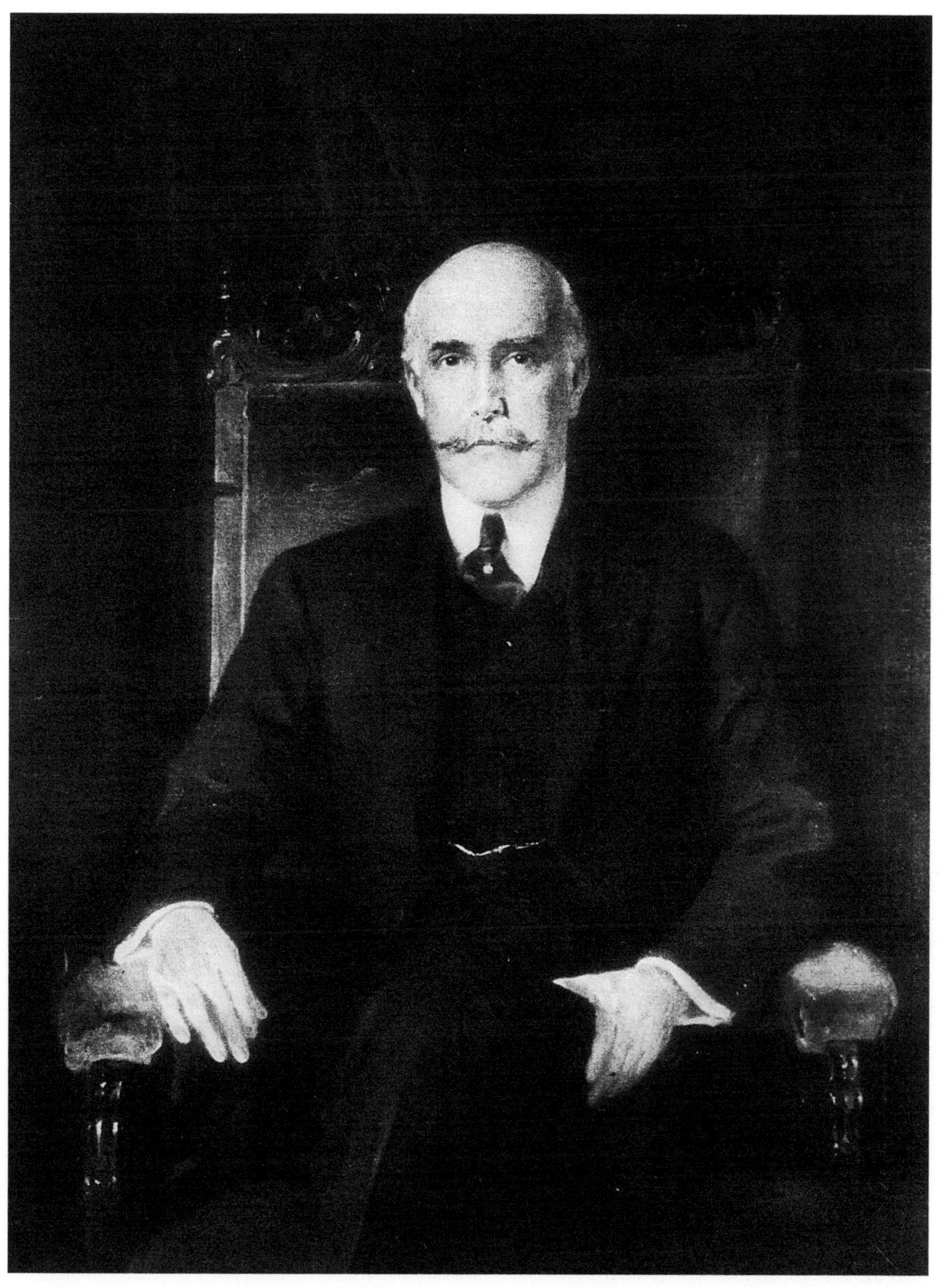

2.1 Madison Grant, portrait by Kyohei Inukai, 1925. Reproduced by permission of the Wildlife Conservation Society Archives.

Grant was the son of a prominent physician, and the offspring graduated from Yale and then Columbia Law School. An avid conservationist, he was secretary of the New York Zoological Society and served on the board of the American Museum of Natural History. With his magnificent, impeccably trimmed mustache, Grant even appeared to be the embodiment of a patrician, which, in truth he was, in every properly bred cell of his body.

Grant would have remained a minor figure in history—at best—remembered only in the obscurest of society pages, if not for his authorship of a memorable work. *The Passing of the Great Race* summed up the arguments and fears of a particular segment of Americans, and a particular era, as well as any work that has done before or since. Published in 1918, the volume portrayed an America at the brink of self-destruction. Grant clearly understood the perils of class warfare: "In America we have nearly succeeded in destroying the privilege of birth"; this was a tragedy, since, "True aristocracy is government by the wisest and best, always a small minority in any population."[7]

Thus, we arrive at the crux of his argument. America, like the rest of the world, was inhabited by a variety of races. These different groups ranged over a hierarchy, from sublime to degenerate; the characteristics fixed for every member of the group. Under this worldview, the danger was in mixing them; when a dominant strain mated with a regressive, the latter's traits prevailed. If a Nordic, in other words, procreated with a Negro, the offspring would not only retain a dark skin tone but would possess all of the inherent, inferior traits of the latter race. Yet, despite these facts, America was letting in people from all over the world, letting them breed their inferior stock at far greater rates than their superiors, and these lesser beings would soon be the majority. Hence the title, *The Passing of the Great Race*, and the widespread use of the term "race-suicide."

While it is easy to scoff at Grant's theories in hindsight, no one should underestimate their strength at the time, nor the number of people who were influenced by them, especially among those with wealth, power, and influence, society's decision makers, in other words. To the elites, the city was the home to their racially inferior neighbors, and to the mongrels who would destroy American society altogether.

In part due to writers like Grant, the elites' sense of the metropolis and its residents was more negative than anything else. In 1888 Allan Foreman, writing in *American Magazine*, penned language that was frankly chilling to both his contemporaries and to modern readers, albeit for different reasons. "In the great 'dumb-bell' tenements," he argued, "in the rickety old frame buildings, in the damp, unwholesome cellars, on the sidewalks and in the gutters reeking of filth and garbage, is a seething mass of humanity, so ignorant, so vicious, so depraved that they hardly seem to belong to our species."[8]

The cause of all this problem, incidentally, was government, not the private sector that ran the factories and built the tenements without regulation. "Congress," an author explained, "with its suicidal *laissez-faire* policy on immigration, by permitting Europe to send us any kind of immigrant it pleases, was directly responsible for the overcrowded tenements in the city." "It is the plain duty of Congress," he intoned, "to stop this immigration, or else assume the responsibility for it instead of putting it on the shoulders of New York."[9]

Whatever the cause of this crisis, the result was clear. Districts like this were "a menace to the public health, a prolific source of contagion. Worst of all, it is a sink of crime and immorality." The urban, working-class, immigrant neighborhood "is one of the city's most hideous features, one of its most violent and forbidding contrasts; summing up, it "is not credible to New York." And thus, clearly, not a legitimate subject for art, let alone art that was great and eloquent.[10]

Instead, the urban elites saw themselves as the only appropriate subjects for painters when it came to urban art. As Sven Beckert noted, in his description of a political climate that also applied to the era's arts, "The well-to-do antisuffragists saw the city as belonging to its propertied citizens"; it was clear to the upper crust that when it came to depicting the city, they were the only connoisseurs and judges, as well as the natural subjects, of painters and sculptors. Even such a luminary and *salonista* as Mabel Dodge condescended to the rest of Gotham when she spoke of the reaction to a showing by Alfred Stieglitz in his Photo-Secession Gallery, how, "the public. The great, blind, dumb New York Public, had never seen anything, had" never been interested in modern art. Only the elites could appreciate real art, and only their class could pay for it. Not surprisingly, because the elites considered themselves the only legitimate subjects of paintings, the works they sponsored portrayed this vision of the city.[11]

A prime example of this elite attitude when it came to painting, surprisingly enough, was impressionism. While it was radical in style, its subject matter frequently depicted a limited vision of the city.

No matter how novel their approach—in fact, their very definition of art—when it came to urban subject matter, impressionist artists often embraced an upper class and bourgeois approach, eschewing immigrant, working-class districts. For many (though not all) of the impressionists, the city was a domain of grand boulevards and genteel strolls, not of workers forging new neighborhoods; in some of their portrayals of the city, the latter did not exist.[12] As David Shi observed, "Like the purposeful urban promenaders and shoppers who frequented city streets, the impressionists took voluptuous delight in the bourgeois life. . . . Degas and other French impressionists . . . populated their canvases with fashionable people in shops, cafes, theaters, ballet and opera houses, at city parks and gardens." In Degas' *Place de la Concorde*, for example, while the setting is decidedly urban, it is also expansive, almost pastoral, rather than depicting the density that was the hallmark of urban life (*fig. 2.2*). The central male figure is a gentle

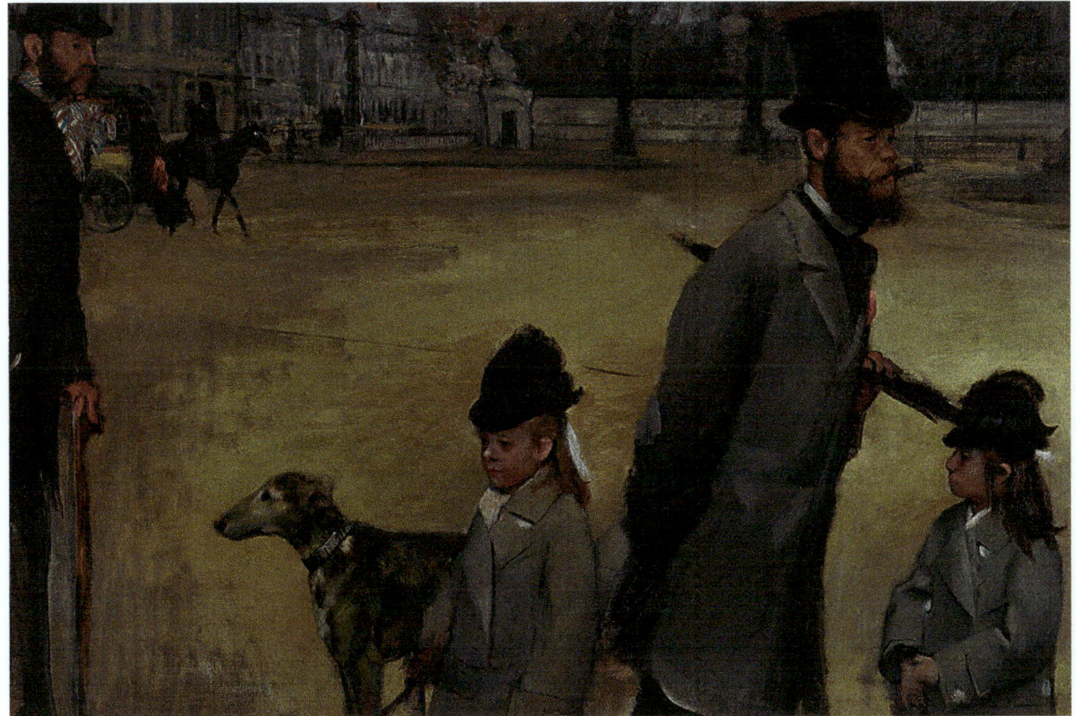

2.2 Edgar Degas (1834–1917), *Place de la Concorde (Viscount Lepic and His Daughters Crossing the Place de la Concorde)*, oil on canvas, 78.4 × 117.5 cm. France, 1875, Inv. no. ZK-1399. The State Hermitage Museum, St. Petersburg. Photograph © The State Hermitage Museum/photo by Vladimir Terebenin.

soul, well dressed and leisurely, who is taking a stroll. Nearby children wear expensive attire and are accompanied by a handsome pet; a carriage and even a mansion stand in the background.[13]

There is a clear sense of the upper class here. In *The Painting of Modern Life*, T. J. Clark argued, "There is a rule to these paintings. . . . Industry can be recognized, but not labor; the factories have to be kept still, as if that were a guarantee of their belonging to the landscape. . . . Industry must not mean *work*." In Claude Monet's *Argenteuil, la berge en fleurs*, for instance, the city and its factories are only background, for the pastoral arbor of flowers that commands our attention (*fig. 2.3*). Grit and smoke do not mar their beauty, nor do they impose on our viewing of them.[14]

Edouard Manet's *The Railway* is a study in contrasts (*fig. 2.4*). The title denotes the epitome of Victorian grit, an institution that propelled progress and left soot—and workers—everywhere. This image, on the other hand, personifies soft gentility, with a lady, dressed in fancy hat and choker, reading a book while a precious small dog rests in her lap; her little sister, meanwhile, in lovely light blue dress, peers into the distance. A small plume of steam can be glimpsed

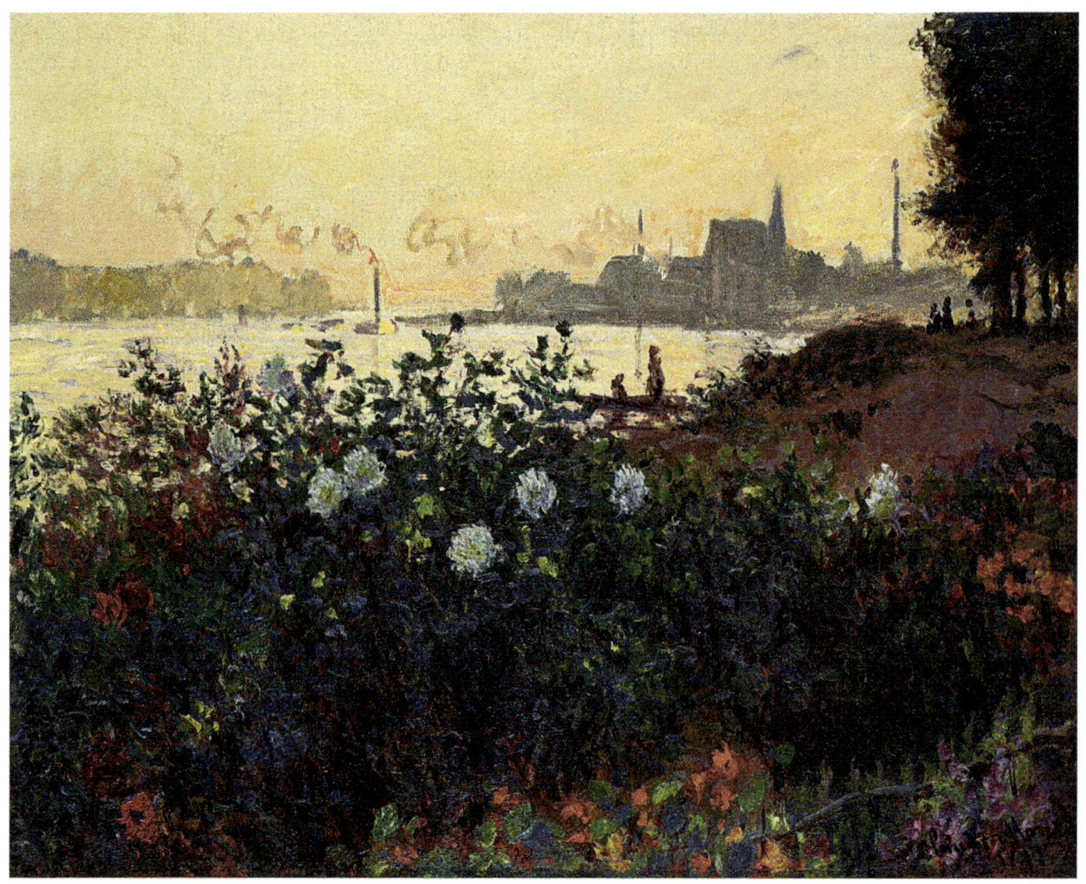

2.3 Claude Monet (1840–1926), *Argenteuil, la berge en fleurs*, 1877, oil on canvas, 53.8 × 65.1 cm; 32.2 × 25.63 inches. Pola Museum of Art, Sengokuhara, Japan. Gift of Suzuki Tsuneshi.

through the bars; notwithstanding the title, this is the sole imposition of industrialization upon the otherwise tranquil scene. Both literally and figuratively the city is being kept at a distance.

Clark arrived at the powerful conclusion that, for the impressionists, "it is not enough to say that they were bourgeois artists; it needs stressing, rather, that their practice as painters—their claim to be modern—depended on their being bound more closely than ever before to the interests and economic habits of the bourgeoisie they belonged to."[15]

American impressionists adopted both the novel style and subject matter of their forebears in Paris. In terms of artistic style as opposed to subject matter, this new artistic form was the revolution, was the new and the modern, was the place to be; one modern historian referred to impressionism as the "daring idiom" of the age.

Their canvases, however, also captured the class biases of the French painters, which in turn reinforced the prejudices of the American elite. As the authors of *American Impressionism and Realism* delicately surmised, "Despite their openness to fresh ideas regarding style and subject choice, the American Impressionists were ambivalent about social change." Instead, as William

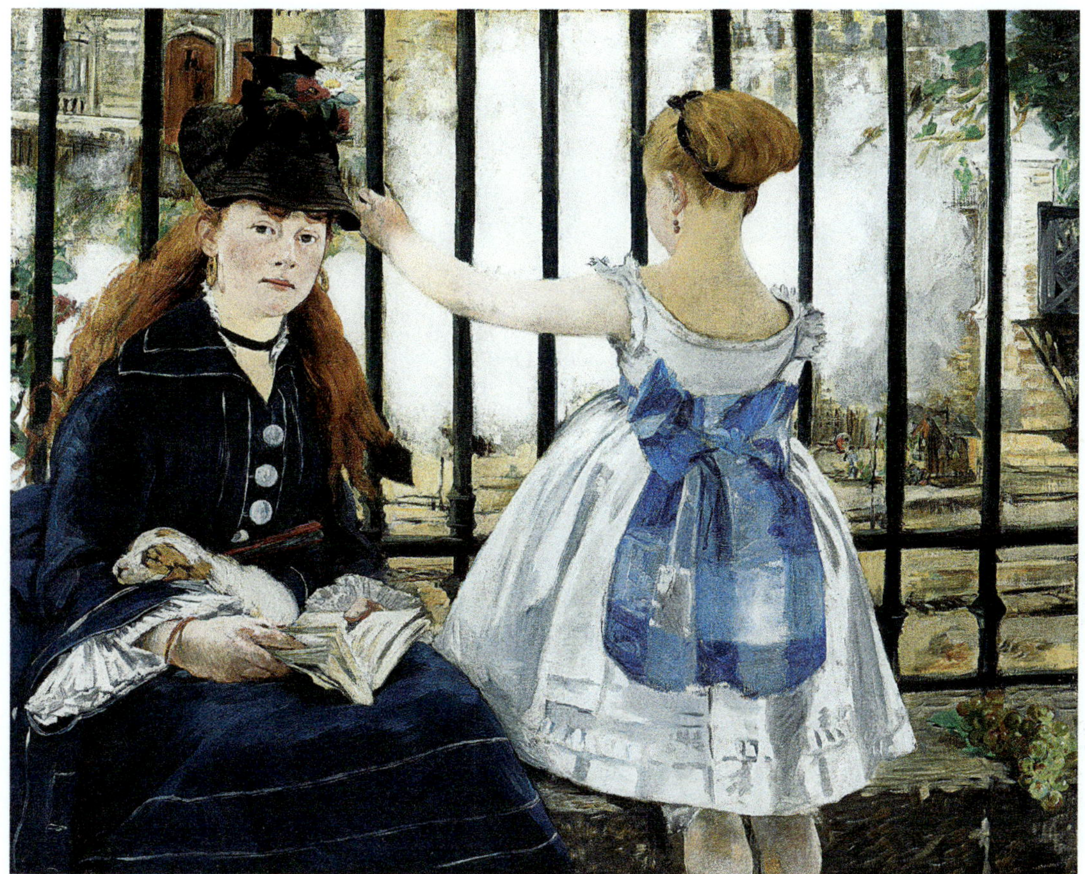

2.4 Edouard Manet (1832–1883), *The Railway*, 1873, oil on canvas, overall 93.3 × 111.5 cm; 36¾ × 43⅞ inches, framed 113 × 132.7 × 5.4 cm; 44½ × 52¼ × 2⅛ inches. National Gallery of Art, Washington, DC, USA/Bridgeman Images.

Gerdts explained in *Impressionist New York*, "Americans working in the Impressionist mode created pictures for a clientele who wanted the best of their own existence reflected in the works they hung on their walls, images that would serve as role models for themselves . . . enshrining the stereotypes of social position and social behavior peculiar to their class."[16]

Not surprisingly, these artists, according to Gerdts, "shunned" the Lower East Side of New York, "choosing instead to depict the distinctive skyline of lower Manhattan," a perspective that focused on the contributions and lifestyle of the elite. They eschewed narrow streets, immigrants, and the waterfront, choosing instead, as was the mode in Paris, to draw beautiful images of "great long avenues with their disparate crowds of casual strollers." One biographer of John Sloan, premiere Ashcan artist, simply stated that in the era of the impressionists, "The city was pictured seldom, and then it was Fifth Avenue only."[17]

In many ways Willard Metcalf's painting *Battery Park* best personifies the impressionist relationship to the city (*fig. 2.5*). In the foreground is an elevated station, an urban symbol if

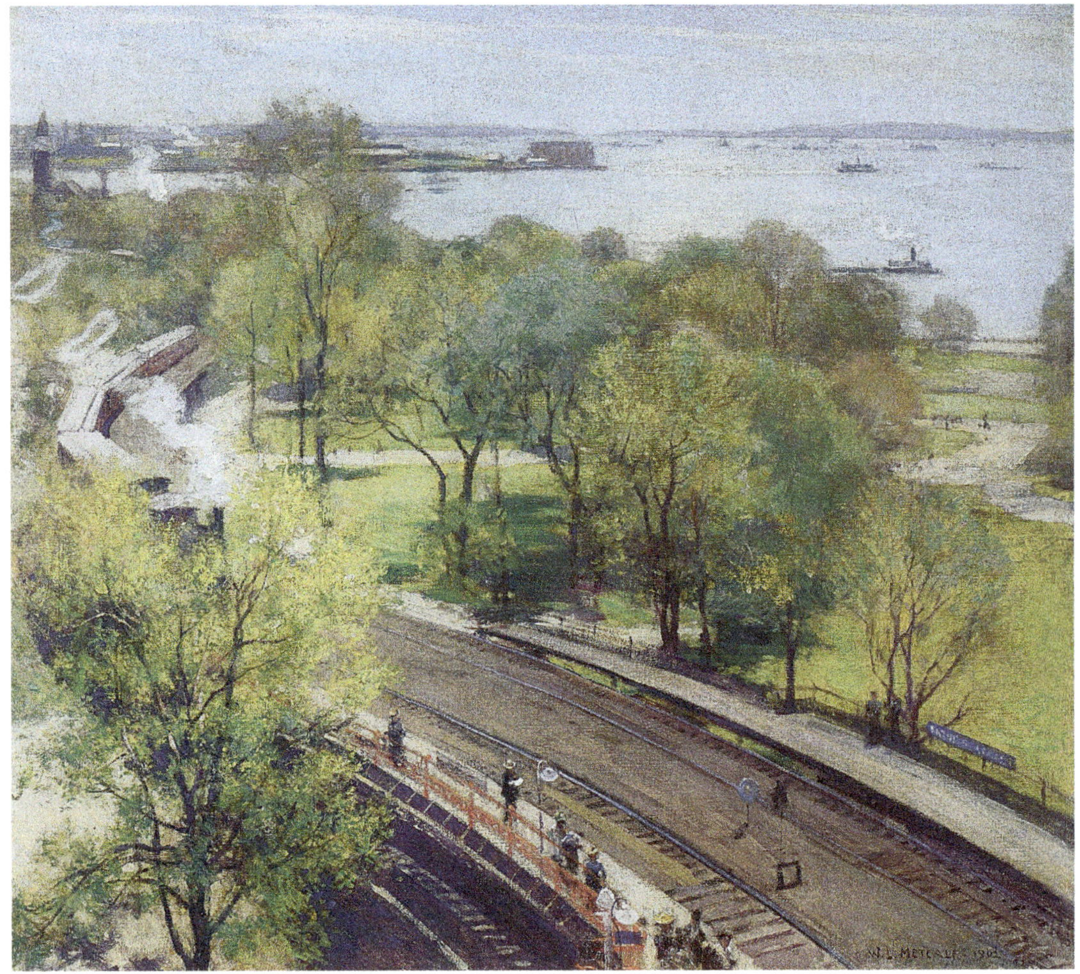

2.5 Willard Metcalf (1858–1925), *Battery Park*, 1924, oil on canvas, 66.04 × 73.66 cm. Public domain, private collection.

ever there was one, and one that Ashcan painter John Sloan would portray frequently. A train, led by a steam engine belching smoke, is close at hand.

Despite these features, however, the scene is hardly urban. The overwhelming context is that of an arbor, with graceful trees framing everything, a soft seaside in the background. One gets the impression that no rush hour intrudes on this station, that there are never crowds, and that no workers ever stand on these platforms.

Childe Hassam was the leading impressionist painter of urban themes in the United States, and his work displayed this movement's class perspective. According to Gerdts, Hassam was "considered the greatest exponent of Impressionism in America, was the American painter who most devotedly addressed himself to depicting the metropolis over the course of his long career."[18]

Hassam was a variant of Horsham—not, as critics claimed, of Middle Eastern origin. He was no child of the slums and, despite his name, hailed from old stock New England rather than recent immigrants; his maternal ancestors included Nathaniel Hawthorne and William Morris Hunt. After a few trips to Europe and working at assorted jobs, he established himself as a freelance magazine and book illustrator in Boston. In 1886, however, he and his new bride took up residence in Paris, where he became an apostle of impressionism, when most American students were still ignoring this style. According to the critic Sadakichi Hartmann, "At the time Childe Hassam began painting, the spirit of Impressionism, with its new discoveries of vibration and colour, was in the air, and he . . . tacked himself enthusiastically to the movement, and from the start stoutly advocated its theories." Hassam returned to the states in 1889, where he would make New York his home for the rest of his life.[19]

In love with his new and permanent abode, Hassam explained, "To me, New York is the most wonderful and most beautiful city in the world. All life is in it. . . . No street, no section of Paris or any other city I have seen is equal to New York." At this point, he became, in the words of Philippe de Montebello, director of the Metropolitan Museum of Art, "the city's principal . . . Impressionist chronicler."[20]

Though Hassam was a pioneer of style—introducing impressionist vistas of the city—in terms of substance, his viewpoint mirrored Herbert Spencer's, in that he extolled and chronicled the downtown crowd exclusively; to Hassam these were the only residents, the only sections of the city that mattered. Elizabeth Broun, writing a complimentary piece on Hassam in *American Art*, nevertheless agreed that "his letters and memberships in various associations make clear that his sympathies were with the wealthy industrialists who were his patrons. . . . For Hassam, the narrative was about the forces shaping America, rather than the people behind those forces." She also noted, "Like many of his contemporaries, Hassam believed in Aryan superiority."[21]

As a reflection of this worldview, Hassam's vision of New York was lovely but limited. Hassam sought, as one writer reflected, "the enclosed safety of the domestic sphere," and he became known as the painter par excellence of Fifth Avenue. Though H. Barbara Weinberg of the Metropolitan Museum of Art noted that Hassam's images "vary in the seasons and the times of day," she admitted that his New York scenes "are one-dimensional and uniform from a sociocultural standpoint."[22]

Hassam's great painting of genteel New York was *Washington Arch, Spring* (*fig. 2.6*). Picturing one of those bright, magnificent days in the city, the streets are full of sunlight. Prominent in the foreground, an elegant lady with a parasol takes a stroll, while behind her a servant wheels a baby carriage. Back toward the arch, gentlemen are out for a walk; over on the side, a carriage with top-hatted coachman waits for its employer. Despite the setting in the heart of Manhattan, there is abundant open space; trees and greenery are everywhere. This is Fifth Avenue at its finest; the Lower East Side might as well have been in Mongolia.

The one representative of the city's masses here is the streetcleaner, in the foreground left. He is literally cleaning up for his economic betters. Art historian William Gerdts felt that

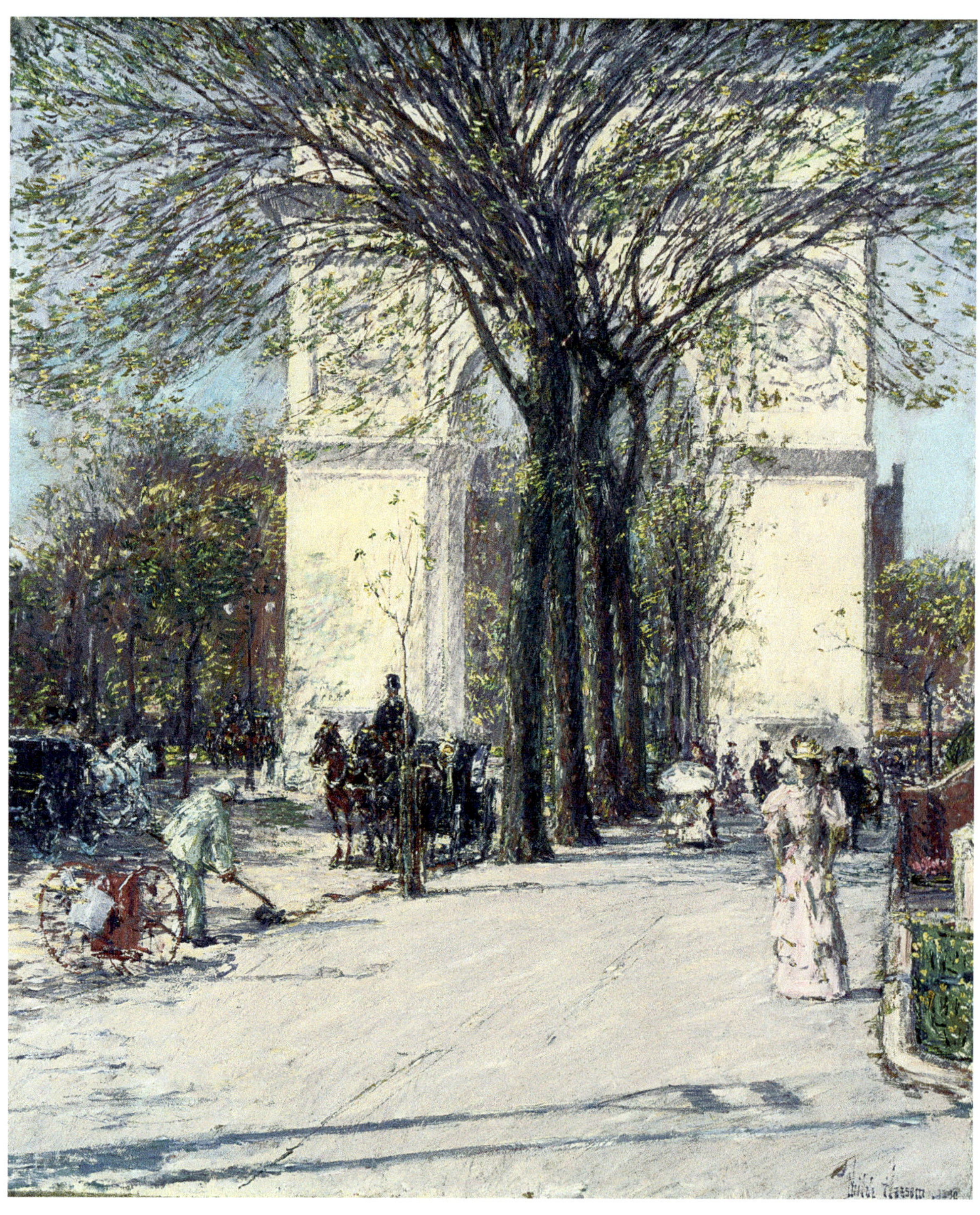

2.6 Childe Hassam (1859–1935), *Washington Arch, Spring,* ca. 1893, oil on canvas, overall 26⅛ inches × 21⅝ inches; 66.3575 cm × 54.9275 cm. Acquired 1921. The Phillips Collection, Washington, DC.

this worker took "his place as part of the system of support for a traditionally elegant way of life. . . . The concern with order, the denial and deletion of squalor, are characteristic of Hassam's assessment of New York."[23]

A similar depiction of the city is evident in Hassam's *The Manhattan Club* (*fig. 2.7*). Both the buildings and the people are elegant: these are magnificent structures, alongside ladies and gentlemen of distinction and culture, who, like the architecture, are well dressed. The only lower-class imposition of the rest of the city is contributed by a figure in the left foreground, a newsboy. Even he wears a matched suit, there is no sense that he is a ragamuffin child of the streets. This is an idealized and sanitized version of New York, what the wealthy believed their city looked like.

For the city's elites—both from old and new money alike—places like New York were *their* home, only about them. They shared among themselves a powerful new philosophy—Social Darwinism—that justified their wealth and condemned those without it. Waves of immigrants, and the growth of the urban working-class sector, were irrelevant and potentially dangerous; if nothing else, dark and fearful. A radical new style of art—impressionism—captured this

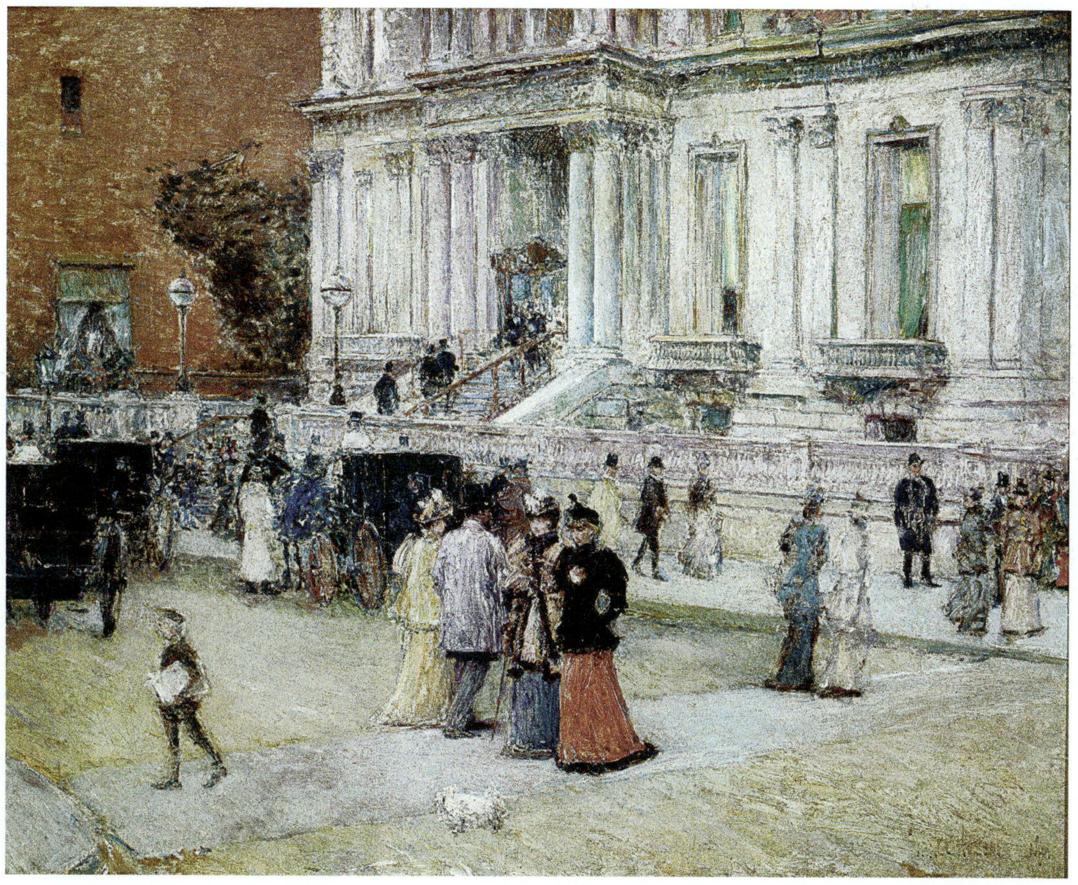

2.7 Childe Hassam (1859–1935), *The Manhattan Club*, ca. 1891, oil on canvas, 22⅛ inches × 18¼ inches. Santa Barbara Museum of Art. Gift of Mrs. Sterling Morton to the Preston Morton Collection.

worldview and often made it beautiful. It did not reflect all of New York, however, and at the turn of the century another group of civic leaders set out to rectify this omission.

At the same time as the elites, another segment of American society became obsessed with urban life, yet with a very different perspective, and new and seemingly enlightened goals. Reformers took heed of the emergence of the city as a national issue, seeking to inform the public about their own perceptions of the metropolis and its denizens, and propose unique solutions to its problems.

Thus, this group, just as much as the elites, saw the city as a social challenge. Their prescription, their cures, were quite different, however. In many ways, the urban reformers represented the epitome of enlightenment. Like their wealthier countrymen, they recognized the rising importance of the city; but instead of upholding the status quo, they sought beneficial change and worked to ameliorate conditions. Their signal accomplishment and unifying thread was that, notwithstanding the many downsides of their movement, they at least rejected the laissez-faire of Social Darwinism and actively worked to make the cities better places.

But there were serious problems here. To the reformers, even the most well-meaning of them, the people who lived in the city were simply casualties of the new industrial order, nothing more. While their intentions were good, especially in contrast to the attitudes of the elites, this view denied any sense of agency, of workers and immigrants not only controlling their own destiny, but of enjoying a life they made for themselves . . . in the city. Thus, the reformers perceived—and depicted, both in words and in images alike—working-class urbanites as eternally helpless victims rather than as participants in a viable community. The city thus became solely a den of misery rather than a vibrant environment that housed potential for beauty in all of its neighborhoods. With views equally as restrictive as those of the business elites, reformers ignored the bulk of the urban experience and instead portrayed a single aspect of the city.

There were real issues here. Christine Stansell, in *American Moderns*, noted how "progressive reformers were still highly class bound, their projects imbued with a conviction of the rightness of middle class hegemony." They did not accept this new metropolis or its denizens, in other words, but sought to remake it—and them—in their own image.[24]

The reality was far more problematic than just a rejection of some neighborhoods; many of these progressives were not even comfortable with the city itself, which would impact how they depicted it. Paul Boyer felt that they, all too often, "tended to fall back with a vengeance upon the wicked-city stereotype." Angela Blake, in the provocatively titled *How New York Became American*, recognized that many urban reformers held a "negative view of the city as the site of poverty and disease, the domain of 'darkness.'" In 1906 William McAdoo, a former police commissioner of New York City, posed the question, "Is New York an unusually vicious city?" and gave a portentous, weighted answer, "Reform organizations . . . would probably say 'yes.'" Reformer Frederic Howe called the city, "a hideous phantasmagoria of hunger, disease, vice, crime and despair," and as modern critic Mark Thomas Connelly observed, among Howe's colleagues there "was the conviction that traditional mechanisms of moral control . . . had broken down in the cities."[25]

That last line pointed to the city's other feature that so disturbed many of the reformers, the hordes of new immigrants. Helen Marot, a feminist and union organizer, caused a stir in 1911 at the Women's Trade Union League when she stated that the organization should work with "American girls" rather than Jewish sweatshop employees. And the eminent sociologist Edward Ross observed, "The immigrant . . . lacks the facility of abstraction. He thinks not of the welfare of the community but only of himself."[26]

One of the most important works of the reform movement was Robert De Forest and Lawrence Veiller's seminal piece, *The Tenement House Problem*, that led to improved building codes in New York, and then cities across the nation. Filled with statistics, charts, and maps, it was to the housing program what Charles Booth's surveys were to London, a foundational work that spurred generations of reform.

In many ways, this was the model of enlightenment; De Forest and Veiller argued that conditions, not character, were the cause of poverty. One essay, "Foreign Immigration and the Tenement House in New York City," for example, included this ringing rebuttal to the elite view of the poor, as it was embodied in Social Darwinism: "It is easy to see that the tenement house was admirably calculated to foster the most undesirable characteristics of these immigrant people, and to choke out . . . the very good characteristics they might develop." The report continued, "It was not merely easy to be dirty in the wretched, crazy, crowded dwellings; it was almost impossible to be anything else."

And yet, despite this, there were passages that demonstrated other feelings toward immigrants, a sense that while no one should live in these sweat houses, some of these residents were still from inferior racial stock. The same essay noted, "The original character of the immigrants, however, has to be taken into account." All immigrants were poor, "but the Irish showed decided traits of out-and-out pauperism. . . . Intemperance and violence were other noteworthy Irish characteristics."[27]

A typical example of this genre, which displayed both the strengths and the shortcomings of the reformers' approach, was Robert Hunter's famous 1904 treatise, *Poverty*. Hunter's work displayed both the heights to which these advocates could rise, and the limitations that constrained them.

In many ways, *Poverty* is a paragon of progressive thought. In the introduction, Hunter argued, "The book . . . has one aim; namely, to show the grievous need of certain social measures calculated to prevent the ruin and degradation of those working people who are on the verge of poverty." He then chastised his readers, stating, "I am at a loss to understand why well-known and generally recognized poverty-breeding conditions, which are both unjust and unnecessary, are tolerated for an instant."

Hunter concentrated on the economic rather than the behavioral or genetic causes of poverty, dismissing arguments that claimed that these conditions were solely the result of bad habits, or bad breeding. In blunt language, he explained that the poor "are bred of miserable and unjust social conditions, which punish the good and the pure, the faithful and industrious . . . men are brought into misery by the action of social and economic forces." Speaking to a middle-class audience, he reminded readers how "it is obvious to inquiring persons that society, as a result of its industries, its tenements . . . causes a large part of the poverty which exists amongst us." Social Darwinism, in other words, was both directly confronted and repudiated here.

Yet there was a discordant note as well. The poor were depicted as helpless victims, totally unable to affect the conditions of their life, or even to make simple decisions on how to undertake day-to-day business. Near the end of the book, Hunter described how his colleagues "were busy from morning until night in giving them opportunities . . . to become independent of relief. . . . They always promised to try; but as soon as we expected them to fulfill any promises, they gave up in despair." He thus concluded, "this entire class of dependents must be cared for in some way." The poor could not be in charge of their own lives.

Particularly telling was Hunter's analysis of youth. David Nasaw, in *Children of the City*, argued that young people's days were filled with choices, over whom to play with, the rules of their games, and where the boundaries of neighborhoods—of safe and dangerous zones—began and ended.[28]

Hunter saw none of this authority and liveliness. Instead, "all children from the tenements, and even from many apartment houses, should be classed in poverty," and thus in tragedy as well. This was "a city which has forgotten the child," despite the presence of a wonder world of amusements, from penny arcades to diving off the docks to street life itself; the Ashcan artists would devote great quantities of paint and canvas to the interaction of youth with the urban environment. Hunter definitively stated, however, that "the city child becomes criminal because it can almost be said that in these districts the only things to do worthy of a boy's spirit are those things which are against the law."

Hunter, in other words, recognized the ills of the new industrial order and wanted to change society for the better. At the same time, however, he assigned no agency to the urban working class, which transformed them into helpless victims rather than active players, let alone legitimate subjects for beautiful paintings. He used the term "dependent class" fourteen times in his narrative, the words "dependent classes" another twelve times. In a *New York Times* discussion of Hunter's book, the reviewer spoke of the "dim, silent millions among us."[29]

Thus, the reformers shared one perception with their arch-opposites, the elites. Both groups refused to see the poor or the working class as real people, with dreams and the ability to realize them, enjoying their lives in the city. At least the reformers had some sense of pity for society's downtrodden and wanted to change their conditions. But they recognized only the underclass, instead of the majority of working New Yorkers.

Of all the authors who attempted to bring reform to the city, the best known, and in many ways the most important, was Jacob Riis. Riis was different from other reformers. A photographer as well as a writer, Riis influenced through his images more than from his words. But he was the leading artist to visually present the reformers' perception of Gotham.

Although the reformers' vision of the city, of poverty and despair, did not inspire any school of artists, impressionist or otherwise, it did manifest itself in a wealth of visual terms; reformers used images—maps, diagrams, and above all, photography, particularly the expose of photojournalism. Riis pioneered in using this new medium to try and bring change to the city, and his photographs and writings captured not only what this group was attempting to achieve but the ways in which they perceived the city and its inhabitants as well.[30]

Riis himself was an immigrant. Arriving from Denmark in 1870, after a series of odd jobs he became a reporter, eventually assigned to the police beat. In 1888 he signed on with the *New York Evening Sun* as a photo journalist and began to experiment with flash powder, which enabled him to capture dimly lit interior scenes.

Riis' focus quickly shifted from the crime scenes themselves to the conditions he felt generated illegal acts. He traveled to the various slums of New York, gaining access and capturing these environments on film as no one had done before or has done since.

One of the original muckrakers, Riis sought to do much more than just take pictures. Beginning in 1888, he transformed his work into a traveling lecture and slide show, urging his viewers to take action and clean up these horrid conditions.

As much of a showman as he was an evangelist, Riis put on a stereopticon presentation, with almost one hundred slides of an unprecedented nature. Using two projectors, he presented a ten-foot square image, embroidered with anecdotes, stories, and in some settings even background music.

Because he preached to an audience of middle-class reformers, he understood perfectly the limits of their thinking. His pictures and first-person caricatures would grab their hearts above all, then spur them to action; few, if any, had seen anything like his images or even dreamed that such conditions were possible. In contrast to the elites, he highlighted the background causes of crime, how high unemployment and poor wages led to children wasting away and malnutrition inciting disease that spanned neighborhood boundaries. "I could not stand by and see the Republic built on a pigsty," he averred, declaring that those who believed as he did must act to make their city a better place. "When a thing is right," he insisted, "it is bound to come, if we make it come."[31]

In 1890 Charles Scribner's Sons published his masterwork, *How the Other Half Lives*. Filled with powerful words backed by devastating photographs, this was, and is, a book that captures attention; indeed, it is still frequently assigned in classrooms for subjects ranging from social work to photography to urban history. A reviewer for the *New York Press* at the time called it "a plain, unvarnished tale . . . and yet the incidents are thrilling. The characters he has drawn and their surroundings have made most dramatic and pathetic pictures." In 1938 the historian Allan Nevins claimed that it "did more than anything else to prepare the way for the housing investigations and new tenement-house codes of the next decade." When Riis died in 1914, former president Theodore Roosevelt eulogized him as "the ideal American citizen."[32]

There is no question that Riis' campaigns led to better conditions in some of the city's worst neighborhoods, and for these efforts, he should be honored. But the manner in which he portrayed the metropolis and its denizens is another issue altogether, and it reveals a very different side, not only of Riis, but of his generation of urban reformers.

Thus, for the elites, the city was magical, if bound by class. It was glamorous and sparkling, an exciting place, for any gender and at any age, a fine setting if one was a banker, or an ingénue, or raising a child. No one else mattered.

The reformers took this to the opposite extreme. Their city was dark, dismal, impoverished, and horrid. As in the rich man's version, there was no solid working class here, just the dregs of the lowest stratum, most of them undesirable immigrants. New York was a terrible social problem to be cured, much like a contagion rather than a place to ever be enjoyed by the working class.

Riis shared this outlook completely. The *London Quarterly Review* opened its article on *How the Other Half Lives* by observing, "From a superficial reading of this . . . book, one might easily get the impression that New York was one vast slum."[33] Riis saw streets, for example, not as places of activity and discovery, as urban pedestrians of every income had found, but instead, as historian Cary Goodman noted, "as an institution that contributed to the disintegration of character and the destruction of communal bonds in the slum." He quoted Riis himself regarding the city's effect on children, concluding that it is all detrimental, "because character implies depth, a soil, and growth. The street is all surface: nothing grows there; it only hides a sewer."[34]

Even more problematic were the people who lived there. Because Riis believed that no one should live in such grim conditions, he called on people of goodwill to change the situation. But that does not mean he accepted these New Yorkers as anything approaching equals, or even wished them to be his neighbors. Instead, his vision exclusively perceived them as victims, with no will, no agency, no personality, no qualities other than as subjects to be investigated and reformed. As Bonnie Yochelson and Daniel Czitrom pointed out, "He ascribed little or no role at all to tenement dwellers themselves. . . . He admired the honest laborer as long as he or she remained unorganized and politically mute." Rather, Riis "comprehended his subject as a faceless and dehumanized mass." Samuel Freedman, in the *New York Times*, described how Riis and other muckrakers "pleaded the case of the lower class by relentlessly portraying its degradation."[35]

The New York that Riis photographed was real; his images are accurate. But they are a portrait of the slum, nothing more. Combined with the art of Childe Hassam, in the total of both of their collections, there was no working class, no lower middle class, no lively districts crowded with markets and restaurants, churches and synagogues, saloons and lovers. Like Hassam, Riis depicted one part of the city but missed all the rest. His districts existed, were distressed, and worthy of reform. But the other parts of the working-class city were never seen, never explored; what he does *not* show is far broader than what he does. The Broadway chronicler

Mark Hellinger put it best, with precious irony, when he described a fictional character who appeared in one of his stories: "His tenement home was one of those holes that the reformers take such delight in finding. Poverty lurked in every corner, and there was no attempt to turn the spot into anything that might resemble a home."[36]

During this era, while photography was considered an incredibly powerful new form of media that was far more accurate than painting, even photographers could have an agenda and lack sensitivity to aspects of the human experience. Life in Riis' city was hopeless; as he emphatically stated in the introduction to *How the Other Half Lives*, "We know now that there is no way out. . . . in the tenements all the influences make for evil." Everything is squalor; in *Bottle Alley Mulberry Bend, x shows where the victim stood when shot*, there is filth everywhere, all encompassing (*fig. 2.8*). One lost soul sits, the only human in the image, surrounded by trash.

The people who live in places like this were beyond redemption. Note how the woman, depicted within the photograph *In the Home of an Italian Ragpicker, Jersey Street*, simply stares into space (*fig. 2.9*). There is no sense of life here, no control over the conditions of one's environment. She is subject to the winds exhaled by those more powerful than her, to be pitied and aided, not respected.

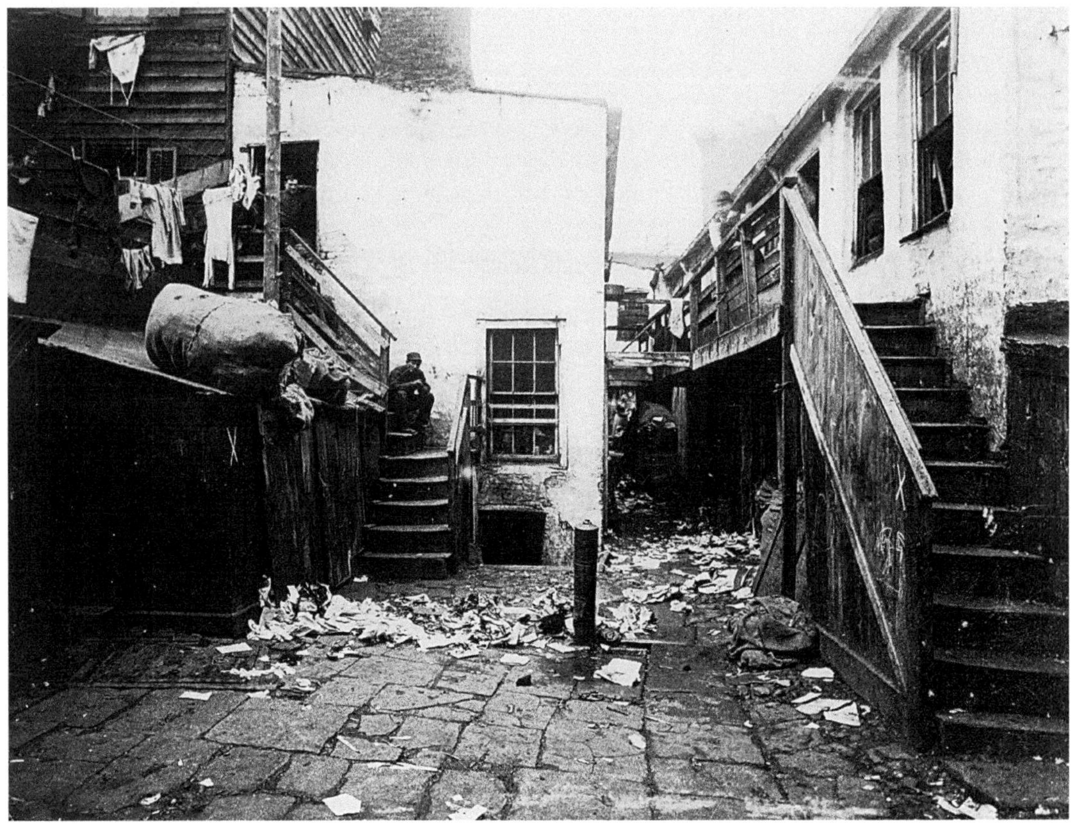

2.8 Jacob Riis (1849–1914), *Bottle Alley Mulberry Bend, x shows where the victim stood when shot*, ca. 1895. Museum of the City of New York. Photo credit: The Museum of the City of New York/Art Resource, New York.

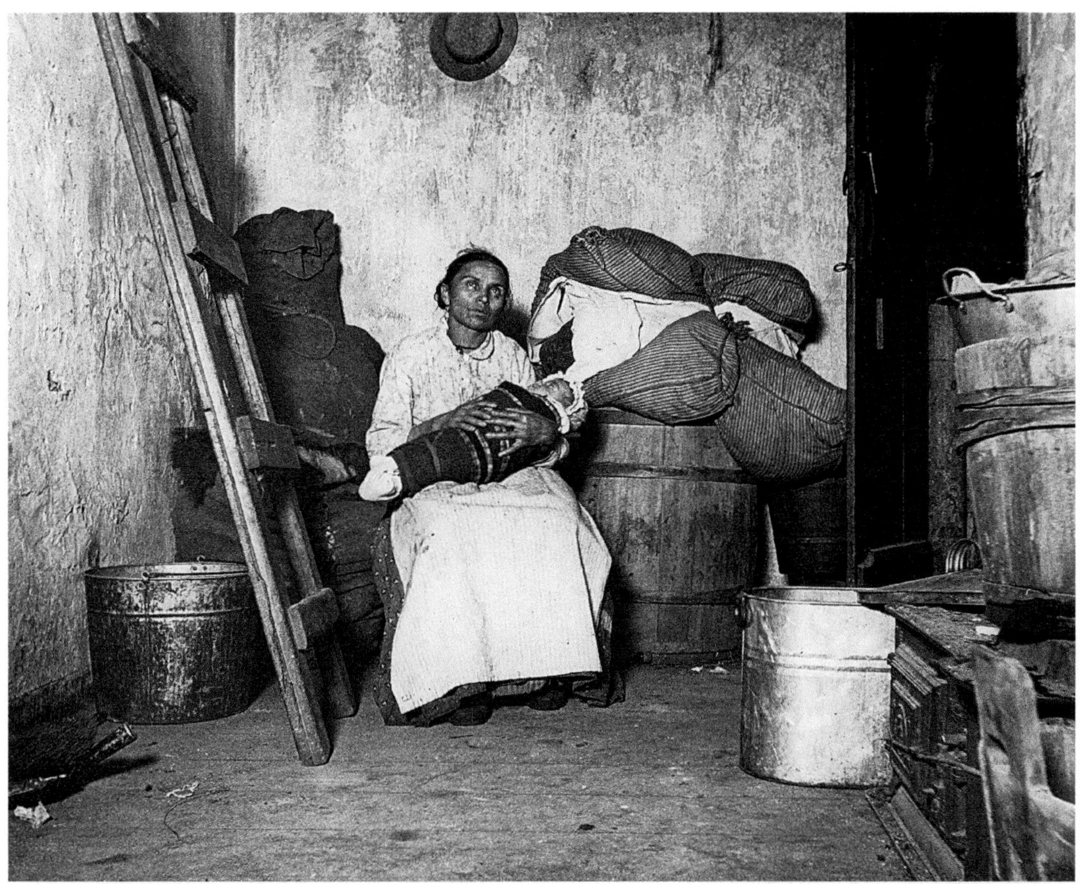

2.9 Jacob Riis (1849–1914), Italian mother and her baby in Jersey Street or *In the Home of an Italian Ragpicker, Jersey Street*, from *How the Other Half Lives*, New York City, ca. 1890. Museum of the City of New York. Photo credit: The Museum of the City of New York/Art Resource, New York.

Above all, there were the children. For Riis, they were the symbol of what the city represented. In response to Riis' photographs, Marianne Doezema observed that they "spoke eloquently of what was *lacking*, such as cleanliness, order and appropriate space."[37] In this case, however, the absences were far more poignant; they are, instead, the laughter and the games of youth. The power of choice that David Nasaw discovered in *Children of the City*, the right to choose games and rules, playmates and territorial boundaries, was replaced by a power that ground down human beings at the earliest ages and never stopped. When it came to the city, children were like their parents; they feared their environment for good reason: it could only hurt, never enrich them. They epitomized powerlessness and victimization.

In *Two Greek children in Gotham Court debating if Santa Claus will get to their alley or not. He did*, for example, the young boy on the right looks scared, possibly intimidated by the older boys on the left (*fig. 2.10*). The little girl stares out, seemingly oblivious of everyone and everything around her.

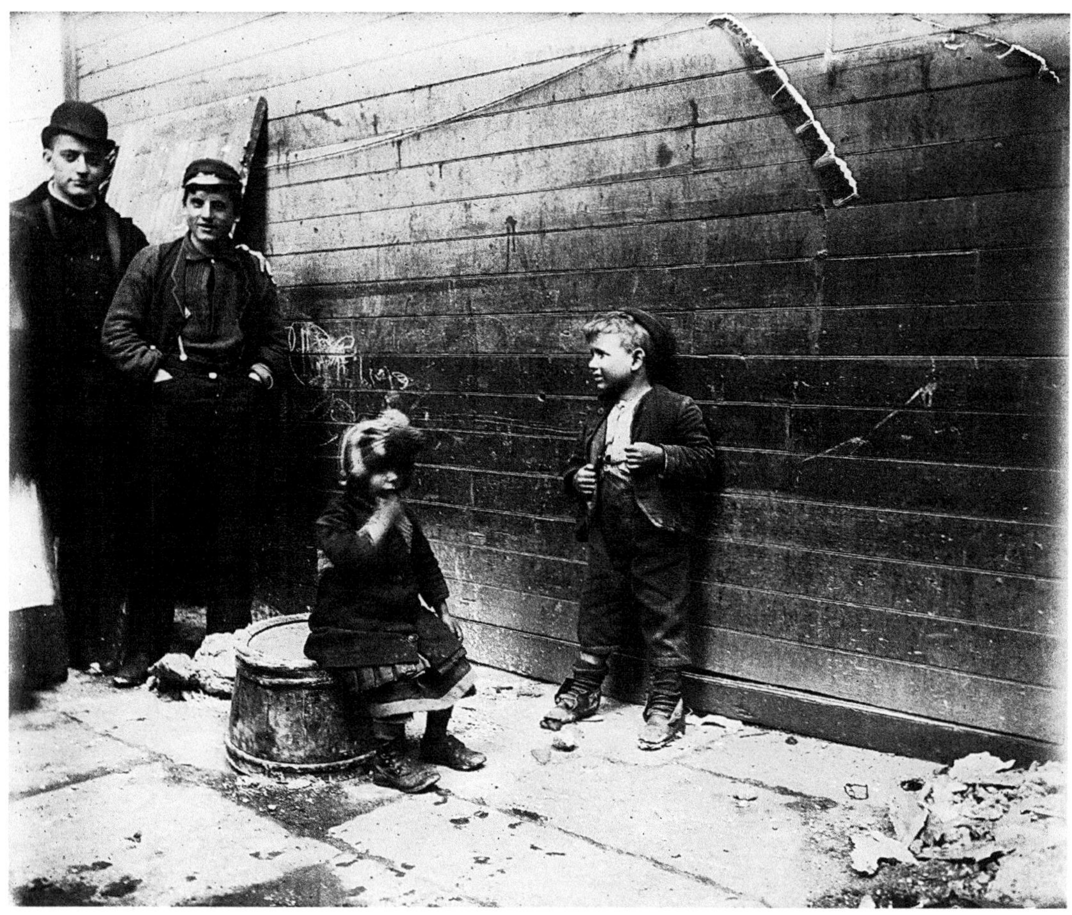

2.10 Jacob Riis (1849–1914), *Two Greek children in Gotham Court debating if Santa Claus will get to their alley or not. He did*, ca. 1890. The Museum of the City of New York. Photo credit: The Museum of the City of New York/Art Resource, New York.

Even worse, in his image *Minding the baby; Baby yells a Whirlwind Scream, Gotham Court* there is real fear on the little boy's face, as the adult rushes to grab the smaller girl (*fig. 2.11*). It is not clear if the woman is the mother of either or both of them, a neighbor, or even a stranger. But it remains apparent that, despite his clenched, determined grip, he will be powerless to stop the larger force.

Riis' work, while factual, portrayed only a single facet of the city. Art historians Rebecca Zurier and Robert Snyder explained how this muckraker "editorialized, sensationalized, and sometimes disparaged the very immigrants whose lives he hoped to improve. . . . Far from being objective, these pictures serve their own agenda by deliberately omitting much of what" the Ashcan school artists would attempt to capture.[38]

Photography did not have to be used in this way, as a later generation adopted a far different approach. Although Lewis Hine took pictures of people with the same economic status and

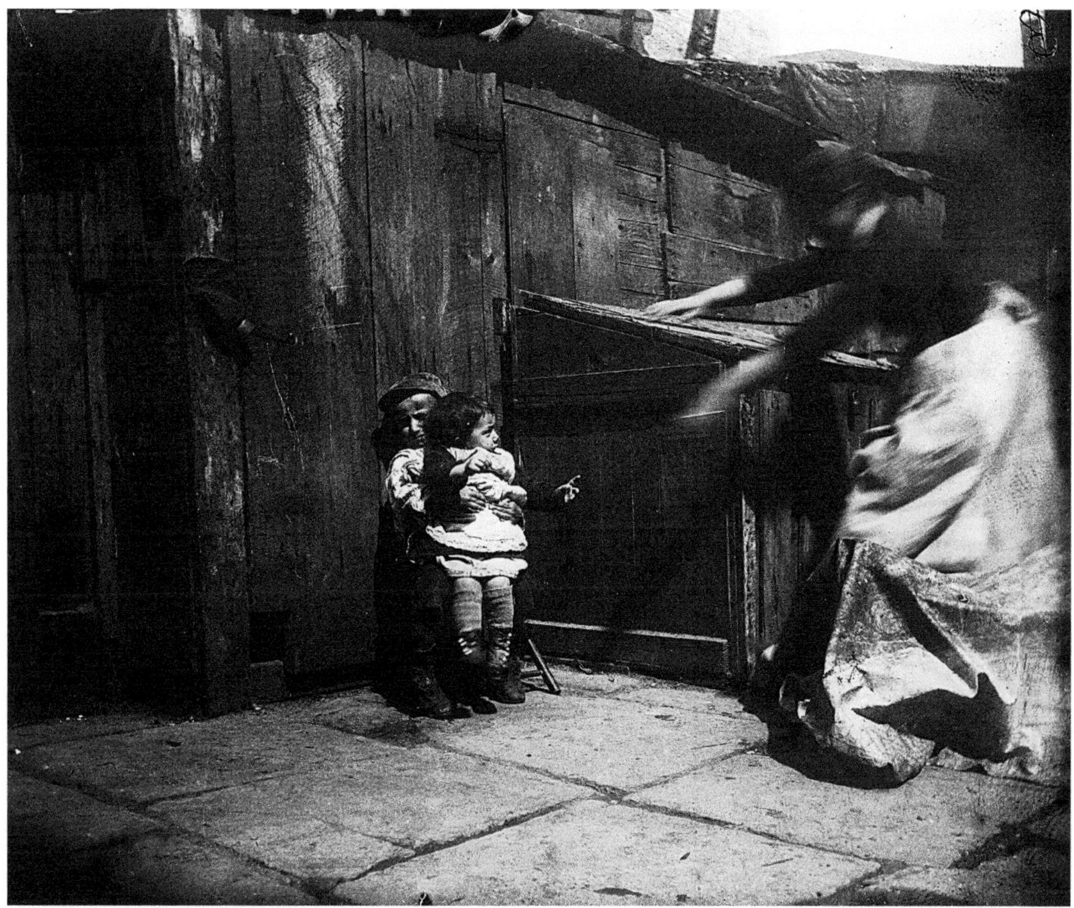

2.11 Jacob Riis (1849–1914), *Minding the baby; Baby yells a Whirlwind Scream, Gotham Court*, 1890. Museum of the City of New York. Photo credit: The Museum of the City of New York/Art Resource, New York. Title in Art Resource invoice is A *young boy holding a baby, a woman reaches for them.*

national origin as Riis' subjects, he did so from a unique and dissimilar perspective. As a result, his work contrasts sharply with that of his predecessor and highlighted what Riis and the reformers missed.

A native of Wisconsin, Lewis Hine moved to New York in 1901, eleven years after the publication of *How the Other Half Lives*. By 1904 he was employed by the Ethical Culture Society and became involved with a project to photograph immigrants who had just arrived at Ellis Island. Within a few years he began working for the National Child Labor Committee and in 1908 accepted a regular position there, visually documenting nationwide the abuses that were their chief concern. Hine, in other words, was creating images of the same groups that Riis captured: the immigrant, the economically distressed, and children.

Yet, Hine saw these Americans in a totally different light. While he hated degrading work, he saw honest labor as redemptive and felt the industrial classes were the heroes of this new America. The art historian Kate Sampsell-Willmann wrote that Hine "never wavered . . . from his dedication to the dignity of work and joy in labor." Unlike Riis, who "blatantly objectified and openly disliked his subjects," Hine "made pictures of beauty and grace persevering in the midst of ugliness, exploitation and filth." This artist chose to "depict society's powerless with dignity."[39]

Hine's finest portrait tackled, for example, one of the foremost social issues of the era, the immigrant. His work took him to the place where this was at its most raw, to Ellis Island, where newcomers had not even stepped on American soil and begun the process of assimilation. Yet, his 1905 image *Jewess at Ellis Island—1905* is a thing of beauty (*fig. 2.12*).

In this image, Hine does not portray her as a faceless member of a teeming mass but rather presents both an individual, and as Sampsell-Willmann explained, "a delicate and beautiful young woman." Ellis Island is merely the background; it is the person, not the institution, that dominates this photograph.[40]

These qualities are also abundantly on display in the photos Hine took at the steelworker enclave in Homestead, Pennsylvania. Hine never tried to cover up misery; in his work for the pathbreaking report *Homestead*, he painstakingly depicted the grimness of a steelworker's life.

Hines' image of a tenement house, *A One-Room Household*, could have just as easily come from Riis' camera (*fig. 2.13*, pg. 34). It is disturbingly crowded, there are children with no space, and the floor is dirty.

The difference is that in Hine's body of work there is a sense of balance, a representation of other aspects of a working-class community, of the warmth that Riis missed. In *The Street Market* the scene is hardly middle class, but it is also lively (*fig. 2.14*, pg. 34). In the middle right children play, while on the left they help mother pick out foodstuff, clambering all over the vendor's cart. Contrary to popular belief, they often kept their streets and their neighborhoods clean. Notwithstanding Riis' images, the working class was not always dingy or filthy.

Hine's photographs of children further rebuffed Riis' despairing approach. In part due to "his own sensitivity and playfulness," the photographer smiled "at the fact that wonders of childhood survive even in the most brutal surroundings." Hine saw "agency in the faces of his subjects, belief in their own free will." These youngsters, like the woman framed in Ellis Island, were transformed from being an "object in the photographer's narrative to subject in his or her own story."[41]

These elements of joy are clearly on display in Hine's image, *In Carnegie's Footsteps* (*fig. 2.15*, pg. 35). This image is striking due to its subjects' alertness and ease of bearing. Taken at their eye level rather than from an adult's perspective, it portrayed young men, who, from their clothing and the setting, are clearly from the working class and poor. All the same, they are standing at attention, happy to be photographed, confident enough to look directly at the man taking the picture instead of gazing down and away; most amazing of all, they are smiling. They seem proud, looking forward to the rest of their life. The image is happy, rather than fearful.

More joyous, still, are the subjects of *The Brook in Munhall Hollow* (*fig. 2.16*, pg. 35). The caption describes how dank the waters they are standing in really are, referring to the setting as "an open drain," as "a crime against health and childhood."

In spite of these conditions, however, Hine seems incapable of restraining himself. The children in this picture are not just grinning, they are openly laughing. Yes, the site of the picture must be cleaned up, and yes, there is danger here. But it's also, at the same time, a lot of fun and should be replaced by something equally playful. Mud and children combine and pleasure is the result. These children, like all children—rich, poor, and in-between—have still figured out how to enjoy themselves. This implies both power and the capacity to adapt an environment to one's needs.

Better still is the picture of *Laura Petty, a 6-year-old berry picker on Jenkins farm, Rock Creek near Baltimore, Md.* (*fig. 2.17*, pg. 36). This child is not just happy, she is feisty. As with most

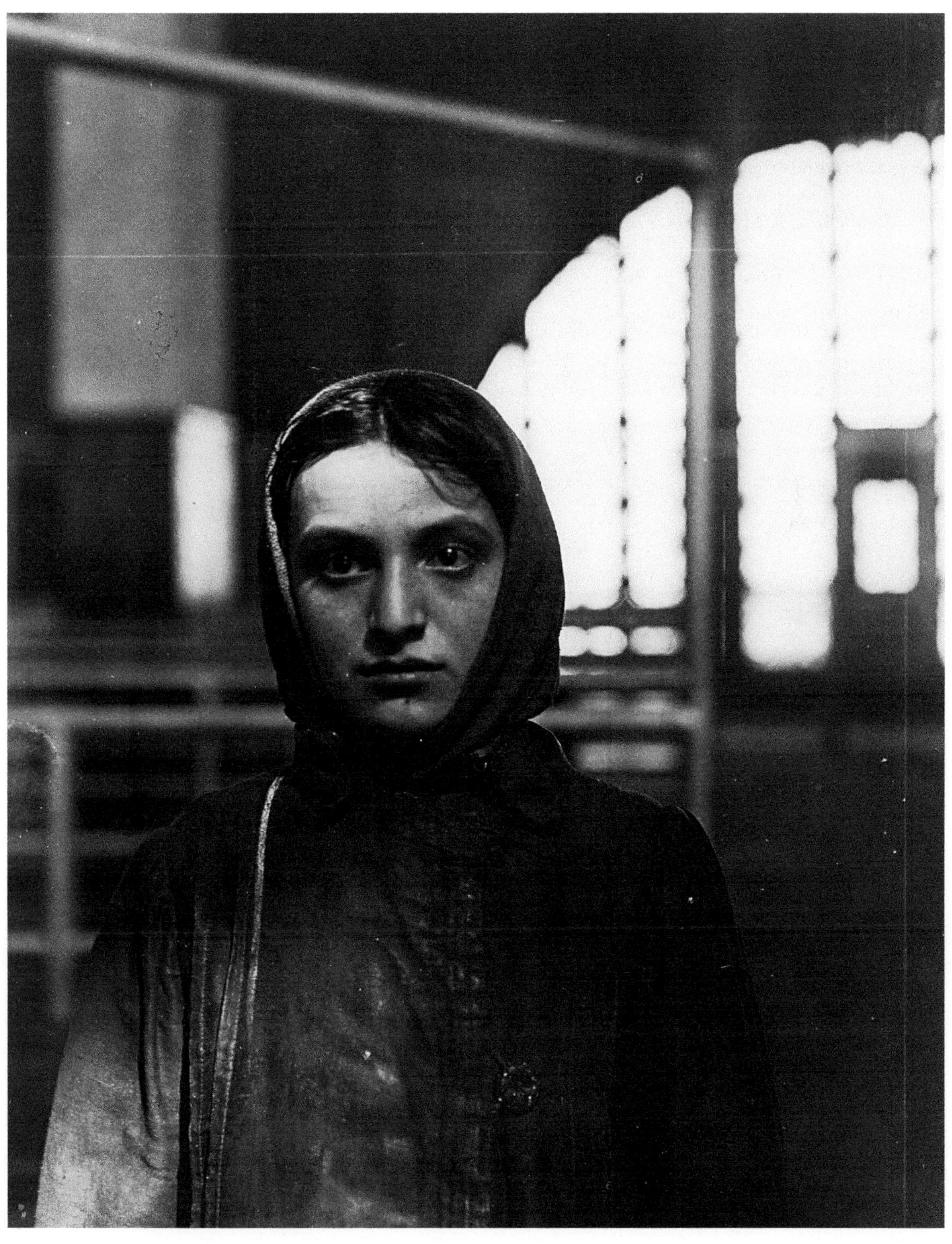

2.12 Lewis Hine (1874–1940), *Jewess at Ellis Island—1905*, 1905, gelatin silver print, image: 24.1 × 19.1 cm. 1977.0177.0151. George Eastman Museum, Rochester, New York.

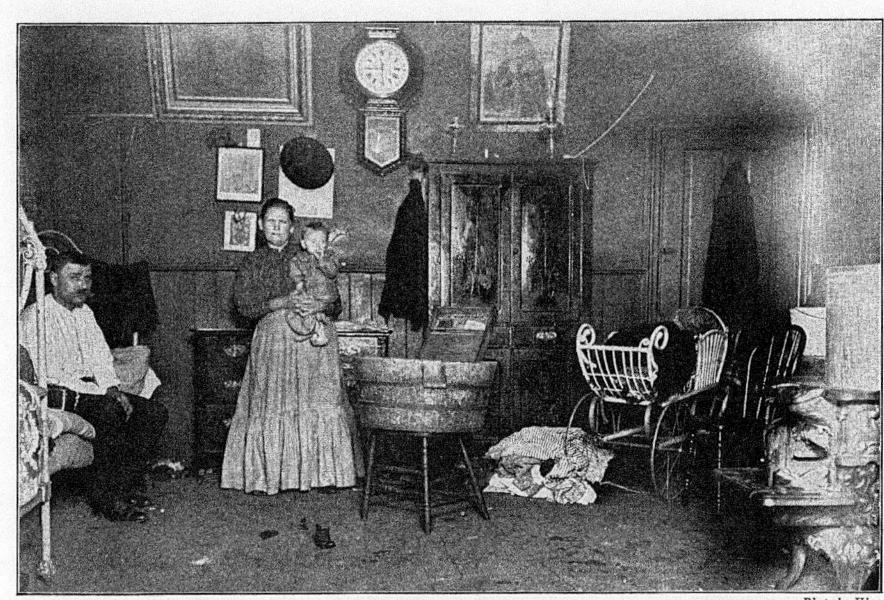

A One-room Household

2.13 Lewis Hine (1874–1940), *A One-Room Household*, opposite page 53, Margaret Byington, *Homestead* (New York: Pittsburgh Survey and Charities Publication Committee, 1910).

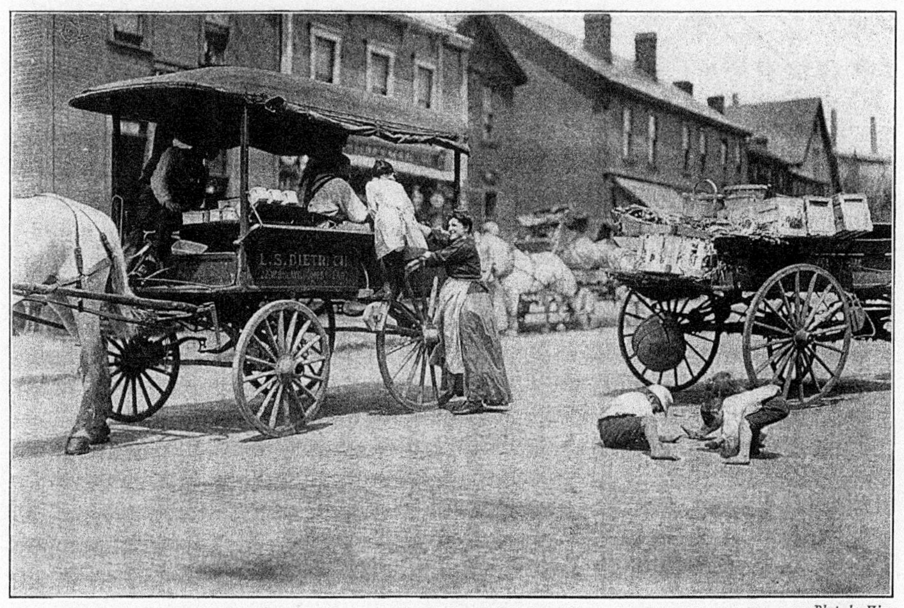

The Street Market

2.14 Lewis Hine (1874–1940), *The Street Market*, opposite page 73, Margaret Byington, *Homestead* (New York: Pittsburgh Survey and Charities Publication Committee, 1910).

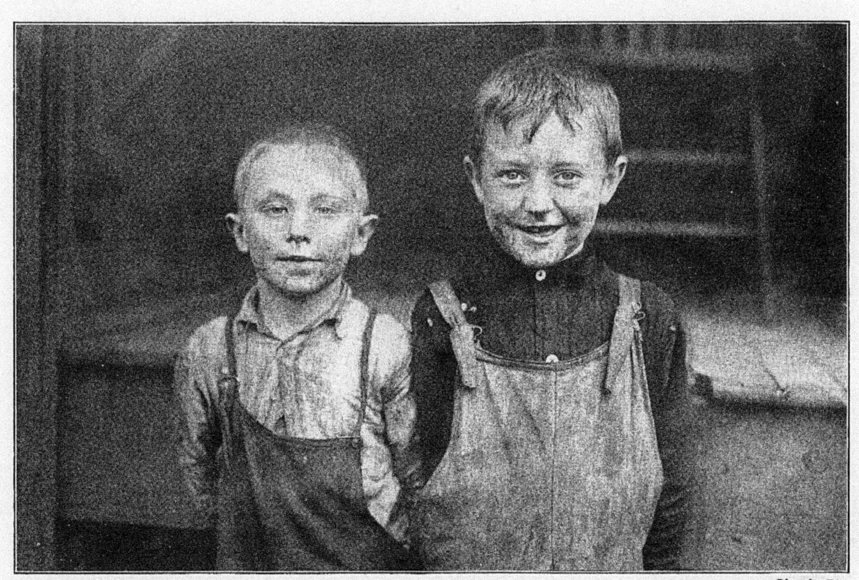

2.15 Lewis Hine (1874–1940), *In Carnegie's Footsteps*, from Margaret Byington, *Homestead* (New York: Pittsburgh Survey and Charities Publication Committee, 1910), facing page 119.

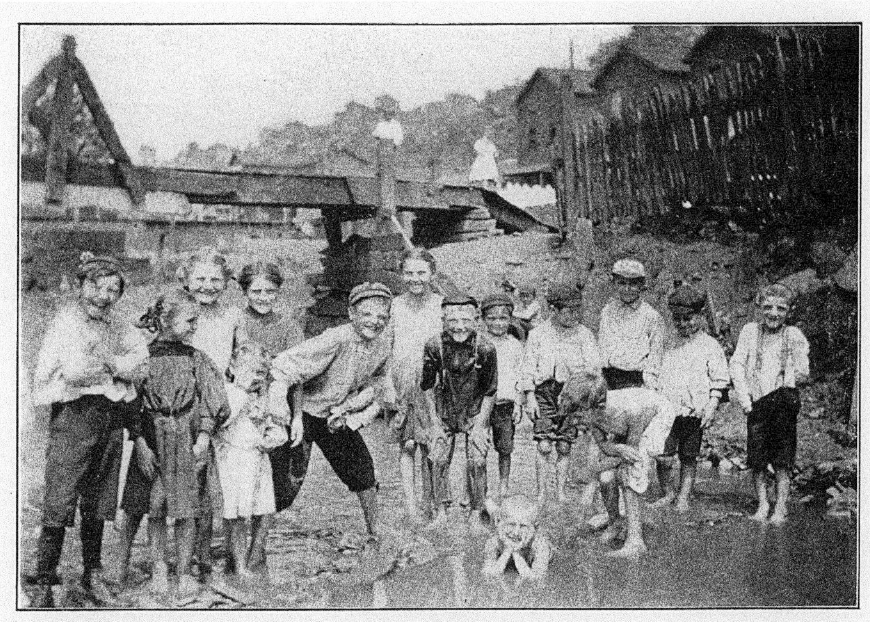

2.16 Lewis Hine (1874–1940), *The Brook in Munhall Hollow*, from Margaret Byington, *Homestead* (New York: Russell Sage Foundation, Charities Publication, 1910), facing page 121.

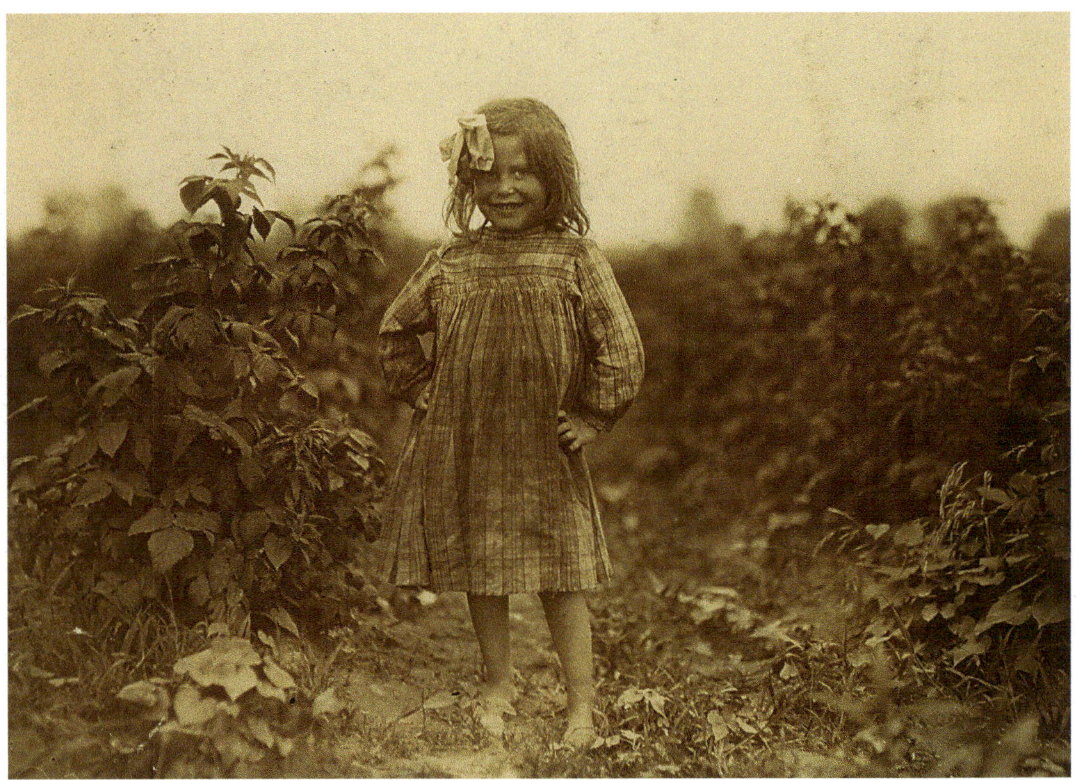

2.17 Lewis Hine (1874–1940), *Laura Petty, a 6-year-old berry picker on Jenkins farm, Rock Creek near Baltimore, Md.* "'I'm just beginning.' Picked two boxes yesterday." (2 cents a box). (See my report July 10, 1909.) July 8, 1909. Location: Baltimore, Maryland. 1909 July 8. Photographic print. Reproduction number: LC-DIG-nclc-00003 (color digital file from b&w original print) LC-USZ6-1197 (b&w film copy negative). Call number: LOT 7475, v. 1, no. 0829 [P&P]. National Child Labor Committee Collection, Library of Congress, Washington, DC.

children, she has the world by the tail. And she knows it; note the placement of the hands on her hips, as if daring all commers to check her out. The caption reads, "'I'm just beginnin.' Picked two boxes yesterday." "Look at me," she seems to be saying, "Aren't I something?!?"

Best of all is a joyous image (*fig. 2.18*). The toddler here is dirty and laughing, pointing to something wonderfully compelling. Hine's subject is simply . . . a child.

For all their limitations, Riis' images served as a powerful bridge to the Ashcan school painters. By 1900 Americans understood the importance of their vastly expanding urban civilization and learned about it through a series of images that depicted the top and the bottom of the city, exclusively. As a new century dawned, the Ashcan artists would make their mark by offering up a totally different metropolis than the ones that had been envisioned by either the elites or by Jacob Riis.

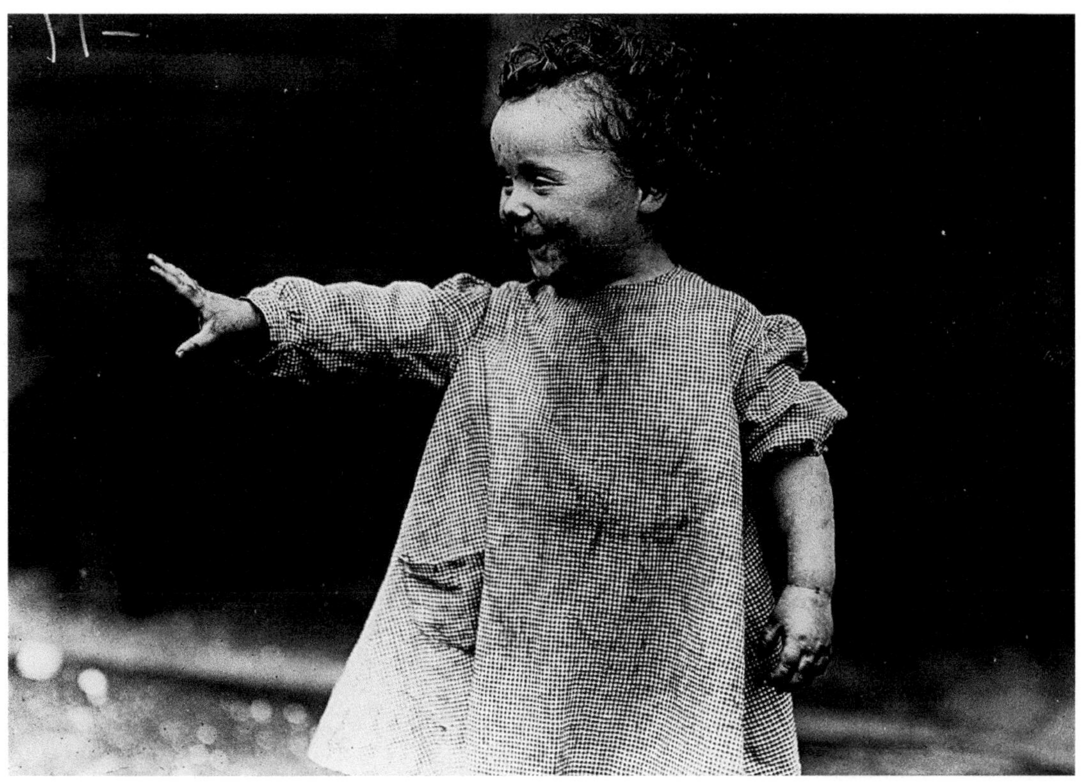

2.18 Lewis Hine (1874–1940), *Tenement Child—1909*, "No Soap for me," Steelworker's child—Pa., 1909. Gelatin silver print. Image: 11.7 × 16.7 cm. 1977.0187.0114. George Eastman House, Rochester, New York.

CHAPTER THREE

Vision from an Ashcan

The Ashcan school represented a challenge to its era. In a fundamental reinterpretation of art's appropriate subject matter, it threw down a gauntlet, of canvas and paint, to the art world both of the right and of the left. It did not see the city through the narrow peephole of the elites, instead introducing new landscapes, new characters. But these perspectives were also different from what the reformers saw. This new approach painted the rest of the city, with beauty, endowing urban and working-class individuals of all ages and genders with agency and will. In so doing, the Ashcan artists created one of the great American art forms.

First, they reconceptualized art as well as the city itself. To artists trained in the National Academy, landscapes were the stuff of rural settings, pastures and farmers, and nature's grand tableaus. Elite urban artists expanded this notion, by showing how downtown settings, with broad boulevards and well-dressed residents, could also be fitting subjects for their talent. As Michael Owen wrote in the foreword to a catalog for an Ashcan exhibit, "the near banishment of the pretty girl in the garden was replaced with a new awareness of urban realism."[1]

The Ashcan artists took this one giant leap further. First and most significantly, they embraced the urban experience in all its diversity. Instead of depicting the city as consisting only of Washington Square, or else as sections grim and dirty and foreign, they understood and sought to paint the sheer excitement of the urban experience. They captured tall buildings but also workers and construction sites, railroads and seagoing barges. Not just the Easter Parade but bustling immigrant neighborhoods; not just elegant salons but decent, cramped, working-class apartment life. John Loughery, in his biography of John Sloan, explained how "Sloan the walker in the city, the explorer of neighborhoods near and far, the spectator of little scenes and daily dramas, ultimately came to the conclusion that it was in the streets he traveled every day, rather than in the studio or the rural areas outside the city limits, that he might find himself as an artist."[2]

A few perceptive individuals understood this shift. One New York writer, in a 1903 article for *Scribner's Magazine*, observed, "What American cities most need to render them beautiful is an artist who will body forth to our duller eyes the beauty already there." Jerome Myers, a powerful, yet largely unacknowledged artist in the Ashcan school, in a 1940 autobiography described himself "with a solitary crayon pencil, peering at the crowded East Side of New York City. . . . At nightfall the surcease of a great city, the repose in the parks, or on the recreation piers, the aged gossip, the children at their endless play—a panorama which was for me unceasing in its interest, thrilling in its significance." His sentiments are clear, as is his sense of the city's power: "My love was my witness in recording those earnest, simple lives, those visions of the slums clothed in dignity, never to me mere slums but the habitations of people who were rich in spirit and effort."[3]

It is this ethos, first of all, that defined the Ashcan school of art. As everyone who has ever loved New York—or London, or Paris—understands in their soul, the city is an exciting place to be, and in that excitement, there is beauty.

Nobody captured this better than John Sloan, the premier artist of this genre. His *Six O'clock, Winter* is a masterpiece of this emotion (*fig. 3.1*). Everything is movement and power. Yet this is not the force depicted in a portrait of a monarch in royal garb, but rather the rumble of a city, and a working city at that. There is no genteel soul strolling here in fashionable clothing. Instead, the people depicted here wear middle-class garments and are pressed together in the rush hour after work. There are masses of them as well; their strength truly is in the infinite number of human threads twisted into the urban fiber. This is an epic painting, in a metropolitan setting. Overhead bellows a subway train, a monster of modern industry, not heroic myth; it is held up by pillars and bracing of iron and steel, not the bones of a dragon's skeleton.

Above all, everything is movement, the city's hallmark. As the train blasts overhead, against a passionate blue sky, crowds of individuals shuttle back and forth. Most are returning from their

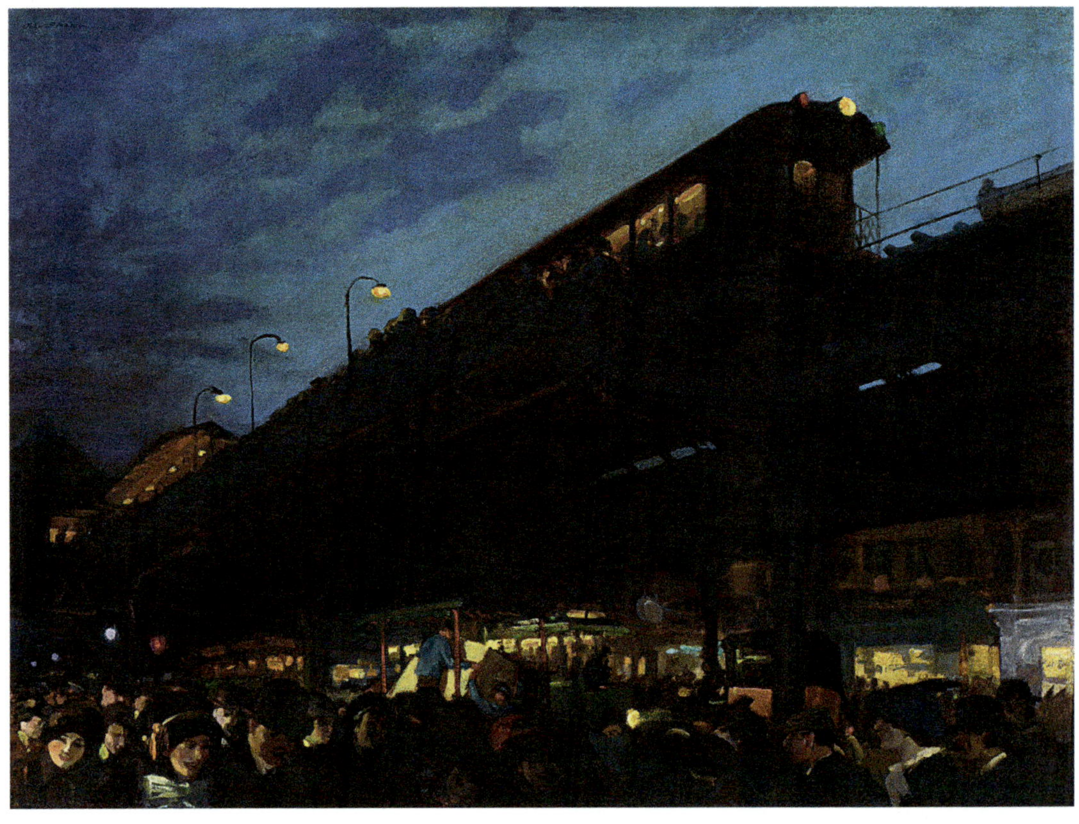

3.1 John Sloan (1871–1951), *Six O'clock, Winter*, 1912, oil on canvas, 26⅛ × 32 inches; 66.3575 × 81.28 cm. Acquired 1922. © 2009 Delaware Art Museum/Artists Rights Society, New York. The Phillips Collection, Washington, DC.

jobs, but some are still on the job; note the taxi and bus drivers, and the figures in the middle erecting a stand. Throughout there is a sense of movement, as the diagonal line of the elevated pierces the canvas. The notion that winter is a time that hems one in, limits chances, denotes death, is vanquished here. Instead, Gotham's technology pushes back winter, provides freedom and movement. The figures here are not gloomy; they are happy, despite the dark season. Sloan's image is an illustration of a great city's excitement and dynamism. His metropolis is neither elite heaven nor underclass hell. It is a throbbing creature, filled to the brim with life with working-class residents, busy lively people with full lives who make choices to determine how they will handle Gotham.[4]

Sloan was also capable of capturing a different mood, albeit one that was still intensely urban. In many ways, *Sunset West Twenty-Third Street* (*fig. 3.2*) looks like a tableau of the Monument Valley from a John Ford western. While the scale is equally epic, the setting is urban and working class. Thus, the view remains profound, and vast in scale. But these are skyscrapers, not buttes, and the lights are electric, not from stars. The beauty here is real, but shaped and created by humans in that greatest of their inventions, the modern city. This, too, shows how the Ashcan artists reconceived the physical, and how they endowed Gotham with beauty by reinventing old forms to fit a new setting.

And the figure on the side, providing scale, in not a lone cowboy or Native American, but instead a woman doing the wash on a rooftop. She is someone with limited resources, making use of what space the urban setting offers to unfurl her clothesline. Regardless, she does not

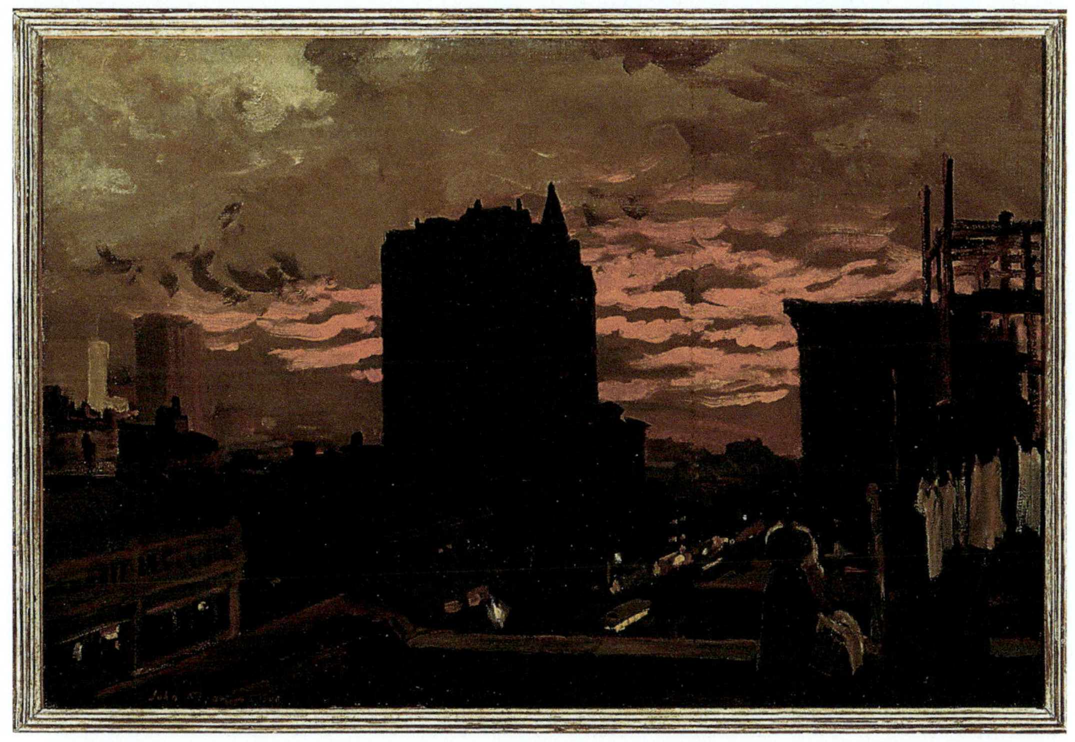

3.2 John Sloan (1871–1951), *Sunset West Twenty-Third Street* (23rd Street, Roofs, Sunset), 1906, oil on canvas, 24⅜ × 36¼; 61.91 × 92.1 cm. Joslyn Art Museum, Omaha, Nebraska. 25th Anniversary Purchase, 1957.15.

seem cowed by the panorama; rather, she seems contemplative, admiring and pondering what lies before her, just as one would do when gazing on the Grand Canyon. Her situation in life is apparent, yet she seems fully capable of grand thoughts, of appreciating the beauty that Sloan has laid before her. Despite her hard work, she takes it all in, luxuriates in the view, and invites the viewer to think about and admire the city with her. The city can be among God's gifts to America, too. Rather than drones or the downcast, its working-class residents are sentient creatures who are fully capable of appreciating the beauty here.

The Ashcan school, however, shared at least one element with elite painters like Childe Hassam, and that was that both groups used the impressionist technique. Ashcan artists, however, did not use this method to guide their subject matter but rather as a tool, a fluid technique to capture the city's movement. As noted in the introduction to *American Impressionism and Realism*, "They had at their disposal a vigorous style that was particularly effective for interpreting a dynamic time in a democratic place."[5] This technique, however, made no departures from the canon; instead, their contribution, their grand thrust, lay elsewhere. As Judith Zilczer pointed out, "Compared to their French counterparts, the American Eight were hardly revolutionary in style." John I. H. Baur, director of the Whitney Museum, in his assessment of what was novel about the Ashcan school, and what was not, asserted that these artists pressed for "a social liberalism as radical in its day as their styles were conservative."[6]

In George Luks' *Thompson and Bleecker Streets* (*fig. 3.3*), we see what made the Ashcan school both original and traditional. On the one hand, there is the style, the characteristic

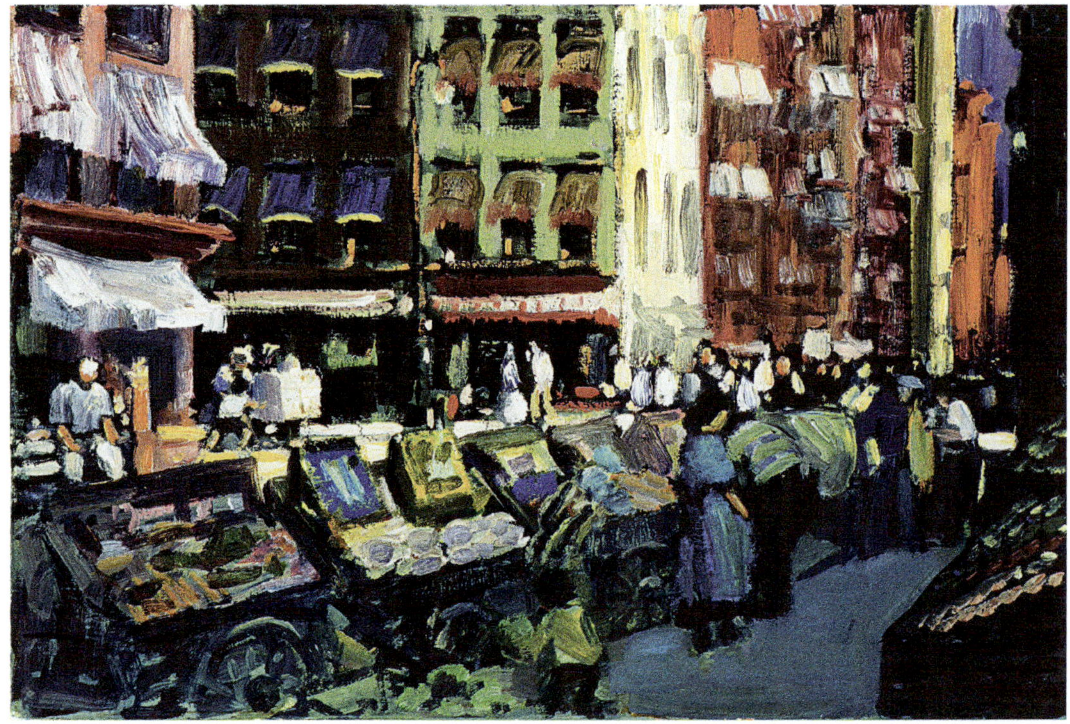

3.3 George Luks (1867–1933), *Thompson and Bleecker Streets*, ca. 1905, oil on canvas, 20 × 30 inches. Palmer Museum of Art of the Pennsylvania State University. Gift of James and Barbara Palmer. 2005.14.

impressionist style, the dappled images. Yet the subject matter stands out; here this method is used to portray the congestion of a crowded immigrant shopping district, of women rummaging through pushcarts. This, too, shows how the Ashcan artists reconceived the physical, how they endowed Gotham with beauty, reinventing old forms to fit a new setting. Thus, the great rebellion of the Ashcan school was in *what* its artists chose to draw, rather than in *how* they drew it. Their hallmark was in making beautiful subjects no artists had deemed fitting before, urban landscapes and the working classes who dwelled within them. As historian Peter Conn asserted, "Theirs was a concern primarily with new subject matter, not with new technique."[7]

This can be seen in George Wesley Bellows' classic *The Cliff-Dwellers* (*fig. 3.4*). Here is the working-class city: boisterous, smelly, full of life. Nothing is glamorous here, yet this is animation,

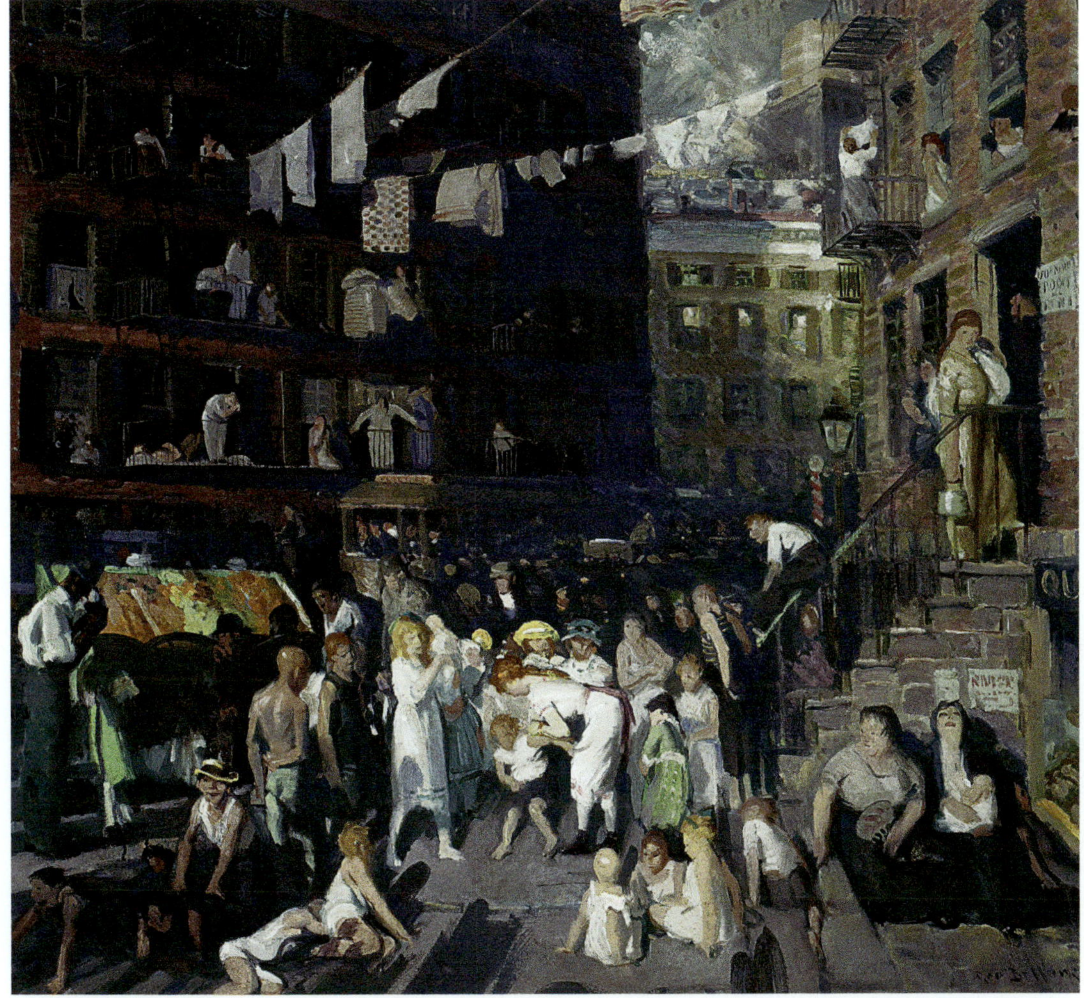

3.4 George Wesley Bellows (1882–1925), *The Cliff-Dwellers*, 1913, oil on canvas, 40³⁄₁₆ × 42¹⁄₁₆ inches; 102.07 × 106.83 cm. Los Angeles County Fund (16.4). Los Angeles County Museum of Art, Los Angeles, California. Digital Image © 2016 Museum Associates/ LACMA. Licensed by Art Resource, New York.

not depression. Theodore Dreiser wrote a review of this painting that began, "It is so direct, so forthright." There are no hidden nuances, "any more than the broad accurate face of life anywhere." This is hardly a charming scene, as "the walls are so red and dirty. And by day and night, at this time of the year, hot. . . . And the houses and gutters smell just as do the people— sweaty and weary." Yet the image is flush—with people, wash lines, pushcarts. These people are not strutting, nor are they defeated. It's just another hot day in the city for ordinary people, a neighborhood, as Dreiser put it, "packed with . . . vibrant, necessary or unnecessary life."[8]

Thus, the Ashcan school redefined what was the fitting subject for a painting in a fundamental way. They understood that a new America presented new scenes, new people to draw. William Taylor, in his study of New York City, *In Pursuit of Gotham*, complained, "The visual properties of modern cities like New York must have seemed a kind of antipastoral vision of the beautiful. It was one thing to portray people scattered across fields, at work and at play; it was quite another to depict them against a background of concrete, glass, and asphalt." Moreover, Taylor continued, "there was something, too, about man in relation to machine that seemed initially incongruous, even grotesque. Tall building . . . blocked the horizon; created dark, sunless canyons; overshadowed waterways; and dwarfed those bits of vegetation. . . . It proved difficult to portray people in such settings without dwarfing or dehumanizing them."[9]

And yet, those were exactly the kinds of places that the Ashcan artists made beautiful with their art. George Wesley Bellows' *Blue Morning* does fine work at capturing the city's aesthetic appeal (*fig. 3.5*). This is a study in soft, luxuriant tones, a gentle blue predominating. The colors are suited to a painting of an early summer's evening on a farm, with earth colors in the foreground as hands tend to a flock of sheep.

Except that the subject here is the excavation of Pennsylvania Station, on Ninth Avenue between Thirty-Third and Thirty-Fourth Streets in Manhattan. A massive urban structure dominates the background, while the foreground contains various elements of work in the city: a crane off to the right, laborers toiling with large hammers, and a fence to keep out bystanders, which adds contrast and brown tones.

The artist, therefore, portrays the city as an epic experience, just as a century prior, the Hudson River school had captured beauty in the Catskills' forests. But the density here is not represented by trees or plant life, but by city folk and buildings. Marianne Doezema, in her perceptive study *George Bellows and Urban America* referred to this image as "the gleaming white station building in construction, rising up out of the great hole," making it sound like a goddess emerging; but Bellows subject is a work site in New York City. In a 1917 interview, Bellows protested descriptions that called his work innovative, even when they captured the exact elements that made his art fresh. "I have been called a revolutionist," Bellows complained, "if I am, I don't know it." Rather, he asserted, "First of all, I am a painter, and a painter gets hold of life—gets hold of something real, of many real things. That makes him think, and if he thinks out loud he is called a revolutionist." Yet Bellows was indeed an innovator because of what he chose to paint, of where he found beauty.[10]

And so, the Ashcan artists broke from rural, pastoral tradition in American art by discovering the physical beauty of the urban setting and its residents. John Corbin, writing in 1903, five years before the Macbeth exhibition, thought the city "grotesque" and "formless" yet still sought "an artist bent on divining new forms of beauty" in this environment. Louis Baury, in a 1911 article in *The Bookman*, went even further, capturing what the Ashcan school had accomplished. "Only a handful," he realized, "had sensed the fact that the vital message of the age is flashed forth in the incandescent signs on Broadway and graven on the park benches which are set down here and there among the metropolitan mountains of men." Baury recognized what was happening with the Ashcan movement, how "these few painters are artistic pioneers; to them the

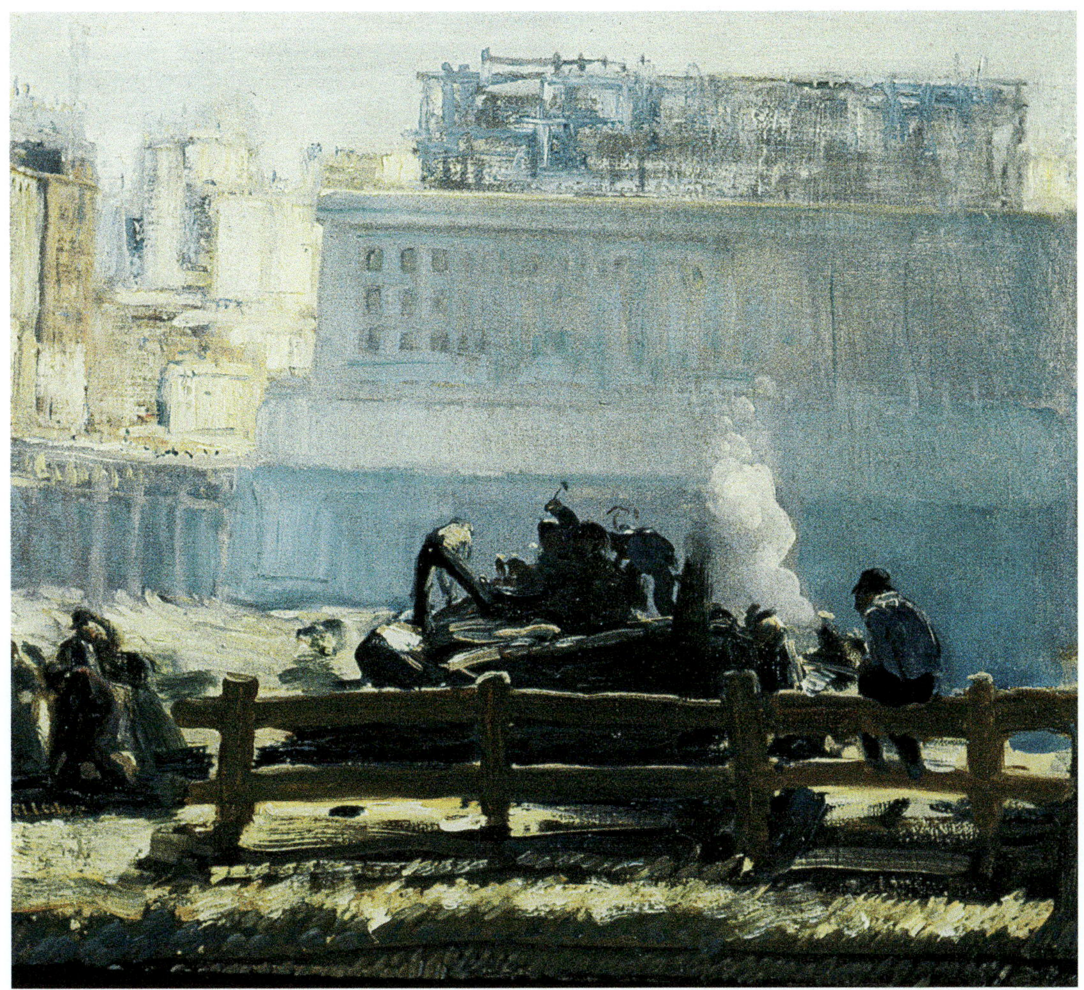

3.5 George Wesley Bellows (1882–1925), *Blue Morning*, 1909, oil on canvas, 31½ × 43½ inches. Private Collection/Bridgeman Images.

many-tongued voice of the city is speaking in definite, insistent terms. For them this Occidental sphinx has become articulate."[11]

From this concern with the urban setting blossomed one of the Ashcan school's most powerful concepts. Because of their subject matter, they implicitly argued a revolutionary doctrine, that beauty was not bound by class. If Hassam made a breakthrough with the notion that landscapes did not require rural or natural settings, the Ashcan artists took another even greater leap toward modernity. Unlike Hassam, unlike the Social Darwinists, they did not believe that vast wealth, or even the power of elites, inherently or exclusively formed subjects that were attractive and worthy of attention.

A portfolio of three of John Sloan's images illustrates this idea, representing the most powerful of the Ashcan school's innovations for American urban painters.

In the first, *Carmine Street Theater*, Sloan portrays a typical working-class neighborhood with grace and affection (*fig. 3.6*). Yet the class notes are apparent throughout the work. The children are happy and tidy, but neither wealthy nor in despair. A loose dog, rummaging through garbage, symbolizes disorder. On the left middle, a nun placidly strides, in an era when most Americans considered Roman Catholicism the religion of immigrant working-class masses. The theater's name implies that this is an Italian neighborhood. Behind it there is a fire escape and the windows of a tenement building. The scene is urban and its characters are of lower status. Yet it is a beautiful painting.

In *The Wake of the Ferry II*, Sloan presents one of his most striking images (*fig. 3.7*). This is a ballet, with the tugboats shimmering, delicately weaving through the traffic and the stormy weather, *Swan Lake* performed by sailors. All the signs, however, point to modest circumstances. The view is from a ferry boat, a type of mass transit. Oceangoing vessels push heavier boats

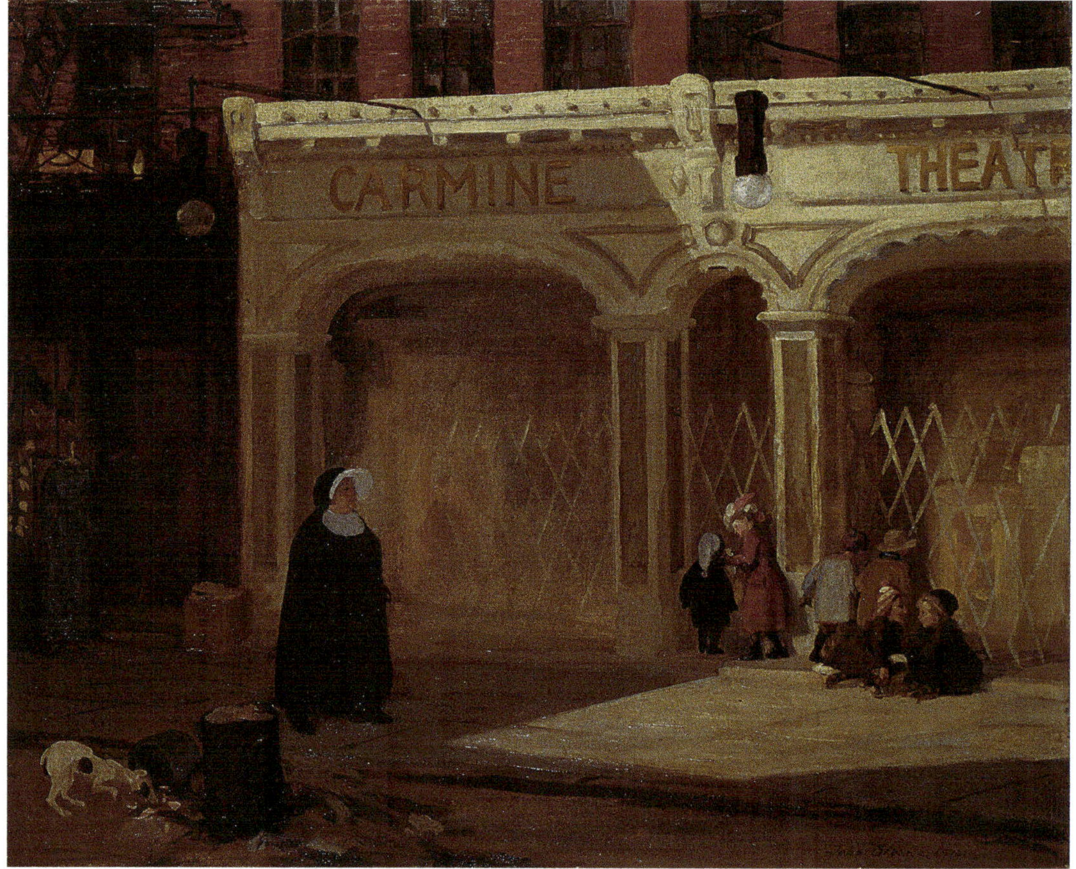

3.6 John Sloan (1871–1951), *Carmine Street Theater*, 1912, oil on canvas, 26⅛ × 32 inches; 66.1 × 81.2 cm. Hirshhorn Museum and Sculpture Garden. Smithsonian Institution. Gift of the Joseph H. Hirshhorn Foundation, 1966. Photography by Lee Stalsworth. © 2016 Delaware Art Museum/Artist Rights Society (ARS), New York. Hirshhorn has it as *Carmine Theater*, but ARS has it as *Carmine Street Theater*.

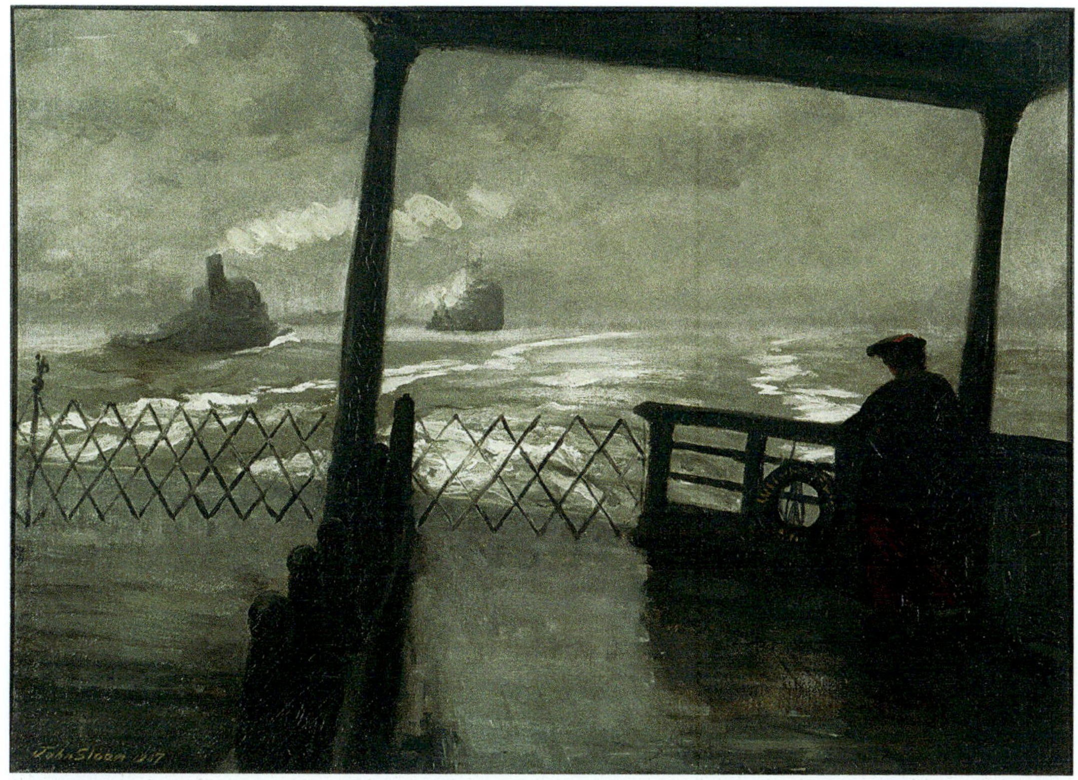

3.7 John Sloan (1871–1951), *The Wake of the Ferry II*, 1907, oil on canvas, 26 × 32 inches; 66.04 × 81.28 cm. Acquired 1922. © 2012 Delaware Art Museum/Artists Rights Society, New York. The Phillips Collection, Washington, DC.

along with blunt brawn; there are no first-class accommodations here, no *Normandie* or *Titanic*. Yet there is a sublime quality to this painting, a sense of larger forces at work, at peace with themselves and the universe. John Dos Passos described the working-class beauty of such a scene: *"Tree gulls wheel above the broken boxes, orangerinds, spoiled cabbage heads that heave beneath the splintered plank walls, the green waves spume under the round bow as the ferry, skidding on the tide, crashes, gulps the broken water, slides, settles slowly into the slip."*[12]

Finally, there is his 1907 work, *Election Night* (fig. 3.8, pg. 48). Filled with boisterous life, this is a vibrant painting, one that captures the excitement of the city in compelling fashion. Its subjects wear working- and middle-class clothes. Tall buildings press in close, hemming in the scene. Overhead a subway train bellows, all electricity and strength, oblivious to the merriment below. Beneath it, in the heart of the city, horns blow, and people celebrate and laugh and jostle one another. This is better, wilder, and happier than New Year's Eve. In an image that modern-day observers can still view with admiration, as well as with a smile, Sloan has made New York's politics and its masses not only attractive but festive. Art historian Michael Lobel felt it was "a veritably timeless sense of carnivalesque celebration, akin . . . to one of Pieter Bruegel's peasant scenes, or to a bacchanal by Titian or Nicholas Poussin." Sloan's drawing personified the joy of everyday life and the events that punctuated it, but the charm, the beauty, was that of an American city, not the European countryside. The *New York Tribune* called

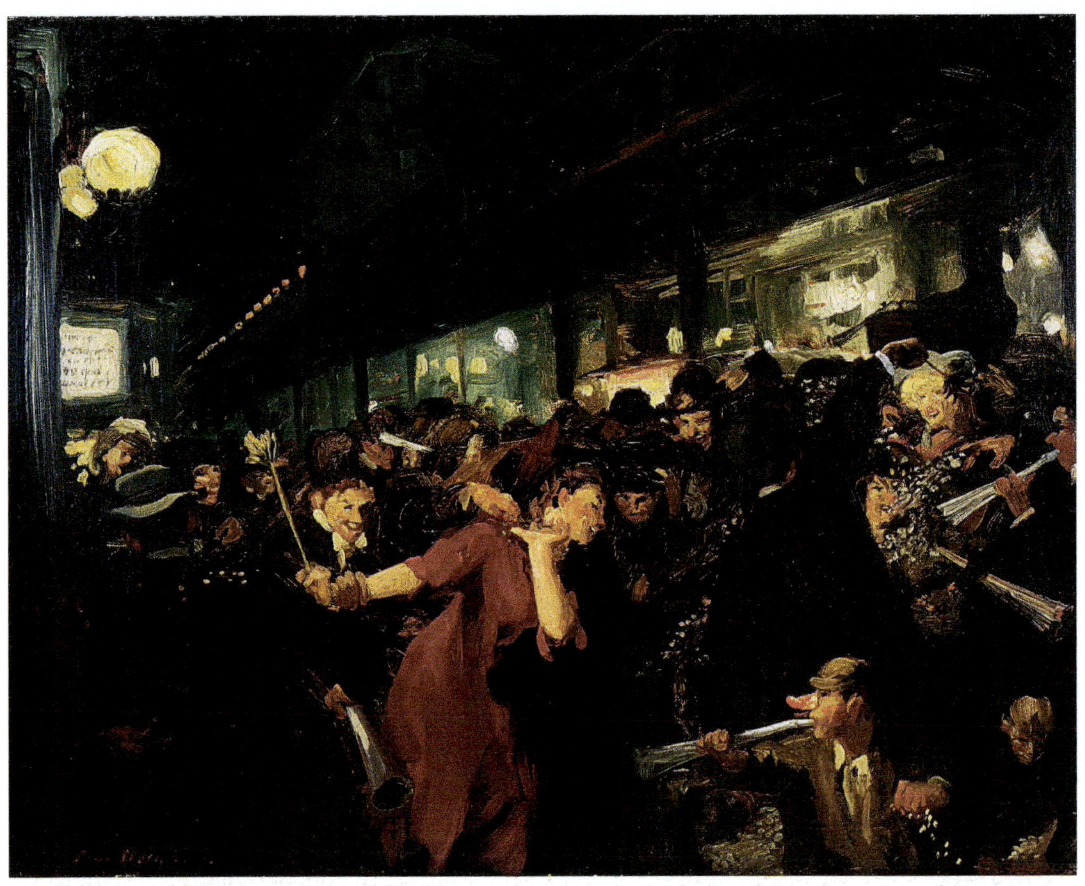

3.8 John Sloan (1871–1951), *Election Night*, 1907, oil on canvas, 25⅜ × 31¾ inches.
Marion Stratton Gould Fund, 41.33, Memorial Art Gallery, Rochester, New York.

this "the kind of crowd that has become typical of New York. . . . big, unwieldy, restless, and excitement seeking."[13]

Even more, this is an ode to the power of the ordinary citizen. Democracy was not just practiced in the heart of the city; it is exalted. At the same time, it was also held in less than solemn reverence; note the boy in the lower right with fake nose and horn. The city houses important values. But it is also fun.

For the Ashcan artists, Gotham housed all classes, and not merely the elite or the downtrodden. To explore that totality, and to capture it, took a new sensitivity. Rebecca Zurier, in her study of the Ashcan school, *Picturing the City*, described how these artists encountered the urban form: "Only an insider would possess the . . . knowledge necessary to organize the plethora of sights that to a stranger would read as random overload. Only an outsider would take the time to record and marvel at details that more jaded viewers cease to notice." And what details they were: "The buildings that frame the streets burst with information: architectural ornament, sagging shutters . . . windows forming an irregular pattern of closed and open with figures and laundry spilling out. Pushcarts overflow with fruit and clothing. Street signs advertise a frothing glass of beer." Deborah Fairman, in an article on the theme of spectacle in Ashcan school painting, noticed how "some chose to portray the 'underside' of the city, some its expansive beauty, others its vast and disorienting scale." Two paintings display this understanding of the complexity of urban life particularly well.[14]

George Luks' *Street Scene (Hester Street)* is a crowded urban tableau (*fig. 3.9*). Many of its figures are middle class; the lady on the right wears a proper summer hat, and the man in the left foreground with the cigarette appears to share her status. But on either side of him and back are Orthodox Jews, quite possibly immigrants.

There is a lot going on here. Commerce is depicted through the lady with the basket, and by the shopkeeper arguing with his customer on the right. A pushcart used to display flowers for sale sits in the foreground, and a peddler selling children's toys plies his wares in the middle of this scene. The store window displays carcasses, a butcher shop's merchandise.

The background also depicts a moving, dynamic city. Piling into the intersection, multitudes of shoppers seem to be arriving here. All around are multistory apartment buildings with fire escapes, the kind of structures that were the hallmark of urban density. These are not symbols of despair, as they were to the reformers, but the habitats of the mixed and lively people who reside in the city.

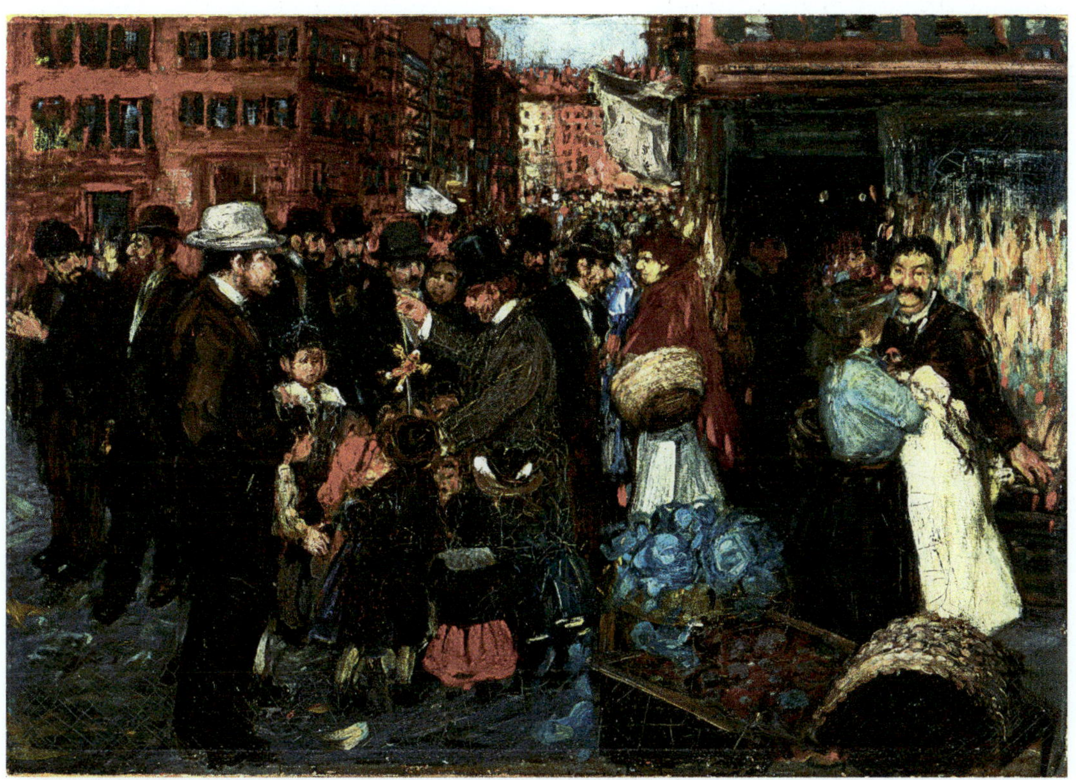

3.9 George Luks (1867–1933), *Street Scene (Hester Street)*, 1905, oil on canvas, 26 × 35 inches. Brooklyn Museum, Dick S. Ramsay Fund, 40.339. Photo credit: Brooklyn Museum, Brooklyn, New York.

John Sloan's etching *The Show Case* illustrated other features of the Ashcan perspective (*fig. 3.10*). Most notably, this is an image of the middle class. The girls who are the focus wear dresses and stockings and flowery hats. Ashcan school art, therefore, is not a portrait of the lower depths. Yes, these places existed, and yes, they were deserving of serious attention. But they did not represent the majority of the city, as the reformers' single-minded concentration would have led viewers to believe. To the Ashcan school the city was a much more diverse place, hence, the image here. Diversity appears in cross-class ways as well, with the girls flanked by an upper-class couple but with members of the working class in the background.

There is another novel feature here, as well, yet one that will be a constant of the Ashcan school. The city is not only populated by adults: children have an important place here, too. In Bruce Weber's study, *Ashcan Kids*, he explained how the subjects of his monograph "figure as emblems of vitality, promise, and hope. . . . the message is clear: children will not be ignored or forgotten."[15]

These youngsters, thus, are neither proper little ladies and gentleman of elite art nor downtrodden, destroyed victims of the reformers. Rather, Sloan depicts them as people with modest means, still capable of window-shopping and dreams of consumer delights (such as Madam Ryanne's corsets) and purchasing power. Above all, they are happy, like the children

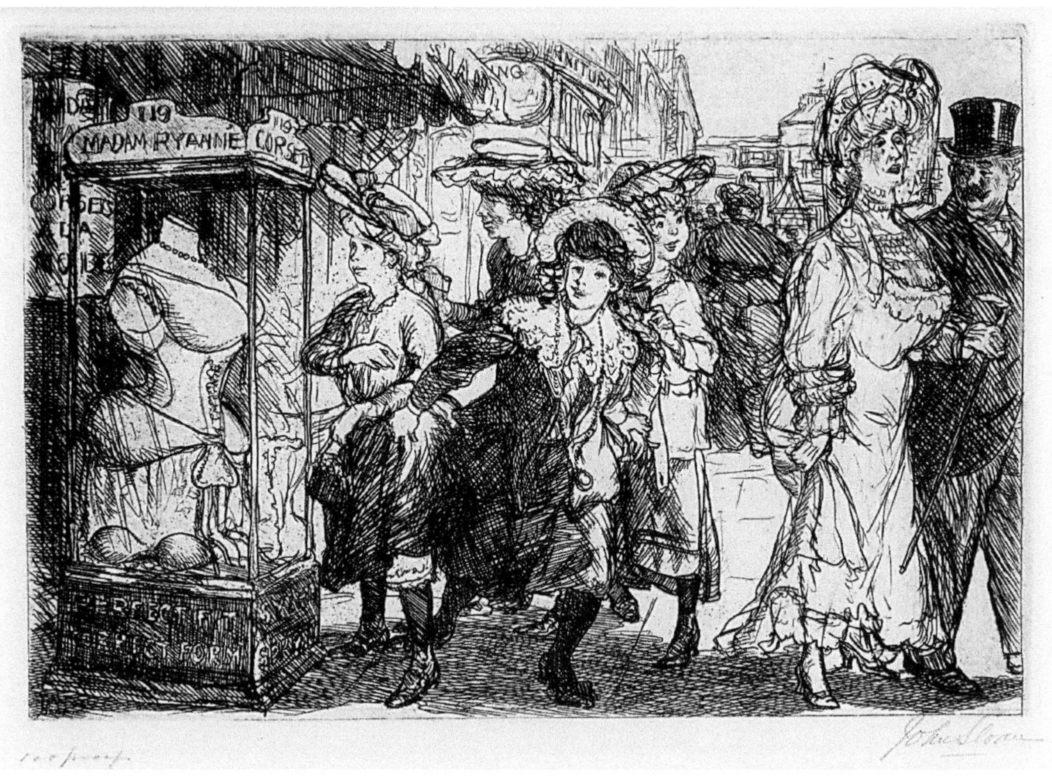

3.10 John Sloan (1871–1951), *The Show Case*, 1905, etching, ink on paper, 5 × 7 inches; 12.7 × 17.8 cm. Private Collector. Courtesy of Swann Auction Galleries. © 2016 Delaware Art Museum/Artists Rights Society (ARS), New York."

Hine photographed. Laughing, skipping, being entertained by the sheer joy of shopping, they are *enjoying* the city.

Thus, the Ashcan artists created a new definition of humanity, to fit a modern age. Their universe, their concept of fitting subjects for great art, was inclusive and expansive, introducing a whole spectrum of personalities, characters, and experiences that artists had never captured before, the life of the working-class urbanite. As one of these painters argued, other artists would frequently "draw an arbitrary line across God's works and say, 'In this half of His works He has been successful, but over here in the shadows . . . the seamy side, He has failed.'" Instead, Robert Henri, spiritual leader of the Ashcan artists, "encouraged his pupils to . . . see beauty in what is familiar to others, often in what may seem drab or ugly to the callous mind." As a result, the Ashcan artists painted the members of the urban working class, who had never been captured on an American canvas before.[16]

Note how apolitical this was, and how the Ashcan artists bypassed the leading artistic motifs of the era. John Loughery, in his biography of John Sloan, commented how, for Jacob Riis, "for the novelists who had discovered the theme of the tenement and the prostitute, the American city was a moral nightmare, the mark of a society that had lost its soul." Add to this mix the editors of *The Masses*, who saw in urban life the very rationale of socialism. Meanwhile, at the other extreme, "for painters like Childe Hassam . . . it was the emblem of a culture come of age, with New York as a version of a European capital, a worthy subject for well-made art."[17]

Sloan had taken a position at *The Masses* as art editor, but he soon left; his vision was different than theirs. Rather than trying to prove a point about the political state of America, or of its status among nations of the world, he simply wanted to depict everyday life in the city as having beauty of its own. And in that simple concept lay the revolution of the Ashcan school.

The artist and his colleagues expressed this better than any of the others, even better than Robert Henri. "It was interest in life and the poetic beauty of things seen when I moved about the city that made me want to paint pictures," he explained. "Love of the people came into it—not what they call social consciousness now, the working man bulging with muscles . . . or bowed down under his burden." Instead, "we began to paint things of the city because they were . . . interesting." Above all, his wife, Helen Farr Sloan, recalled from memory his explanation of how he felt about New York: "I saw it with an innocent poet's eye. The subjects I found for the paintings were bits of joy in human life." This was best summed up in a 1972 master's thesis at University of California–Berkeley, whose author summarized this artist beautifully when he stated that Sloan's work was "a gentle statement of humanitarian good will."[18]

This insight was spiritual, in that it dedicated art to a more realistic portrayal of life, to a better rendering of the human condition. Lloyd Goodrich of the Whitney Museum claimed that "the chief motivating force of Sloan's art was his interest in human beings—not humanity as a vague abstraction but actual men and women. . . . He liked what was common, everyday, and universal. . . . He liked the places and occasions when people got together for sociability and enjoyment." For Sloan, the attraction was "character, in people and places, and the humor of daily life." George Wesley Bellows remarked, "I was always eager to do the tremendous, vital things that pressed all about me." He felt that "an artist must be a spectator of life; a reverential, enthusiastic, emotional spectator, and then the great dramas of human nature will surge through his mind."[19]

Commentators recognized this approach and how novel, how important, it was. In 1916, James Huneker, one of the preeminent art critics in New York during that period, sketched a word portrait of the Ashcan artist George Luks for the *New York Times*. Huneker began by observing that Luks' "favorite expression is: 'Yours for happiness.' He means it. It is the leading motive of his life." This fit a man who "still loves the familiar, the homely, the simple." Above all, Huneker detailed Luks' preferred subject matter and explained how, "in the Yiddish restaurants where old men with Biblical heads drink coffee and slowly converse; on Houston Street, when, apparently, the entire population is buying fish Shabbas Abend . . . there Luks captures some gleam of humor or pathos. . . . a human trait which emerges to the surface of this vast boiling kettle." It was clear to the critic that "the east side is yet to boast its Dickens," and yet, "Dickens would have enjoyed" this art.[20]

No surprise, John Sloan himself articulated this appreciation of everyday life as well as anyone. In his diary, for example, he recorded how he "painted one picture of the Bowery, a rainy night with beautiful subtle color in the sky." Yet one feature of the scene disturbed him: "You hardly realize that there is this old man walking down the street under the elevated. . . . I have never liked to show human beings when they are not themselves. I think it is an insult to their human dignity." In *The Gist of Art*, he argued, "The artist seeks to record his awareness of order in life." For Sloan, this meant that he "went on painting and etching the things [he] saw around . . . in the city streets and on the roof tops." Why? What did this represent to him? Bluntly, he asserted, "The real artist finds beauty in common things."[21]

Sloan's *Woman and Child on the Roof* epitomizes this spirit (*fig. 3.11*). On one side, the setting is urban and dense. Given that the subjects are seeking relief on the roof, their dwelling is probably narrow and tight. A few towels pinned overhead provide shade. Yet there is love here. The child happily plays with a stuffed animal. The mother smiles as a mother will, appreciating her offspring. She wears proper shoes and a dress; though urban, she is not impoverished. Above all, there is a sense of ease, of people in the city who are at peace with life.

Another key feature that differentiated Ashcan school art from works that preceded them, especially by reformers, was that they portrayed the working class as having *agency*, the ability to determine many of the terms of their own life, rather than being helpless pawns of larger forces, whether they be sweatshops or Tammany Hall. They recognized that the city's working classes as capable of forming communities, or of carving out their own little pocket within the metropolis where they could live life the way that they wanted, rather than having it imposed upon them. As Patricia Hills, an art historian at Boston University, commented, "These artists, therefore, came to believe, as did Whitman, that *individualism*, the belief in the primacy of individual states and interests, was not the exclusive province of the upper classes, creative artists, and 'men of genius,' but was manifest in each unique individual of whatever sex, race, or class."[22]

A pair of John Sloan works depict this quest for independence. *Three A.M.* is an important demonstration of this principle, because it crosses gender lines and possibly rebuts the most sanctimonious modes of propriety (*fig. 3.12*, pg. 54). Sloan had glanced at this scene from the rear window of his apartment on Twenty-Third Street, and according to an entry in his diary it remained "stewing in my mind for some weeks." He assumed that the girls were sisters, and that when one arrived home, even at that hour at the bottom of the night, "the other rose from her slumbers and prepared a meal. This picture is redolent with the atmosphere of a poor, back gaslight room. It has beauty, I'll not deny it; it must be that human life is beautiful."[23]

While this scene has all the traits Sloan described, it also contains much more. The women are in charge of their own lives, not bound by a boarding house's schedules or subject to a chaperone's tirades. They come and go as they please and fill their stomachs when it suits them, rather than an arbitrary time when dinner is served. The lady on the left is casually dressed and animated, as her sibling participates by preparing a repast, without any sense of coercion. Women, therefore, are depicted as being free and in charge of their own lives, not bound by the conventions of late-Victorian society. They are also depicted as being happy, rejecting both the elite vision that excludes them and the reformers' insistence that the urban working class must be miserable and in despair.

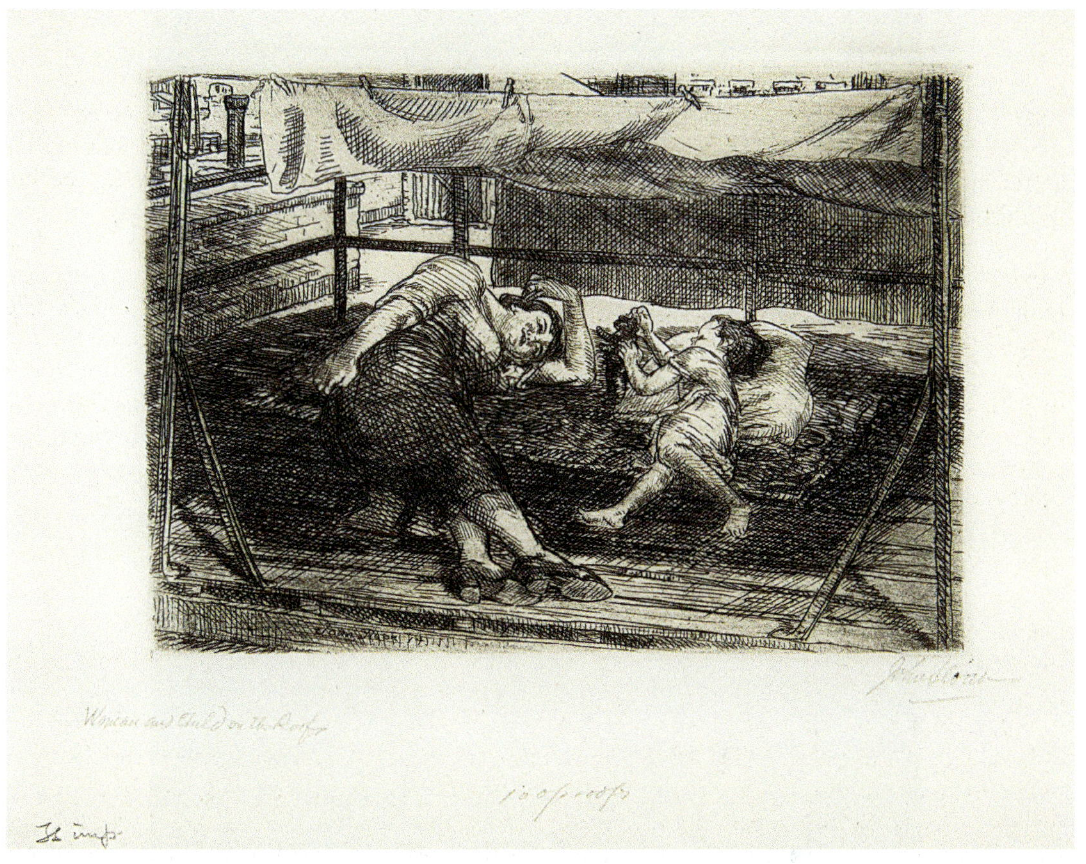

3.11 John Sloan (1871–1951), *Woman and Child on the Roof*, 1914, etching, plate: 4⅜ × 5⅞ inches, 11.1 × 15 cm; sheet: 6⁹⁄₁₆ × 10 inches, 16.7 × 25.4 cm. Metropolitan Museum of Art, New York City. Gift of Ernest Shapiro and Family, 1995. Accession Number: 1995.411.42. © 2016 Delaware Art Museum/Artists Rights Society (ARS), New York. Image copyright © The Metropolitan Museum of Art. Image Source: Art Resource, New York.

There is even one other interpretation, which carries this argument much further, that the working class defied convention and enjoyed the power of deciding how to live their own lives. Suzanne Kinser, in the article "Prostitutes in the Art of John Sloan," argues that, given the extreme hour, the tightness of the dimly lit apartment, and attire of the returning sister, she, and possibly both of them, were ladies of the night. It is questionable if this is accurate, since Sloan described the setting as "a curious two room household, two women and, I think, two men," which makes it sound as though a pair of couples lived there. Nevertheless, the late hour, the festive garb of the one who came in from unknown places, and the fact that Sloan noted how "their day begins after midnight," lends powerful evidence in support of Kinser's thesis.[24]

Whether or not this is true, the independence of the women is evident. Patricia Hills, in "John Sloan's Images of Working-Class Women," pointed out the subject's "unconstrained

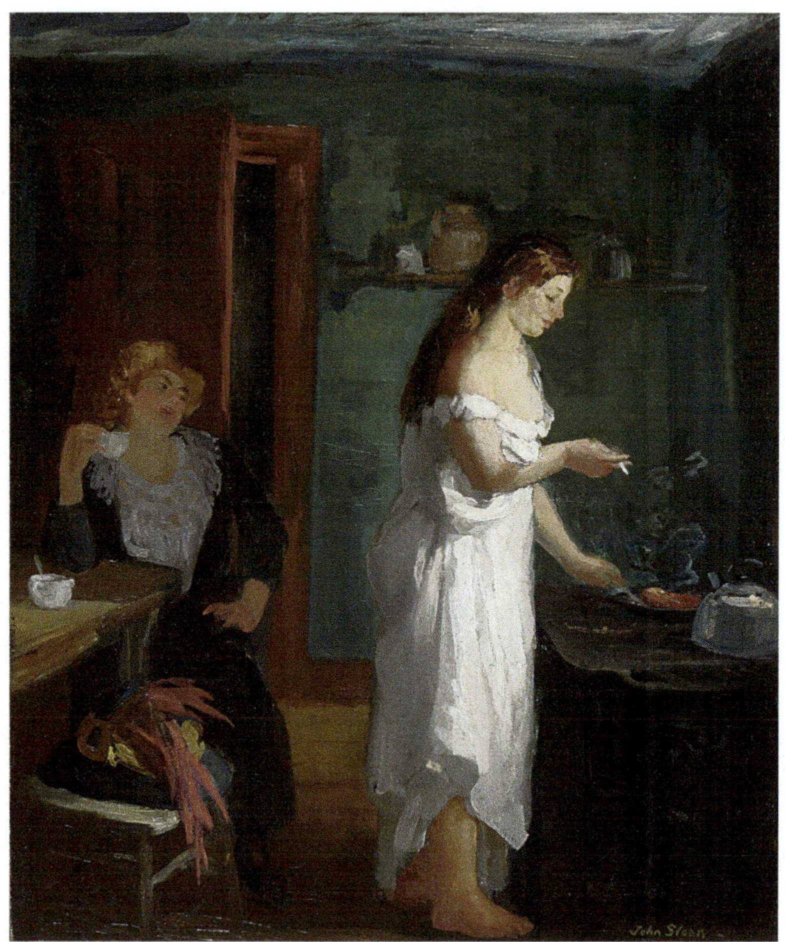

3.12 John Sloan (1871–1951) *Three A.M.*, 1909, oil on canvas, 32⅛ × 26¼ inches. Gift of Mrs. Cyrus McCormick, 1946. (1946-46-10.1). Philadelphia Museum of Art. © 2016 Delaware Art Museum/Artists Rights Society (ARS), New York. Photo Credit: The Philadelphia Museum of Art/Art Resource, New York.

freedom to move about within her clothing and, as suggested by the sketchily rendered open door in the background, to move as well into the spaces outside the room, even into the city." In a world of Victorian gender rules, that is a powerful statement.[25]

The setting also tells us a lot. It is neither sentimentalized nor an idealized portrayal of life in the city. Rather, it is small, tight, messy, and clean. Not at all Victorian, but very urban. And its residents are still enjoying life.

Crossing from gender to class issues, Sloan provides this same authority to male workers in *Salute* (fig. 3.13). The workman depicted here is engaged in a dangerous profession. Judging from the framework that surrounds him, he likely manipulates heavy iron or steel beams in some way, performing this task at daunting heights. Yet unlike Jurgis Rudkus, the protagonist of Upton Sinclair's *The Jungle*, he does not seem cowed. His platform is quite high, judging from the panorama of buildings below him, and his perch is frighteningly narrow. All the same, he accepts the admiring glances of an onlooker and child and fancifully waves his hat to salute them. Despite his hardy labors, he is in charge of his environment, sufficiently that he is capable of lighthearted, amusing gestures. He is not a person to be bypassed or sidelined and appears to derive both status and pleasure from his work. In a world of formidable metal, he remains master of his fate, at least within the high-rise latticework. At the same time, his wave adds

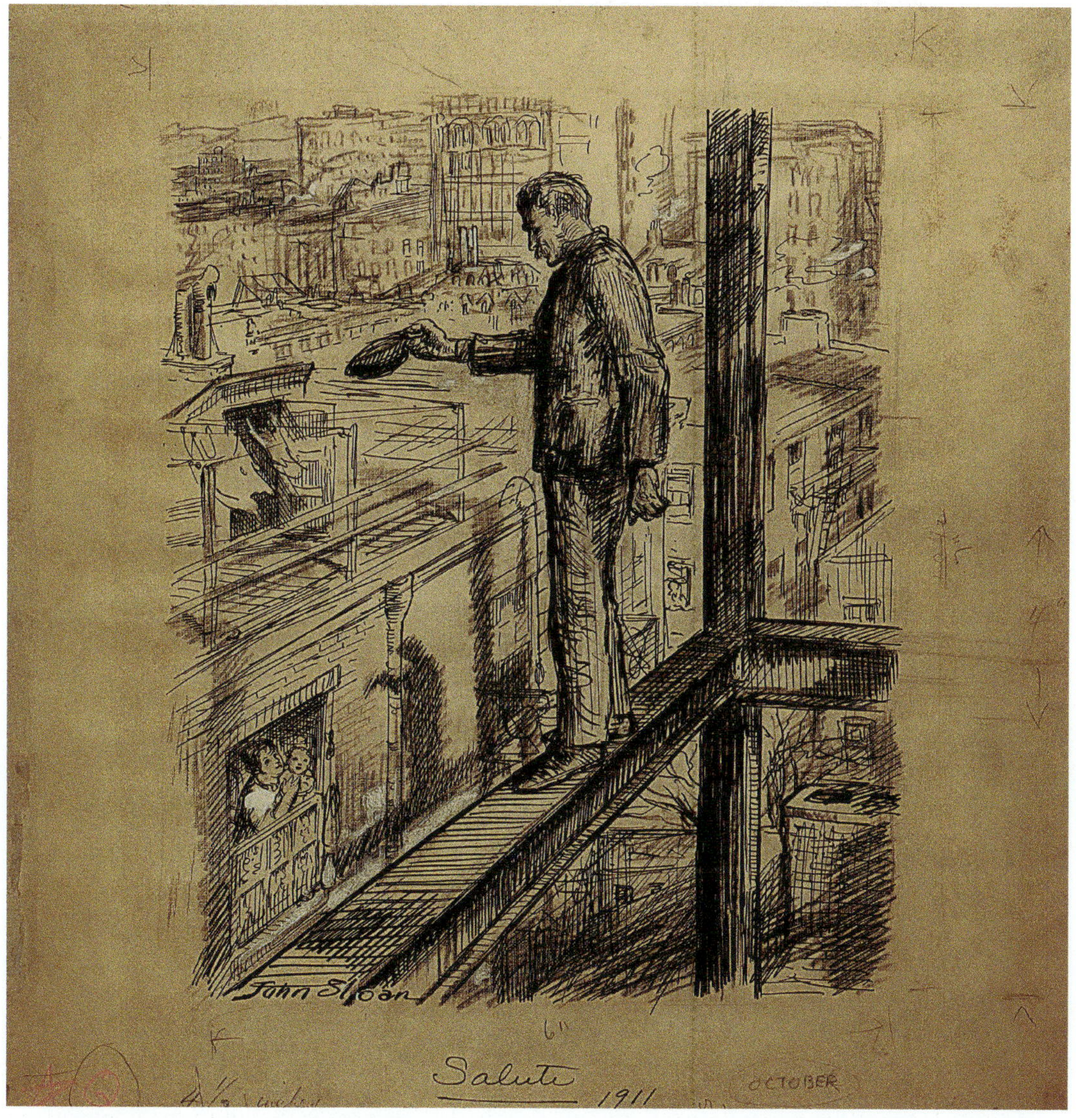

3.13 John Sloan (1871–1951), *Salute*, ca. 1911, ink, charcoal, and zinc white paint on paper, 14¹⁵⁄₁₆ × 14⅛ inches. Delaware Art Museum, Wilmington, USA/Bridgeman Images. © 2016 Delaware Art Museum/Artists Rights Society (ARS), New York.

charm and tenderness to the city, a piece of drama and human personality amid the hubbub, to make the child and mother smile.[26] In his self-assurance, he makes the city humane.

The Ashcan artists' appreciation of the city also affected their artistic perspective. In making sense of incredibly dense neighborhoods, they sought out the tiny, human, element that summed up some essence of the larger urban experience. Meyer Schapiro, in his survey *Modern Art*, observed how they "took as their chief objects smaller and smaller bits of landscape, interesting for some personally savored nuance of color, light, and air."[27]

Everett Shinn's *The Laundress* is a fine example of this kind of insight (*fig. 3.14*). The scene depicted here is not just small; it is miniscule. All the viewers see is a section of an alley, not even an entire block, cramped and even further divided by fences into parcels the size of napkins. That space is precious here is further illustrated by the clotheslines outside; there is no room in the apartments all around to hang laundry. Buildings intrude into this slim territory, further restricting our gaze. Sheds take up even more room. Yet, despite this constriction, this is a painting of light and color, of hominess and community. People live and grow here, and there is evidence of family and tranquility as the woman pulls her household's items from the basket and hangs them. Despite the exceedingly minimal vista, Shinn has grabbed a piece of city life.

Another feature of urban life the Ashcan artists grasped came in their embrace of spontaneity. They interpreted this as the need to get out of the studio and explore the city's streets and its people. They wanted the full measure of Gotham, and like Henri Cartier-Bresson decades later, hoped to stumble upon the "critical moment," hoping to commit it to memory, then portray it on canvas.

The founding advocate of this approach was Robert Henri, the great mentor of Ashcan artists. In a 1901 article for *The Press*, Henri railed against the falseness then current in art schools and discussed alternatives. "The real study of an art student," he proselytized, "is generally missed in the pursuit of technic." Instead of learning how to become artists, "students have become masters of the art of drawing, like some others have become masters of their grammers. And like so many of the latter, brilliant jugglers of words, having nothing worthwhile to say they remain little else than clever jugglers of the brush."[28]

Later, in his treatise on painting, *The Art Spirit*, Henri made clear what he sought instead. "Real students," he felt, "go out of beaten paths, whether beaten by themselves or by others, and have adventures with the unknown." The acolyte matures, until "the sketch hunter has delightful days of drifting about among people, in and out of the city, going anywhere, everywhere, stopping as long as he likes—no need to reach any point, moving in any direction following the call of interests." This seeker in the city is "looking for what he loves, he tries to capture it. It's found anywhere, everywhere. . . . The hunter is learning to see and to understand—to enjoy."[29]

Everyone around Henri picked up on this spirit. John Sloan wrote, "Henri said paint life and never mind about art." George Wesley Bellows believed, "There are only three things demanded of a painter: to see things, to feel them and to dope them out for the public. You can learn more in painting one street scene than in six months' work in an atelier."[30]

The master himself captured this quality in *Snow in New York* (*fig. 3.15*, pg. 58). His scene is fleeting, a quick glimpse of a street as one fights to see through a snowstorm. Only one on the lookout for the beauty of the city would even notice it, notice the subtle, soft colors, the contrast of the earthen buildings and the variegated colors of the horses, taxis, and huddled pedestrians against the muted shade of the lance of sky that dominates the center.

This embrace of life refuted one of the major criticisms against the Ashcan school, that these artists were guilty of sentimentalism, an argument that occurred early on and has continued in modern works by Wanda Corn and Amy Goldin. In all fairness, there were tinges of this outlook

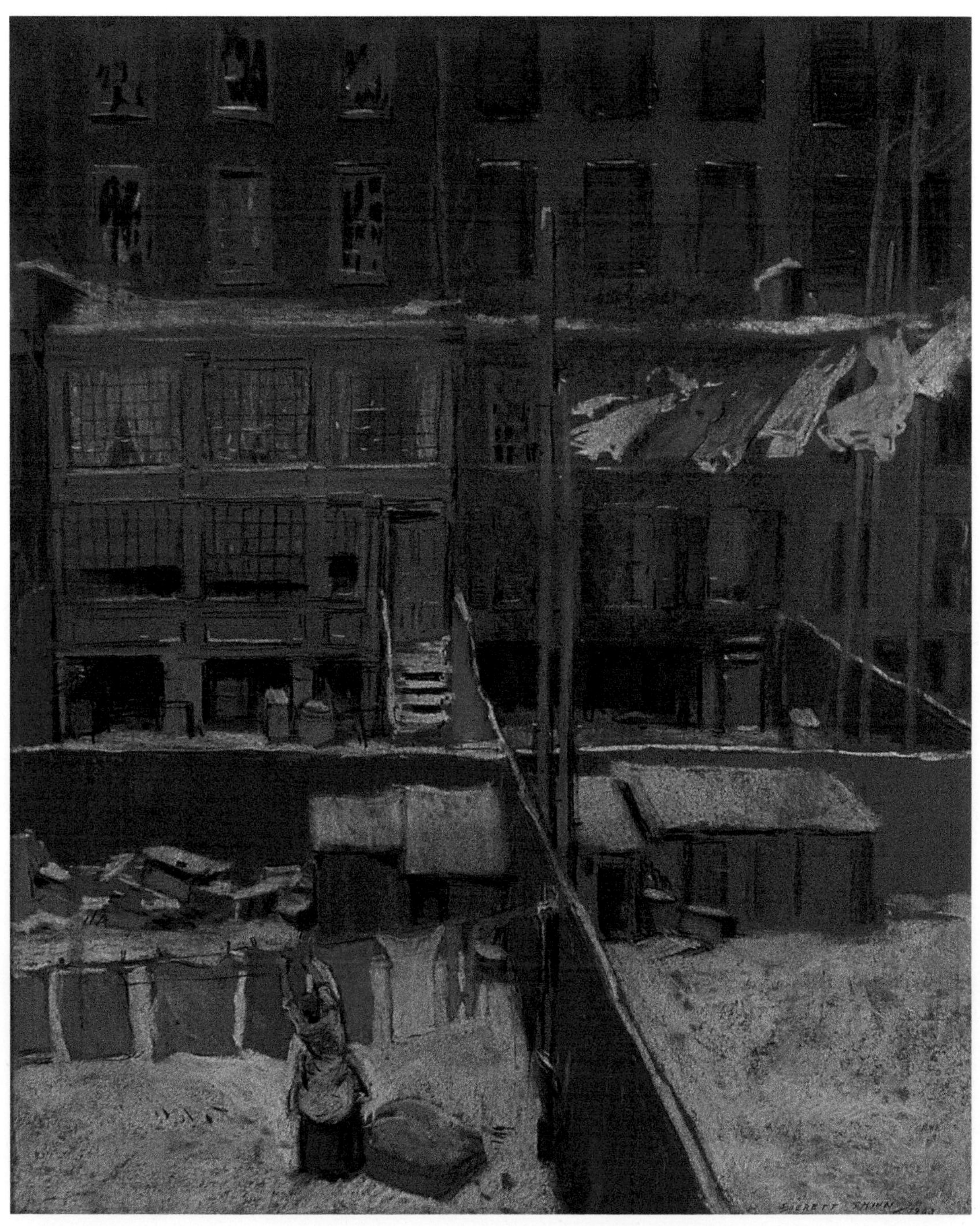

3.14 Everett Shinn (1876–1953), *The Laundress*, 1903, pastel, 25⅞ × 20¾ inches. Collection of James R. and Barbara R. Palmer. Palmer Museum of Art, University Park, Pennsylvania.

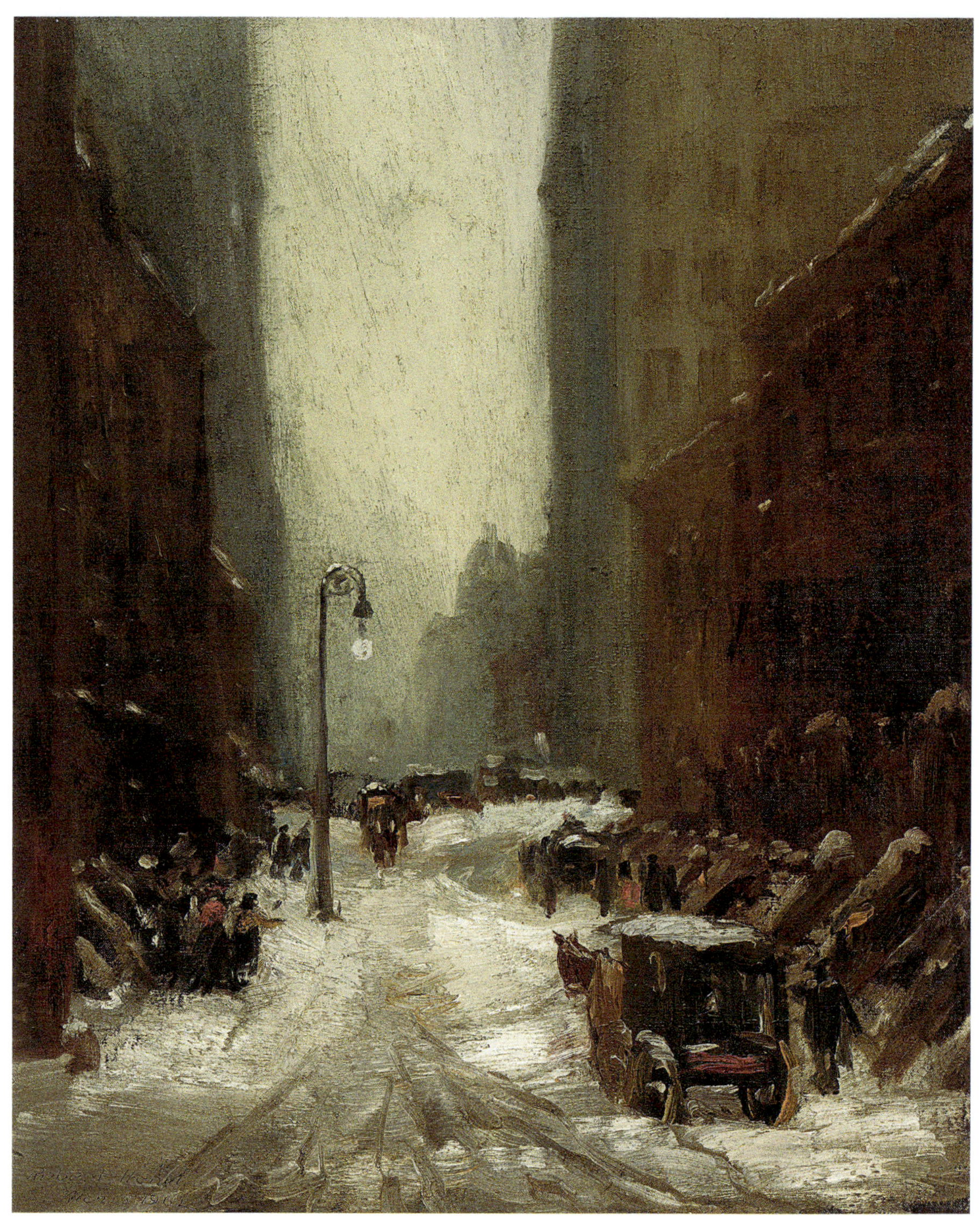

3.15 Robert Henri (1865–1929), *Snow in New York*, 1902, oil on canvas, 81.3 × 65.5 cm; 32 × 25¹³⁄₁₆ inches. National Gallery of Art, Washington DC, USA/ Bridgeman Images.

early on, as some critics romanticized of the plight of the poor. Louis Baury, in a 1911 article, ecstatically captured the myth of the noble savage when he wrote, "The slum folk are not to be pitied. Far from it. Generally speaking, they are better than we—better because more genuine."[31]

But other critics' analysis, other evidence, brings these claims into question. In her doctoral dissertation, Emily Kies observed that Ashcan paintings "display warmth and emotionalism (not to be confused with sentimentality)," an idea that John Sloan had expressed decades prior when he claimed, "There is a profound difference . . . between sentimentality and sensitivity." Instead, Sloan explained, "We came to realism in revolt against sentimentality and artificial subject matter and the cult of 'art for art's sake.'" In this new style, he and his colleagues were not about to substitute one form of mawkishness for another, simply labeling it "urban" instead of "pastoral."[32]

Rather, the Ashcan artists knew that the working class did form communities, did participate in institutions like family and church that nurtured them, did enjoy aspects of their lives. Showing these features, while a challenge to orthodoxies of both the right and the left, remained an accurate portrayal. Ashcan artists depicted working-class life with sensitivity and respect, not with the sentimentality that critics charged them with. Their approach was not to romanticize the city, but to show its many parts with honesty and as places where city folk were capable of living their own lives, elements that both elites and reformers missed. Sloan despised "those 'sentimental scrawling of bearded Jews' in which 'seven thousand years of suffering' were 'expressed in a rotten line with sloppy tones.' Or drawings of negroes by Southerners who 'just loved' the downtrodden. In all this kind of work . . . the artist was showing superiority . . . a cheap kind of condescension." This was the sentimentalism that the Ashcan artists rejected in lieu of far fuller and more nuanced depictions of their subjects.[33]

The Ashcan artists' goals were more universal, more human. The catalog copy for a 1988 exhibit of Sloan's works observed that "Sloan infused the painting of scenes of everyday life . . . with a zest, humor, and honesty that were new to American painting in the early years of the twentieth century." This style was "not condescending or satirical . . . nor was it propagandistic, as some other artists would have it; it was a caring but detached view of American life as it was lived by ordinary Americans." Marianne Doezema felt that George Bellow's approach was "free of condescension," that "he depicted the working class . . . without patronizing them, sentimentalizing their situation, or relying on stereotypical . . . types."[34]

But there was far greater significance to what the Ashcan artists achieved. One contemporary who picked up on the appeal of this kind of work was Theodore Roosevelt, who believed that "the Bowery is one of the great highways of humanity, a highway of seething life, of varied interest, of fun, of work." This quote is of extreme relevance because of what its author stood for. More than almost any other figure of his age, Teddy epitomized what it meant to be an American, both for his countrymen and for people around the world. He thus pointed to the single greatest contribution of the Ashcan school.[35]

In 1905, shortly after Sir Caspar Clarke had taken over the reins of the Metropolitan Museum of Art, he summed up the state of affairs in art collecting: "America appears to be concerned with the art of every land save that of America." Galleries in cities across the national continent seemed like mausoleums with lavish, decorated coffins. Sloan saw that as well, how art in this country was at its lowest ebb, due to its "pursuit of visual imitation."[36]

Henri had the antidote. "Here in America we have a country filled with energetic people," he proclaimed. "We are a distinct people; we have tremendous ideas to express. And often it seems to me that I cannot wait to hear the voice of these people. . . . the thing that we have to say as a people."[37]

George Moore, in *Modern Painting*, a volume that Sloan referred to as his "bible," took this even further, arguing that the American people sought "the calm of national character in our art. A national character can only be acquired by remaining at home and saturating ourselves in the spirit of our land until it oozes from our pens and pencils in every slightest word, in every slightest touch." Henri added, "What is necessary for art in America, as in any land, is first an appreciation of the great ideas native to the country and then the achievement of a masterly freedom in expressing them." In an article about John Sloan's approach to gender and class, Patricia Hills picked up on this concept when she wrote of Ashcan images how "to conservatives they posed a threat to 'Anglo-Saxon' values. To reformers they lived as the squalid victims of an inhuman system. . . . To the group of artists around Henri they represented a new spirit that would infuse American life with its vitality."[38]

Painters, writers, and cinema stars would later flesh out the elements of this new, American vision. Henri argued that there was "only one reason for the development of art in America, and that is that the people of America learn the means of expressing themselves in their own time and their own land. . . . What we do need is art that expresses the *spirit* of the people of today." Dreiser concluded that the Ashcan artists had intended to "paint every day New York life," that to these practitioners "a Hester Street pushcart is a better subject than a Dutch windmill." These components of the city were not just represented in oils, charcoals, and watercolors, either. Charlie Chaplin, one of the masters of the great, emerging visual form of the era, exclaimed in 1919, "There is beauty in the slums!—for those who can see it despite the dirt and the sordidness."[39]

This then, became the most important contribution of the Ashcan school, even ahead of their revolutionary ideas on cities and art and class. Rather, by depicting the urban scene with unprecedented insight, they fostered the development of a true native art form for America.

CHAPTER FOUR

THE ASHCAN ARTISTS

THE ASHCAN ARTISTS PRODUCED A NEW KIND OF ART BECAUSE THEY WERE PART OF A NEW America. From old stock and not immigrants, they were still modern and urban, and they often honed their craft working in one of the most dynamic new industries, the great burst of newspaper growth around the turn of the century. Leading this coterie was a most unusual presence—a philosopher, recruiter, advocate, and leader with a heritage of gambling.

Robert Henri's father was a dreamer, an innovator, and a dead-on shot. Throughout the postbellum West, John Jackson Cozad—Cozad was Henri's birth name—planned and built towns, bridges, a myriad of different projects. In 1882 Nebraska, the entrepreneur was working in a dry goods store when he got into in a fight with one of the employees. Amid narrow aisles stacked high with goods the argument raged, till his opponent shoved Cozad, toppling him. As he fell, John Jackson pulled a small caliber revolver typical of that era and killed his assailant with a bullet to his forehead, fine shooting then or now. The family fled town, changing its name. Young Robert, only seventeen at the time, adopted his own moniker, becoming Robert Henri.

Robert began to pursue his dreams of becoming an artist. Enrolling in the Pennsylvania Academy of Fine Arts in 1886, he studied under Thomas Anshutz. Two years later he journeyed to Paris for formal training, at the Académie Julian. Although he returned to the United States in 1892, to take a position at the Pennsylvania School of Design for Women, he maintained ties to the continent via frequent trips. During one of these excursions, in 1898, the French government purchased his painting, *La Neige*, and hung it in the Musée du Luxembourg, a most prestigious setting. Henri's reputation as a painter of international reputation had been forged.

Coming home, he obtained a teaching job at the Chase School of Art. This was a marriage with failure built in, as William Merritt Chase epitomized the conservative, National Academy approach, in everything from his ego to his painting. Henri, on the other hand, was a bolt of novelty; he stood out from the crowd, in both his physical presence and in his ideas. At a time when the average height was modest by modern standards, Henri was tall and slim and angular, just over six-foot-one, with eyes variously described as "Russian" or "Oriental." One witness claimed the artist moved "with the natural elegance of a man . . . accustomed to horseback riding" and compared his presence to that of later heroes Gary Cooper or Jimmy Stewart. Henri wore a handlebar mustache, spoke with a soft Nebraska drawl that had lingered from his youth, and pronounced his adopted name "Hen-rye."

Everything about him was distinctive. He composed letters in a big sprawling handwriting that was strikingly clear, even through the lens of an imprecise modern-day microfilm reader. Though artistically sloppy when he began his career, one of his later wives attended to his wardrobe, and Henri took to wearing tailor-made wool suits, with bespoke silk underwear. He would appear in class with a silk smock over his suit, and a visit to his quarters in the evening would find him in a mohair smoking jacket. His studio had always been orderly, with one wall covered by shelves filled with art volumes and his sketch books. The kitchen table served as his palette, yet he was scrupulous in cleaning up after each session. Everett Shinn, another Ashcan artist, wrote that "order was the dominant feature of his studio, immaculate and set for his own exacting inspection."[1]

George Wesley Bellows recalled that while his mentor was always late to class, he then "strode into the space between the easels and looked about him with slanting, penetrating eyes." Though he stopped in front of each work and spoke in private tones to its creator, many students would lay down their drawing instruments and follow behind him like so many ducklings. A contemporaneous article in *Vogue* claimed, "No one could see and talk with him for five minutes, meeting him as an absolute stranger, without feeling the force of his personality." In 1922 a critic observed that "his admiring pupils hung upon his inspired word like grapes upon the parent stem."[2]

What Henri taught was in defiance of the convention taught in American art schools at that time, and rarely practiced on canvas. With all his power, he believed, and preached, an art that was both democratic and American. In his most powerful expression of this philosophy, Henri declared, "There is only one reason for the development of art in America, and that is that the people of America learn the means of expressing themselves. . . . What we do need is art that expresses the *spirit* of the people of today." In the single volume that he authored, *The Art Spirit*, the master expanded on this philosophy. He felt that art had to be organic, that "when fully understood," it became "the province of every human being. It is simply a question of doing things, anything, well. It is not an outside, extra thing. . . . Museums . . . will not make a country an art country." Forbes Watson, in his introduction to Henri's book, summarized these beliefs: "He ardently believed in the close relationship of Art to Life—believed that Art is a matter in which not only professionals and students, but *everyone* is vitally concerned."[3]

Henri applied this outlook to both to his fellow artists and to his subject matter. In *The Art Spirit*, he wrote, "There are painters who paint their lives through without having any great excitements. One man said to me, 'I lay it in in the morning, then I have luncheon and I take a nap, after which I finish.' Certainly a well-regulated way for a quiet gentleman and quite unlike the procedure of an idea-mad enthusiast who works eighteen hours at a stretch." Florence Ruthrauff, in a 1912 review of Henri's significance for *Fine Arts Journal*, remarked on "his desire that the painter be an individual and not a mere reproducer, who will take his work as a matter of vital importance to the world." Henri observed, "The true character of a student is one of great mental and physical activity."[4]

Henri's broader philosophy mirrored that of another great thinker of that rebellious era, W. E. B. Du Bois. In his 1903 masterwork, "The Talented Tenth," the African American leader provided insight for the ages, "If we make money the object of man-training, we shall develop money-makers but not necessarily men." Echoing these lines, the artist Guy Pène du Bois noted how "Henri himself believed that he was creating a class of men. The student of art must be a man first, with a good strong conscience and the courage to live up to it. Art could come later." In his biography of John Sloan, Van Wyck Brooks cited how "Henri presented an artist's life as a virile occupation that was fit for the 'commanding' and the 'energetic.'"[5]

Above all, Henri sought to redefine beauty, arguing that "the whole value of art rests in the artist's ability to see well into what is before him." The future Ashcan savant dismissed those who had paid a high price for a Rembrandt portrait of a gentleman but "turn with disgust" from a study of a beggar by the same painter. While noting that Rembrandt was sufficiently renowned that these different works now hung in museums side by side, Henri maintained, "The idea still remains, that beauty rests in the subject."[6]

Thus, what made Henri a visionary more than anything was where his gaze fell (*fig. 4.1*). Rockwell Kent observed that "Henri was in a very deep and true sense a man of the people. . . . He was a democrat, not by compulsion of a philosophic mind, but naturally and from his heart." The new element, however, was that he found that humanity, that subject matter, not, as others before him had, in the rural yeomanry but on the working-class streets of dense modern gothams. He sought grace in "a sketch that is the life of the city and the river."[7]

That sensitivity is what he taught to his students, what made him leader of a new wave in art. Henri is less remembered as an urban artist (he turned to portraiture after 1902)[8] than as a thinker, an innovator who saw things few had seen before him, who convinced others to recognize the charm of urban settings, so that they too could endow them with beauty.[9] Pène

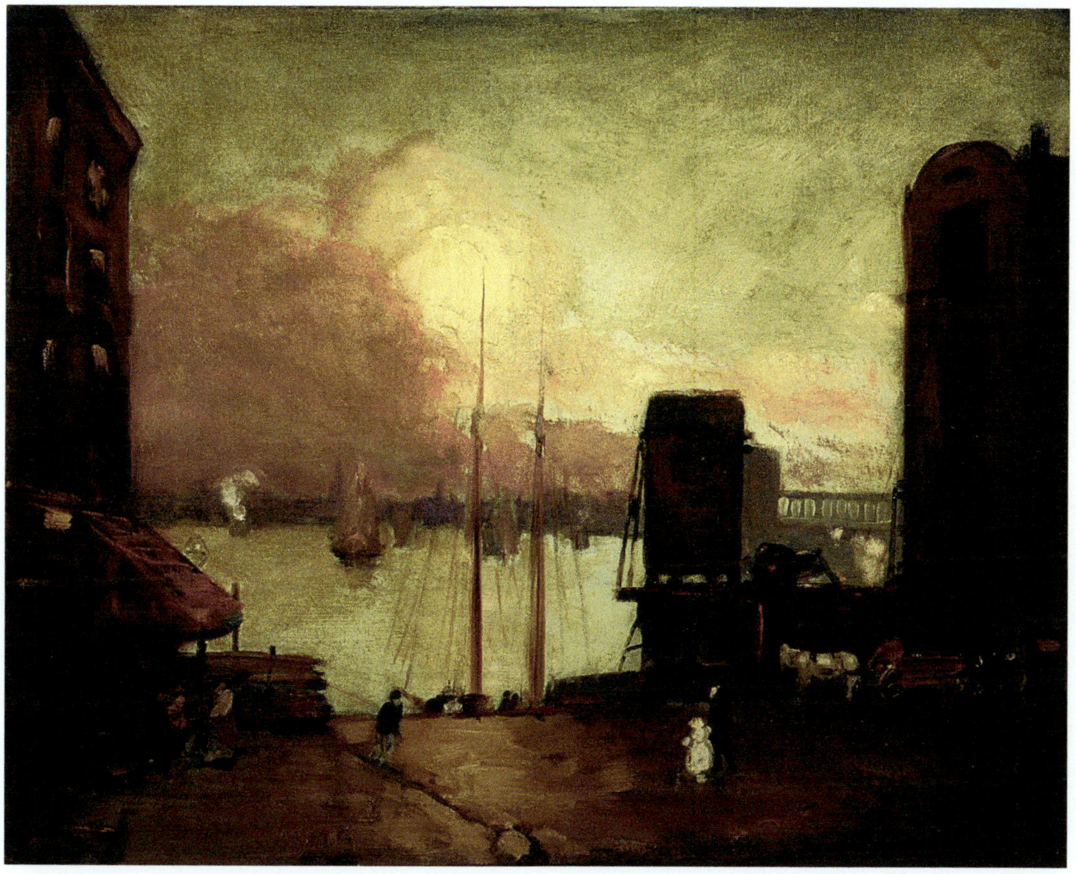

4.1 Robert Henri (1865–1929), *Cumulus Clouds, East River*, 1901–1902, oil on canvas, 25¾ × 32 inches; 65.4 × 81.3 cm. Gift of Mrs. Daniel Fraad in memory of her husband. Smithsonian American Art Museum. Photo credit: Smithsonian American Art Museum, Washington, DC/Art Resource, New York.

du Bois remembered how "the Henri class . . . was the seat of the sedition among the young." A young Ariel Durant felt these sessions became her "first impression of freedom, of respect, of education, of beauty, of the world." Even Emma Goldman gushed that he "helped to create a spirit of freedom in the art class which probably did not exist anywhere else in New York at this time." Henri was coming into his own at roughly the same time that a radicalized Bohemian culture was arising in New York.[10]

Henri then sent his students, naïfs yet painters of promise, out to discover the urban milieu and its industrial and working-class scenes. Frances Cranmer Greenman, a pioneering female artist, explained how every morning he exhorted them to "forget the elegant rubbish of stylish studios and go down to the docks, to prize fights, to the slums. And paint what we saw there." In truth, Henri and the Ashcan artists never chronicled true poverty at its lowest, saddest level but instead focused on working- and lower-middle-class residents and scenes of commerce and construction. Yet, that was still unprecedented. John Sloan observed, "It was really Henri's direction that made us paint at all, and paint the life around us." Helen Appleton Read asserted that "life seemed to the Henri student to flow stronger and fuller in Bowery bars and riverfront alleys than in the Knickerbocker Hotel or the fashionable streets of the upper east side." that had previously been the sole terrain of urban artists.[11]

Thus, whatever his role may have been, as an artist or as a teacher, Henri's influence was enormous. William Innes Homer, in his challenging biography of this innovator, pronounced how Henri "gave his students, not a style . . . but an attitude, an approach. . . . It is safe to say—and it is saying a great deal—that he was the single most important teacher and force for artistic change in his generation." The list of those who studied under him, and who in turn testified to his importance, is striking, and it includes George Wesley Bellows, Edward Hopper, Rockwell Kent, Guy Pène du Bois, and Walter Pach. At the end of his life Henri estimated that he had worked with thousands of students. George Wesley Bellows referred to his teacher as a father-figure and described this relationship simply, "My life begins at this point." Edward Hopper, who went on to achieve greater fame than any of the earlier Ashcan artists, still believed that "Henri was the rallying-point and leader. . . . No single figure in recent American art has been so instrumental in setting free the hidden forces that can make the art of this country a living expression of its character and its people." Even Big Bill Hayward made it a point to visit Henri's studio when the radical leader would stop in New York. The noted critic Sadakichi Hartmann, in a 1906 review, proclaimed, "It is Henri's personality first of all that has made a mark in our American art life," adding, "we younger men have always looked at Robert Henri as a typification of the new movement in our art."[12]

The closest Henri came to a full-blown protégé was John Sloan, who acknowledged, "I don't think I would have become a painter if I had not come under his direction." In his diary, the young man trumpeted, "Henri is the best teacher of art in this country, if not the world—'Them's my sentiments.'" In response to an inquiry about whom one should study art with in New York, Sloan replied, "Henri, none other." Until the Armory Show, he referred to Henri as his "father in art."[13]

Sloan was Henri's foremost associate, and the greatest painter of the Ashcan generation. And he was the product of older stock, descending from paternal ancestors of Scottish cabinetmakers as well. While growing up in Philadelphia, Sloan watched his father become a successful traveling salesman for a line of books, fine stationery, and greeting cards. The first of these entranced the young man, and he devoured literature, finishing Dickens and Shakespeare before he was twelve. Without any prompting, he produced his own, illustrated version of *Treasure Island* and copied all the artwork from the family's dictionary.[14]

With a growing portfolio, Sloan found work in the art department of the *Philadelphia Inquirer*, illustrating the entertainment pages and the fiction stories that were published in the Sunday supplement. At the same time, he began classes at the Pennsylvania Academy of the Fine Arts, taking sessions with, among others, Thomas Anshutz. The senior artist rebuked his pupil because, during a session, Sloan had moved his chair to the wall and began sketching his classmates; as Van Wyck Brooks noted, "He was much more interested in the life about him." That same year he met Robert Henri at a party, and the two quickly formed a bond. Among Henri's circle were the future Ashcan artists George Luks, William Glackens, and Everett Shinn. With Sloan and the others, they would form a lively group that met regularly in Henri's quarters.

In 1904 Sloan felt "the necessity of New York as a residence." On an exploratory trip, he stayed with Henri (who had moved there in 1902) and garnered sufficient freelance assignments to make the jump possible. At that time the city was home to twenty illustrated periodicals with a combined circulation of 5,500,000, so it was likely he would have found success. In April 1904, he made the jump. Married, five-foot-ten, with jet-black hair, Sloan was about to join the New York art scene, the last of the Ashcan artists to do so.

Sloan and his first wife, Dolly, established not just residence but an expansive life in their new environs. Their first apartment was on Fifty-Seventh Street and Sixth Avenue, in the same building and on the same floor as Henri's studio. That fall they moved to Chelsea, to 165 West Twenty-Third Street, between Sixth and Seventh Avenues. This put them on the edges of both the Tenderloin—a district known for dance halls, bars, and whorehouses, as well as artists—and, to the west, one of the city's primary African American neighborhoods, prior to the emergence of Harlem. The couple remained there through the glory years of the Ashcan movement and in 1912 moved to the artistic regions of Greenwich Village. Although Rockwell Kent remembered the Chelsea digs as "the top floor walk-up studio apartment of a reasonably dilapidated old brown-stone house," Theodore Dreiser, who had expected something exotic, was disappointed by its pedestrian appearance. Sloan wrote that the novelist "saw at a glance that I was not leading the right kind of artist-life for his purposes: no rich furnishings and none of the typical trappings like fish-nets and spinning wheels which were the earmarks of the 'studio.'" Plagued by nearsightedness and astigmatism, Sloan often used binoculars to observe the neighborhood around him.[15]

Sloan's artistic approach matured as he viewed the city around him (fig. 4.2, pg. 66). Guy Pène du Bois noticed how he could "not remember a still life by Sloan. . . . He devotes his art entirely to things he has seen in life." Just as in Henry James' short story masterpiece "The Real Thing," Sloan painted from remembrances "the realized thing seen in the mind," which were "more real . . . than the things look." In other words, he painted the essence of a scene, rather than a documentary recreation. Never painting out of doors, he would put down a hasty sketch and then fetch hurriedly to his studio to begin work, returning to the original scene only to "soak it up," never to draw. His second wife, Helen Farr Sloan, told how he would walk the streets endlessly, till a "human incident" gave him the "final" idea, and he'd head back to the studio and work from memory. Pène du Bois claimed that Sloan had "often been accused of mixing too much literature with his paint.[16]

Yet, underwriting this art was a broader perspective. In 1906, during a walk through the East Side immigrant districts, Sloan found "healthy faced children, solid-legged, rich full color to their hair. Happiness rather than misery in the whole life. Fifth Avenue faces are unhappy in comparison." Van Wyck Brooks opined that "in most of Sloan's work . . . one felt a kindly humor—one of his mottoes was 'Draw with human kindness.'" Avis Berman, in an article for *Smithsonian*, explained that the artist's view of urban life consisted of "flashes of joyous humanity reveling in whatever pleasures their surroundings had to offer." Sloan remarked that

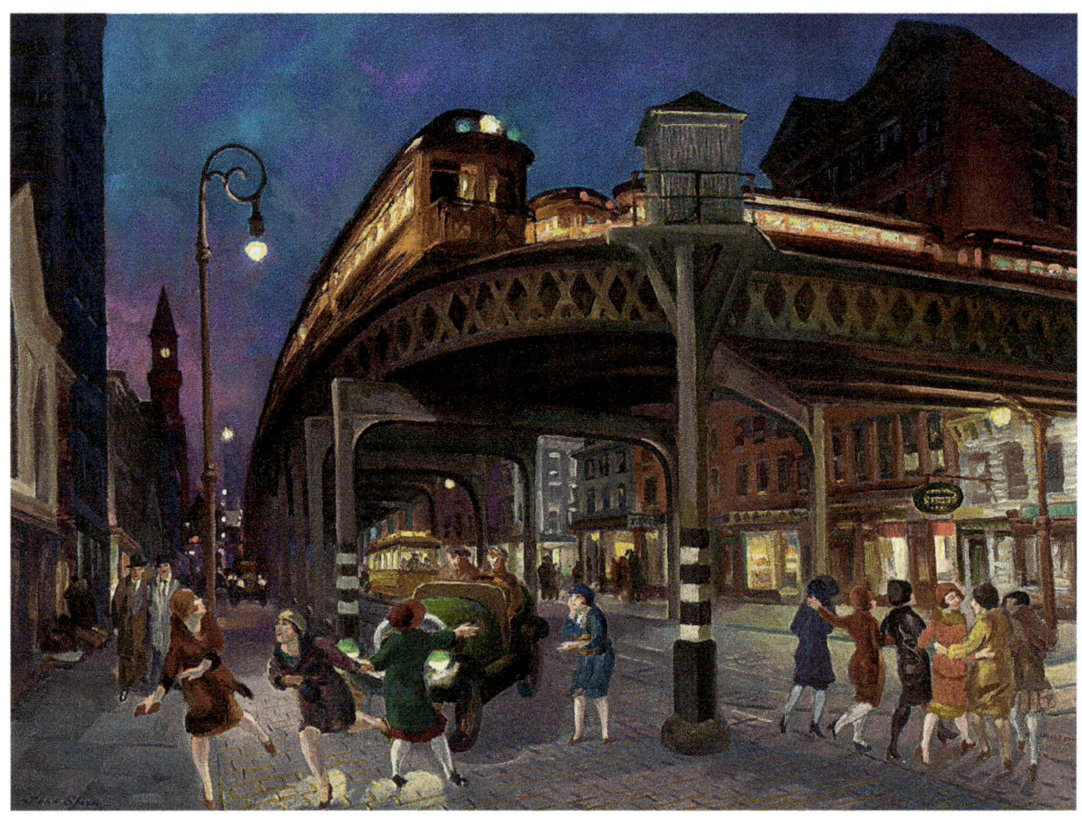

4.2 John Sloan (1871–1951), *Sixth Avenue Elevated at Third Street*, 1928, oil on canvas, 30 × 40⅛ inches; 76.2 × 101.9 cm. Whitney Museum of American Art, New York; Purchase 36.154. © 2016 Delaware Art Museum/Artists Rights Society (ARS), New York Digital Image © Whitney Museum of American Art/Licensed by Artists Rights Society.

he was pleased that Germany had lost the First World War, because it symbolized "the defeat of efficiency."[17]

In later years, Sloan would stay true to these ideals. Having joined the Socialist Party, in 1912 he became art editor for *The Masses*, drawing graphic images as well as handling layout. Several years later, however, he withdrew, on grounds that the magazine would have been better off depicting the whole of urban life rather than just party propaganda. Rebecca Zurier, author of the leading work on this famous and influential publication, wrote how Sloan "considered his paintings documents of 'humanism'—'interest in humanity, at play, at work, the everyday life of city and country'—but resisted attempts to give them a more political reading." Decades later, through the self-righteous, conservative twenties and into the thirties of Depression and New Deal, he taught at the Art Students League, still instructing students to "draw what you see around you. . . . Make life documents. . . . Do illustrations for a while. It won't hurt you. Go out into the streets and look at life. Fill your notebooks with drawings of people in subways and at lunch counters." After his death, the Whitney's Lloyd Goodrich, in a memorial address for Sloan at Dartmouth College in 1951, remarked that "the American art world today is a freer, more democratic and healthier world . . . in no small part due to him."[18]

The other blooming star of the Ashcan movement was a young, athletic painter named George Wesley Bellows. A Midwesterner, Bellows was born and raised in Columbus, Ohio, part of a world where he was "surrounded by Methodists and Republicans." Bellows began nurturing his talent on long, dull Sundays, which his mother demanded be spent inside to keep the Sabbath holy. According to a 1921 article, Bellows by "the time he was five wanted little but to draw and paint." While his father, a local architect and contractor, urged the son to take over the family business, his mother advocated a career in the ministry. More interested in art, Bellows attended Ohio State University, taking every class in which he could wield a brush or charcoal, drawing for the school paper, and excelling at the exciting sport of that era, baseball. Upon matriculation, he received an offer from no less a team than his home state's Cincinnati Reds. He chose instead to take on the New York art scene.[19]

Bellows entered a magical world. An imposing figure with a prematurely bald head, he stood six-foot-two above his size twelve shoes, with a solid build and a lyrical, commanding voice, ready to take the place by storm. With his father providing an allowance, Bellows began classes in 1904 at the New York School of Art. Fellow students remembered him as being all too sure of himself, "insufferably cocky," but Bellows had the sheer talent to back up this personality.[20]

The class he took was taught by none other than Robert Henri himself, who provided entree to a much wider circle of artists. Though Bellows was a generation younger than most of his contemporaries, he shared their outlook on life and, above all, their artistic approach. He and Henri became more than close, in what one art historian labeled "a comfortable father-son relationship"; years later the younger man could recite Henri's philosophical utterances verbatim. Possibly because of this, more likely because of Bellows rampant self-assurance, Bellows and John Sloan never clicked as friends. According to one account, Sloan first encountered the young athlete when he was filling in for Henri as a temporary instructor. With the flush of youth, the young man rejected this substitute for the real thing, and when Sloan approached his canvas, Bellows turned his back. Sloan later described his junior in unflattering terms, how "as a painter he was a great ball-player . . . you can see the feet of clay."[21]

Bellows, meanwhile, wasted scarcely a New York minute in earning his reputation. In 1907 he exhibited a series of boxing pictures and won public acclaim and the Hallgarten Prize, an award of note. The following year members elected him to the National Academy, the youngest artist to ever receive that distinction. To this day, Bellows' prizefight paintings remain the most famous works of Ashcan art, iconic images (*fig. 4.3*, pg. 68).

Yet Bellows had developed a perspective that placed him firmly within the Ashcan school. A 1911 editorial in the *New York Sun* noted how the artist "refuses to see his city through the rose colored glasses of Childe Hassam. . . . One applauds George Bellows and at the same time shudders at his truth telling ugliness." The artist himself described his subject matter this way: "Wherever you go, they are waiting for you. The men of the docks, the children at the river edge . . . prize fights, summer evening and romance . . . young people, old people, the beautiful, the ugly." In words Henri must have appreciated, Bellows stressed that "an artist must be a spectator of life; a reverential, enthusiastic, emotional spectator." This sensibility, he explained, must be like "the joy of the child. . . . is not the joy of the child greater, more joyous, more wise, even, than the cynicism of our pseudo-cultured adults?" The artist died young, of a ruptured appendix at forty-two, in 1925. By then he had become the most famous contemporary painter in the country. In 1965, *New York Times* art critic John Canady referred to "an art that was essentially provincial in its optimism . . . the honest picturesqueness of the common man and the beauty of the visual world."[22]

For all his confidence, Bellows was never known as the extrovert of the Ashcan collective. That honor went to the Rabelaisian figure of George Luks.

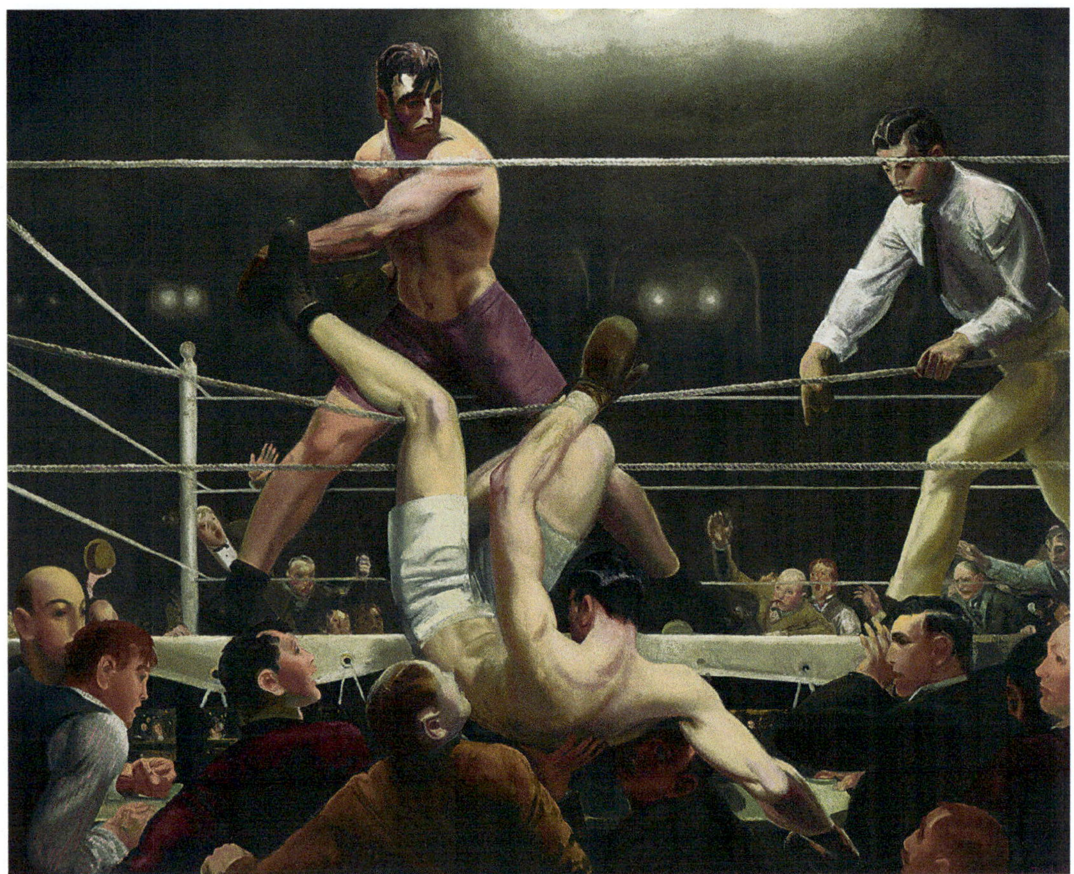

4.3 George Bellows (1882–1925), *Dempsey and Firpo*, 1924, oil on canvas, 51⅛ × 63¼ inches; 129.9 × 160.7 cm. Whitney Museum of American Art, New York. Purchase, with funds from Gertrude Vanderbilt Whitney, 31.95. Digital image © Whitney Museum of American Art.

Not much is known about Luks, born in 1866 to what art historian John Loughery referred to as "a moderately cultured family" in one of Pennsylvania's coal-mining sections. By 1893 he was on the art staff of the *Philadelphia Press* and joined the group around Robert Henri there, including Sloan, Everett Shinn, and William Glackens.[23]

Three years later, Luks moved to New York and stepped into history. The newspaper scene there was dominated by the all-consuming rivalry between Joseph Pulitzer's *World* and William Randolph Hearst's *Journal*. In 1896, just a mere two months after Luks had joined the *World*'s staff, Pulitzer produced a masterstroke, one that would change newspapers and, even more, graphic art, up to this day and far into the future.

A bold claim, with modest origins and a touch of genius. Seeking a new feature, Pulitzer set artist Richard Outcault to drawing the world's first comic strip. Known as *The Yellow Kid*, its star was an urchin with an oversized noggin perennially attired in a long sunflower overshirt. Set in the fictional Hogan's Alley in Hoboken, New Jersey, a world populated by wise and humorous young people with thick accents, kind of a combination Bowery Boys and *Peanuts*, it was a success the instant readers found it in the folds of the *World*.

Given the nature of their competition, it was impossible that Hearst would not respond. In a heartbeat, he snatched up Outcault, luring him to the *Journal* along with his popular character. Pulitzer, unfazed by such treachery, brought out a second *Yellow Kid* feature, with the same urban patois and setting, and turned the assignment over to new hire George Luks. This piece met with equal acclaim, and Luks became known as the "premier humorist artist" at one of the most important newspapers in New York. He kept this assignment for a year and a half, till he left for the war in Cuba as a combat artist, attached to various correspondents. But as the text analysis of the only volume to collect the *Yellow Kid* panels notes, Outcault's and Luks' "depictions of urban life would alter the course of painting in the United States" and led to Dick Tracey, Superman, and *Maus*. Moreover, a recent article by Richard Gambone argued that these cartoons were the predecessors of Luks' later work, that they "provoke questions about tensions between a presumed democratic society and challenges to the established social order."[24]

After drawing the Cuban war, Luks returned to New York and joined his fellow ex-Philadelphians to create the Ashcan school. Painting old men and young children alike, he frequently journeyed to the Lower East Side for subject matter (*fig. 4.4*). Later, in his Art

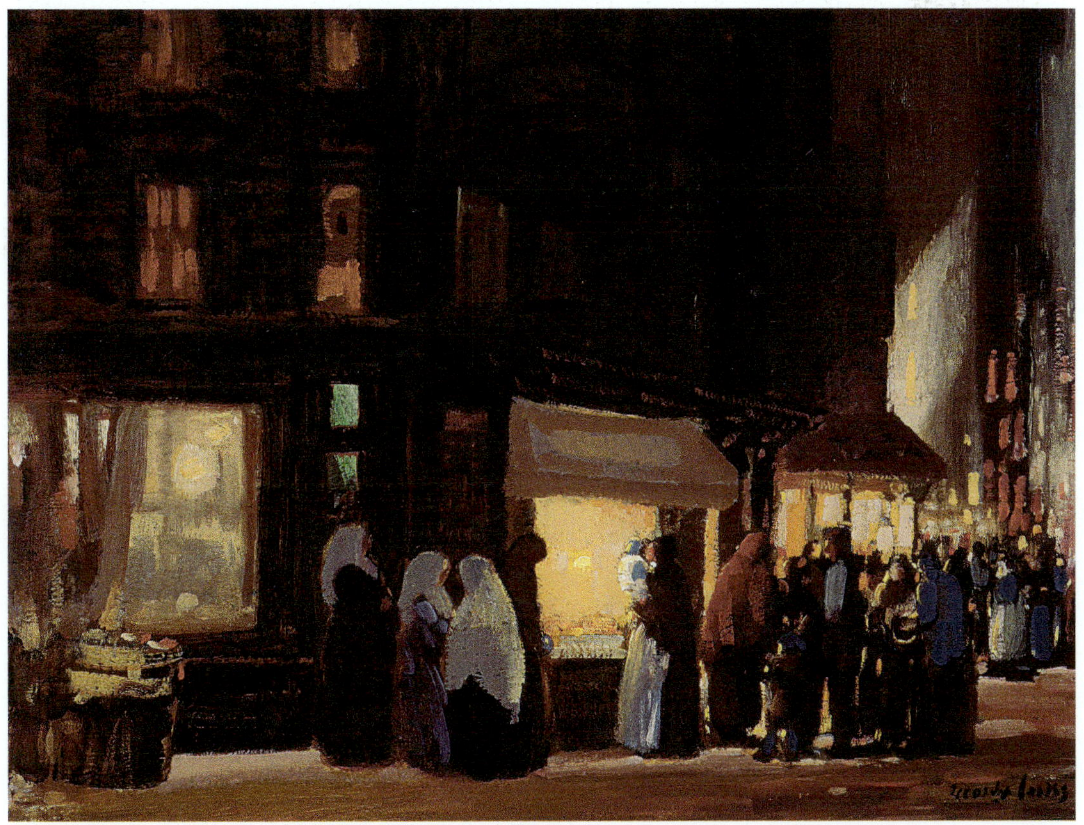

4.4 George Benjamin Luks (1867–1933), *Bleecker and Carmine Streets, New York*, ca. 1905, oil on canvas, 25 × 30 inches; 63.5 × 76.2 cm. Milwaukee Art Museum. Gift of Mr. and Mrs. Donald B. Abert and Mrs. Barbara Abert Tooman. M1976.14.

Students League classes, he taught students to go out and draw the city. Good to his word, he would corral bums or streetcleaners and present them as his session's models and subjects. Guy Pène du Bois explained Luks as "a dealer in the riches he finds around him."[25]

The leading critics of the era took notice of the artist's approach and his skill. Sadakichi Hartmann held that Luks "sees life and paints it. It is not a life without vulgarity . . . but it is the vulgarity of ordinary mankind. . . . Sane and healthy and beautiful for all those who can see beauty in what is generally classified as ugliness." Luks' foremost champion was James Huneker, one of the great journalists of the time. Huneker explained how Luks "loathes 'movements' and refers to . . . cubists . . . impressionists and futurists, in words that curdle the blood." Although some referred to the artist as "a naughty painter," Huneker found that the "real Luks . . . is the Luks interested in the byways and highways of life; the Luks who knows the heart of darkness on the East Side; sympathetic and brilliant painter of men, women and children as they joy or sorrow, thrive or die." Gambone wrote of Luks' vision, of "the vital, energizing spirit he saw in the slums, a viewpoint diametrically different from that advocated by most social reformers, who saw nothing but the debilitating effects of poverty." Instead, Luks portrayed "slum dwellers as the social equals of the middle and upper classes, filled with a very American drive and energy to get ahead." In an expression of one of the fundamental tenets of Ashcan art, Luks himself told an interviewer, "Humanity is essentially the same," regardless of relative income or location of abode.[26]

Luks was a character, with a self-destruct mechanism built into his very fiber. At five-foot-five-and-one-half, he was hardly a towering presence; Rockwell Kent described his friend's physique as "stocky rather than rotund." Like the similarly displayed Falstaff, the artist enjoyed practical jokes, would wake up Everett Shinn early in the morning, barge into the sleeper's bathroom, lather up the mirror profusely, then stroke the foam off his own reflection. Guy Pène du Bois recalled that Luks' "dinner-table manners could shock the least squeamish people. His conversation was heavily larded with obscenities."[27]

As befitting such an extrovert, Luks was anything but modest, yet he backed up his claims with astonishing skills. He boasted that he was one of only two truly great artists in the history of the world (Frans Hals was the other). All the same, one observer caught him working with both hands as he completed a sketch. One digit worked the foreground image while the other concurrently filled in the borders.[28]

But in true Hemingwayesque fashion, Luks also liked to drink. And fight. Often simultaneously, till inevitably, at the wrong place and time. One art historian wrote that the artist "*enjoyed drinking—in fact he loved to get drunk. It was the only thing worth doing besides laughing and painting and women.*" In a letter from John Sloan to his wife Dolly, Sloan recalled a visit to Luks' residence. "There was a bottle of whisky, which George used considerably. . . . when I left George was in a most stupid mess." Sloan and others testified that he "would often pick a fight in a saloon, say something nasty and get things going and then leave the place, with people who had nothing to do with the argument left to finish the fracas."[29]

A nasty game, inevitably ending in tragedy. In 1933 Luks' body was found under the el tracks, smashed, presumably the victim of a barroom fight. The press covered it up, claiming that he had been sketching the city when he was struck by a sudden illness; his friends knew better. On his sixtieth birthday, he had told an interviewer, "A man's just out of school at sixty. . . . I'm just getting started." An obituary in *The Art Digest* began, "One by one the great individualists of American art have passed."[30]

John Sloan considered William Glackens the best sketch artist of the Ashcan group, describing him as "the greatest draughtsman who lived on this side of the ocean." Referred to by friends as "Butts," Glackens was, in Sloan's words, "quiet, gentle, handsome." Some remembered how it seemed impossible to get mad at their colleague; on one occasion, he had the temerity to advise John Sloan that Henri's teaching was a negative influence yet lived to see the next dawn.[31]

Glackens was an intimate member of the Ashcan circle. Attending classes at the Pennsylvania Academy of the Fine Arts, he befriended fellow student John Sloan and became so close with Robert Henri that they roomed, and even traveled to Europe, together.[32]

Glackens' skills as a penciller were legendary (*fig. 4.5*). He had "an incredible visual memory, frequently going out on assignment without pencil or paper and producing accurate drawings when he returned." Everett Shinn claimed his colleague "could make a drawing of a fire engine almost detailed enough to construct one from, after merely seeing it go by on the street." On

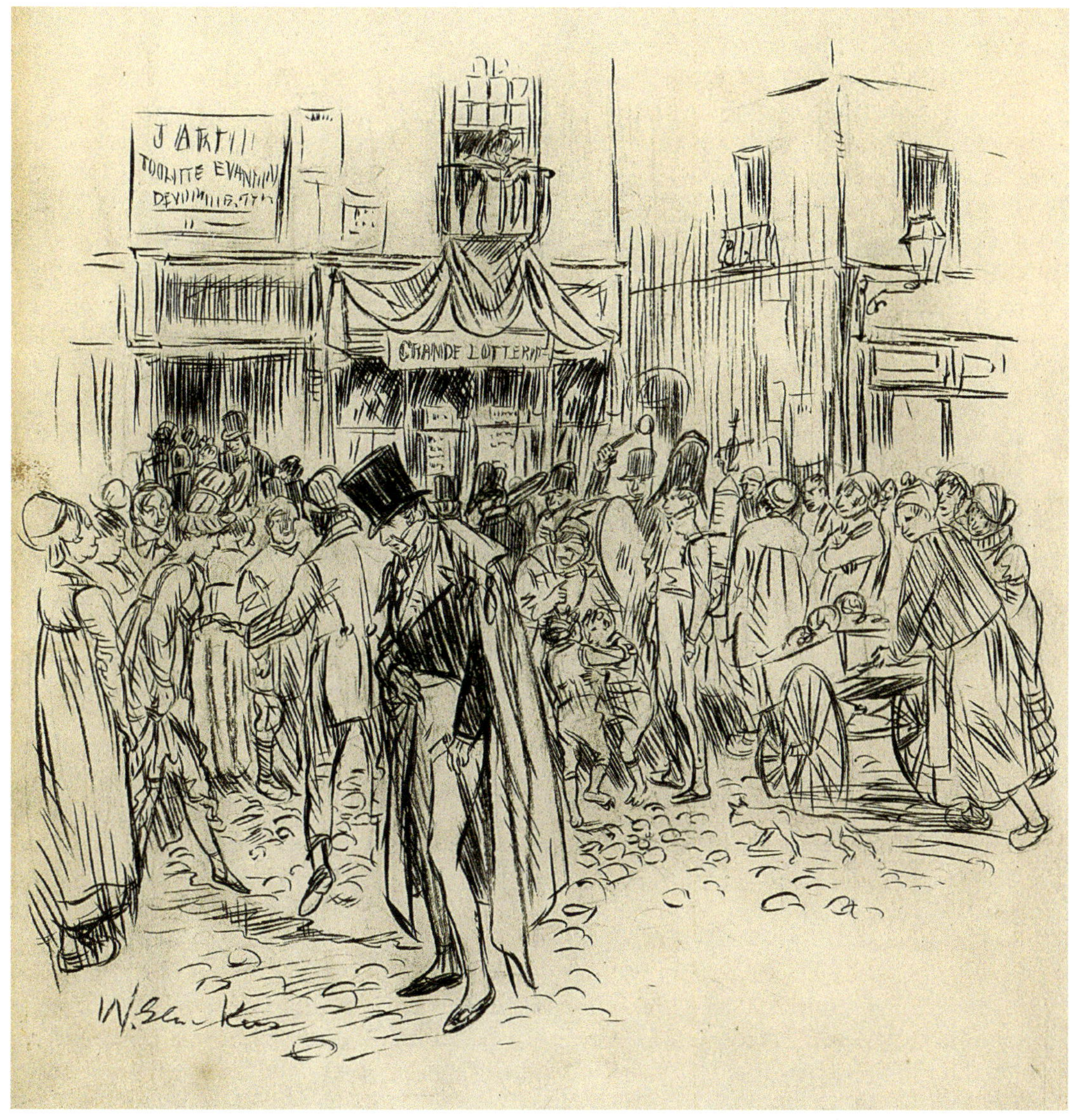

4.5 William Glackens (1870–1938), "He noticed he was in front of the lottery office," ca. 1902. Drawing: pen and ink over graphite underdrawing, 28.6 × 24.2 cm. Reproduction number: LC-DIG-ppmsca-05864 (digital file from original drawing). Library of Congress Prints and Photographs Division, Washington, DC.

another occasion, while vacationing in Long Island because of summer heat, an acquaintance announced that she planned to take a special trip into New York City, to see what a special lamp post looked like. From memory, Glackens produced a meticulous rendering of the object in question and saved her the trip.[33]

This type of work took guts as well as skill. Ira Glackens, his son, narrated one story from his father's newspaper days, involving a murder scene. The evil deed had taken place in a barn, which police had locked. But the editor wanted a drawing, and William was small, so friends boosted him through a narrow window, a feat that deposited him into a pool of the victim's blood. Glackens was also known as *the* man for handling crowd scenes; according to Shinn, "none of us . . . could do a crowd quite like Glackens. The editors considered it his specialty."[34]

Glackens wandered far and wide over Gotham, providing art for Abraham Cahan's stories of the Lower East Side, as well as drawing uptown neighborhoods. When he died, his wife wrote to John Sloan, "Nobody need mention Time the healer to me. I know life will be sadder and more lonely and regretful every day. If it were not for the hope of finding a proper housing for his pictures I shouldn't have any object in living at all. I know everybody who knew him will never forget him."[35]

Referred to as "Eve" by his friends, Everett Shinn was a natty dresser, thin and of medium stature. Even late in his life, an interviewer described him as having "ballroom gallantry. Instead of reticence, there was the garrulity of a man whose life has been crammed with excitement and activity and who has so hugely enjoyed every moment of it." Theodore Dreiser was so taken with the artist that Shinn became the model he used for his depiction of the artistic life in *The "Genius."*[36]

Coming of age in New Jersey, Shinn studied mechanical drawing in Philadelphia, where he worked for a chandelier manufacturer. Only sixteen years old and filled with dreams, he got caught by his boss drawing street scenes in the margins of his regular work. Yelling, "Art school, young man, art school. You're no good to me here," the supervisor fired him.

Grand idea, but classes at the Pennsylvania Academy of the Fine Arts cost money, so Shinn became a staff artist at the *Philadelphia Press*. This not only provided him with an income; soon he was sharing a room with coworker George Luks, who in turn introduced him to Robert Henri. In 1897, the Spanish-American War was in full bloom, so the great dailies sent most of their reporters and artists to cover the story. New York was hiring replacements to handle local news, so that year Shinn moved to Gotham.[37]

Shinn worked for the *World*, and soon joining him in New York were the other members of the Philadelphia pressroom crew. But for Shinn it was love at first sight. John Sloan commented that Shinn's paintings were "love letters to the great lady of his heart—Manhattan." The city's response was positive. A *New York Times* reviewer felt that Shinn "has only to go forward to fill the full measure of success." His drawings appeared in *Harper's* and *Vanity Fair*.[38]

Outside of his commercial work, Shinn's artistic interests began with the classic Ashcan preoccupation, street scenes of the vibrant metropolis laid out before him (*fig. 4.6*). His interest was more in a sense of the scene than in specific portrayals. One modern art reviewer noted how "Shinn was more concerned with capturing the overall experience of the urban street rather than individual characterizations . . . the weather conditions upstage the human presence and exaggerate the energy and movement of the crowd."[39]

By 1908 Shinn's interests had moved uptown. Ironically, though that would be the year of the epochal exhibit of Ashcan painting, Shinn had fallen in love with the theater and became its great artistic chronicler, as well as drawing stage panels for David Belasco's emporiums. One

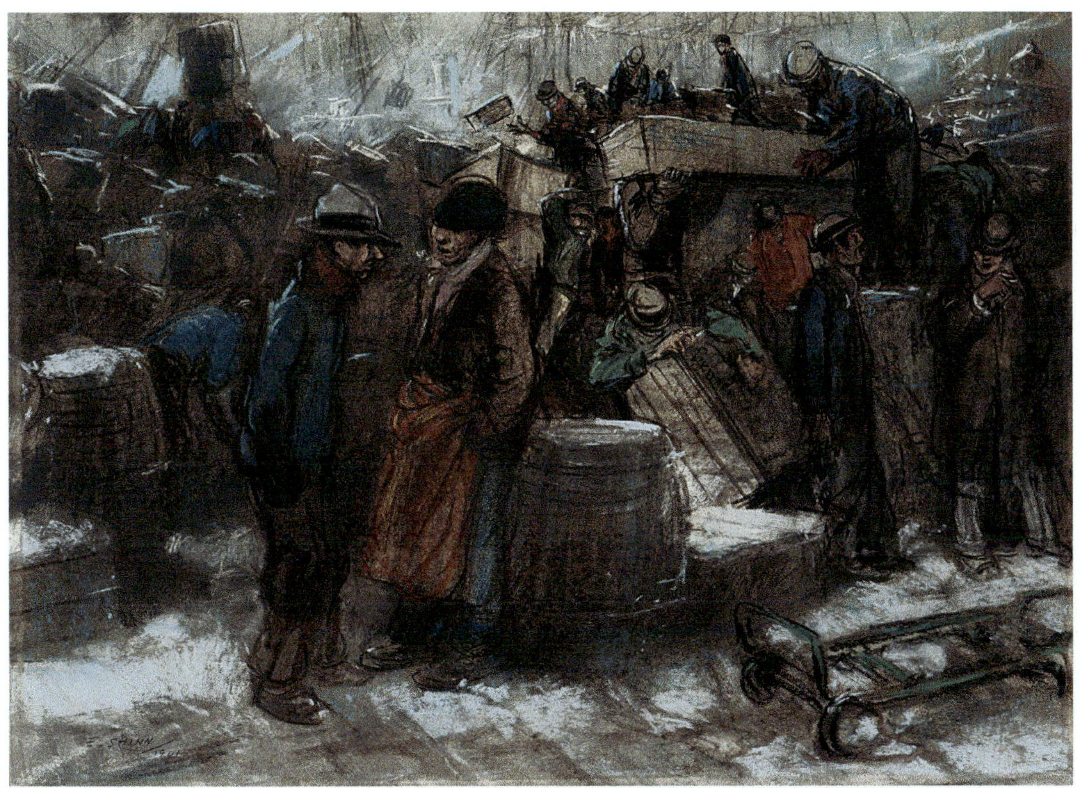

4.6 Everett Shinn (1876–1953), *The Docks, New York City*, 1901, pastel on paper, 15.5 × 22 inches; 39.37 × 55.88 cm. Munson-Williams-Proctor Arts Institute. Photo credit: Munson-Williams-Proctor Arts Institute/Art Resource, New York.

critic lyrically described this life as, "It was a Jimmy Walker, straw-hat world, and Shinn enjoyed every moment of it."[40]

Five of the artists just memorialized—Henri, Sloan, Bellows, Glackens, and Shinn—were part of the pioneering Ashcan exhibition in 1908. One other practitioner of this approach to art, who was not included in that exhibit, also bears mention.

Unlike so many of his contemporaries, Jerome Myers was not from the Northeast but was born in Petersburg, Virginia. By the time he was nineteen, however, he had made it to New York City, working as a scene painter in the theater district. Two years later he was studying at the Art Students League and about to launch his career as a serious artist. After taking a studio across the street from John Sloan's, the two became good friends. Myers never fit in the larger clique, nor was he included in the pathbreaking exhibition of 1908 that made the term "Ashcan" part of American art history. As William Innes Homer noted, "Sloan always thought Myers should have been invited, but Henri blocked the idea. Myers was not a member of the circle, and Henri objected to the sentimentality of his work."[41]

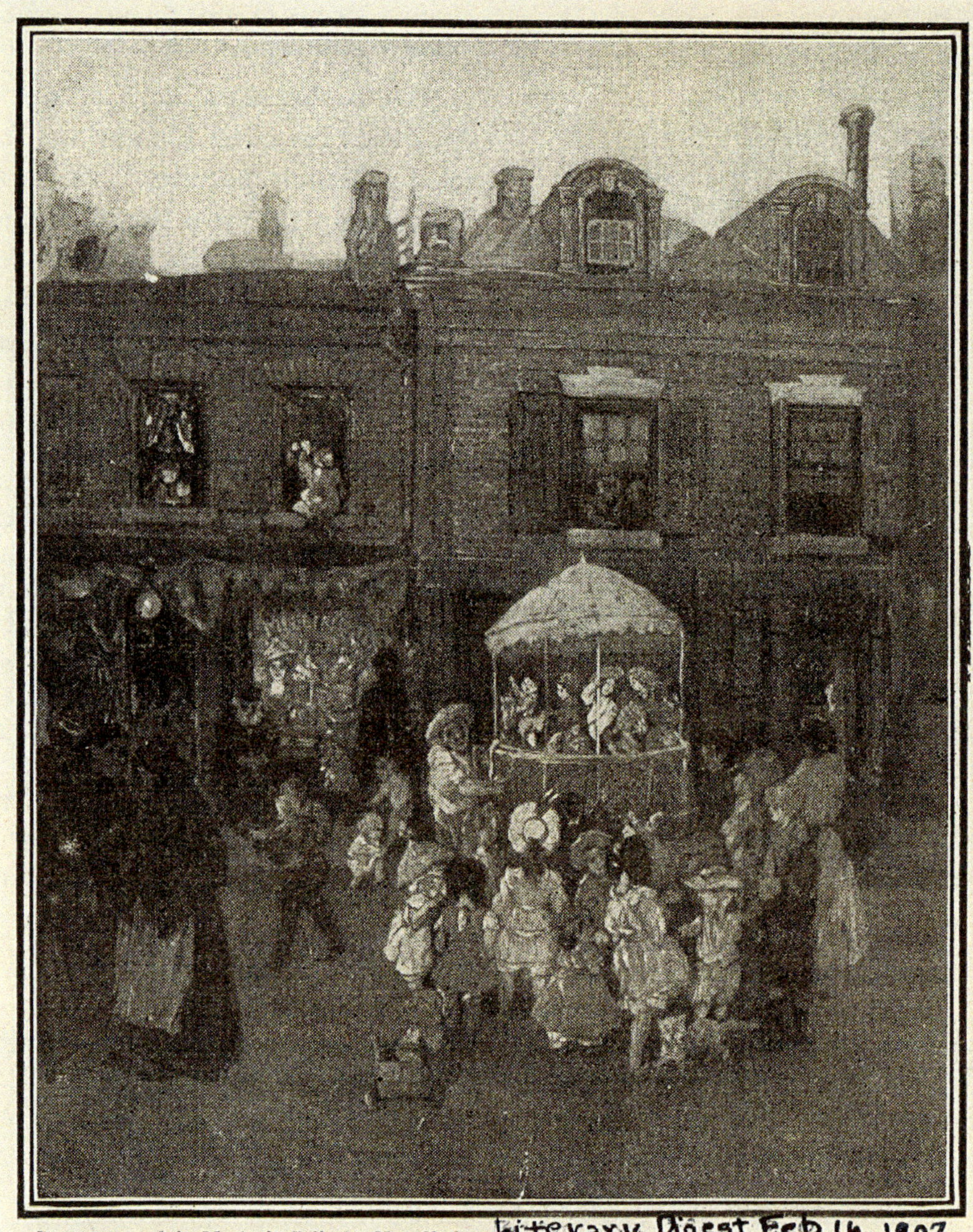

By courtesy of the Macbeth Galleries, New York.

"THE STREET CAROUSEL, EAST SIDE, NEW YORK."

From a painting by Jerome Myers.

This artist, in the judgment of a critic, reproduces, "in the great tradition of *genre*," the "visions of our slums."

4.7 Jerome Myers (1867–1940), *The Street Carousel, East Side, New York*, 1907, print, 5½ × 3¾ inches; 14 × 10 cm. The New York Public Library. Photo credit: The New York Public Library/Art Resource, New York.

Still, Myers shared the Ashcan approach to art (*fig. 4.7*). Of the Lower East Side, he wrote, "Others saw ugliness and degradation there, I saw poetry and beauty." Citing American history, he wondered, "If Abraham Lincoln had been an artist. . . . I wonder whether his sympathies would not have led him . . . to paint the common people, who he said were made by God." John Sloan felt "a grave, idiosyncratic quality is displayed by Jerome Myer. . . . He paints dark pictures . . . and has a feeling for the night, for the mystery and fear of dark corners." A 1915 word portrait in *The Craftsman* spoke of how, in his work, "there is the joy of receiving his humanity, his kindness, his humor, his understanding of all of the great and small tragedies of humble life." Grant Holcomb III referred to him as "the gentle poet of the slums."[42]

In terms of personality, their traits ranged from Sloan's shyness to Luks' garrulousness. What they shared was an appreciation of the city, a love for its vastness and exuberance, and for the humanity of its residents.

Even more, the Ashcan artists came to New York as journalism, and the city, were booming. Nurtured by a philosopher-king, they developed a new approach, and a new American art. They were ready to take on New York City, and in their wake, and the art world as well. Their triumph would not last long, but it has endured.

CHAPTER FIVE

The Art Scene

Nothing exists in a vacuum. Before the Ashcan artists emerged, some creators had rebelled against the Academy by taking individual paths and finding their own way. By so doing, they pointed the nation's art scene toward the later, pathbreaking work of the Ashcan artists.

The real godfather of the Ashcan school was Walt Whitman. As the art historian Ruth Bohan put it, "Today, 150 years after its first publication, *Leaves of Grass* remains a landmark of American literary achievement." Van Wyck Brooks extolled, "for the first time, [he] gave us the sense of something organic in American life."[1]

Whitman had much of value for the Ashcan artists. Essayist Kathleen Kennedy Townsend observed, "What's most shocking about his writing today is not that he loves men or describes 'the body electric.' What's stunning is his democratic sensibility." Whitman's masterful poem "I Hear America Singing" begins:

I hear America singing, the varied carols I hear,
Those of mechanics, each one singing his as it should be blithe and strong
The carpenter singing his as he measures his plank or beam,
The mason singing his as he makes ready for work, or leaves off work,
The boatman singing what belongs to him in his boat, the deck-hand singing on the steamboat
    deck,
The shoemaker singing as he sits on his bench, the hatter singing as he stands,
The wood-cutter's song, the ploughboy's on his way in the morning, or at noon intermission
    or at sundown,
The delicious singing of the mother, or of the young wife at work, or of the girl sewing or washing,
Each singing what belongs to him or her and to none else.

Even more powerful for these urban artists were the words of "Mannahatta":

The down-town streets, the jobbers' house of business, the houses of business of the ship-
    merchants and money-brokers, the river-streets,
Immigrants arriving, fifteen or twenty thousand in a week,
The carts hauling goods, the manly race of drivers of horses, the brown-faced sailors,
The summer air, the bright sun shining, and the sailing clouds aloft,

The winter snows, the sleigh-bells, the broken ice in the river, passing along up or down with
*   the flood-tide or ebb-tide,*
The mechanics of the city, the masters, well form'd, beautiful-faced, looking you straight in
*   the eyes,*
Trottoirs throng'd, vehicles, Broadway, the women, the shops and shoes,
A million people—manners free and superb—open voices—hospitality—the most courageous
*   and friendly young men,*
City of hurried and sparkling waters! city of spires and masts!
City nestled in bays! my city!

There is no question the Ashcan artists took Whitman's lessons to heart. William Innes
Homer, in *Robert Henri and His Circle*, described Whitman as one of two of Henri's "idols" (the
other was Ralph Waldo Emerson), indeed as the influence who formed "the basis for many of
his ideas." Henri described the poet thus: "Walt Whitman was such as I should have proposed
the real art student should be. His work—nothing greater has been done at any time—is an
autobiography—not of haps and mishaps, but of his deepest thought, his life indeed." Van Wyck
Brooks found that John Sloan shared these sentiments, that Sloan was "deeply drawn" to the
poet, that he "had given Henri a fine copy of *Leaves of Grass* and Whitman from the first had
been a bond between them." Sloan's memory of a captivating walk across the Brooklyn Bridge,
which possibly presaged his *The Wake of the Ferry (no. 2)*, told how "on the bridge I thought
of Whitman's Brooklyn Ferry."[3]

The first giant among these early rebels against elitism was Thomas Eakins. Lloyd Goodrich,
whose biography set up all future discussion of this artist, intoned, "Seldom has there been
such a realist as Eakins. . . . He used the material that lay closest around him. Every figure
he painted was a portrait, every scene or object a real one." The catalog for a 1967 exhibit at
the Brooklyn Museum, *The Triumph of Realism*, described Eakins as "the most uncompromising
of the American realists and artistically on a par with Homer. . . . Prettiness and artificiality,
pleasing colors and cleverness in thematic choice were diametrically opposed to his desire to
give a genuine, unadulterated view of the people and things he was daily exposed to." Goodrich
noted that "the commonest complaint about his art was that it lacked 'beauty' and poetry.'"
Eakins and Whitman were good friends, and Eakins gave the poet a black-and-white print of
his masterpiece *The Gross Clinic*.[4]

Eakins' influence on the Ashcan artists went far beyond merely what he put on canvas.
Goodrich added to the laurels he bestowed by declaring, "Among American artists of the last
generation, Thomas Eakins was one of the strongest, leaving behind work of inescapable power"
but also "exercising a widespread influence as a teacher." Another artist, Walter Pach, lamented
that Eakins "was only the 'teacher' to many who did not see the great power of the man."
Robert Henri considered him "the greatest portrait painter" America had produced up through
the 1920s, describing him as "a man, strong, profound and honest, and above all, one who
had attained the reality of beauty in nature as it is." Eakins drew portraits, but the kind that
Henri called "a beautiful portrait; not a pretty or a swagger portrait, but an honest, respectful,
appreciative man-to-man portrait."[5]

Yet Eakins sought more, pursued subject matter that the Ashcan artists would later embrace
as well. Goodrich observed that the artist painted "ordinary people in ordinary settings, and
commonplace themes like sports, prizefights, surgical operations, and scenes from everyday life."
By so doing, he captured "the accent peculiar to America."[6]

In other words, he represented the beginnings of a new, fundamentally American art. Eakins
recognized this quality, this goal, toward the end of his life. In 1914 he told an interviewer, "If
America is to produce great painters and if young artists wish to assume a place in the history

of art in their country, their first desire should be to remain in America," as opposed to making the seemingly mandatory pilgrimage to Paris. Only by exploring local sources, "will we create a great and distinctly American art."[7]

Eakins came to these values from strange roots. Born 1844, in Philadelphia, he was of traditional stock, Scots-Irish, English, and Dutch; none of those Hibernian or Teutonic influences that were flooding America's shores with immigrants. His father, appropriately enough for a budding artist, was a writing master, a connoisseur of elaborate script, in demand for drawing up official documents, as well as an instructor in the fine art of gracious penmanship. This brought in a tidy income, and the family was solidly middle class, both in terms of standing in the American social hierarchy, as well as in income. Prudent investments by his father—in traditional ventures such as real estate and stocks—ensured a lifelong income for the young man. Thomas Eakins never depended on painting for his daily bread, which provided him freedom, the most valuable commodity for any human being, artist or not, the power to choose his own course, to pursue his own definition of art.[8]

But not at first. First, he had to learn the established mode. And there was only one place on the face of the earth, at that time and place, that one could study with the best the human race had developed, at the center of the art world. In 1866, at the age of twenty-two, he went to Paris.

Paris, which was about to be shocked by a revolution called impressionism, was the citadel of orthodoxy, with the Académie des Beaux-Arts and its training institutes, the Ecole des Beaux-Arts and the Académie Julian, far more despotic than anything in America.

His response to this world of art foretold his future career. Considered a hick from the hinterlands, at first Eakins plunged eagerly into his new Parisian life. He took classes in which a student sat for four to six weeks and did pencil studies of a sculpted bust. After this traditional stint, however, he rebelled. Technical excellence was not the end of his striving, but rather, great and powerful art. Looking at the world around him, he sought to render its moods and nuances, and gifted scribbling served only as a useful tool in that pursuit, nothing more.

Eakins returned to Philadelphia four years later, in 1870, where he set up a studio in his parents' home. Although he started with innocuous scenes—his sisters at the piano or playing with their cat—he soon became consumed by the issues of the day. Thomas was in a major industrial metropolis at the start of a boom time, the dynamic burst of growth known by Mark Twain's potent description of an era, *The Gilded Age*. Yet he was still a product of a class background—in this case very respectable middle class—and that shaped his perspective. Eakins was not interested in the growing legions of workers but rather in what was happening to his own people.

The big fear for men at this time, which would carry over to the next century, was effeminization. Creative, striving males were no longer setting up farms, or even factories. More and more, they did not haul or hammer, mold iron, or craft leather. They were not even entrepreneurs. They did not even stand. Instead, they sat. In offices. And pursued the growing demands required by paperwork. Men were becoming flabby, both in their bodies and in their spirits. Physical fitness became a fad for office drones, and writers like Theodore Roosevelt extolled the masculine virtues, while painters turned to images of men engaged in uniquely male activities.

Eakins shared these sentiments, these fears; like anyone else, he remained a product of his times. Decades before George Wesley Bellows achieved prominence by painting boxing scenes, Eakins looked to the prizefighting ring.

Two pictures portray Eakins' vision of realism: *Between Rounds* and *Salutat* (figs. 5.1 and 5.2, pgs. 80–81). Certain features about this collection leap out at the viewer, a study in contrasts. On the one hand, Eakins is a pioneer, because he exposes his audience to a garish, popular sport, one that exposes the human body. There are crowds and naked torsos here, which people comment on from the galleries.

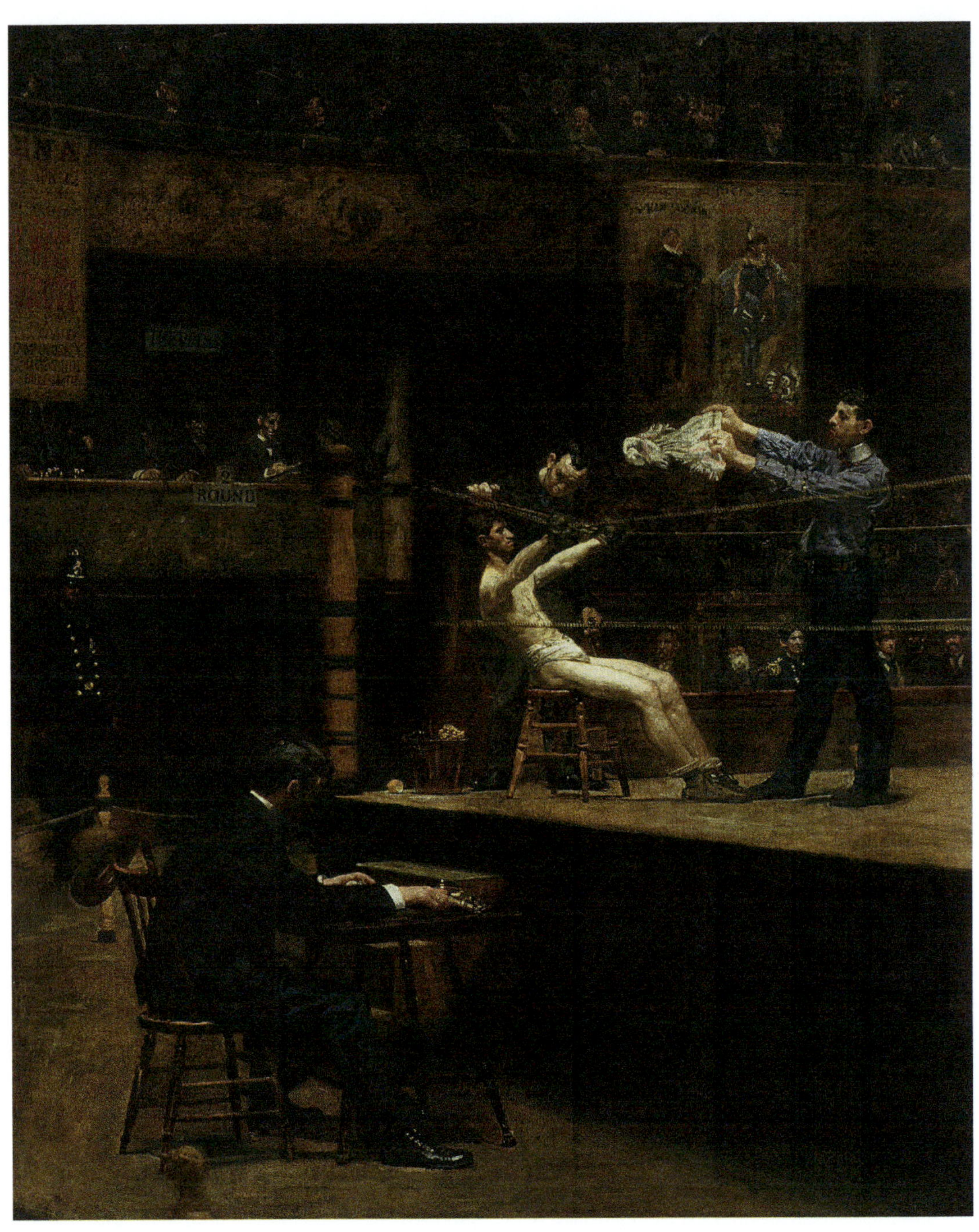

5.1 Thomas Eakins (1844–1916), *Between Rounds*, 1898–1899, oil on canvas, 50⅛ × 39⅞ inches; 127.3 × 101.3 cm. Gift of Mrs. Thomas Eakins and Miss Mary Adeline Williams, 1929. (1929-1854-16). Philadelphia Museum of Art. Photo credit: The Philadelphia Museum of Art/Art Resource, New York.

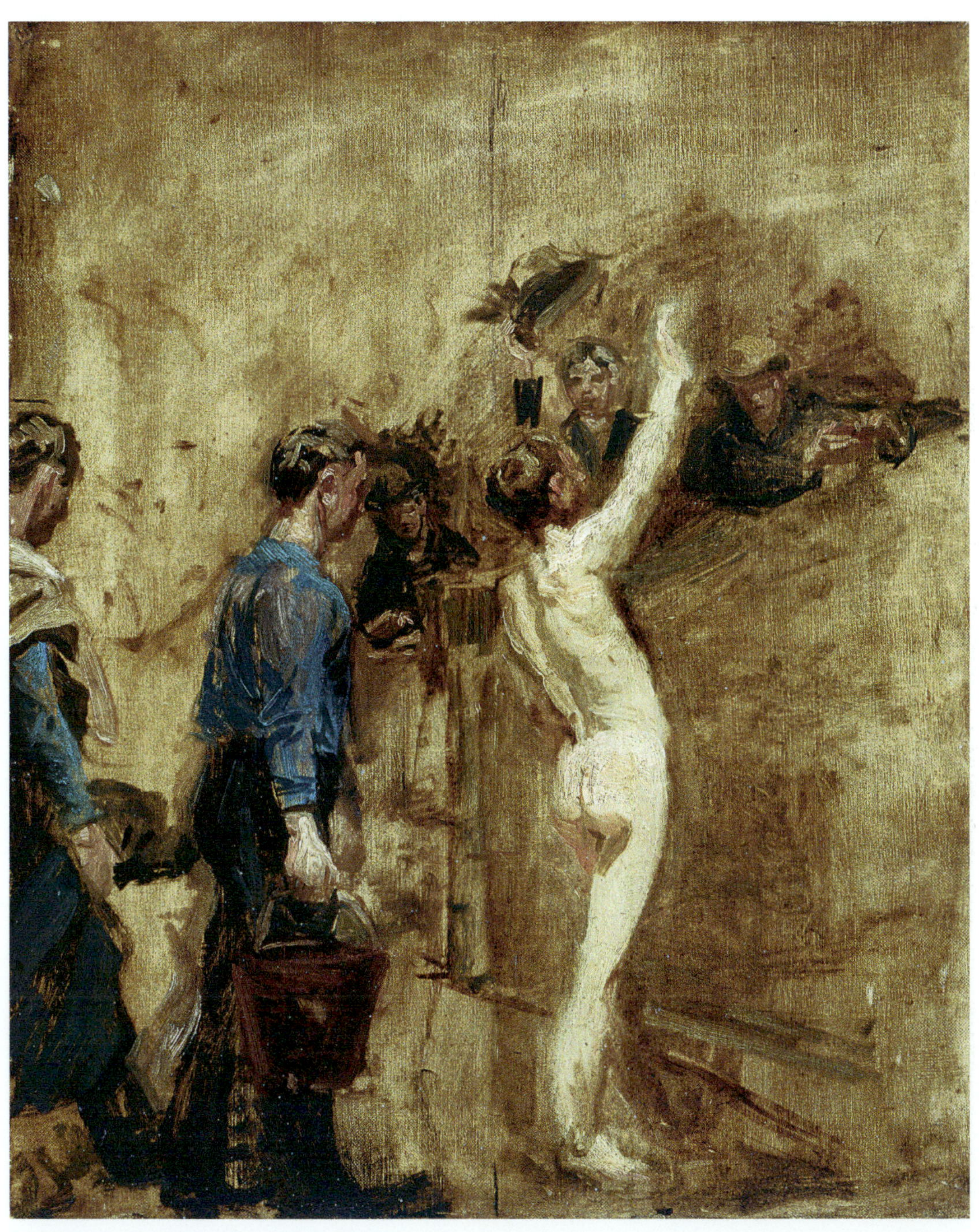

5.2 Thomas Eakins (1844–1916), study for *Salutat*, 1898, oil on canvas, 20⅛ × 16⅛ inches. Carnegie Museum of Art, Pittsburgh. Gift of Mr. and Mrs. James H. Beal, 81.54.1.

But beyond that significant contribution, real limits appear. For one, unlike the real thing, all these settings are immaculately clean; not a scuff, speck of dirt, nor a drop of blood taints the vista.

Most astonishing of all, despite the fact that these are boxing pictures, there is no violence. *There is no boxing here.* Rather, we get what Eakins preferred, a series of superb figure studies. These figures, in other words, presented what was great and novel, yet also what was limiting in realistic art before the arrival of the Ashcan school.

Eakins produced two masterpieces. The first, *Max Schmitt in a Single Scull* (*fig. 5.3*), captures masculinity in the late nineteenth century, constrained by class boundaries. For the middle-class male, rowing seemed the perfect antidote to industrialization and office duties. It was a sport carried on outdoors and involved the strengthening of muscles in the arms and back.

While this work is almost pastoral in its tranquility, it is also a slice of urban life, with modern bridges highlighted in the background. Schmitt is engaged in an everyday, recreational pursuit, although one enabled by the economics of his standing in life. Sculls of this sort cost real money, unimaginable to a laborer. Unlike a workman, the subject is able to take an afternoon off to partake of nonremunerative sport. Eakins is venturing into new realms for figure drawing yet still bound into his world.

In *The Gross Clinic*, Eakins took his interests, in portraiture and in exploring unfathomed aspects of real life, to new depths, shocking the art world of his time (*fig. 5.4*). In this painting,

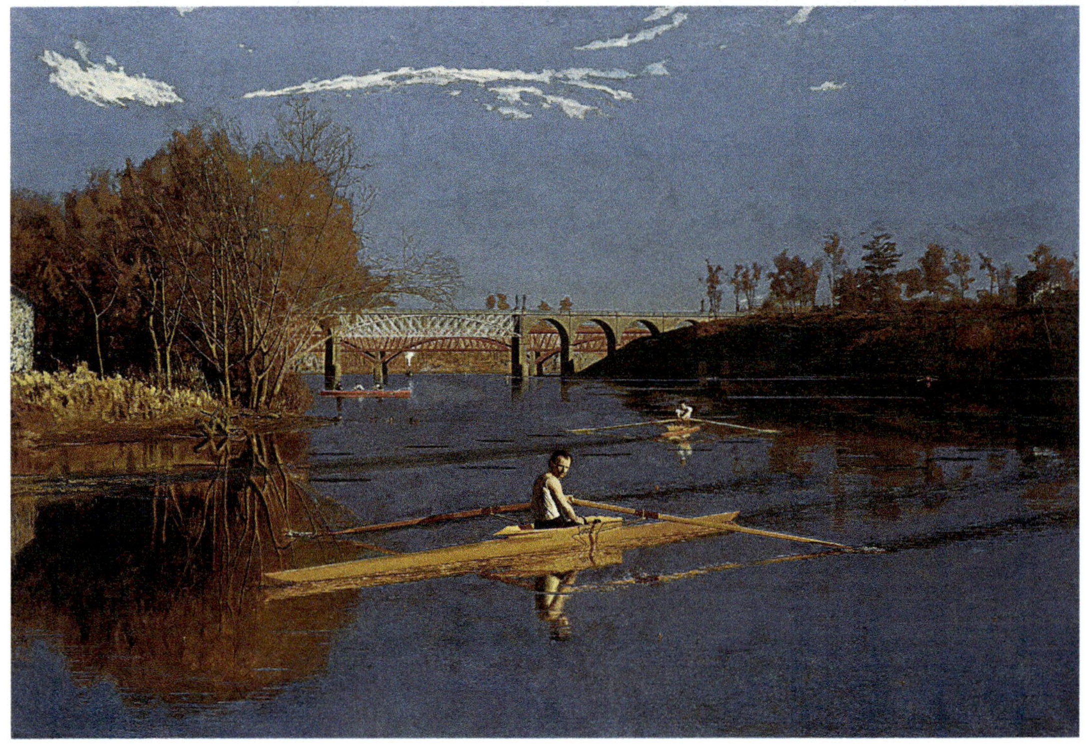

5.3 Thomas Eakins (1844–1916), *The Champion Single Sculls (Max Schmitt in a Single Scull)*, 1871, oil on canvas, 32¼ × 46¼ inches; 81.9 × 117.5 cm. Purchase, The Alfred N. Punnett Endowment Fund and George D. Pratt Gift, 1934. (34.92). The Metropolitan Museum of Art. Image © Metropolitan Museum of Art. Image source: Art Resource, New York.

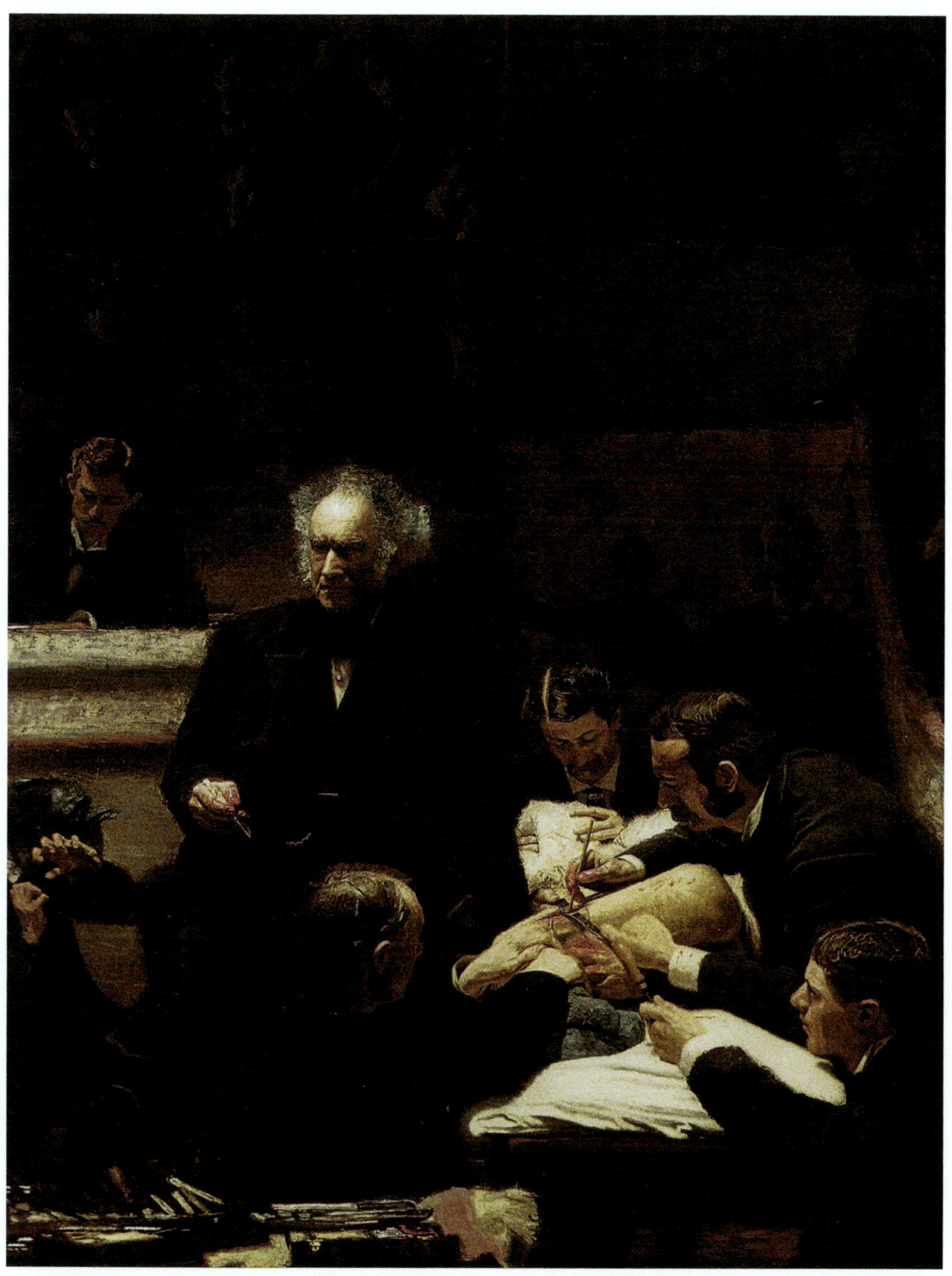

5.4 Thomas Eakins (1844–1916), sketch for *The Gross Clinic*, 1875, oil on canvas, 26 × 22 inches; 66 × 55.9 cm. Gift of Mrs. Thomas Eakins and Miss Mary Adeline Williams, 1929. (1929-184-31). Philadelphia Museum of Art. Photo credit: The Philadelphia Museum of Art/Art Resource, New York.

Eakins brings classic portraiture to everyday life, an unprecedented bridging. Historian Elizabeth Johns bluntly stated, "Thomas Eakins was a painter of portraits"; in 1918, art critic Horace Traubel remarked, "personally, I consider him the greatest portrait painter America has produced." *The Gross Clinic* itself was literally epic in scale—eight feet by six feet—worthy of the masterpieces of antiquity.[9]

Yet it is stark in its depiction of medical procedure, previously a private part of life, while at the same time being extremely nationalistic. Philadelphia was one of the centers of medical learning at the time, and with this painting Eakins trumpeted to the world his city's eminence in that field. The hands Eakins paints are bloody, and we see the results of an incision into the human body; a spectator to the left shields the eyes from sheer horror. Yet there is the feel of humdrum, of a day-to-day activity. Gross, the center of this scene, seems droll and unaffected, lecturing to his students, who continue working, while a young man to the left takes class notes. In this time before germ theory, everyone wears proper street clothes of suit and tie. Instead of a heroic episode or a pathbreaking medical event, this is an episode in everyday life. The painting is filled with mundane details—an anesthesiologist clasps the patient's head in an ether-soaked fabric, assisting doctors hand up instruments from a tray that might come from a hardware store, physicians hold the patient's lower limbs steady—rather than a lyrical romanticism, or the stalwart rectitude of one of society's leaders caught in a formal pose.[10]

Reaction to the painting was vigorous and often strident. To citizens of that era and the middle class, its depiction of human blood must have been received like a slasher movie in the twenty-first century. Though some critics thrilled to the expertise of this American painter, others blanched at his subject matter. While one wrote, "We know of no artist in this country who can at all compare with Mr. Eakins as a draughtsman," another questioned "the propriety of introducing into our art a class of subjects hitherto confined to a few of the more brutal artists and races of the old world." This could be, in other words, the work of people of inferior genetic makeup, primitives and savages. Even in 2010, a modern critic in the *New York Times*, referred to *The Gross Clinic* as "a bloody union of human progress and frailty." After initial display, the canvas remained in a private medical school, rarely brought out for exhibitions, and did not win an award till 1904. The jury at its initial showing, offended and put off by its frank depiction, refrained from hanging it in the regular section of the exhibition. Elizabeth Johns recorded that "it made people uneasy, even angry." One reviewer described it as "a picture which even strong men find it difficult to look at long if they can look at it at all." Real existence was unbearable to the art world at that time, a harbinger of critical reaction to the subsequent Ashcan school.[11]

Eakins' foremost pupil, Thomas Anshutz, followed in his teacher's footsteps but began to break through the iron wall of class. Anshutz began his studies at the National Academy, but in 1875 he moved to Philadelphia to work with Eakins and became his assistant at the Pennsylvania Academy of Fine Arts in 1878, succeeding him as teacher in his own right in 1886. He adopted his mentor's idea of embracing sincerity and truth, eschewing artifice. Anshutz' aim was to "make as accurate a painting of what I see in front of me as I can." His art was "based on knowledge, and knowledge on fact."[12]

But Anshutz' gaze turned to sectors of American life that Eakins never contemplated. On his father's side, relatives owned and ran iron mills, and the young artist had spent a long period growing up in Wheeling, West Virginia, a small city where iron mills played an oversized role. From these roots, the artist chose to paint something rarely attempted in the American art world, the lives of ordinary workers.[13]

In many ways, this is a pioneering impression. In *Ironworkers*, we see toilers coming off the job (*fig. 5.5*). Instead of middle-class suits, the subjects of this painting are in crude dress; the highlighted figures in the foreground are wearing bright red tank tops, even in the twenty-first

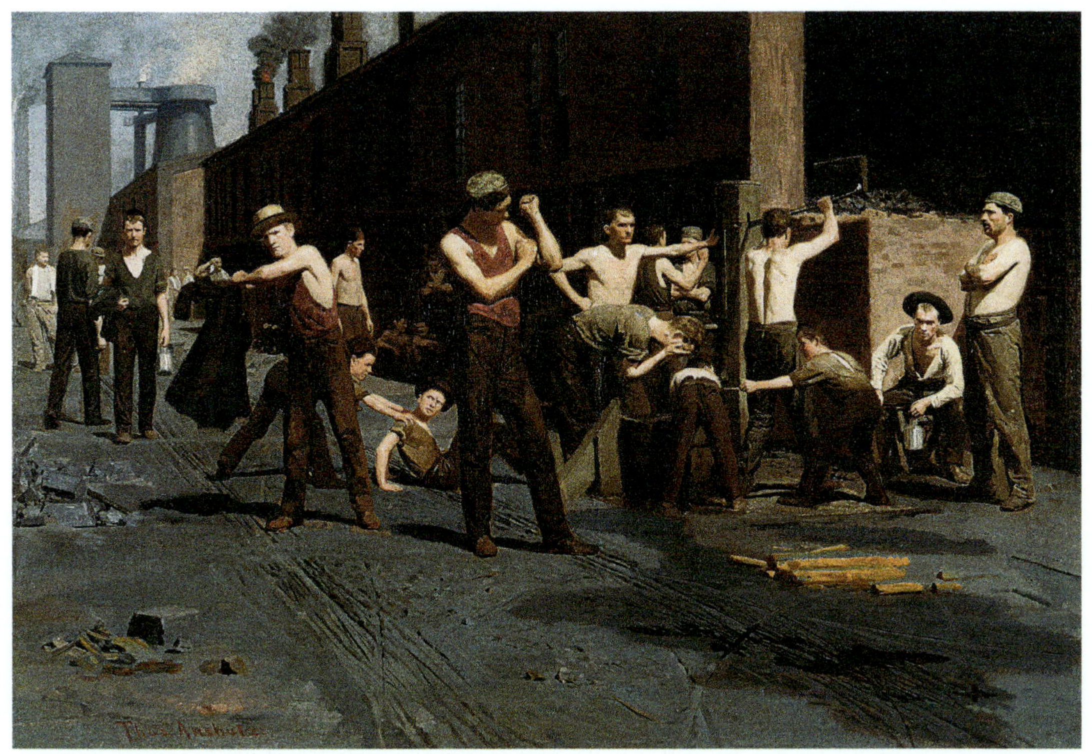

5.5 Thomas Pollock Anshutz (1851–1912), *The Ironworkers' Noontime*, 1880, oil on canvas, 17 × 23⅞ inches. Fine Arts Museum of San Francisco, Gift of Mr. and Mrs. John D. Rockefeller 3rd. 1979.7.4.

century often seen as working-class garb. Even more striking to its 1880 audience, one of the men in the center background, and three others on the left, wear no shirt whatsoever, a shocking depiction in a painting designed to be exhibited to mixed-gender audiences in late-Victorian America. This seems accurate and appropriate, however, exactly the kind of behavior men would demonstrate, after coming from a long day working around blast furnaces. On the left, meanwhile, one of the men carries a metal pail. This may be nothing more than his meal tin, but this might also illustrate the ritual known as "rushing the growler," wherein workers would take a receptacle like this one to a local tavern, during lunchbreak or at the end of the day, and return with it full of beer.

Anshutz' portrayal of working-class life here also has its limits. Despite the setting, there is no dirt, highly unusual given their place of employment. Not a speck can be found, either on the walls, or even on the abundant bare flesh. Possibly as a symbol of such cleanliness amid the implied presence of grime, Procter & Gamble adopted this image for one of their advertisements (in all fairness, they added a tub to the right of Anshutz' original art, so there would be some direct reference to their product).[14]

Beyond that, this painting was a milestone. All of its figures demonstrate the athleticism that comes from healthy toil; their musculature represents a significant departure from the elite views of either a puny middle class or nonexistent workers—or the despondent victims of Jacob Riis' photographs. As Randall Griffin, the leading scholar studying Anshutz, cogently observed, the artist "created a new image of the American factory worker, one remarkably mundane and unmelodramatic." Anshutz saw his subjects neither as heroic gods of the forge nor as industrialized and in despair. Rather, he "focused on the men as individuals" and made "the factory worker seem strikingly human."[15]

The Ironworkers' Noontime remains Anshutz' most famous painting by a considerable margin; nothing comes even vaguely close to this standard. As recently as 1972, it was sold for $250,000. Yet, his importance rises over and beyond this work, by providing links to the next generation of painters to tackle this human subject matter in the new century. Starting in 1886, one of his students was Robert Henri, who referred to his teacher reverently, as "a great influence . . . a man of the finest quality, a great friend." John Sloan and his first wife, Dolly, were also close for a while, Dolly writing her husband, "I wish you would write to Tommy Anshutz," and the older man commented in a letter to John on "a good thing by Bellows" (George Wesley Bellows, one of the other Ashcan painters). The two eventually broke when Anshutz reprimanded Sloan, taking the former's drawing class, for drawing his classmates instead of the formal model on display. Sloan walked out, never to return.[16]

Compared to these giants, Joseph Pennell was not as well known, yet he still tackled the new subject matter. Born and raised in Philadelphia, he received his art training in that city, eventually sojourning to Europe and taking up residence in London, till, relatively late in life, he returned to the United States.

First and foremost an etcher and lithographer, Pennell is best remembered for his poster for the fourth Liberty Loan campaign in 1918, an archetype of that genre. It depicts an embattled New York Harbor, the city in flames as fighting planes cruise overhead, the Statue of Liberty still standing, albeit with her head and torch arm in shambles on the ground.

But earlier, Pennell had been fascinated by the new world that produced the war, the world of factories and cities. Art historian Marianne Doezema noted, "He, more than any other American graphic artist, may have demonstrated that the feats of the steel maker and the civil engineer were an appropriate subject for art." In books and articles, Pennell wrote about this new subject matter that so enthralled him. "Work today," he intoned, is the greatest thing in the world, and the artist who best records it will be best remembered." Comparing ancient and modern monuments, he believed that, "while in other days popes and princes built churches and palaces which are still the wonder of the world, to-day commerce and Industry are doing work equally impressive. . . . Our mills are as well worth painting as medieval churches."[17]

Even more than Eakins or Anshutz, Pennell did not hesitate to immerse himself in the new America, which made him an important predecessor of the Ashcan school. Thus, in *Edgar Thomson Steel Works, Bessemer*, Pennell depicts the darkness and the beauty of the industrial world, a scene that is dense with dirt that blossoms out of a forest of stacks (*fig. 5.6*). All the same. we can see the symmetry and power of a trestle mounting a gorge, of the might of railroads and factories in harmony.

Pennell also investigated the city. Producing the illustrations for John Van Dyke's 1909 volume, *The New New York*,[18] Pennell ventured into novel territory for artists. In *Across the Bowery Looking East*, the artist seems willing to go under the el train, literally (*fig. 5.7, pg. 88*). Although not as dynamic as the later works by Sloan, Pennell's illustration is beginning to pick up on the dynamism of the city and the strength of its architecture. Not including the pedestrians, we can see two different versions of motorized transport, with a trolley car passing over tracks running on a perpendicular axis, while another vehicle rolls by overhead, far above the ground; the downtown here exists in three dimensions. Multistory buildings stand in the near background, and in the distance a bridge tower dominates the scene.

Jewish Cemetery (Near Bowery) introduces other elements of the urban experience at that time (*fig. 5.8, pg. 89*). Here the metalwork acts as a framing device for a more humane scene,

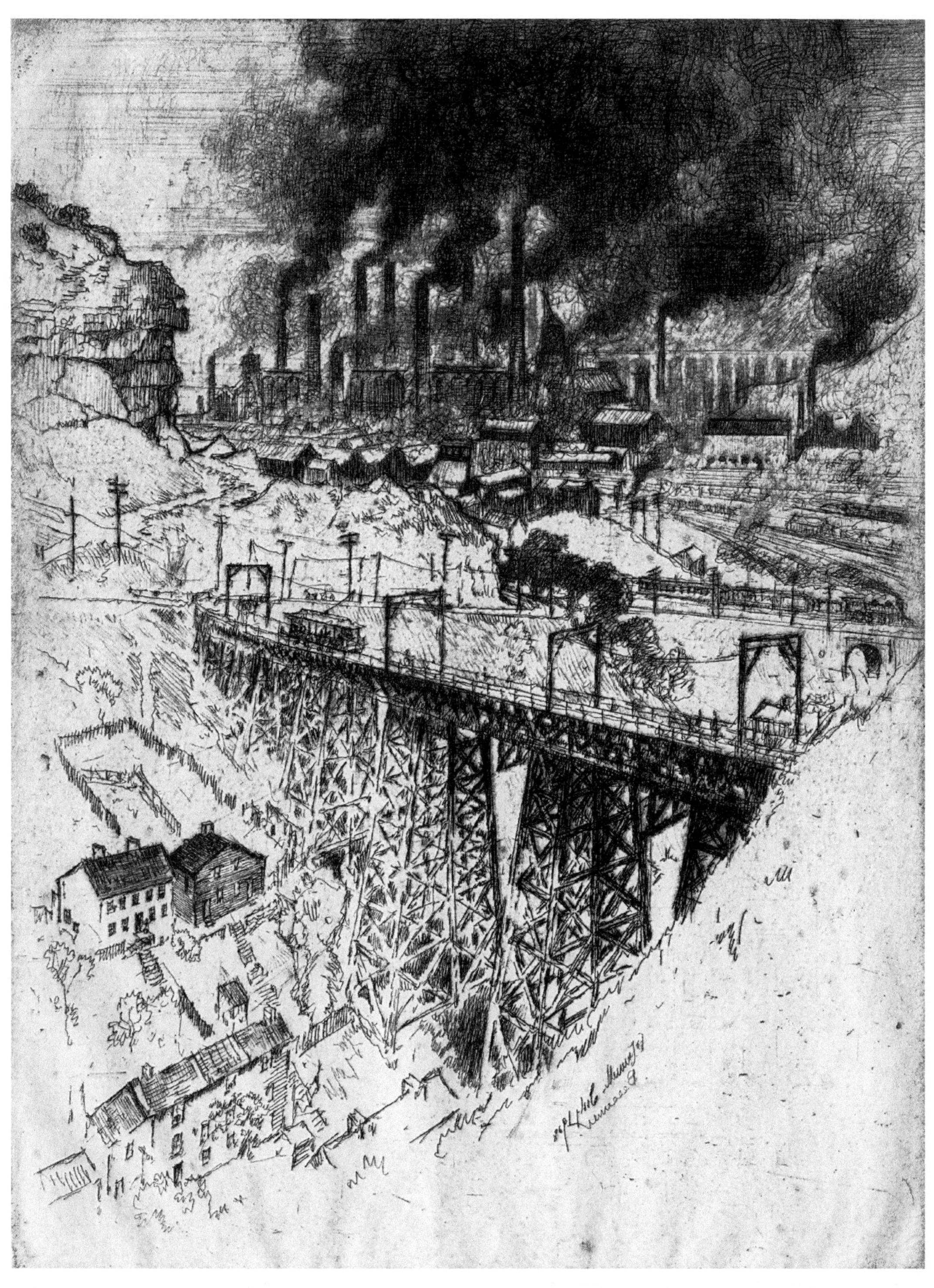

5.6 Joseph Pennell (1857–1926), *Edgar Thomson Steel Works, Bessemer*, 1908, etching, 28 × 20.3 cm. Cleveland Museum of Art, bequest of James Parmelee. 1940.781 © Cleveland Museum of Art.

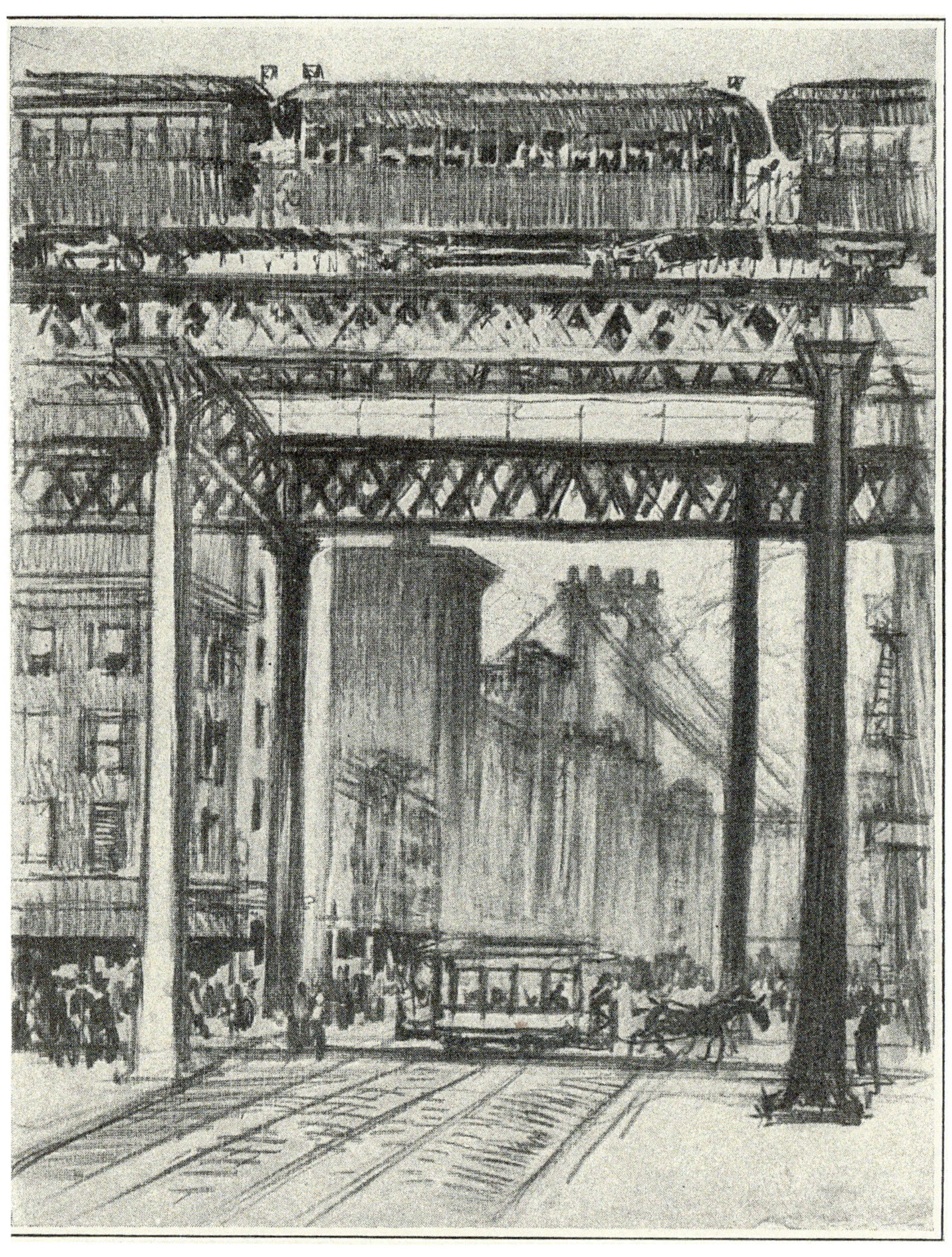

5.7 Joseph Pennell (1857–1926), *Across the Bowery Looking East*, in John Van Dyke, *The New New York* (New York: Macmillan Company, 1909), opposite page 248.

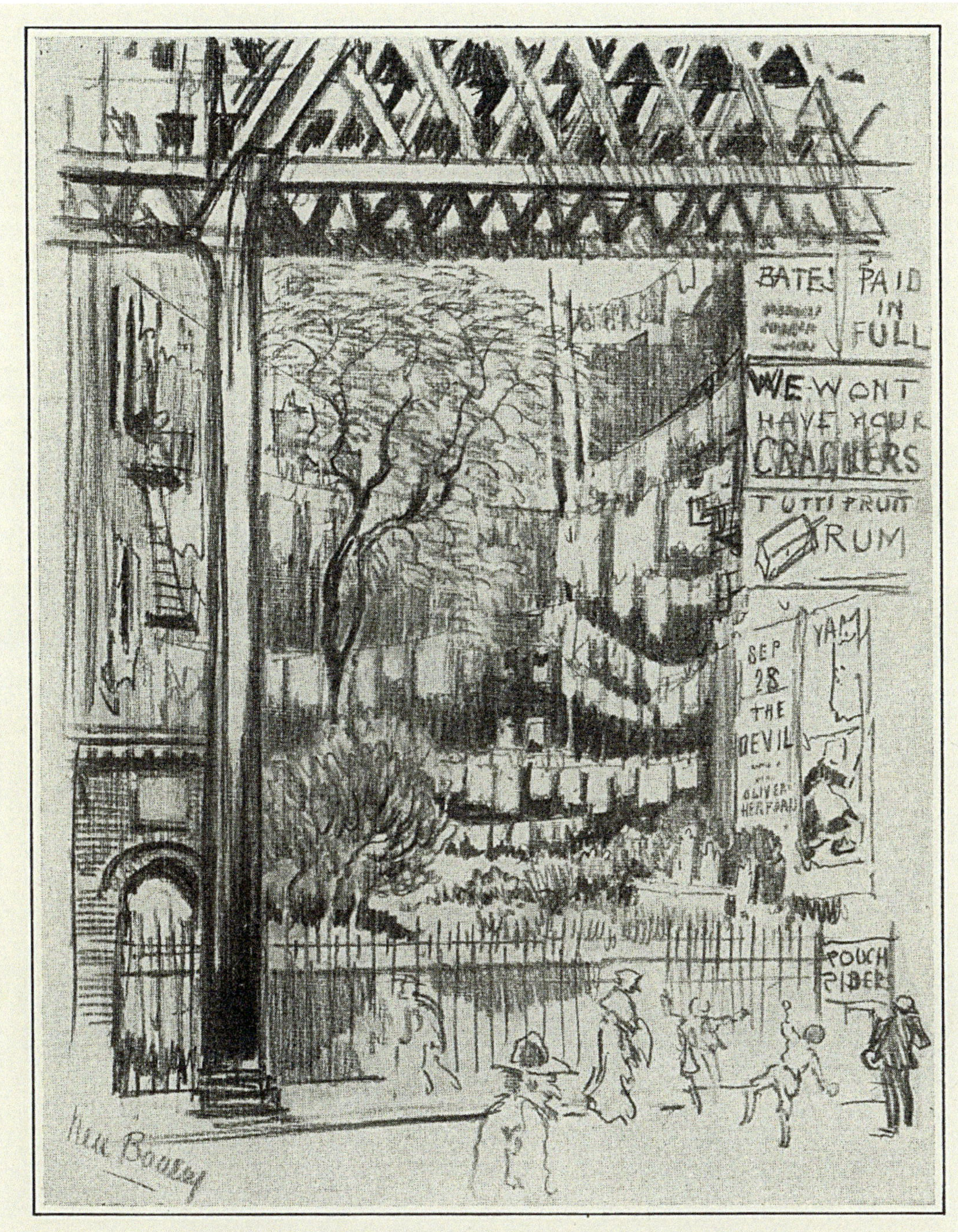

PL. 56. — JEWISH CEMETERY (NEAR BOWERY)

5.8 Joseph Pennell (1857–1926), *Jewish Cemetery (Near Bowery)*, in John Van Dyke, *The New New York* (New York: Macmillan Company, 1909), opposite page 250.

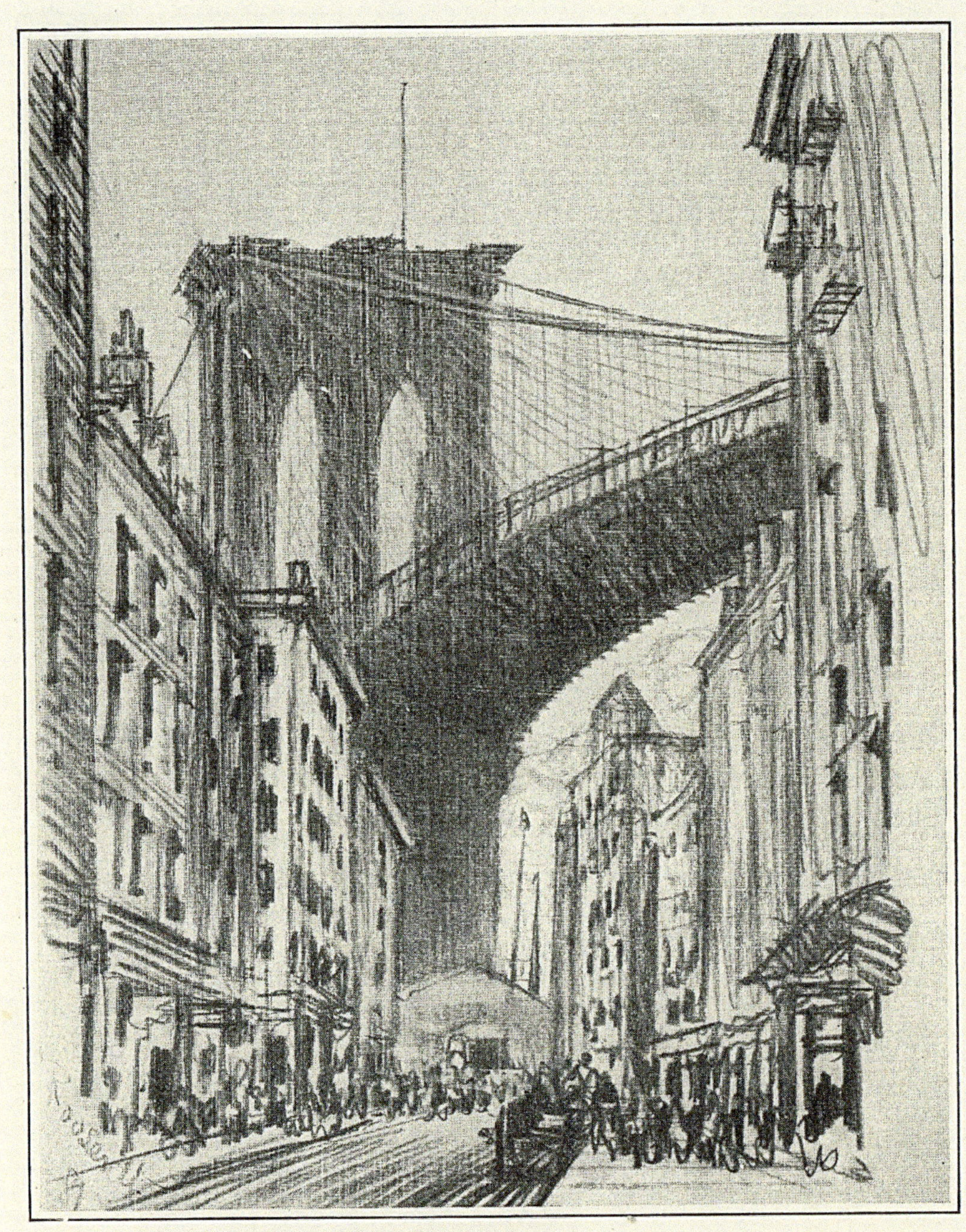

5.9 Joseph Pennell (1857–1926), *Tenements Near Brooklyn Bridge*, in John Van Dyke, *The New New York* (New York: Macmillan Company, 1909), opposite page 261.

providing horizontal and vertical borders. What makes this work unique is that the artist introduces that most vulnerable of residents in the new urban world, children. More similar to Lewis Hine's images than to Riis', the children play. Overhead there looms one of the all-important elements of the city, high levels of human density, depicted here by rows of clotheslines, balanced and juxtaposed against the natural devices of trees and bushes.

Finally, *Tenements Near Brooklyn Bridge*, Pennell's masterpiece in this genre (*fig. 5.9*). Here the analogy to ancient marvels is apparent. Just as the Colossus dominated Rhodes and the Greek universe, here the Great Bridge dwarfs everything around it. Juxtaposed against its transcendent height is the mundane, the far lower heights of the tenements. Pennell has captured both sides of the city, and the ways in which it soared through the imaginations of Americans at this time.

Decades before the Ashcan artists broke through walls of class, genre painting, and reformism, other artists—great artists—broached these subjects and began to paint real life in America, becoming predecessors to the urban school.

Moving On

After the Armory Show, the Ashcan artists all drifted away from urban art, and from its fountainhead, New York City. Everett Shinn wound up in Hollywood, Charles Glackens in France. John Sloan spent much of his time in Santa Fe, exploring different themes entirely. And George Wesley Bellows, the wunderkind who was their brightest and youngest star, never got to see much of the future. Instead, he died in 1925, at the height of the Jazz Age and before the Depression and New Deal, of complications from a ruptured appendix.[1]

In this reshaped art environment, others continued to explore the urban milieu. The most famous of these—in fact more so than any of the Ashcan artists—was Edward Hopper.

There were some links between the Ashcan artists and Hopper. To Hopper, New York was "the American city that I know best and like most," and it was the setting for many of his most iconic drawings. Hopper also recognized Robert Henri's contributions, to both art and to art teaching. He extolled Henri's "courage and energy," which had done so much to "shape the course of art in this country" and complimented his philosophy as, "art is life, an expression of life, an expression of the artist and an interpretation of life." He also described the maître's "enthusiasm and his power to energize students," noting how "few teachers of art have gotten as much out of their pupils, or given them so great an initial impetus."[2]

Aside from these touchpoints, however, Hopper composed a world entirely different from the one presented by the Ashcan artists. To the earlier generation of pioneers, the city was a home, a dynamic place well peopled, capable of endowing status and comfort. Hopper's city, on the other hand, was existential in its capacity for isolation.

The most important difference between the two approaches related to the role of the individual. To the Ashcan artists, its citizens were always part of a community, regardless of their class, ethnicity, age, or race. Streets were always filled, as were the rooftops, and even tenement rooms contained several occupants who would talk to one another, a quality that seemed to relieve the tight physical setting. As Frank Getelein put it in an article on Hopper, "A great deal of this ebullient journalism—more, perhaps than is generally realized—survived into their work, shaped it and gave it its distinctive immediacy. . . . Of all this there is nothing in the work of Edward Hopper."[3]

Hopper, instead, has become a hero because his works personifies so much of the modern condition, above all loneliness in a mass society. He depicts a harsher, much lonelier city than the Ashcan artists did, where there is little contact between people, where density produces isolation rather than intimacy or neighborliness.

Hopper's most iconic painting is *Nighthawks* (*fig. 6.1*). This work has become the personification of the modern city, and even modern life itself. There is no communication here, no contact between the few individuals left in the diner. While Hopper protested these judgments, he acknowledged, "Unconsciously, probably I was painting the loneliness of a large city," the very opposite of a work by Luks or Glackens. Though the corner in *Nighthawks* is probably real—Gail Levin has pinpointed it as Greenwich Avenue at Eleventh Street and Seventh Avenue—it is still an image of the mind's despair and carries no evidence of the life that was implicit in the Ashcan images.[4]

This contrast appeared even more indelibly in Hopper's other paintings. *Night Windows* seems to be right out of John Sloan's sketchbook, with its figure caught voyeuristically through a window. Yet, despite the late hour, she does not seem at repose, or poised to retire for the day.

Teresa Carbone's comments about this work were particularly telling: "Unlike many night-window subjects originated by New York's . . . Ashcan School painters that featured good-natured immigrants minding their neighborhoods or seeking some cool night air, Hopper's figure is a solitary (at least temporarily) and unabashed modern girl in a brief, silky slip." Carbone presents a more apt comparison: "She is a young woman similar to those populating Dorothy Parker's short stories—who rode buses or subways to work each day, suffered the advances of their bosses, and ate their meals in lunchrooms and diners." And usually ate them all alone.[5]

Even more extreme is *Sunday* (*fig. 6.3*, pg. 96). On the one hand, *Sunday* could register as an Ashcan-style illustration of a business street in the city. The mood, however, is entirely different. No one is shopping; *no one is even there*. If the hallmark of a city is human density, this image defies that principle. Rather than a picture of a community, this image presents a desert. As befits a castaway on a deserted island, the lone figure appears forlorn.

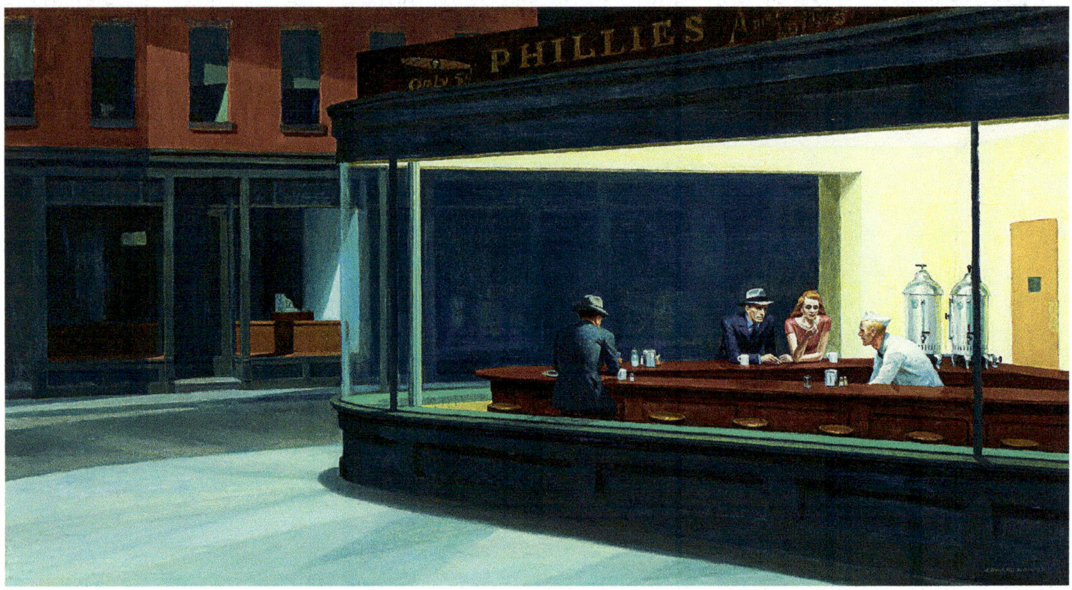

6.1 Edward Hopper (1882–1967), *Nighthawks*, 1942, oil on canvas, 30 × 60 inches. The Art Institute of Chicago.

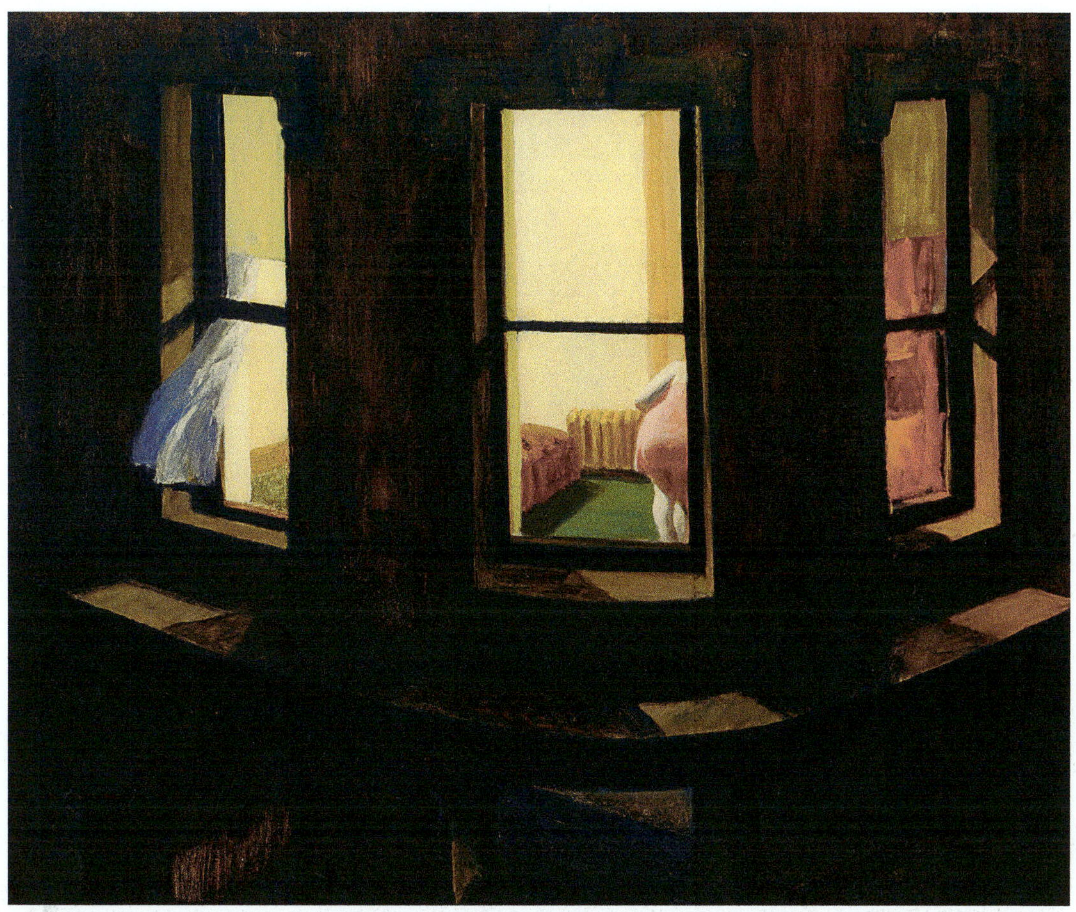

6.2 Edward Hopper (1882–1967), *Night Windows*, 1928, oil on canvas, 29 × 34 inches; 73.7 × 86.4 cm. Gift of John Hay Whitney. Museum of Modern Art. Digital image © The Museum of Modern Art/Licensed by SCALA/Art Resource, New York.

In his loneliness, more than any other characteristic, Hopper's work differs from the streetscapes of the Ashcan. Instead of a lively world, the isolation of his figures is almost painful. They are all alone, with no neighbors, priests, rabbis, or friends to keep them company within the monolith of the city. Suzanne Burrey, in an *Arts Digest* article about Hopper, caught the primary difference between him and his Ashcan school counterparts. Unlike in the drawings by Sloan, among others, the people in Hopper's paintings "express no spirit of optimism, joy or humor." This is not just loneliness; this is the depression that can result from being alone and isolated among the city's millions.[6]

Thus, there is an overwhelming sense of loss in Hopper's work, even when others are present. In contrast to Ashcan works, where people talk to each other (often vociferously, and in groups), sing and play music, while jackhammers and steam shovels clang, Hopper's paintings reveal what one writer described as "the element of silence that seems to pervade every one of his major works." Art historian Peter Conrad noted, "Though the people Sloan watches may be alone,

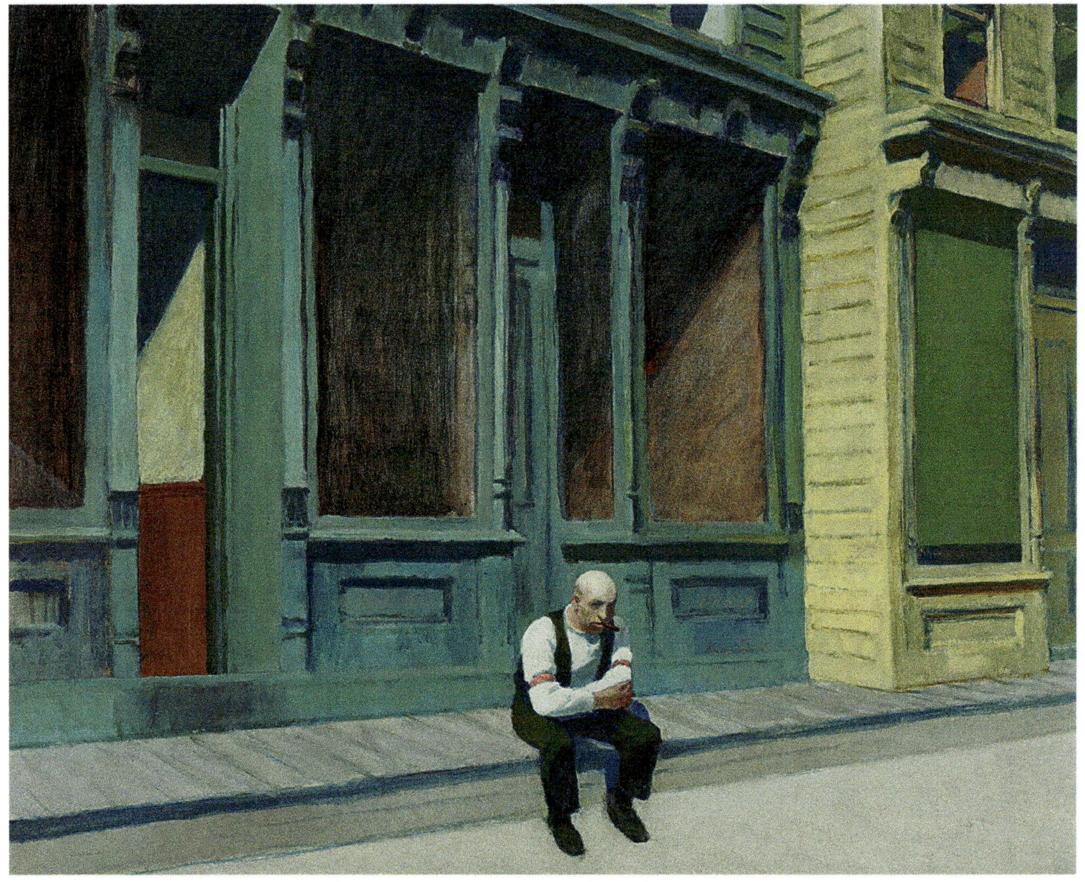

6.3 Edward Hopper (1882–1967), *Sunday*, 1926, oil on canvas, 29 × 34 inches; 73.66 × 86.36 cm. Acquired 1926. The Phillips Collection, Washington, DC.

they're never solitary." In Hopper's world, even when one rides the subway at rush hour, you are all alone.[7]

In this regard, while there are several figures in Hopper's *Room in New York* (*fig. 6.4*), it does not matter. Though they seem to share an apartment, they make no contact. Each might as well be Robinson Crusoe. As Conrad puts it, the figures "carry their solitude around with them and employ it as their protection." In Hopper's paintings, people are trapped; the city is a place of despair and menace, rather than community.[8]

In some of Hopper's works this sense of despair is carried to the extreme; in contrast to Ashcan paintings, humanity no longer even exists. Levin agreed that "Hopper's mature cityscapes were generally undisturbed by human presence. There is often an eerie feeling born of this desertion, this absence of activity."[9]

Skyline Near Washington Square (*fig. 6.5*, pg. 98) is such a scene. Washington Square is one of New York's liveliest spots, usually filled with chess players, roller skaters, mommies with trams, and lovers. Hopper's painting, instead, captures the square during its plague years, stark

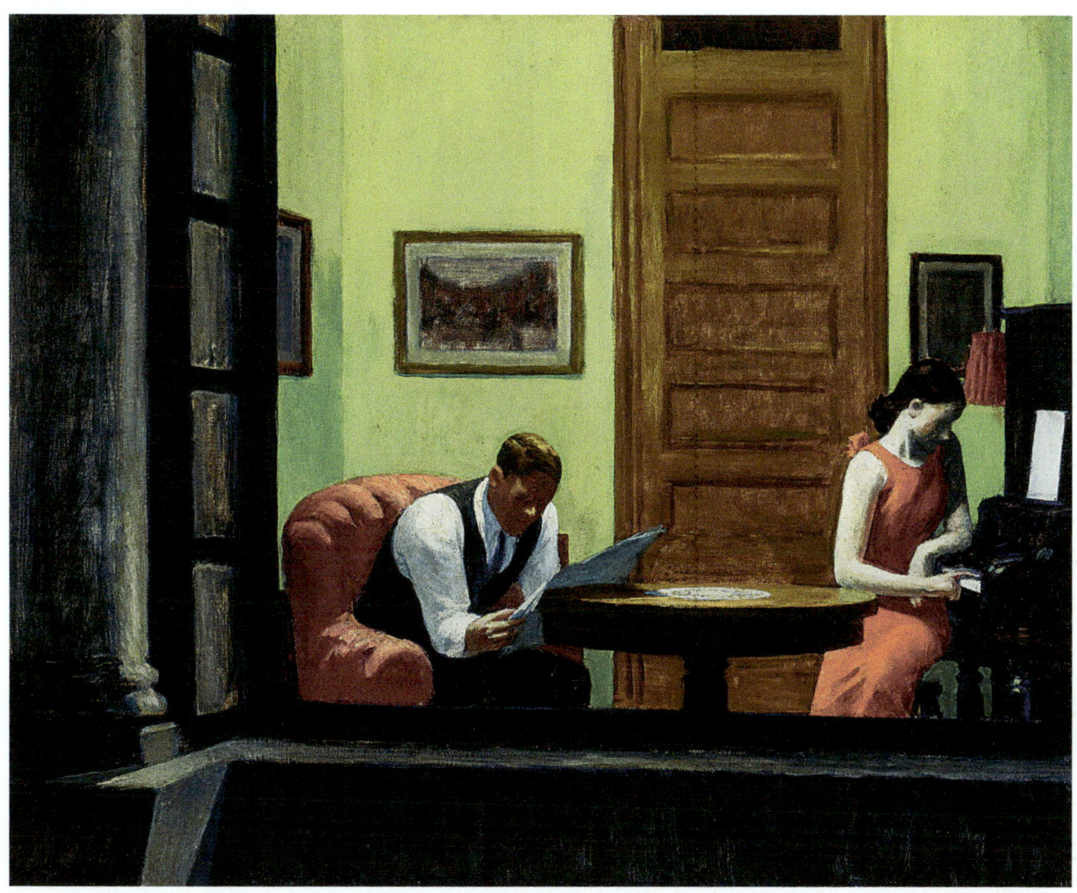

6.4 Edward Hopper (1882–1967), *Room in New York*, 1932, oil on canvas, 37 × 44½ × 4 inches. Sheldon Museum of Art, University of Nebraska-Lincoln. Frank M. Hall Charitable Trust, H-166.1936. © Sheldon Museum of Art.

sunlight illuminating sheer desolation. It is New York after the fall, a scene from total war that left no one standing. Conrad summed this up when he wrote, *"The motive of Hopper's abstraction is fear of and withdrawal from the city, a solemn refusal to represent it."*[10] This is the complete antithesis of the Ashcan School.

The true successor to Ashcan was the New York Social Realism movement of the 1930s. In the era of the Great Depression, it made sense that artists would explore the world around them and respond to it. By 1934 the city's unemployment rate had climbed to a third of its population, and 1.6 million residents required public assistance. Much of the art produced in response was political in nature: Lloyd Goodrich wrote how, at that time, "art without social content was mere formalism and decoration," so instead artists sought social change along class lines. Unlike Sloan and the other Ashcan artists, these painters looked to depict far more than humanity in the city; rather, they had a message to project social change. All the same, this spirit prompted renewed interest in the depiction of middle- and working-class lives. Reginald Marsh, one of

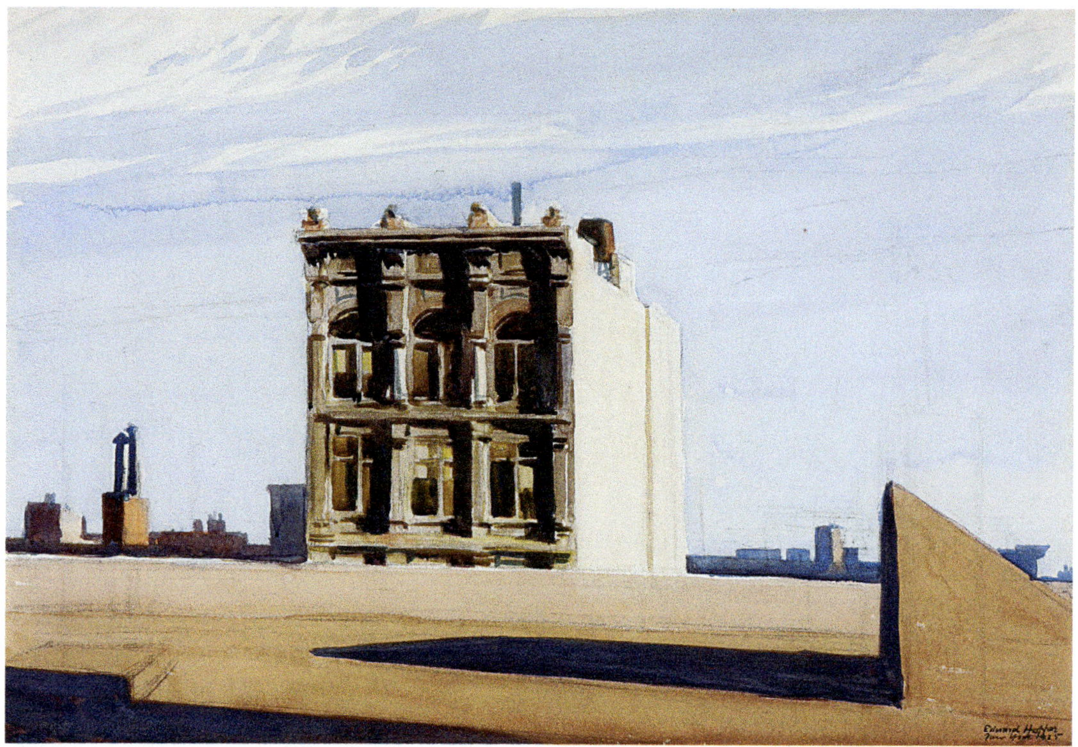

6.5 Edward Hopper (1882–1967), *Skyline Near Washington Square*, 1925, Transparent watercolor over graphite on wove paper, 15¹⁵⁄₁₆ × 21⁹⁄₁₆ inches (overall). Edward W. Root Bequest. 57.161. Munson-Williams-Proctor Institute. Photo credit: Munson-Williams-Proctor Institute/Art Resource, New York.

the leading painters of this renewed interest, remarked how "there is a world of real people, both male and female—flesh, blood, elbows, facial expressions, unbroken necks—a world that has more in it than . . . hors d'oeuvres, cockeyed tables, splintery napkins."[11]

There were several prime influences at work here. The master teacher was Kenneth Hayes Miller, who filled a role similar to the one that Robert Henri had assumed for the Ashcan artists. While Miller was born in upstate Oneida, New York, his parents had moved to the city when he was only four. After studying art and traveling to Europe, he began a stint as an instructor at the Art Students League in 1911, where he would stay for forty years, and step down in another era altogether, in 1951. From that lectern, he mentored generations of students and impressed on them the importance of working-class life. His studio was on East Fourteenth Street near Union Square, and he appreciated the city views from his windows, instructing students about the beauty he saw there. Decades later, a *New York Times* art reviewer referred to him as "a kind of unpolitical social realist."[12]

Other than Miller, there were two important patrons who supported this new approach with more resources than the Eight had ever dreamed of. Lloyd Goodrich was a prime mover here. Although he had studied under Kenneth Hayes Miller, as the Depression erupted he entered the circle around Gertrude Vanderbilt Whitney. The timing was right, since the society leader was just becoming interested in starting a museum dedicated to American art, as opposed to the European concentration at the Met; in later decades, this would become the Whitney Museum of American Art. Goodrich joined this effort early on as writer in residence and in 1935 became Research Curator for her collection. At a symposium on the aesthetics of painting in 1933, Goodrich delivered the keynote address, speaking on behalf of the American realist tradition and against abstract works not anchored in real human experience. Following this lead, Whitney began to invest in New York realist artists.[13]

The other major influence, which enabled the realism movement to expand to greater dimensions than it ever had, or ever would again, was the New Deal's response to economic calamity. In an unprecedented move, part of this was a move to hire artists, under the Works Progress Administration's (WPA) Public Works of Art Project (PWAP). On the grounds that artists were also American workers in need of help, from 1934 to 1942 the PWAP provided a monthly check of fifty-three dollars to ten thousand artists, who produced one hundred thousand easel paintings, eighteen thousand sculptures, thirteen thousand prints, and four thousand murals, figures that do not include works for post offices and courthouses. Even more astonishing was the recognition from the highest echelons of government. The White House hung thirty-two of these paintings on its hallowed walls, another 130 went to the Department of Labor building. While the latter location seemed fitting for working-class art, the House of Representatives displayed another 451. Harold Ickes, the activist secretary of the interior, argued that under this administration, "there exists the greatest official interest in art, the greatest production of paintings the U.S. has ever known." Franklin Roosevelt himself remarked with pride, "One hundred years from now, my administration will be known for its art, not for its relief."[14]

Several paintings demonstrated the link between this art of the thirties and that of the Ashcan artists, all taken from the PWAP archives. Charles L. Goeller's *Third Avenue* (fig. 6.6, pg. 100), in its intimate depiction of street life, mirrors the earlier images if the city but lacks a sense of hustle and bustle.

Lily Furedi made up for this with lack of crowds and energy with her 1934 painting, *Subway* (fig. 6.7, pg. 101). The painting demonstrates several key elements of the urban experience. Drawn at eye level, it indicates the density of urban life, though not truly recreating the crush of rush hour, since individual images would be impossible in such a setting. There is also a cross-class, interracial dimension, regular features of life in the city. In the foreground men wear hats, the emblem of middle-class males, while the news dealer behind them sports a working-class cap. Meanwhile, an African American New Yorker sits on the left. Unlike automobile-centric cities, where commuters are isolated in their vehicles, everyone here rides the subway together. Yet, in another observation of typical New York behavior, no one looks at anyone else, unless they are already friends like the two ladies on the right. Instead, they bury themselves in a myriad of distractions, from magazines to newspapers to makeup.

The foremost artists of this new urban realism were Reginald Marsh and Raphael Soyer, part of what became known as the Fourteenth Street school, after they followed Miller to that quintessential New York address, filled with merchants of every class and description, near to the parades and soap box speakers of Union Square.

Marsh came to his talent genetically, the offspring of two artists. After Yale University, in 1920 he wound up in New York, as was—and remains—typical for artists. While working as a freelance illustrator for magazines like *Vanity Fair* and *Harper's Bazaar*, he enrolled in classes at the Art Students League in 1922 under Kenneth Hayes Miller and began to draw the city around him. Although by the 1930s many of his paintings depicted the effects of the Depression or the horrors of alcoholic life on the Bowery, he also, in the words of one art historian, drew "energetic works of the working class that celebrated . . . the excitement of the city, much in the vein of the Ashcan painters."[15]

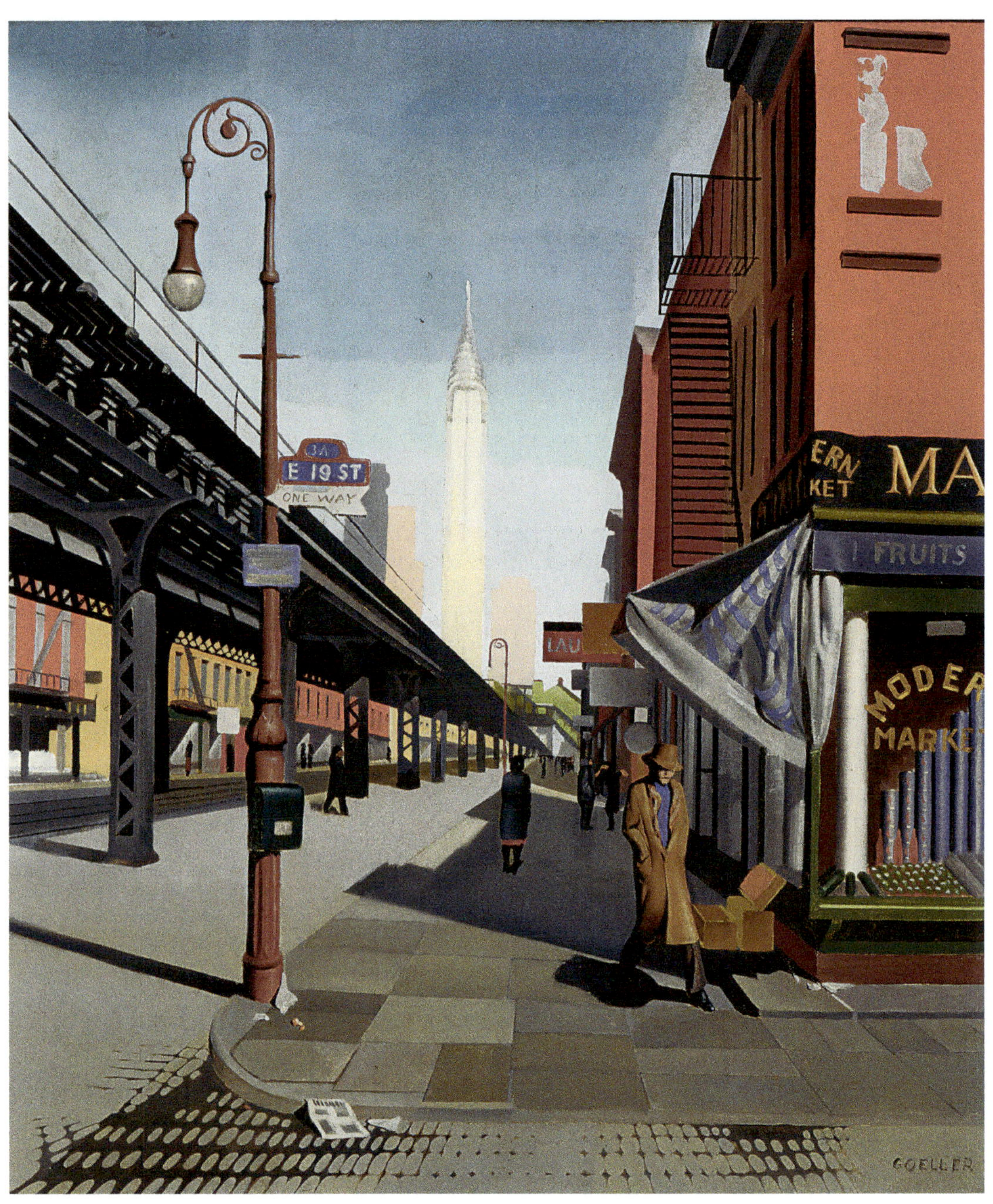

6.6 Charles Goeller (1901–1955), *Third Avenue*, 1933–1934, oil on canvas, 36 × 30⅛ inches; 91.4 × 76.4 cm. Smithsonian American Art Museum. Photo credit: Smithsonian American Art Museum, Washington, DC/Art Resource, New York.

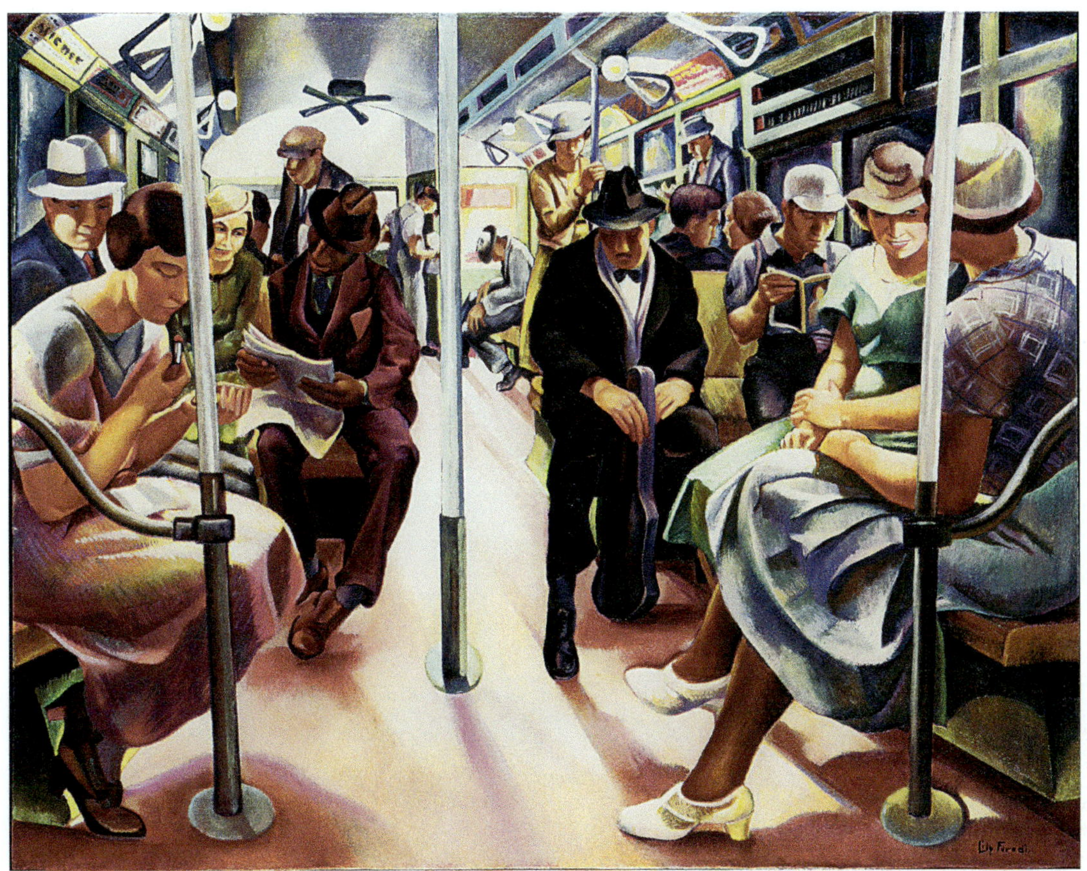

6.7 Lily Furedi (1896–1969), *Subway*, 1934, oil on canvas, 39 × 48¼ inches; 99.1 × 122.6 cm. Transfer from the US Department of the Interior, National Park Service, 1965.18.43. Smithsonian American Art Museum. Photo credit: Smithsonian American Art Museum, Washington, DC/Art Resource, New York.

In Marsh's 1936 work, *Twenty Cent Movie*, he captures the raucous, garish excitement of the city (*fig. 6.8*, pg. 102). There is more entertainment available in this one spot than in most small towns. Overhead are visual displays of three features. Billboards trumpet a wonderworld of acts. At the near right the African American appears to be a performer, while across the entranceway a hustler lounges, prepared to lure passersby to who-knows-what forms of entertainment.

The other artist to reach Marsh's level of renown was Raphael Soyer. Born in Tambov, South Russia, his father was an author and teacher of Hebrew literature and history, and the family emigrated in 1912. Soyer attended classes at Cooper Union and at the Art Students League, where he became friends with Reginald Marsh, and was taught by, among others, Guy Pène du Bois—a Robert Henri student—and even by John Sloan. In 1941 he wrote to Helen Sloan, the senior artist's wife, expressing happiness that John had finished a period of severe illness, only to share his regret that younger artists had forgotten "how much he has influenced our work."[16]

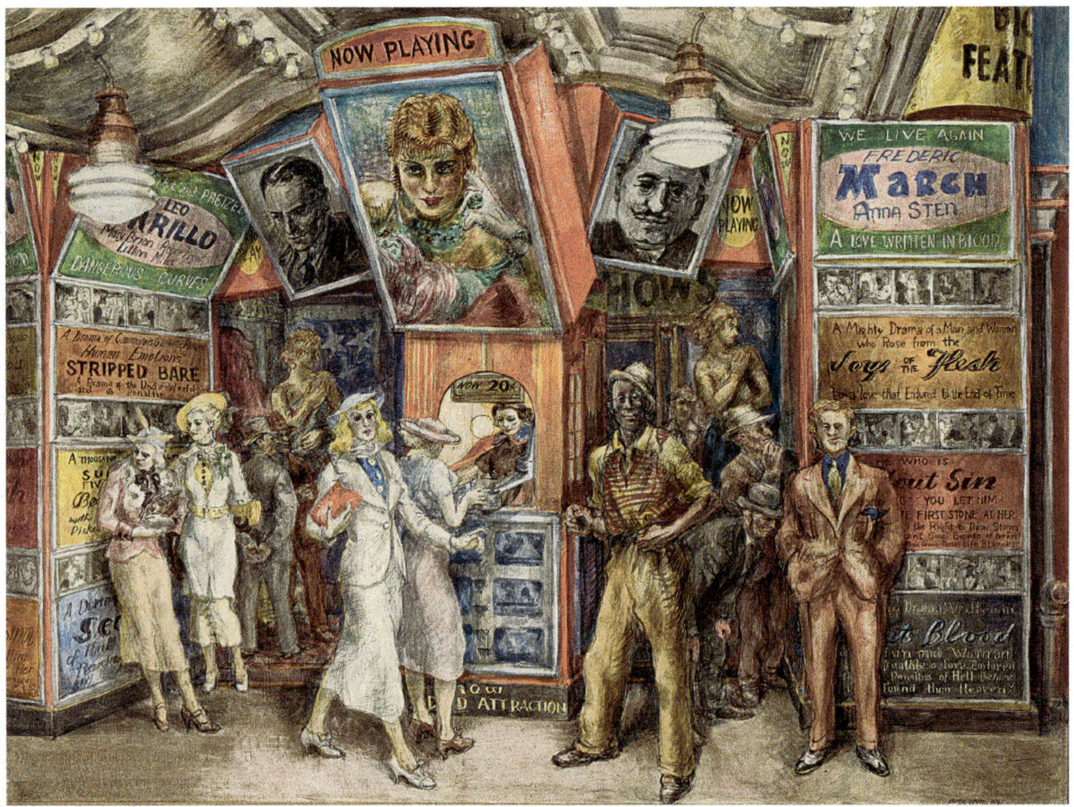

6.8 Reginald Marsh (1898–1954), *Twenty Cent Movie*, 1936, carbon pencil, ink, and oil on composition board, 30 × 40 inches; 76.2 × 101.6 cm. Whitney Museum of American Art, New York; Purchase 37.43a-b. © 2016 Estate of Reginald Marsh/Art Students League, New York/Artists Rights Society (ARS), New York. Digital image © Whitney Museum of American Art/Licensed by Artists Rights Society.

Even more than his predecessors, Soyer was a gothamite; in 1972 he told an interviewer, "I painted only what I saw in my neighborhood in New York City, which I call my country rather than my city." Art historian Matthew Baigell observed that Soyer, "impressed by the great variety of ethnic, religious and economic groups living in relative harmony, . . . found New York to be a microcosm of the entire nation." Soyer remarked, "I always painted only what I knew and saw around me."[17]

Soyer's most famous painting, his 1936 work, *Office Girls*, best expresses this philosophy and geography, depicting the crush of the city (*fig. 6.9*). The image is filled with faces of all kinds, just like a downtown street at rush hour, with buildings hemming everyone in. The blonde on the left, by the way, is Erika, one of Soyer's favorite models.

Along with the end of the Depression, the founding era of urban realistic art reached its conclusion by 1940. In the postwar era modernism trumped all, and realism became hopelessly outdated. No longer was anyone interested in this approach to visual imagery. Before we spend too much time at realistic art's funeral, let us explore the themes the Ashcan school artists pursued in their images.

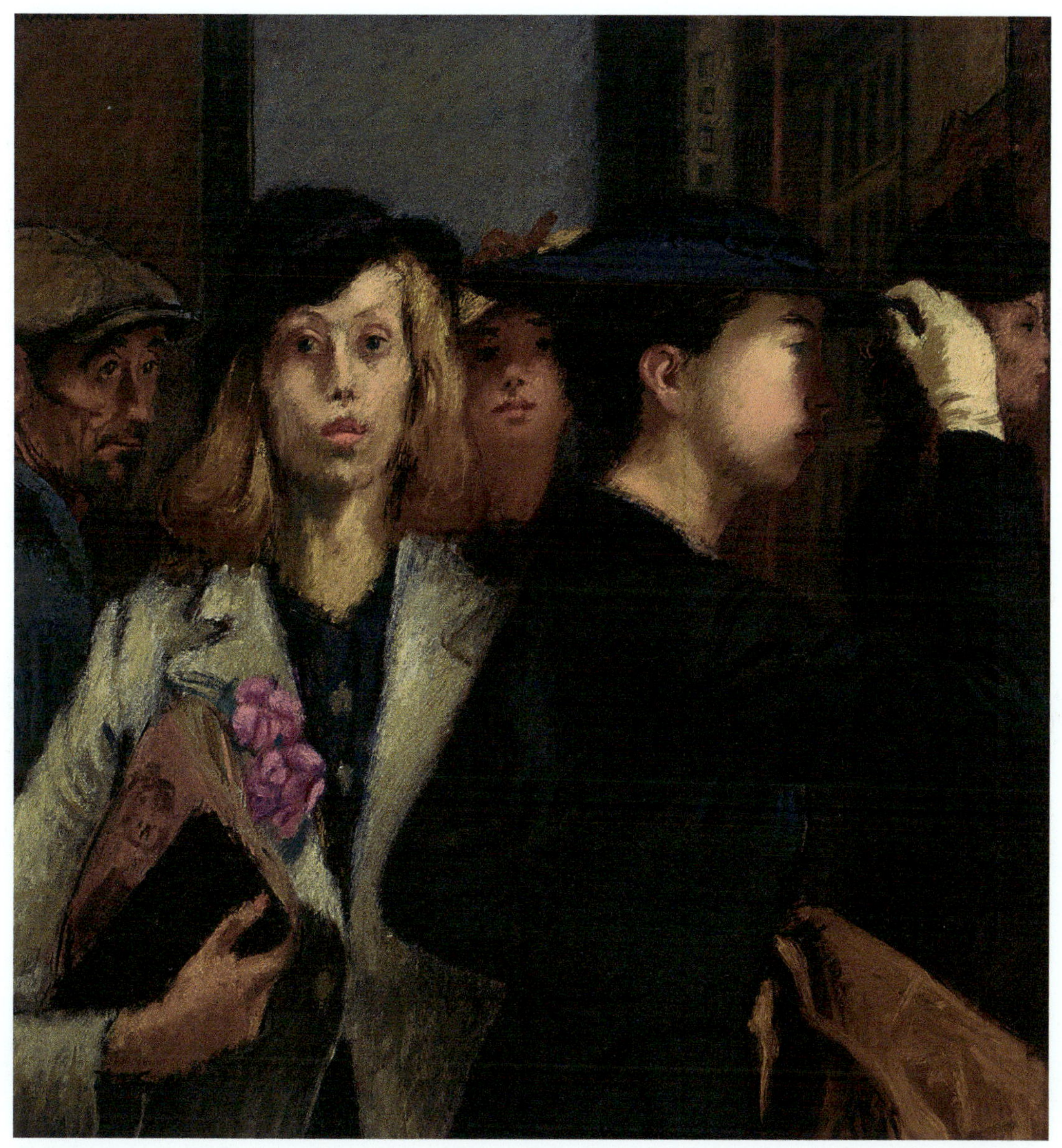

6.9 Raphael Soyer (1899–1987), *Office Girls*, 1936, oil on canvas, 26⅛ × 24⅛ inches; 66.4 × 61.3 cm. Whitney Museum of American Art, New York; Purchase 36.149. Digital image © Whitney Museum of American Art.

CHAPTER SEVEN

THE CITY AS ART

THE ASHCAN ARTISTS REDISCOVERED NEW YORK IN ITS MOST DAZZLING MOMENT; AT THE TURN of the century, New York collected accolades like a young boy hoarding baseball cards. If the city was the throbbing downtown of turn-of-the-century America, its paragon was New York, the focus of the Ashcan painters. To writers like John Reed, "New York was an enchanted city. . . . Everything was to be found there—it satisfied me utterly." When Henry Adams returned there in 1904, "as he came up the bay, he found the approach more striking than ever—wonderful—unlike anything man had ever seen. . . . All New York was demanding a new man." Theodore Dreiser spoke of "the beauty of it. Such seething masses of people! Such whirlpools of life!" Modern-day academics described it as "the quintessential modern city," as "the shock city of its age."[1]

It was not just the elites, or even the middle class, who recognized this vibrancy and were attracted to it. Theodore Dreiser captured in words what the Ashcan artists instinctively understood, that the city—for all its grit—could be exciting, and that the working-class life within it could spawn beautiful art. The author of *Sister Carrie* "once knew" an impoverished, "and very much shriveled little seamstress who occupied a tiny hall-bedroom in a side-street rooming house." Her accommodations were anything but grand; she "cooked her meals on a small alcohol stove set on a bureau, and who had about space enough outside of this to take three good steps either way." In spite of all this, she remarked, "I would rather live in my hall-bedroom than in any fifteen-room house in the country that I ever saw." After this comment, Dreiser observed that "her poor little colorless eyes held more of sparkle and snap in them than I ever saw there, before or after." E. B. White wrote that New York made up for its shortcomings and dangers "by supplying its citizens with massive doses of a supplementary vitamin—the sense of belonging to something unique, cosmopolitan, mighty and unparalleled."[2]

This excitement made metropolis the quintessential American experience of the time. While Herbert Croly, founder of *The New Republic*, called New York "the most national . . . of American cities," William Dean Howells, in his novel *A Hazard of New Fortunes*, had one of his characters declare, "There's only one city that belongs to the whole country, and that's New York." Modern-day historian Angela Blake argued that, at turn of the century, "the image of New York City was the image of America itself."[3] It made sense that this setting would spawn a great American art form.

Thus, one of the two core elements of the Ashcan approach was that these painters saw the city as a place quintessentially American, of beauty, of excitement. They did not limit their vision to the tony sections, a resort for downtown swells. Nor did they see it as a dark creature filled with refuse and poverty, to be analyzed and saved. Rather, they rolled in its power and its movement and its tension, like cats in a meadow, perceiving and then portraying its earthy industrialism and its working class as no other cluster of painters had done before.

More than any other author, even better than Robert Henri in his writings about art, John Sloan captured this feeling in the pages of his diary. On a day that he and his wife "came home by the new 'tube' under the Hudson, quite a novel sensation," he could also revel in "a raw blustery day with a shower now and then, but with a beautiful sky, huge cloud masses," a cluster of rich urban experiences. On other occasions, he would marvel at "the distant city moist blue, jets of steam like white sprites and witches," or how "passing showers made the city beautiful today." Not just the landscapes but his neighbors attracted him: "The women were all out in their beautiful warm weather clothes. The streets seemed pulsing with human life and warm blood and a feeling of animal love, honest animal affection." In 1922 a writer caught how "Sloan is predominantly interested in human beings—he gets them on the run caught in the very act of their most human daily occupations."[4]

The city's beauty took many forms, appeared in many guises. Neighborhood scenes enthralled the Ashcan painters, as they wandered into sections of all classes and ethnicities. Thus, the best place to begin an understanding of the Ashcan approach is with George Bellow's masterpiece, *New York* (fig. 7.1).

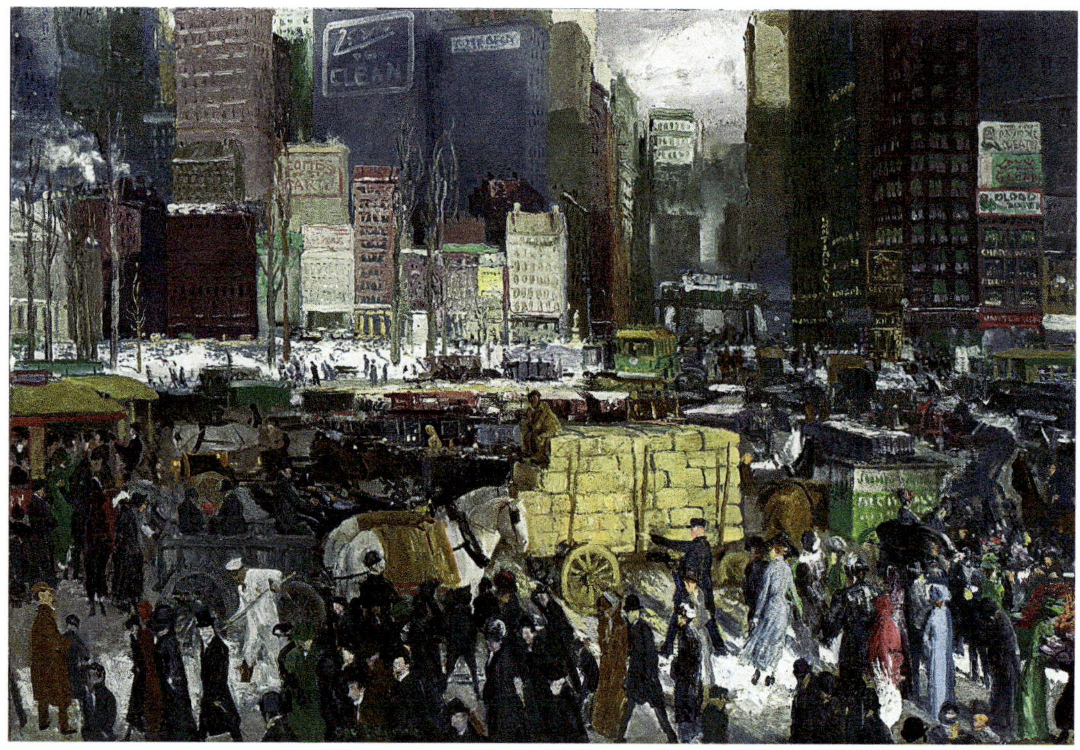

7.1 George Wesley Bellows (1882–1925), *New York*, 1911, oil on canvas. National Gallery of Art. Washington, DC, USA/Bridgeman Images.

This is the city in all its glory, filled with buildings, filled with people, filled with horses and carts . . . just filled. All the elements are here: dense masses of commuters scuffling by, a policeman valiantly trying to direct traffic, just slightly more successful in his efforts than the street sweeper in lower left. Despite the lack of any visible ground space, movement improbably seems to be everywhere, from the pedestrians at the bottom to the elevated on the top of the image. Framing everything are the towers, like a visit from the gods of old, come to take stock of what their charges have wrought. The grim, bustling city has become not just a scene for a beautiful painting, but epic.

This metropolis was made up of its neighborhoods, and the painters wandered through them, regardless of class. Moe Foner, one of the founders of Local 1199 (drug and hospital workers), one of this country's great unions, recalled the world he grew up in: "Williamsburg was a small town in a big city back then. It was a tightly knit community where people knew their neighbors. Some of the boys we grew up with became famous athletes or gangsters or surgeons or millionaire businessmen, but when we were little we all roasted potatoes in the street together."[5]

Jerome Myers, though best known as a painter of immigrant districts, took time and care to capture an urban middle-class setting, recognizing its charm. In *Sunday Morning* the scene is clearly that of a city neighborhood (*fig. 7.2*). Its density is on display in a myriad of ways,

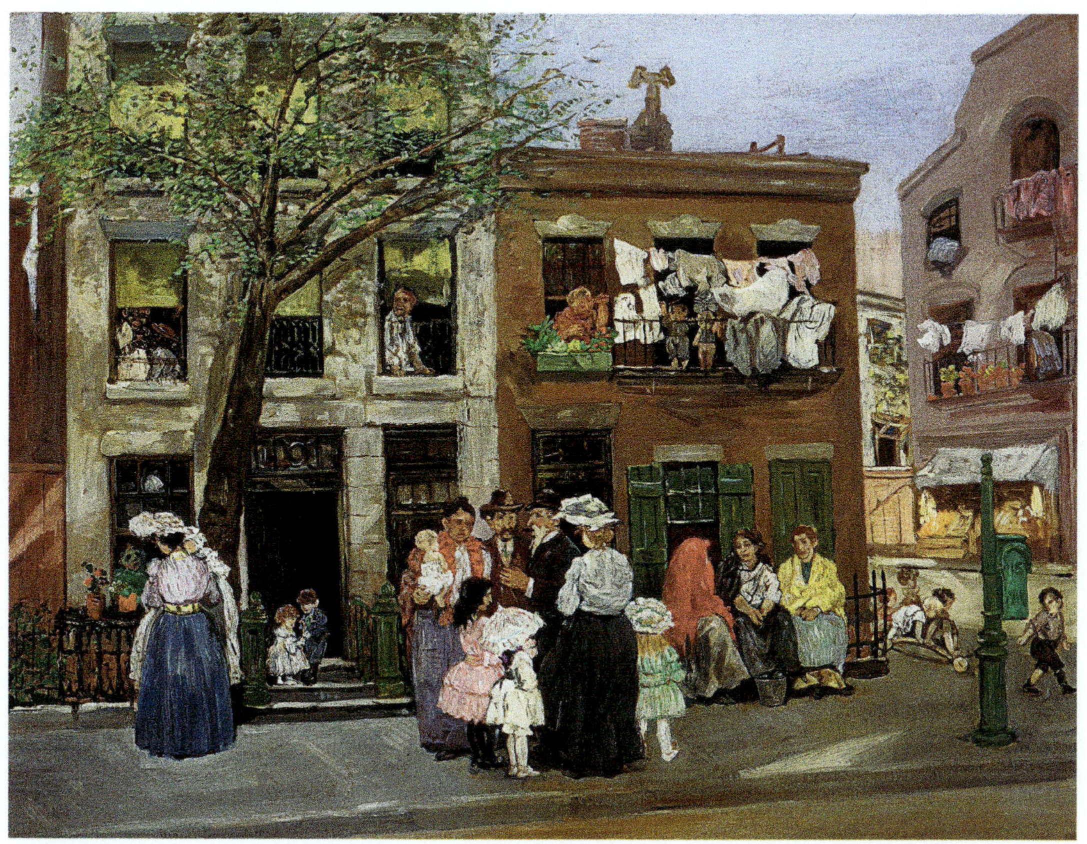

7.2 Jerome Myers (1867–1940), *Sunday Morning*, 1907, oil on canvas, 37½ × 44½ inches; 95.25 × 113.03 cm. Marion Stratton Gould Fund, 98.74. Collection of the Memorial Art Gallery, University of Rochester, Rochester, New York.

from the clotheslines to the window gazers to the children sitting on stoops; there are a lot of people in this picture. Judging from the clothing, however, this is a mixed group. While some of the men look like respectable workers, a number of the ladies on the sidewalk are clearly a step above that, with their fashionable hats, their children well attired.

As the University of Rochester's website explains, there is "no grubby, grinding scene of urban poverty here . . . but rather impeccable streets, spotless, colorful clothes, an infusing spirit of communal contentment." Myers later wrote, "I went to the gutter for my subject . . . but they were poetic gutters."[6]

Myers' contemporaries frequently drifted to poorer settings, yet still treated them with respect. George Luks, in *Allen Street*, captures the color of an outdoor market on the Lower East Side (*fig. 7.3*). Class is depicted by the modest garb of the shoppers and how goods are stacked and hung outside, not displayed in showcase windows. Yet the pigments he uses are bright ones; there is no sense of grime here. Rather, this is a bazaar—hardly a grand one, yet still a place of legitimate commerce, painted with interest, no hint of any condescension. These are urban consumers, nothing more nor less and hence worthy of the artist's brushes.

A more boisterous image appears in William Glackens' *Far from the Fresh Air Farm* (*fig. 7.4*). Though the title is sarcastic, the image is playful. Beyond crowded, this street vibrates with humanity, hums with it. Every store front features another attraction, something else to catch

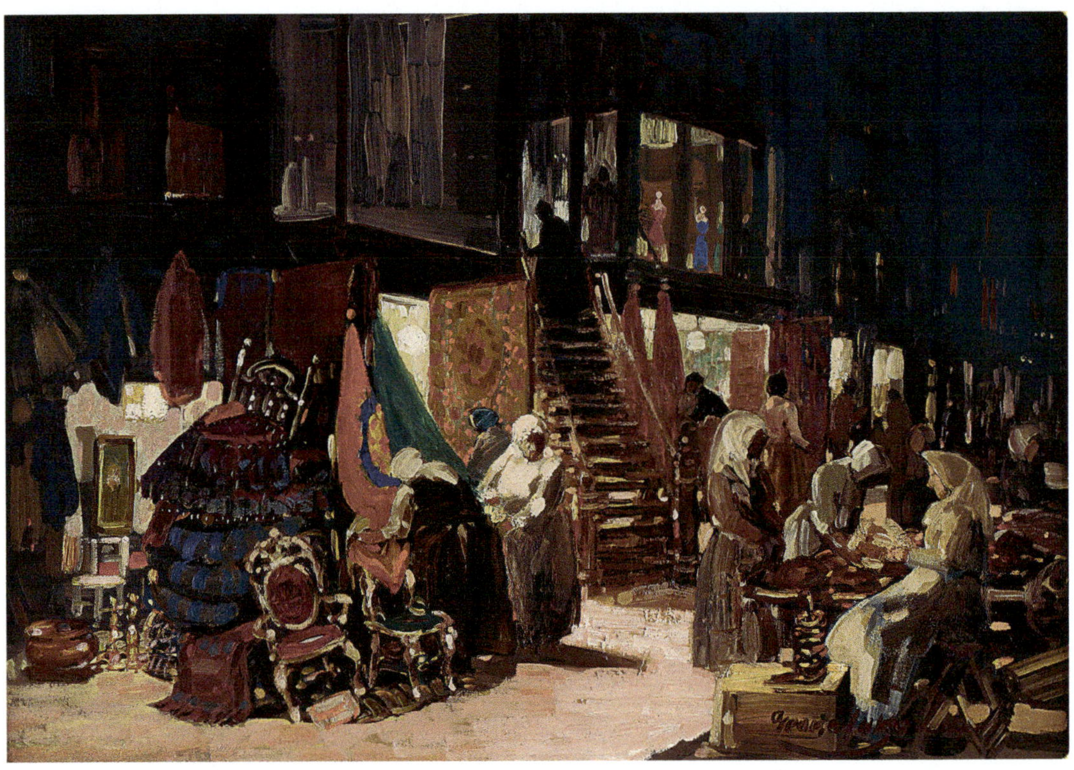

7.3 George Luks (1867–1933), *Allen Street*, 1905, oil on canvas, 32 × 45 inches; 81.3 × 114.3 cm. Hunter Museum of American Art, Chattanooga, Tennessee. Gift of Inez Hyder, 1956.1.

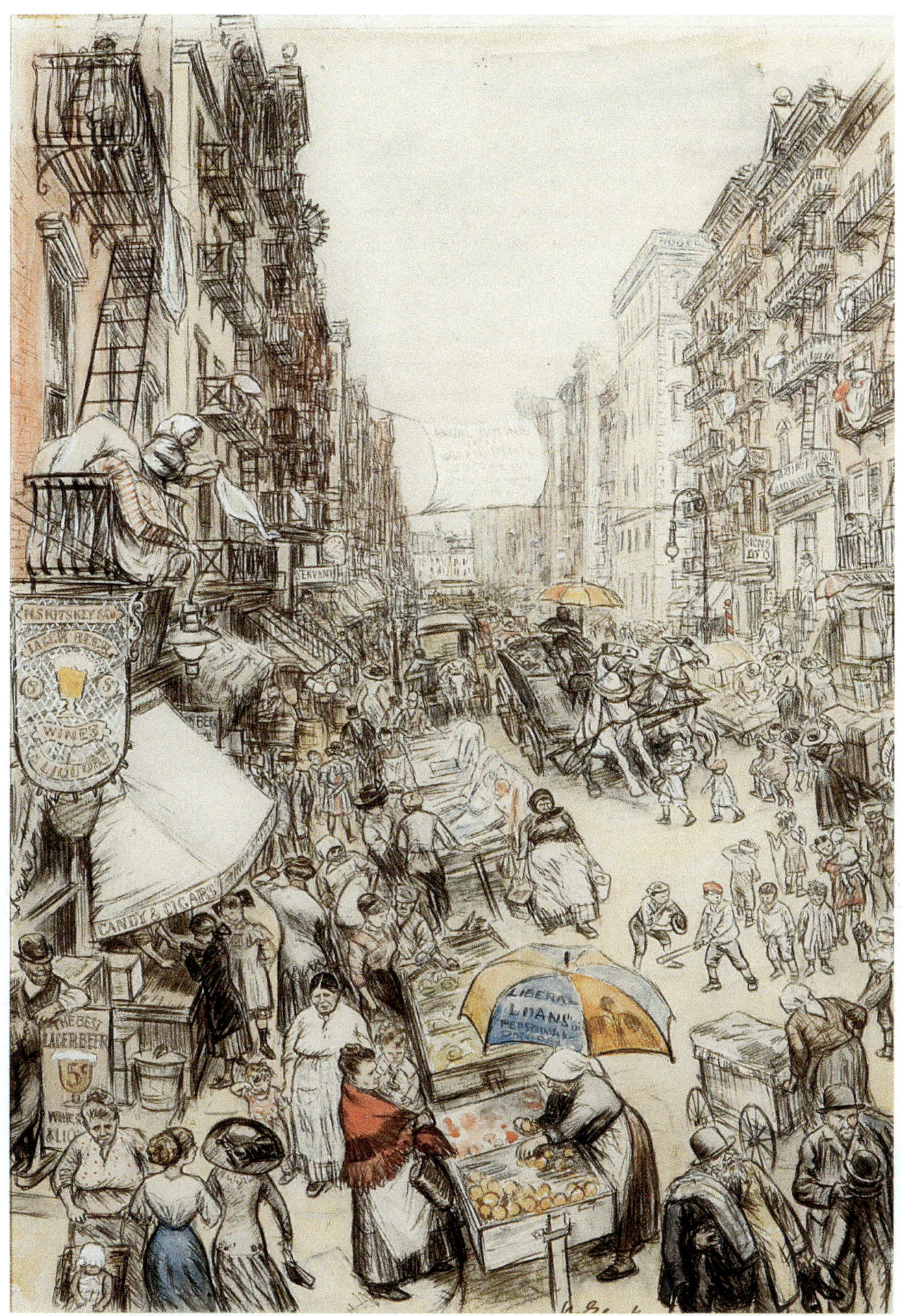

7.4 William Glackens (1870–1938), *Far from the Fresh Air Farm: The crowded city street, with its dangers and temptations, is a pitiful makeshift playground for children*, 1911, crayon highlighted with watercolor on paper, 63 × 43 cm; 25 × 17 inches. NSU Art Museum Fort Lauderdale, Florida. Bequest of Ira D. Glackens, 1991.40.152.

the viewer's eye. Commerce is abundant and varied, from the beer vendor on the left, across to the pushcarts, then up to the galloping delivery truck. High finance is here, too, in the logo on the awning shading the fruit vendor in the foreground. All framed by the tenements surrounding them. There can be joy in the city, and not just on Fifth Avenue.

Several features highlight this picture. First, it is crowded, capturing the high density that is the hallmark of urban life. Judging by both the clothes and the merchandise, it is also clearly an image of a working-class cynosure. Above all, these folks are neither enthralled with their chores nor are they dismayed by them. Rather, these are average men and women, going about life's chores. Yet this reality—neither glamorous nor grim—is transformed into an artwork of lasting quality by an Ashcan artist. John Sloan wrote in his diary, "I walked over 35th Street to a Playground Park near the East River. A long row of tenements . . . which was all gray and melancholy blue. A few children clambering about on the ladder, horizontal bars, etc. Mothers outside . . . pushing 'go carts' with babies. . . . Everything seemed fine this evening."[7] These painters capture life in all its complexity.

Finally, all ages participate; a shopping district is not just for adults. In *A Tree Grows in Brooklyn*, author Betty Smith remarked, "The neighborhood stores are an important part of a city child's life. They are his contact with the supplies that keep life going; they hold the beauty that his soul longs for; they hold the unattainable that he can only dream and wish for."[8]

The liveliness of Glackens' drawing, and Sloan's observations, points to the favorite subject of the Ashcan artists, the people who lived in these neighborhoods. One of the foremost critics of the era, Sadakichi Hartmann, wrote of Luks' work: "He sees life and paints it. It is not a life without vulgarity . . . but it is the vulgarity of ordinary mankind. . . . Sane and healthy and beautiful for all those who can see beauty in what is generally classified as ugliness."[9]

Sloan chronicles an even younger population in *Bonfire* (fig. 7.5). Set amid the tenements of Greenwich Village, these youngsters are having a great time nevertheless. The fire is better than a penny arcade, with characters adding to the festivity with daredevil stunts like jumping through the flames, or watching a bird screech off. It is an urban campout, and the kids here, like kids everywhere, are having a grand time with it.

The most common, and most powerful, motif the Ashcan artists employed in depicting humanity in an urban setting was to highlight a few, or even a lone subject, against the city as background. On January 9, 1906, John Sloan memorialized in his diary, "A clear, very cold day, and the streets very beautiful with snow."[10] Four years later, George Wesley Bellows captured the sense of this urban vista in his *A Morning Snow—Hudson River* (fig. 7.6).

The setting is clearly urban and industrial. Factories line the background on the other side of the river, a commercial vessel is visible at left and some kind of crane next to the dock on the right. Yet, the core of the scene remains an adult walking with her son, watching a workman shovel snow. This is a classic winter scene, worthy of Currier & Ives, with three people set against a lush, snowy setting. The only difference—but the crucial one that marked the historical significance of the Ashcan school—is that the setting is urban, not rural.[11]

These painters were part of an era, in other words, where art discovered the beauty present in the city, especially the greatest city of the New World, New York, adorned by an adjective that denoted its excitement. Theodore Dreiser fell in love with Gotham and told how "in all the city there is no more beautiful sight than that which is contributed by the flight of pigeons. You may see them flying in one place and another, here over the towering stacks of some tall factory, there over the low roofs of some workaday neighborhood; the yard of a laborer, the roof of some immense office building, the eaves of a shed or barn furnishing them shelter and a point of rendezvous from which they sail." All this and more, Dreiser has witnessed: "I have seen them at morning, when the sky was like silver, turning in joyous circles so high that the size of a large flock . . . was no more than a hand's breadth. I have seen them again at evening, wheeling and turning in a light that was amethystine in its texture, so soft that they seemed

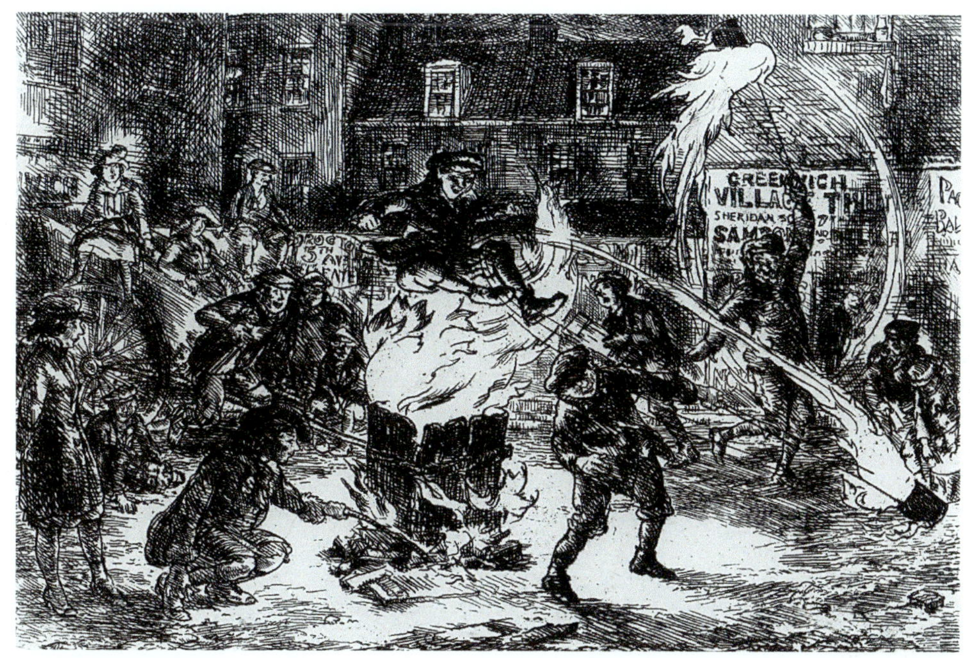

7.5 John Sloan (1871–1951), *Bonfire*, 1920, etching, 5¼ × 7⅜ inches; 13.2 × 18.6 cm. Smithsonian American Art Museum. Given in honor of Janet Flint by the Washington Print Club in September 1984, 1984.104. © 2016 Delaware Art Museum/Artists Rights Society (ARS), New York.

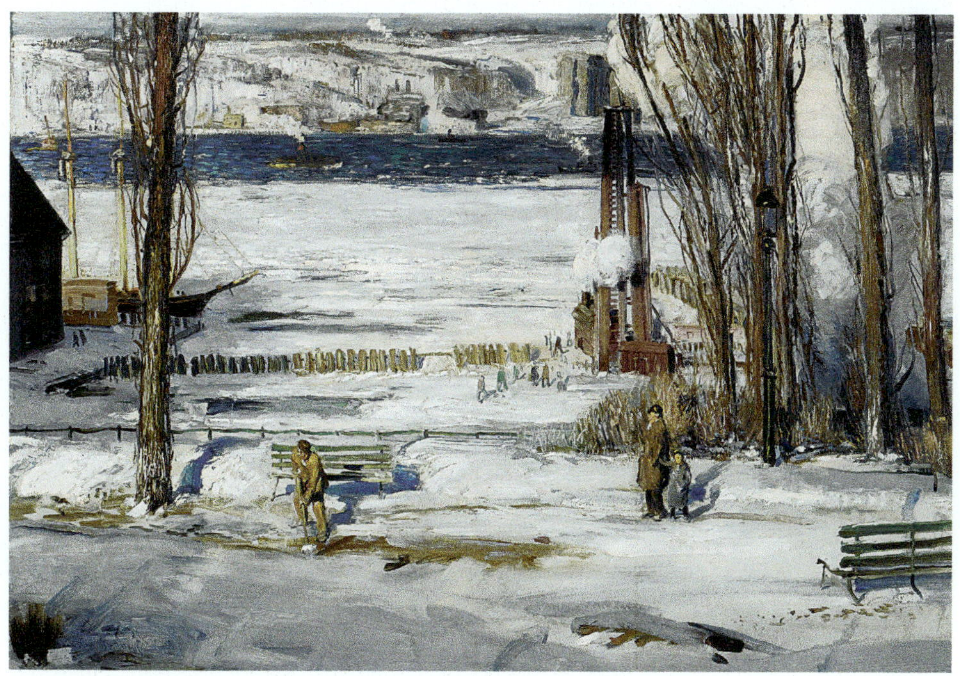

7.6 George Wesley Bellows (1882–1925), *A Morning Snow—Hudson River*, 1910, oil on canvas, 45¹⁄₁₆ × 63³⁄₁₆ inches; 114.5 × 160.5 cm. Brooklyn Museum, gift of Mrs. Daniel Catlin, 51.96. Photo credit: Brooklyn Museum, Brooklyn, New York.

swimming in a world of dream." Summing up what could be found in the city: "In the glow of a radiant sunset . . . when the turn of a wing made them look like a handful of snowflakes, or the shafts of the evening sunlight turned their bodies to gold, I have watched them soaring, soaring, soaring, running like children, laughing down the bosom of the wind, wheeling, shifting, rising, falling."[12]

These birds appear in two of John Sloan's foremost paintings. In *Pigeons*, he portrays a tranquil moment amid the tightness of the city (*fig. 7.7*). This picture is framed on four sides by tall buildings—on both sides, below, and towering above the two lone figures; the frame is narrow, and tight. Despite this, there is pleasure here, as a father and son share a moment of happiness together among their birds. The humans seem at peace, with themselves and with their setting, while the pigeons seem worthy of Dreiser's lyricism. A day out with nature and in sunshine, amid the highpoints of Gotham.

Sloan's *A Woman's Work* has an even tighter box for its scene, an alleyway between buildings (*fig. 7.8*). High walls enclose the sole figure, yet light remains abundant. Working on a narrow

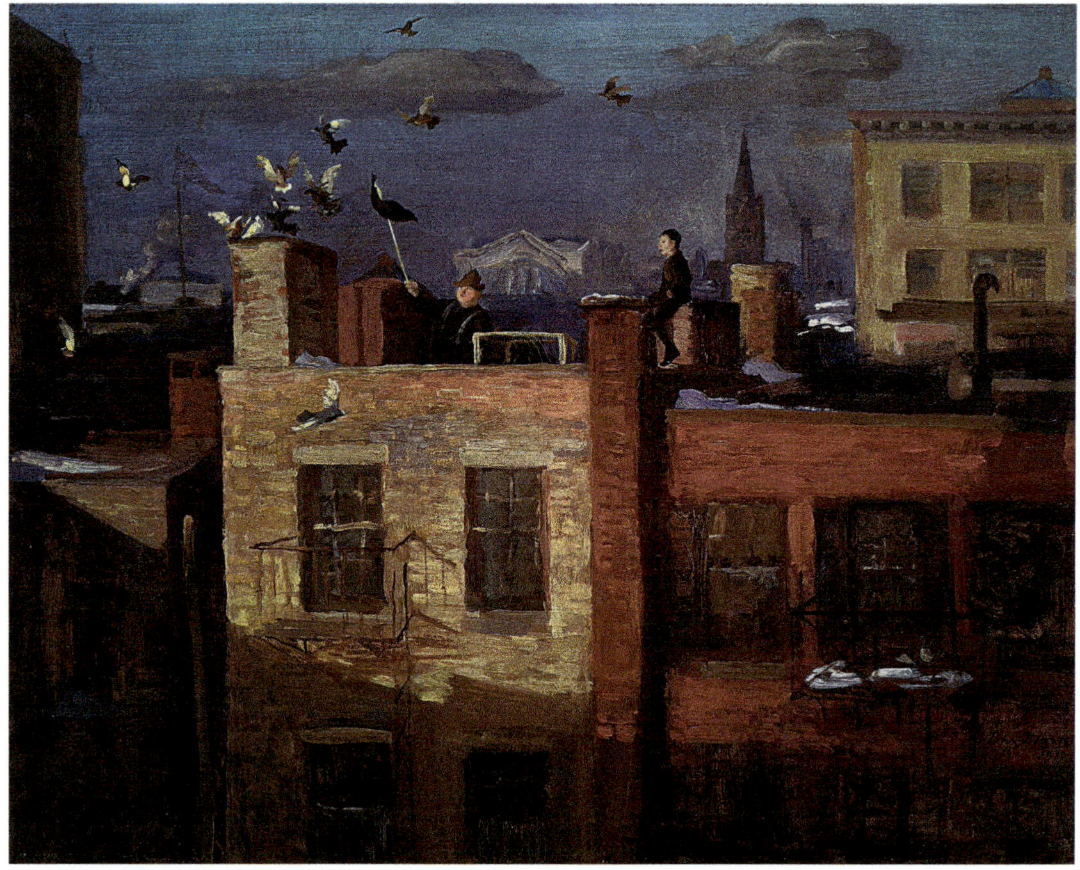

7.7 John Sloan (1871–1951), *Pigeons*, 1910, oil on canvas, 66.36 × 81.28 cm; 26⅛ × 32 inches. © 2016 Delaware Art Museum/Artists Rights Society (ARS), New York. Photograph © 2016 Museum of Fine Arts, Boston, Massachusetts, USA/Melvin Black and Frank Purnell Collection/Bridgeman Images.

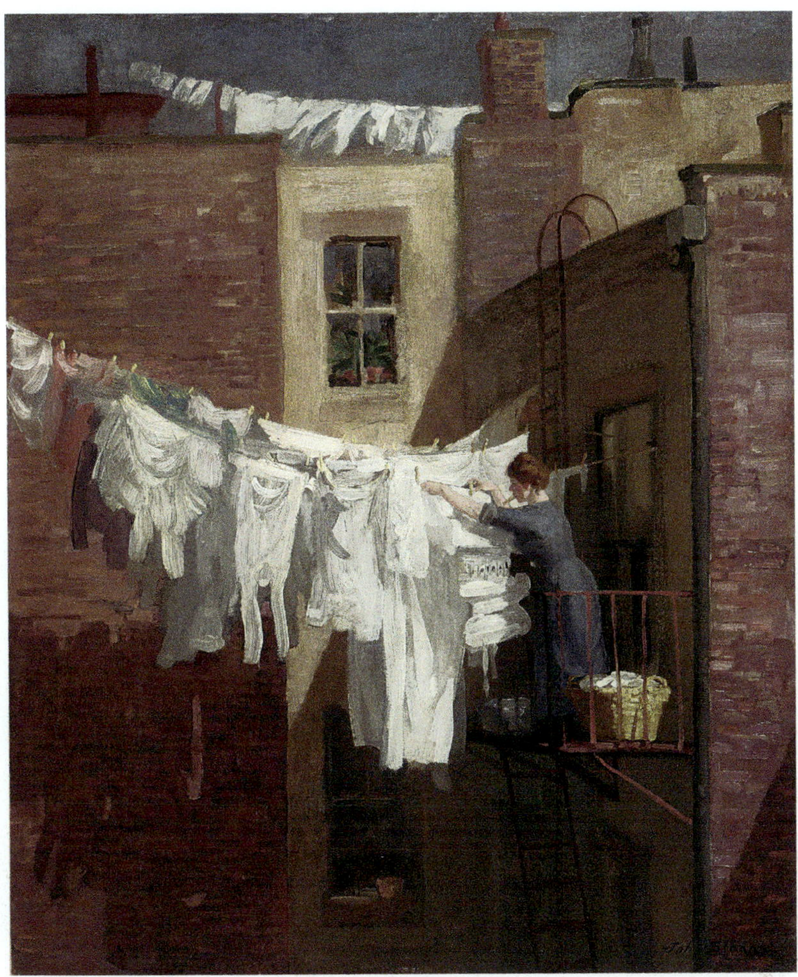

7.8 John Sloan (1871–1951), *A Woman's Work*, 1912, oil on canvas, framed: 97 × 82 × 5.5 cm, unframed: 80.3 × 65.4 cm. Cleveland Museum of Art, gift of Miss Amelia Elizabeth White, 1964.160. © 2016 Delaware Art Museum/Artists Rights Society (ARS), New York.

fire escape, the woman is hanging her laundry but seems somewhat at peace. She is working at a dull chore, and while no smile graces her—nor should, given the task at hand—dark clouds are not seen on her face either. Rather, this remains a brightly lit scene of everyday life in the city, of a person spotlighted amid the myriad colors, not of purple mountains, but of shades of brick. Betty Smith, who grew up in this world, wrote of clotheslines, "On a sunny, windy day. It was pretty to see the lines filled, the square white sheets taking the wind like the sails of a storybook boat."[13]

Yet, part of what makes the city so powerful, so exciting, was the spectacle of modern industry, its machinery and its efforts to create monuments, a very different part of the urban tableau from working-class neighborhoods. George Luks' *Roundhouse at High Bridge* shimmers, its multicolored smoke plumes traversing the length of the frame (*fig. 7.9*). This is industry working hard, with factories alongside a watery concourse, commercial craft passing through, while in the background a train rolls across an overpass. Everything is steel and coal and fire; the painting is livened by eruptions of orange from the factory in lower left.

The Ashcan painting of the city at work discussed most frequently by art historians is George Wesley Bellows' *Excavation at Night*, depicting the building of Pennsylvania Station (*fig. 7.10*). Robert Snyder remembered how, at that time, "the construction of a great building was a dramatic event. New Yorkers routinely peered through the holes in fences surrounding construction sites to monitor the work in progress." So, too, did John Dos Passos respond to this scene, writing, "Across Park Avenue the flame blue sky was barred with the red girder cage of a new building. Steam riveters rattled incessantly; now and then a donkey engine whistled and there was a jingle of chains and a fresh girder soared crosswise in the air." A British journalist

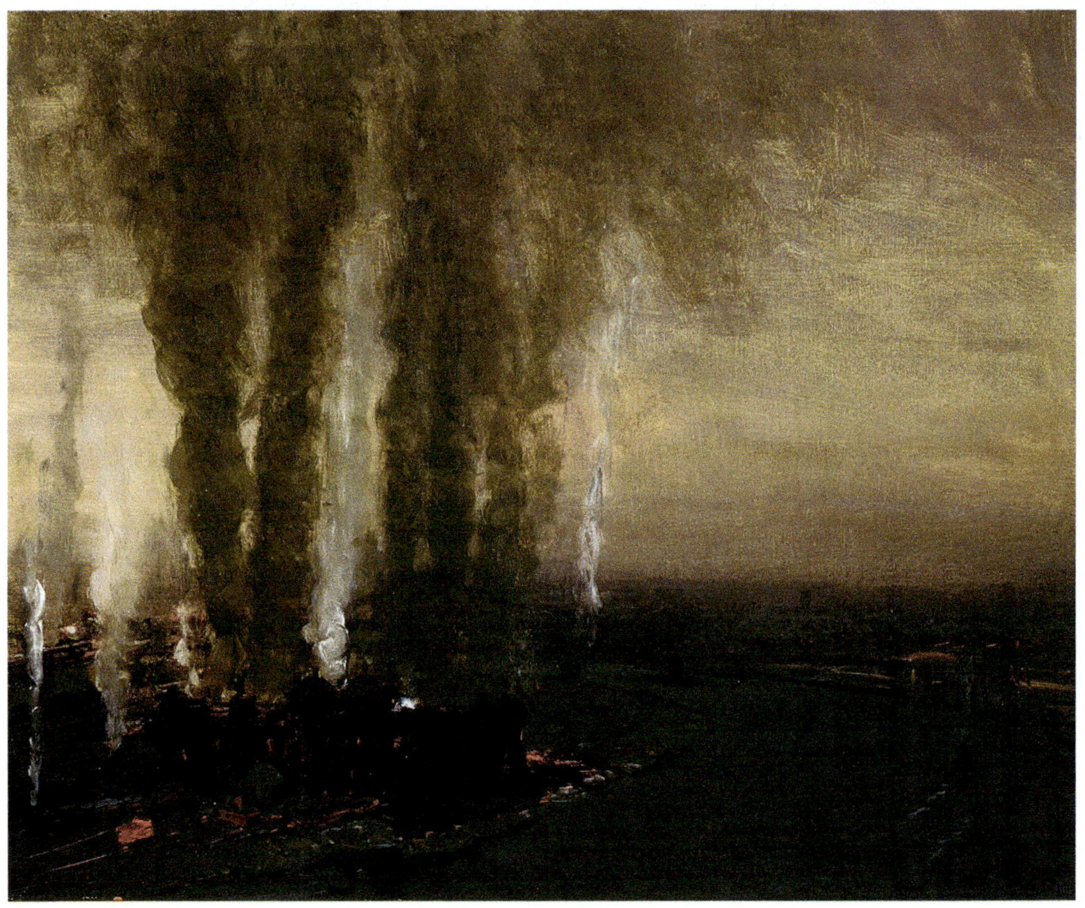

7.9 George Luks (1867–1933), *Roundhouse at High Bridge*, 1909–1910, oil on canvas, framed: 36½ × 32¾ inches, 92.7 × 83.2 cm; overall: 30½ × 30¼ inches, 77.5 × 76.8 cm. Museum purchase. 50.17. Munson-Williams-Proctor Institute. Photo credit: Munson-Williams-Proctor Institute/Art Resource, New York.

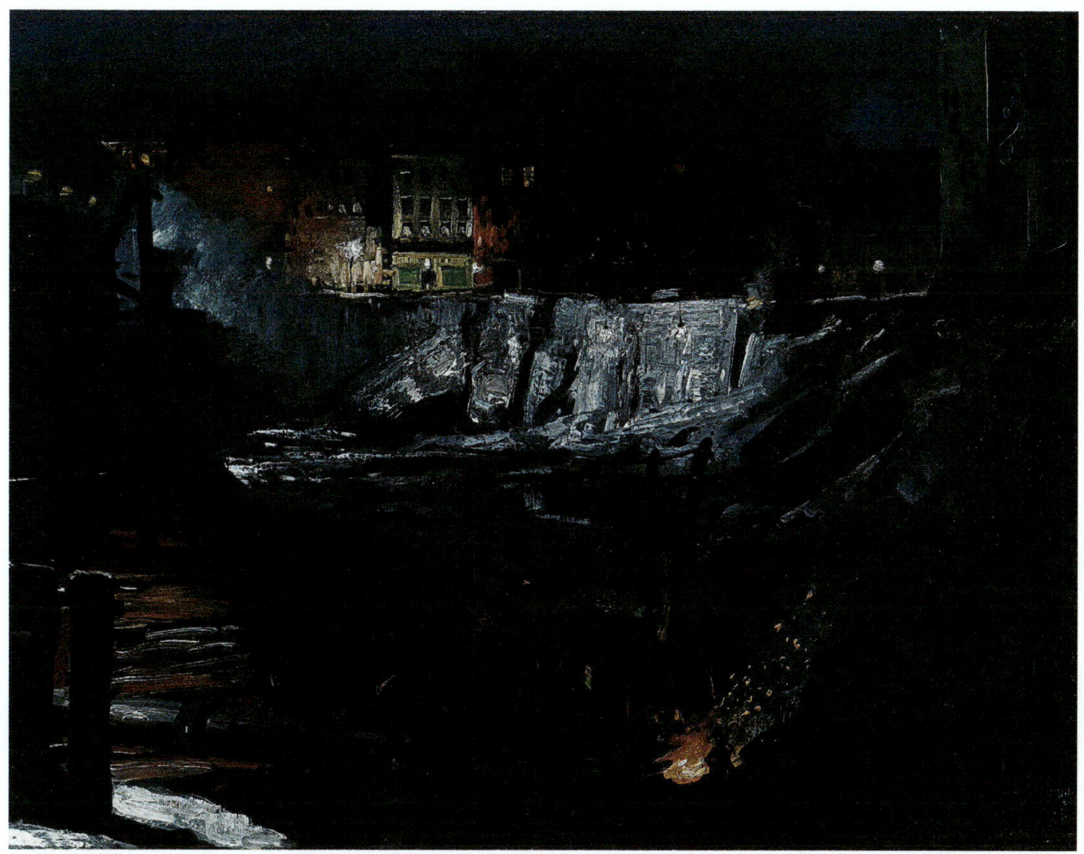

7.10 George Wesley Bellows (1882–1925), *Excavation at Night*, 1908, oil on canvas, 86.4 × 111.8 cm. Crystal Bridges Museum of American Art, Bentonville, Arkansas, 2010.77.

observed that "New York is the greatest mining camp on earth." Marianne Doezema noted how "the scale of the Pennsylvania Station" was another signal that touted New York's importance in the scheme of things and that this kind of project was "appropriate to a national metropolis."[14]

Bellows' canvas is a study in contrasts, highlighting how the Ashcan artists transformed the city into an *objet d'art*, and then into something far, far more important. One glance at this painting can bring up visions of Hades; this is a scene dark and foreboding, where souls go to wither and gain torment. Immense dark patches, so much of this image, speak to despair and to its final stages, nothingness. The frightening glow of hellfire illuminates the bottom and across the top, the latter like a greedy fire, raging and destroying.

A closer look, however, shows the city at work, being rebuilt into something majestic. Great machines are in play here, clawing out the earth to provide space for foundations of steel beam, and later a building that will last for decades or more as an expression of the architect's talent. Light comes from workmen's fires, but also from electric bulbs that will make Broadway talked about across the continent. Lewis Hine spoke of "men of courage, skill, daring and imagination. Cities do not build themselves, machines cannot make machines, unless back of them are the brains and toil of men."[15]

But wait, there is something more here. Yes, it is a city landscape, but as Doezema insightfully pointed out, there is something far greater. "Bellows," she explained, "integrates the visual realities of industrialized urban America into a traditional landscape scheme. . . . By harkening back to a venerable formula of landscape composition, Bellows conveyed a resonance of cultural authority for his picture." The artist, in other words, by painting the beauty of this kind of setting, is doing so much more than just putting oils together in a memorable way. By pulling the city up to the level of a great landscape, he is making the city American, enshrining urban, immigrant Gotham forever as part of a great and growing nation, his people now as much a part of Americana as the figures in Grant Wood's *American Gothic*.[16]

The Ashcan artists had also grasped another unique feature, that the city had become the heartland of America's business, not only where the deals were made, but where a considerable segment of the consumers lived, in high density, and were compelled to shop by the laws of both need and want. New York was the greatest marketplace of the industrial age, the place to get whatever it was you happened to look for. Commerce was not just a matter of spreadsheets tended to by accountants; it was all the consumers enjoying the excitement of products of any kind, everywhere you looked.

This insight was typical of the Ashcan school. Long before social history became an established genre within the discipline, painters and writers were exploring urban life from the bottom up, in all its parts.

They understood that commerce on a crowded street could be an exciting spectacle. John Dos Passos narrated the pace in *Manhattan Transfer*: "Noon on Union Square. . . . Kneeling on the dusty asphalt little boys shine shoes lowshoes tans buttonshoes oxfords. . . . Right this way buddy, mister miss maam at the back of the store our new line of fancy tweeds highest value lowest price. . . . WE HAVE MADE A TERRIBLE MISTAKE. Must vacate."[17] William Glackens captured the importance of shopping to the city in his *Christmas Shoppers, Madison Square*, a scene of tumultuous, democratic fun (*fig. 7.11*). Everything is bustle, as crowds maneuver through the streets, looking for just the right item from the cornucopia now available. This is no small-town general store, with items of every category jammed into a room hardly larger than a shed, but something far greater.

Yet, while the stores were far more specialized than those one-horse burg emporiums, there is still one similarity, and it is vital to understanding why shopping was so important to life in the city. Even in New York, once one came off the big boulevards and off to the neighborhoods, the commercial experience became small scale, with intimate relationships between shopper and proprietor.

New York's commerce covered the full spectrum of enterprises. As Theodore Dreiser memorably described, "One of the most appealing and interesting elements in city life, particularly that metropolitan city life which characterizes New York, is the pushcart man. This curious creature . . . infests all the highways of the great city. . . . He is as hard working . . . as he is ubiquitous." One such entrepreneur took station at Sixth Avenue and Twenty-Third Street, "a dark, gray-headed, grizzle cheeked 'guinea' or 'dago' as he was scornfully dubbed by the Irish policeman who made his life a burden. His eye was keen, his motion quick, his general body make-up active, despite the fact that he was much over fifty years of age."[18]

Shopping, thus, for all classes, became a basic element of the local community in the city. At one level, Joseph Amato observed, "shopping took the form—at least for the prospering middle class—of a privileged and self-congratulatory ambling." But in the local neighborhoods, as Robert Snyder and Rebecca Zurier so insightfully pointed out, shopping districts became "social spaces where residents could count on finding people who spoke their language. . . . Socializing occurs not in the privacy of the parlor but on the sidewalk. Commerce draws people out of their apartments and into a wider community." Thus, in a city where tenements and working-class

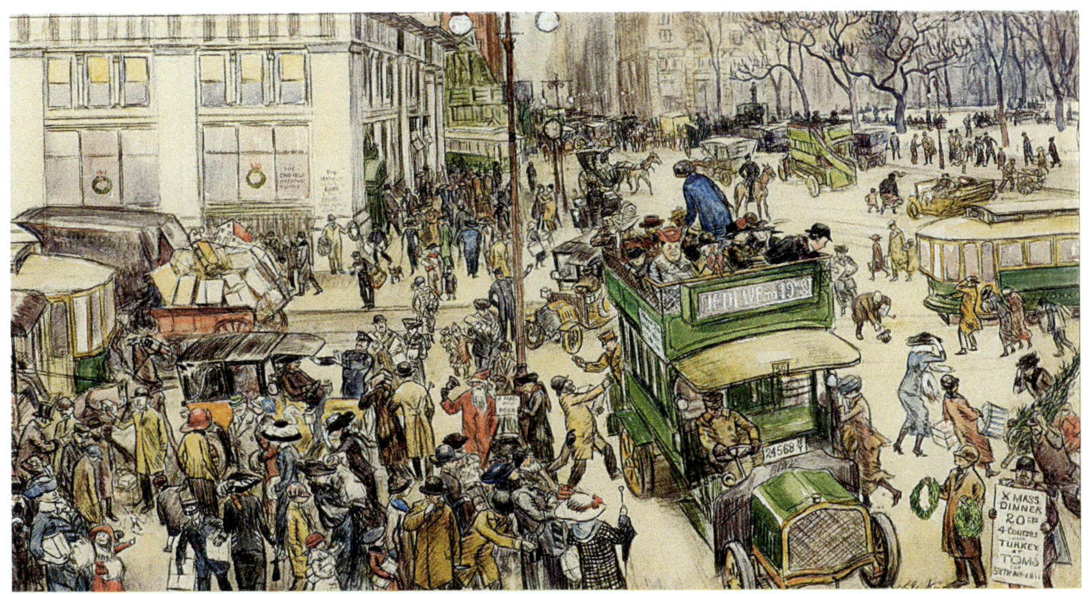

7.11 William Glackens (1870–1938), *Christmas Shoppers, Madison Square*, 1912, crayon and watercolor on paper, 17 × 31 inches; 43 × 81 cm. NSU Art Museum Fort Lauderdale, Florida. Bequest of Ira D. Glackens, 1991.40.106.

apartments are often less than hospitable, city streets served as social spaces as well as commercial spaces. Ashcan art captured the outdoor nature of urban life among those without adequate living rooms or parlors in which they could entertain. The use of public space was central to the urban experience—especially to those with limited means—and no artistic genre captured this more fully or more insightfully than the Ashcan.[19]

Two different Ashcan artists pursued this vision. William Glackens, in *Patrick Joseph Went and Bought Himself a Grocery Store in Monroe Street*, shows what life was like in the city (*fig. 7.12*, pg. 118). The setting is narrow; tall tenements enclose the street, with their fire escapes intruding even further into local space. Yet the street is full and lively, packed with merchants, stalls, and shoppers. Patrick Joseph himself stands on the left, in front of his brand-new shop, watching the street. Shopkeepers like this, watching *their* block, are the best protective service possible. Several children are in the foreground with their respective mothers, and next to them, two ladies—probably neighbors, carry on a conversation.

Jerome Myers draws another such scene in *The Street Market* (*fig. 7.13*, pg. 119). The painting is reminiscent of scenes of market days in eighteenth- and early nineteenth-century small towns, another indication that these artists were creating a new form of American art, replacing earlier pastoral versions with updated urban settings. Though clearly set in an immigrant district, there is much life here. Amid the merchandise, everyone—with the exception of the man in isolation—is carrying on an animated conversation. From the smiles on the faces of both women and girls in the center, foreground, and background, the discussions appear to be pleasant ones. The market is a spot for friendships, a place to make new ones or to renew current relationships.

Glackens' and Myers' art highlights one other novel aspect of the urban shopping experience. Though money is changing hands, not just men are involved. The foremost characters in this

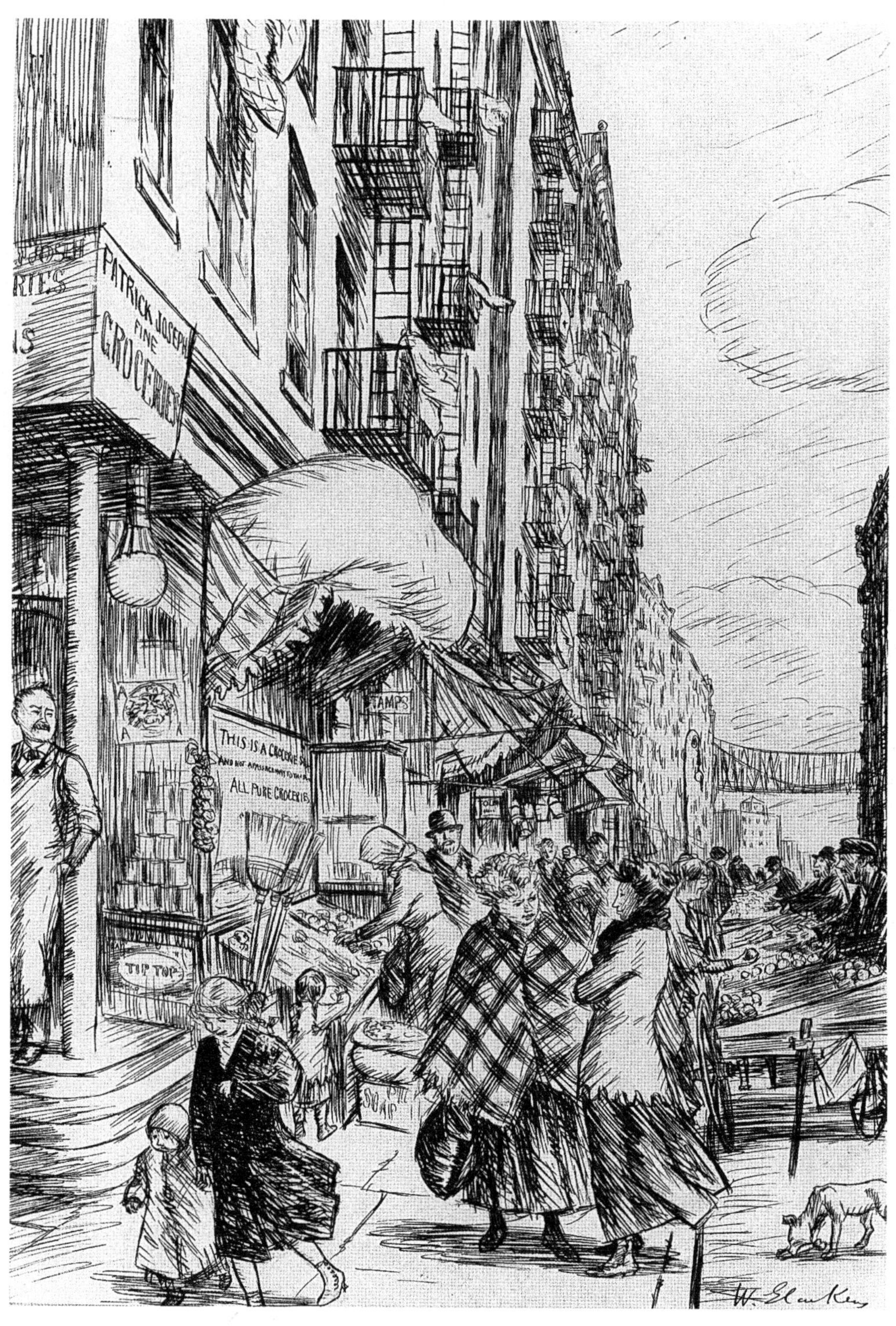

7.12 William Glackens (1870–1938), *Patrick Joseph Went and Bought Himself a Grocery Store in Monroe Street*, 1912. Published as an illustration to E. R. Lipsett, "Denny the Jew," *Everybody's Magazine* 27 (July 1912): 45.

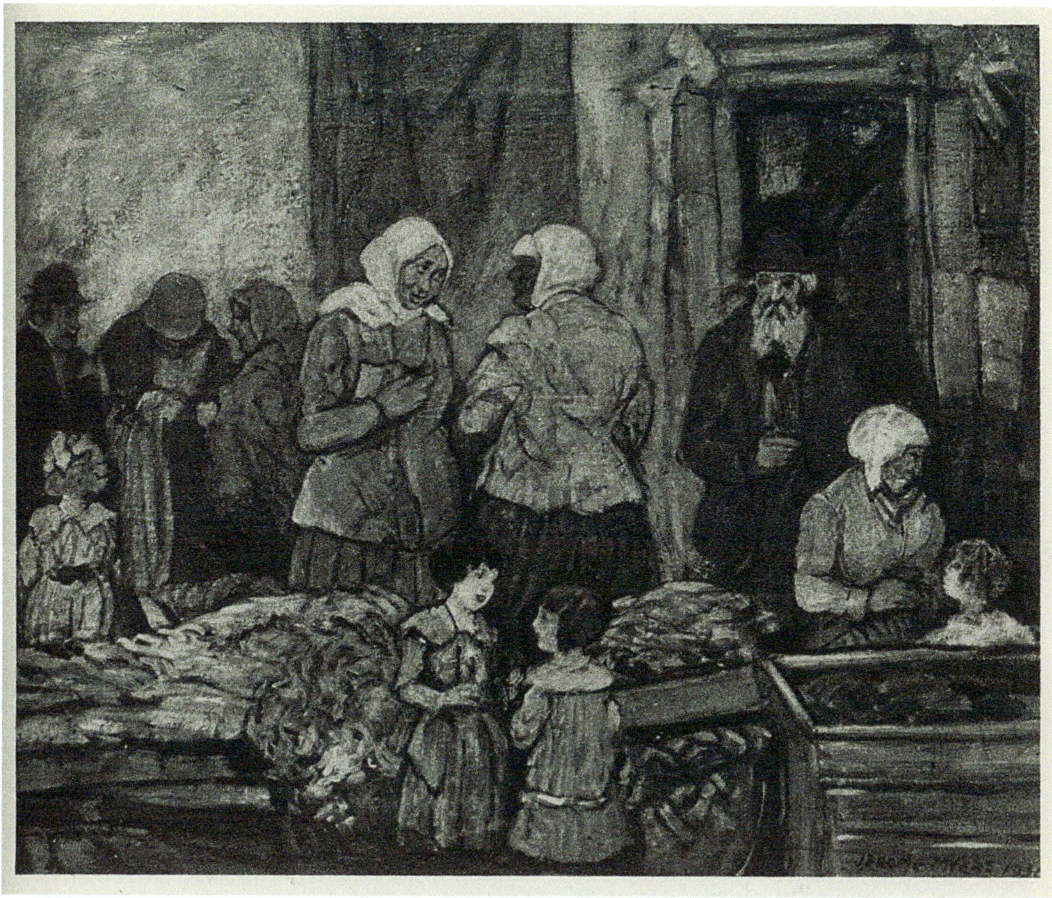

7.13 Jerome Myers (1867–1940), *The Street Market*. Jerome Myers, *The Artist in Manhattan* (New York: American Artists Group, 1940), 157.

drama, the individuals with agency and the power of disposable income (no matter how minimal), are females. As Laurel Weintraub explained, "this new woman is born a consumer."[20]

Even more unusual are young women, who in previous generations were allowed no money to spend and lived in places with little to spend it on. Now, instead, they are free to see everything in the city and can put down their rare penny or nickel where they choose, and for what they desire. As Francie Nolan, the young heroine of *A Tree Grows in Brooklyn*, discovers when she sells some junk, "Francie had a nickel. Francie had power. She could buy practically anything in that store."[21]

John Sloan caught the giddiness of a group of young women, footloose and blissfully free in the city. In *Fun, One Cent*, the girls are clearly neither slum dwellers nor upper class (*fig. 7.14*, pg. 120). Nor are they chaperoned; life is wide open when you go to the mart, even for a girl. Despite this lack of supervision, they are in a nickelodeon, laughing at pictures advertised as "naughty." No matter what your gender or age, the city's commercial sections are exciting and can make you smile.

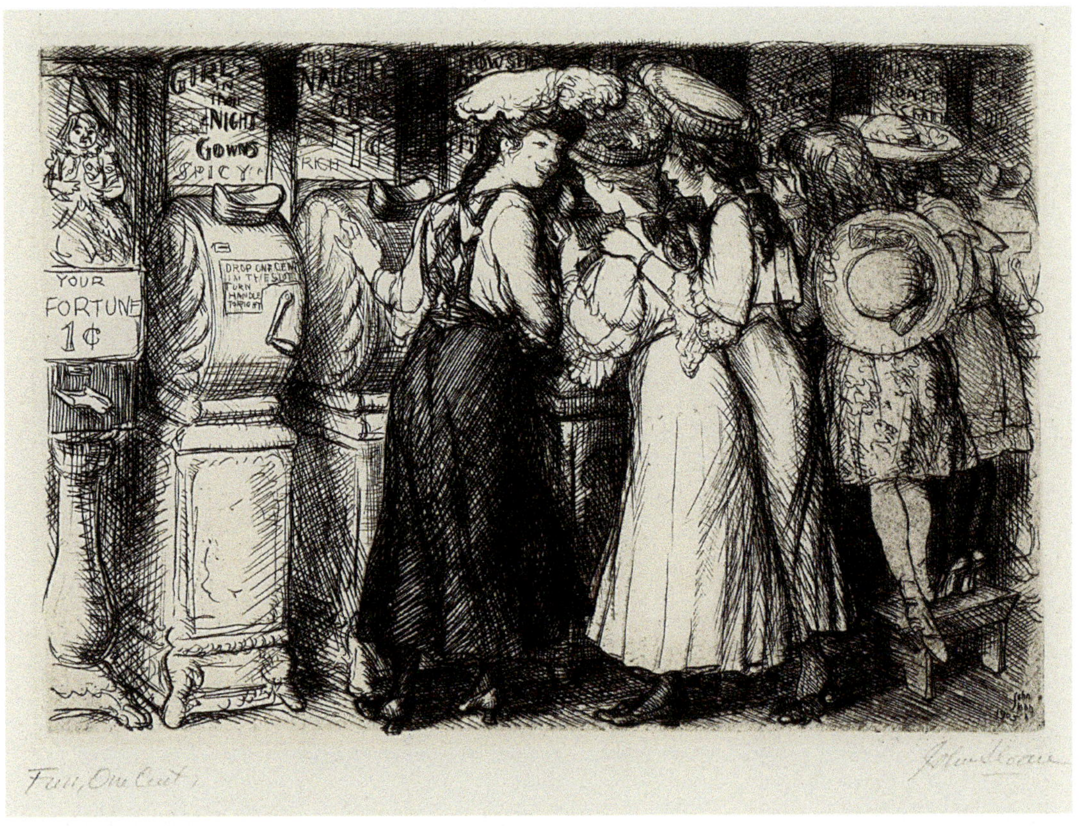

7.14 John Sloan (1871–1951), *Fun, One Cent*, 1905, 7 × 5 inches. Museum of the City of New York, New York. © 2016 Delaware Art Museum/Artists Rights Society (ARS), New York.

All of these groups—different genders and ages and classes—now participated in one of the greatest recreations only available in a city, window shopping. Deborah Fairman noted how, as you perused the shops, "the quotidian, the commonplace things of existence—clothing, furnishings—seemed magical and glamorous; not only a new world of goods but the world itself newly imagined as consisting of goods and their consumption." Fairman added her own commentary, arguing that before, consumers entered a store solely to make a purchase; now they came as voyeurs of materialism, to be charmed by the displays. "The department store," she explained, "literally and intentionally transformed the city street into a spectacle of desire."[22]

Everett Shinn captured this in his pastel *Window Shopping* (*fig. 7.15*). Despite the weather, the young woman is entranced by what she sees in the store windows. Her clothes denote her as coming from modest circumstances, but in the moment captured here, she seems wistful. And why not? She is looking at her dreams. John Sloan wrote his wife Dolly on the attractions of the city: "You should have seen the Sixth Avenue night display of a sheath gown—one of those shops on east side of street near 22nd. The way people looked at it was funny . . . a terrific hat and Directoire cane finished the arrangement." These goods compel attention, and people

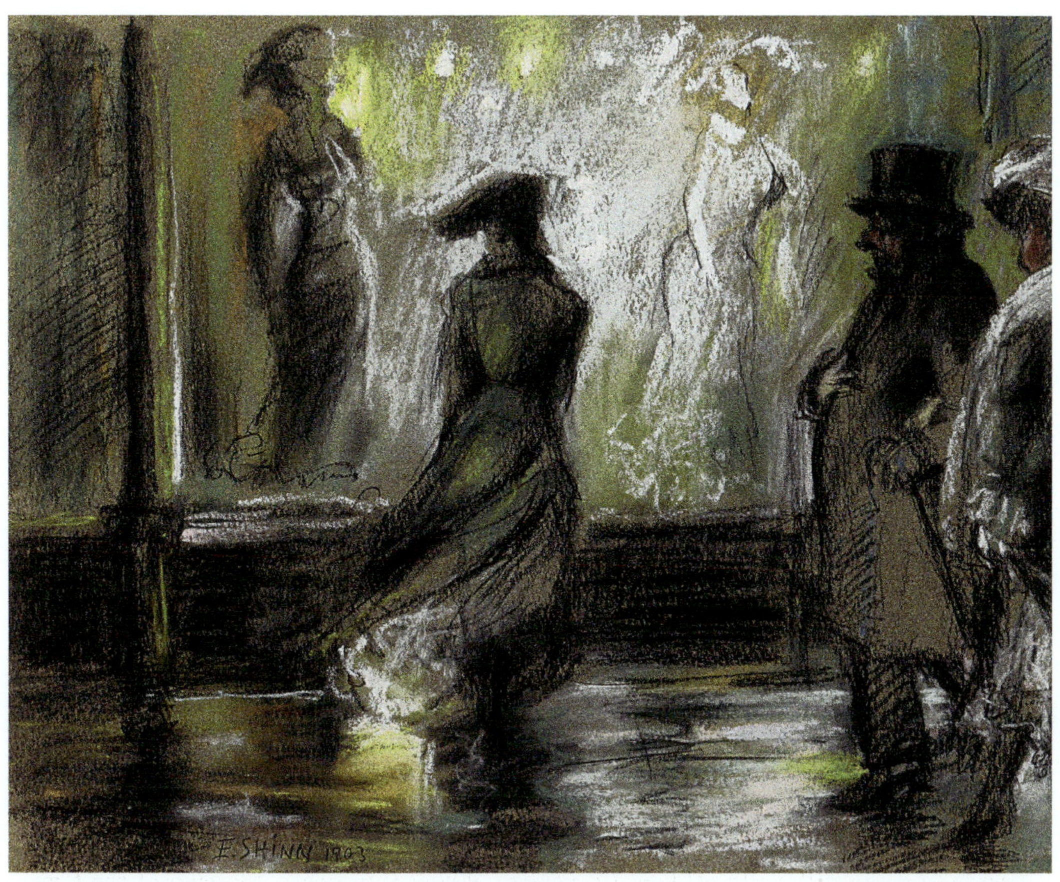

7.15 Everett Shinn (1876–1953), *Window Shopping*, 1903, pastel on paper, 36.2 × 45.72 cm. Private Collection, Pennsylvania. Photograph courtesy of Sotheby's, Inc. © 2015.

gathered to look, to comment, to fantasize. Fantasies now played out, not just in the minds of young women but in the windows of local shops and department stores.[23]

Shinn's painting also points to one of the other features of the city: it was lit by that new invention, electric lights. Electricity pushed back the darkness; Peter Baldwin noticed how, because of urban technology, "streetlights could fill a city block with light." This made the streets relatively safe for women like the single traveler mentioned earlier; even after the sun went down, she could still window shop. This was a new feature of cities that lit up, not only Fifth Avenue but also entertainment districts like Times Square, and even working-class shopping streets. Only the Ashcan artists picked up that last point.[24]

Commercial voyeurism, however, was not limited to goods, but extended to the spectacle put on by the service industries as well. John Sloan captured this in his well-known painting *Hairdresser's Window* (fig. 7.16, pg. 122). This picture was fashioned from memory. On June 5, 1907, Sloan was on his way to visit Robert Henri. Along the route, he "saw a humorous sight of interest." On the street, the artist glimpsed "a window, low, second story, bleached blond hairdresser bleaching the hair of a client. A small interested crowd about."[25]

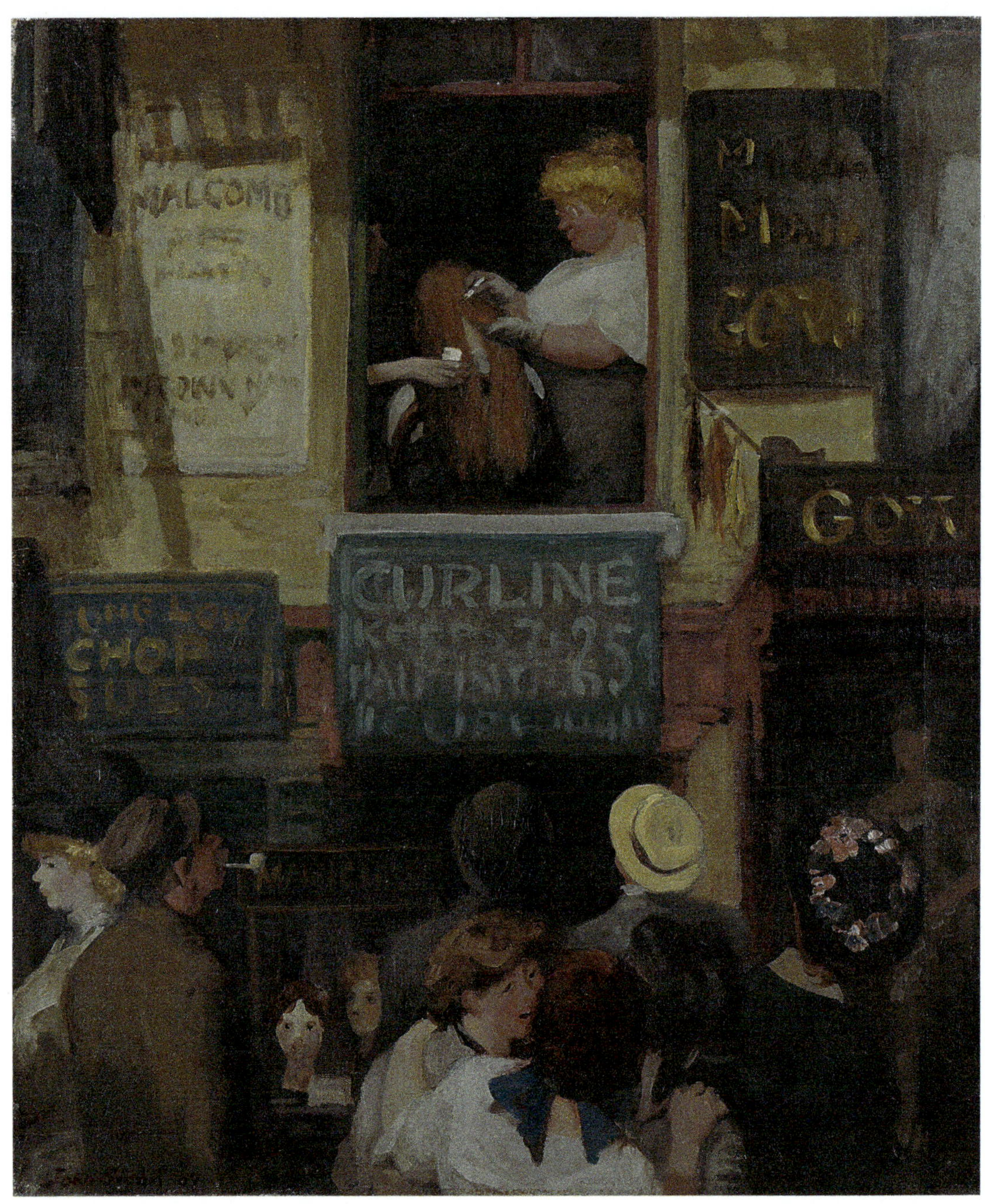

7.16 John Sloan (1871–1951), *Hairdresser's Window*, 1907, oil on canvas, 80.96 × 66.04 cm; 31.88 × 26 inches. Wadsworth Atheneum, Hartford, Connecticut. The Ella Gallup Sumner and Mary Caitlin Sumner Collection Fund. 1947.240. Photography by Allen Phillips/Wadsworth Atheneum.

The vision is a lively one; this street is filled with signage, advertising everything from chop suey to "curline" to gowns—even one storefront on a city street can become a grand marquee. In this tight frame, the hairdresser and her client are the main focus, their inherent interest-worthiness attested to by the fascinated crowd below, some of whom are making animated comments, while most stand transfixed. The task itself is actually mundane; what makes it exciting is the fact that it is on display, in a shop window. The commercial life of the city turns so much into spectacle.

What is remarkable about this painting is that it forces the viewer to not only *see* but to *experience* the fun of this moment; we become, not *external spectators* but instead *participants*, partaking in the fabulous life of the street. Set just above street level, as if one is watching it all from atop a stepladder, in Rebecca Zurier's apt description, "the viewer is placed among them, looking over their shoulders, reading the signboards. The subject is . . . the circuit of gazes and interactions that link people and goods in a city."[26]

Thus, the dense city, with its immense cast, inherently provides entertainment, unlike its small-town cousin. In her study of another great world municipality, Paris, Vanessa Schwartz discussed how the boulevards had become a grand show stage, devoted to mass consumption and, even more, to people watching, what was referred to as "the spectacle of the street."[27]

The Ashcan artists painted the city as unique, and vastly entertaining. Above all, they recognized that it was the most exciting place to be in their America, as well as in ours. This is important because it was an essential part of the Ashcan view of the city: that it is enjoyable, for all classes—thus contesting the views of both elites and reformers.

The city was made for walking. Anywhere; in places like Gotham it hardly matters. Cities like New York, or London, or Paris, you can embark on an unplanned, unplotted excursion. Just head out on foot, and let those two motors be your guide; amble where your shoes take you, and enjoy the sights along the way. Joseph Yardley wrote how "walking can do that to you; take you to places you didn't expect to go, people you didn't expect to meet, entanglements you hadn't planned on. To be sure, walking is usually simply to get you from Point A to Point B, but it can be serendipitous as well." John Sloan recorded in his diary how he "walked across the Brooklyn Bridge for the first time. [He] enjoyed it immensely. There were fine clouds over the sky with sun-ladders of silver one of which struck the Statue of Liberty. This sounds like a romantic touch but it's true nonetheless." Poet Grace Paley extoled how "to walk in the city arm and arm with a woman friend (as her mother had with aunts and cousins so many years ago) was just plain essential. Oh! Those long walks and intimate talks, better than standing alone on the most admirable mountain or in the handsomest forest or hay-blown field."[28]

Sometimes, however, you wanted company. The most common way to accomplish this was to just stop by a friend's abode, unannounced, in hopes of a pleasant visit. You stop by, not necessarily expecting someone to be home, just as today one places a telephone call without being sure the party on the other end will answer. John Sloan wrote his wife Dolly about such an interlude, a casual, unannounced, and unscheduled visit from his closest friends: "The Henris have just gone, they said they expected to find you here; had called Thursday night, while I was away at the opera, hoping to see you."[29]

As indicated in the previous quote, one of the prime attractions of the city was the ease with which you could "go to the show," as they used to say, whether it be a myriad of live forms or that new marvel of the age, the moving picture. This was another new and uniquely urban attraction. In a 1907 article in *Harper's Magazine* entitled "Manhattan Lights," Edward Martin urged readers to "go to the pleasure centre, and you will find a nightly illumination which, they all tell us, no other city in the world can quite hold a candle to." Above all, there is the lure

of an unprecedented sight in human history, a world lit by artificial illumination, so powerful it
even lights up the outdoors and banishes the darkness of the nighttime sky. Martin explained,
"For light itself is beautiful, and though indoors it is easy to have too much of it, out-of-doors
it is hard to misuse it so extravagantly that it will not still please the eye." He described the
various colors ("The long rows of white street lights . . . the orange globes of intense light that
hang by the theatre doors . . .") then concluded, "The show in New York is provided every
night . . . the trouble is to get the perspective."[30]

The Ashcan artists drew this festival, not surprisingly on a small, intimate scale. In Sloan's
Movies, we see a neighborhood hot spot (*fig. 7.17*). The theater is lit and becomes the focus
of the painting, as if hit by a stage spotlight. Everyone is part of the crowd; there are clusters
of women, children, and men. Though the sign seems to announce a "Harem," no one seems
outraged. This is the city, after all, where diverse forms of entertainment are standard. John Sloan
wrote of an evening out, of the spontaneity and the variety of life in Manhattan: "Well, after
dinner I walked out Broadway and the notion came to me why not go to the theatre! I looked

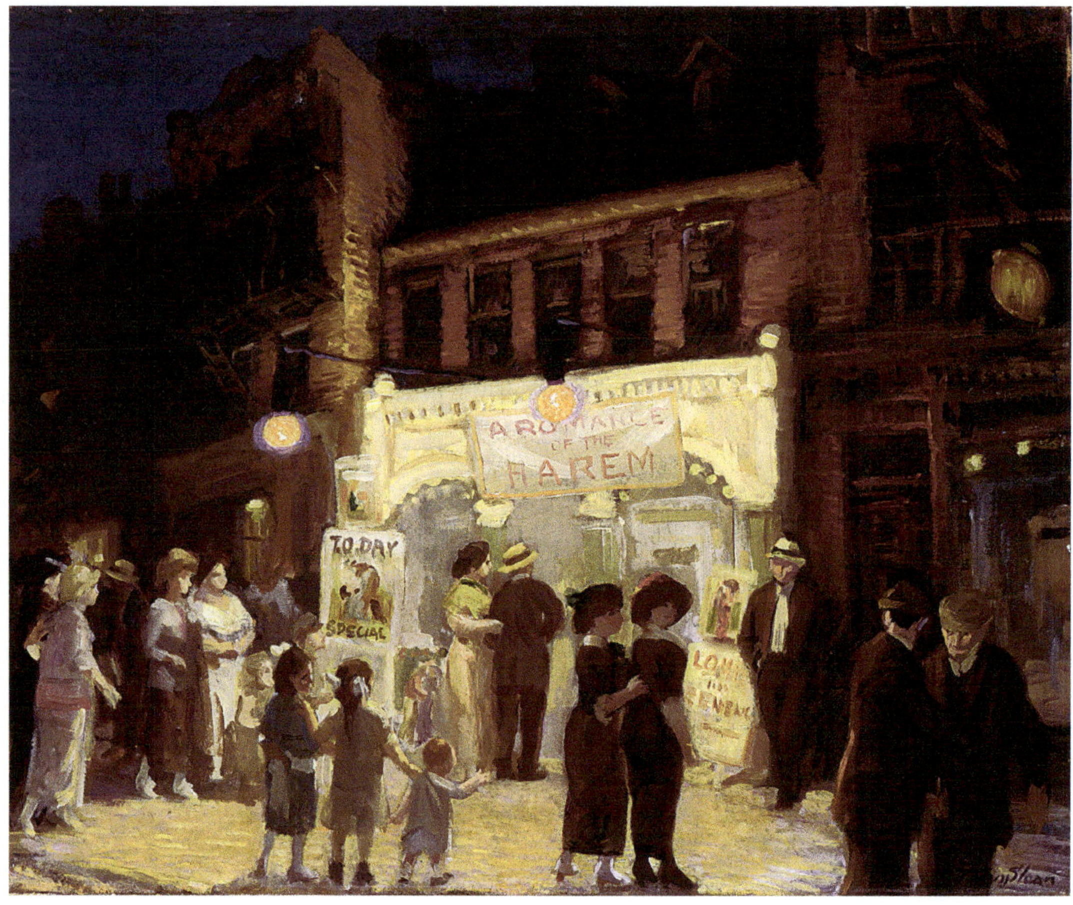

7.17 John Sloan (1871–1951), *Movies*, 1913, oil on canvas, 50.5 × 61 cm. Toledo Museum
of Art (Toledo, Ohio), Museum Purchase Fund, 1940.16. Photo credit: Photography
Incorporated, Toledo.

at the name of plays at the various places I passed and did not feel interested in any of them. Then I found myself in a crowd just thronging into the Metropolitan Opera House. A ticket speculator offered me a ticket . . . and I suddenly decided to go in. *Tannhäuser* was the opera."[31]

Even though this depicts a local setting, Sloan's image captures one of the most important aspects of this new American entity: the city is exciting, above all. Lewis Erenberg, in *Steppin' Out*, argued that "the progressives and the conservatives were unable to understand that most men and women wanted something new in their private lives. The urban world was changing, moving away from being an extension of the private home."[32]

What provided these thrills on a day-to-day basis was not the grand sights, but rather those unique visions and sounds that every urban resident knows makes their town special. Whichever borough you're from, how many times have folks sighed and then remarked, "You could only see that in New York!" Schwartz noted how in Paris, though the opera might have been pricey for the working class, the streets of a great city provided an abundance of free entertainment.[33]

The full glory of an urban avenue is the subject of George Wesley Bellows' *The Street (Spring Blossoms) (June Blossoms)* (fig. 7.18, pg. 126). Beneath the dark el tracks casting grim shadows the crowd seems undaunted. In the foreground two elegant ladies are taking a stroll to show off their garb, leered at by the gentleman on the left of the frame. Children are everywhere, some being reprimanded by parents, others running loose. Density is intense; the streets are packed, and you have to elbow a way through the crowd. Folks peer out of windows or stand on fire escapes to watch the spectacle. The city puts on its own show.

The missives in the files of the John Sloan Papers at the Delaware Art Museum chronicle, over and over, the continual series of unexpected episodes that enliven life in the city. On March 22, 1909, Dolly Sloan wrote her husband, including mention of how, on her return from the doctor's office, she caught "a fine view of a fire." The year before, Robert Henri wrote his friend Sloan of the night he went to the Grand Opera House. The performance was just fair, "but there was a fight in the gallery (packed) that looked for a while as if half the gallery would tumble into the pit—and I saw a man get handcuffs slapped on for trying to throw another man under a trolley car today—exciting!"[34]

Yes, it was. What Henri noticed, millions of others actually participated in and became part of the show.

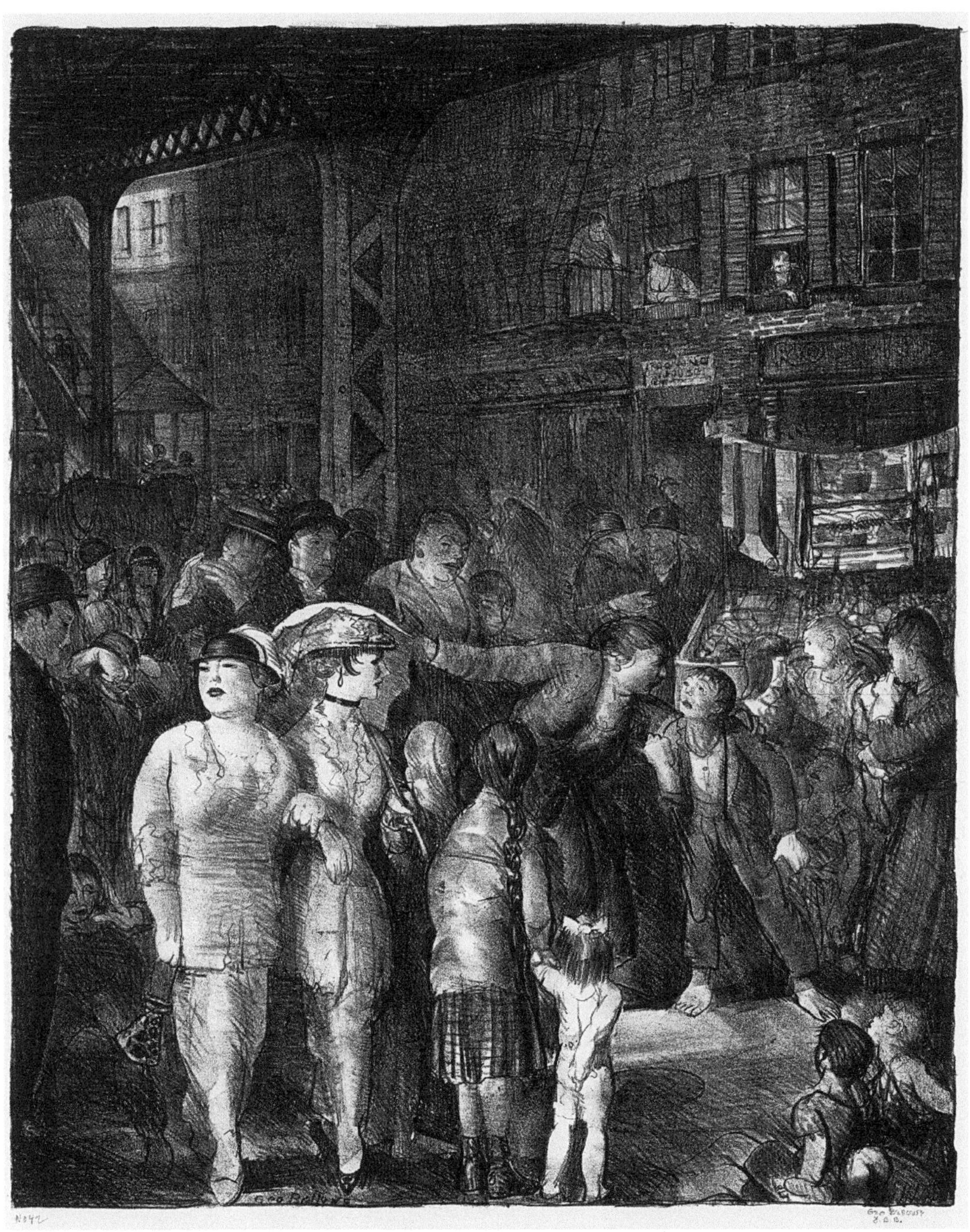

7.18 George Wesley Bellows (1882–1925), *The Street (Spring Blossoms) (June Blossoms)*, 1917, lithograph, image: 19 × 15¼ inches, 48.3 × 38.7 cm; sheet: 25¹³⁄₁₆ × 18⅞ inches, 65.5 × 48 cm. Fletcher Fund, 1971 (1971.514.2). Metropolitan Museum of Art, New York. Image copyright © The Metropolitan Museum of Art. Image source: Art Resource, New York.

CHAPTER EIGHT

PEOPLE OF THE CITY

THE ASHCAN ARTISTS VIEWED THE PEOPLE OF THE CITY FROM A UNIQUE PERSPECTIVE. UNLIKE THE elites, they did not consider these individuals their biological inferiors. Yet they also differed from the reformers, in that they rejected the notion that the people who lived in dense city neighborhoods were inherently subjects of pity. Instead, Henri, Sloan, Myers, and the others painted children and women and men, each from these individuals' own, unique perspective, rather than imposing a worldview on them. By so doing, in their paintings and drawings, they gave working-class individuals agency, showing how these people adapted to the world around them in a myriad of ways, ways that often enabled them to attain a measure of control over some parts of their lives.

Above all, the Ashcan artists captured the vitality of working-class life in the great city. Like urban generations long before, and again today, these painters were inveterate people watchers. Everyone who loves—or even those who just enjoy—the city knows this is one of its greatest attractions, a ceaseless source of anecdote and merriment, the world's greatest show. William Whyte, one of the great sociologists, wrote in *City*, "The street is a stage . . . what is most fascinating about the life of the street is the interchanges between people that take place in it." Or as a *New York Times* reporter trumpeted, "The city as spectacle, as an endless producer of exceptional, theatrical images, a shifting who's who of people and things."[1]

Of particular note was the attention the Ashcan artists paid to the most powerless residents, the children. Instead, they recognized the intense and varied role youngsters played in the city.

The core of their concept of urban childhood was a still radical notion—that the city is not so much a dangerous environment but rather an exciting place to be a child, and one that helps them develop important lifetime skills. This flies in the face of the approach by most charities and reform organizations—even today—that the best thing to do for a city child is to get them as far away and for as long as possible.

Part of these scribblers' perspective derived from their time spent illustrating newspapers. That medium was experimenting with a new innovation, the comic strip. Starting in 1895, *The Yellow Kid* depicted the children in an Irish slum as happy and part of a community, engaging in a series of light adventures, with commentary in thick dialect delivered by the title character. This was the bold new form for graphic artists, and the Ashcan artists paid close attention. What the newspaper cartoonists drew was clearly the city, yet they told their stories with great affection for kids in these urban neighborhoods. In one of his few interviews, Richard Outcault, creator of this format, explained, "The Yellow Kid was not an individual but a type. When I used to go about the slums on newspaper assignments I would encounter him often, wandering out of doorways or sitting down on dirty doorsteps. I always loved the Kid. He had a sweet character and a sunny disposition, and was generous to a fault." George Luks, who took over the strip as its second artist-writer, found that a "child of the slums [made] a better painting than a drawing-room lady gone over by a beauty shop." Later, he elaborated how: "Children seem to have in their eyes a definite glimpse of something, a wonder, a half-awakened expectancy."[2]

Another reason the Ashcan artists picked up on this subject was the inordinate presence children had on the streets of the turn-of-the-century metropolis, especially compared to today. Children were ever present in such large numbers they seemed to be swarming at times. Cary Goodman, in his book on children's games, started his first chapter by telling how "the streets of the Lower East Side Jewish community were like a barrel overflowing with activities and people." John Sloan wrote in his diary on June 7, 1910, about a trip where he "took a walk through the section between Brooklyn and Williamsburg Bridges. Life is thick! Colorful. I saw more than my brain could comprehend, a maze of living incidents—children by thousands in the streets and parks." For these children—unsupervised by wage-toiling parents and without the organizational infrastructure of middle-class life—the streets were everything: playground, community center, ballfield, living room, and hideaway for assignations. Even a 1911 reform study by the Russell Sage Foundation acknowledged, "A hundred activities which in the Fifth Avenue home find their *loci* in parlor, study, den and garden, must among the mass of the people be somewhere outside the limits of the home." A 1915 article on the art of Jerome Myers told how the artist reveled in "the small Italians in Mulberry Bend, shrieking with delight as they hurry from unbeautiful houses to unwelcome schools, or the exultation of the Scandinavian children scampering over Battery Park on their way to new experiences and new lands." Sophie Ruskay, the offspring of immigrants, made clear that, when she grew up, "children owned the streets in a way unthinkable to city children of today." Part of this came from the fact that they lived in small apartments, often with little space for play. Seeking alternative venues, they created a world of fun and amusement in the neighborhood streets. Once outside, away from the adult domination in the factory or the home, these children built their own world, with their own rules, where they were in charge.[3]

Jerome Myers captured a hint of this presence in his *East Side Children* (fig. 8.1). In this drawing, children—while not in abundance—still take over the scene. They are everywhere—standing, sitting, walking with mother, on the stoop, on the trash can, adorning a stone bannister, relaxing in the window. One could not pass this street without being very, very aware of the children all around.

One thing the artists noticed about all these kids was that they were happy, the antithesis of Jacob Riis' terrified urchins. Ruth Gay, a historian who grew up in the Bronx, remembered as a child being constantly reprimanded with, "*Narele, vus lakhste?*—Little fool, why are you laughing?" On a stroll down Ninth Avenue with Jerome Myers, John Sloan found "children swarming in the pools of dirt, sledding down three or five foot slushy heaps—having heaps of fun." A 1911 article in *The Bookman* reported, "The slum kid as you see him running through the streets is the happiest youngster alive."[4]

Several of the Ashcan paintings—including some of the most famous works—capture the joy that many city kids clearly experienced. George Wesley Bellows' classic, *Forty-Two Kids*, portrays this in rich colors (fig. 8.2, pg. 130). This painting was based in fact; street kids all over the city swam off the docks, jumping in, splashing around, cooling off, heedless of the garbage or the dangers. According to a *New York Times* story, kids preferred jumping into one of the city's rivers over going to a municipal pool with its elaborate set of regulations, determined and

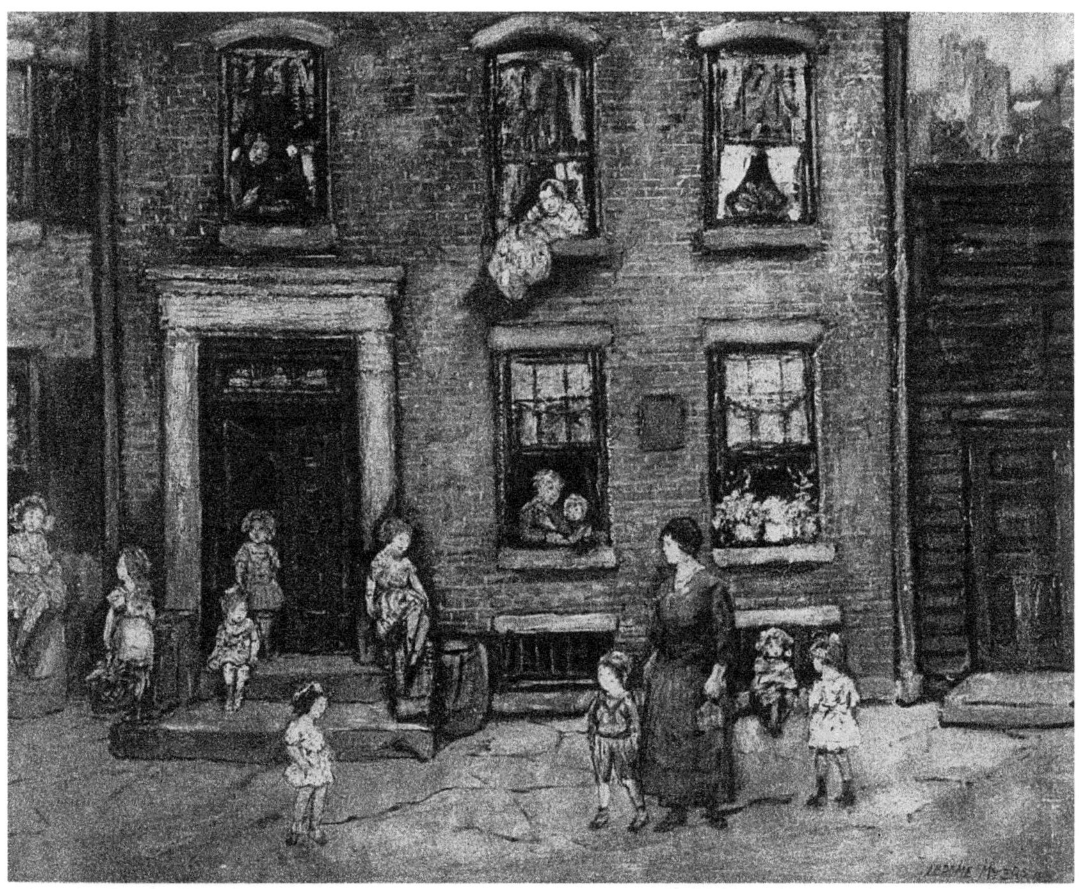

8.1 Jerome Myers (1867–1940), *East Side Children*, also referred to as *In Front of Tenement*. Jerome Myers, *The Artist in Manhattan* (New York: American Artists Group, 1940), 229.

enforced by adults. The paper of record reported that "all the police in New York could not keep these amphibious dock rats on land when the desire for a swim takes passion of them."[5]

The boys in this painting reflect that luxury and are having a grand time, all of their own choosing. Some are active—diving in, swimming, washing, playing—while some just sleep in the sun. Clothing is optional—nobody seems to care—and a few of the boys wear suits but most do not. There is a strong sense of camaraderie here; the boys are part of a community of their own making. Bellows understood what was happening here. Marianne Doezema insightfully pointed out the difference between the title of this painting and another of Bellows' works, *River Rats*: "While 'kids' behaved mischievously, they were thought capable of possessing redeeming qualities. By contrast, river or dock rats were thought to be irretrievably subsumed by temptation and vice."[6]

This subject matter—a frank and joyous painting of one part of a child's life in the city— was unprecedented, and caused reaction. Some caught the point of the painting; a 1912 review of Bellows' work requested that readers see for themselves "if the very joy of pure existence is not its central idea." Joseph E. Chamberlain of the *New York Evening Mail*, on the other hand,

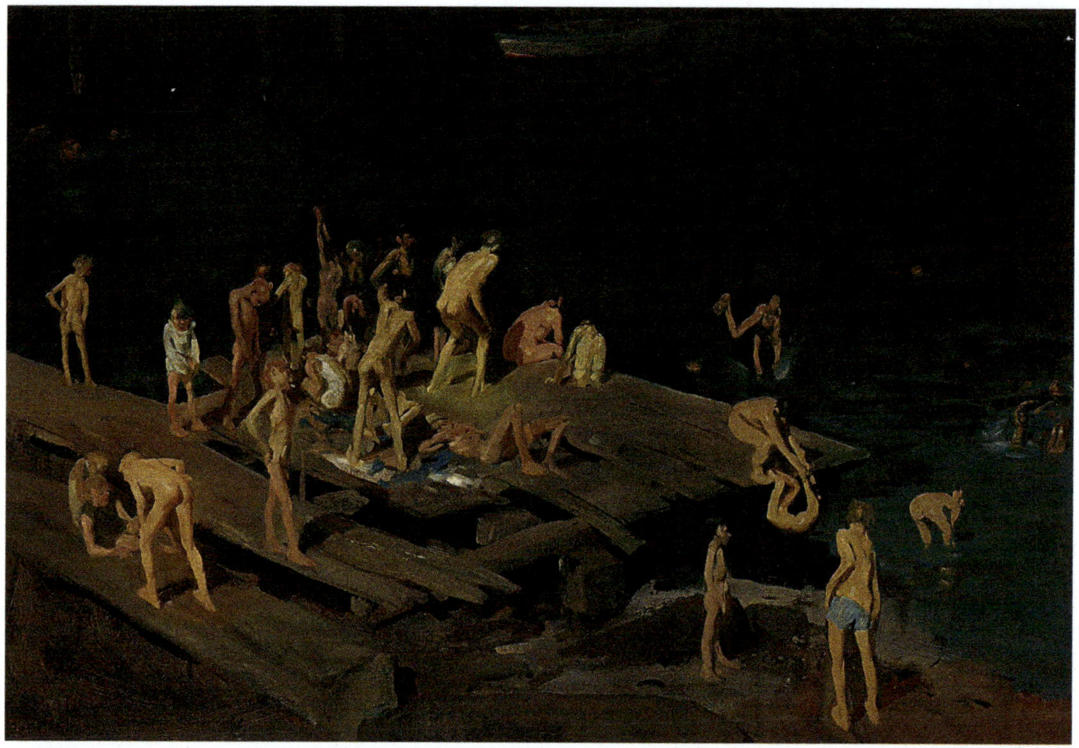

8.2 George Wesley Bellows (1882–1925), *Forty-Two Kids*, 1907, oil on canvas. Corcoran Collection, National Gallery of Art, Washington, DC, USA/Museum Purchase, William A. Clark Fund/Bridgeman Images.

captured the elite response to the Ashcan approach when he described Bellows' work as "a tour de force of absurdity . . . in which most of the boys look more like maggots than humans." Depicting children—even worse, working-class children—as having fun was a controversial notion to many New Yorkers.[7]

Above all, the painting that captured the Ashcan spirit of children enjoying the city is George Luks' *The Spielers* (fig. 8.3). This painting can be summed up easily: these city kids are having a lot of fun. They are grinning from ear to ear, their bodies keeping the beat and swinging in harmony. Whether it be the jitter buggers of the forties or the rock and rollers of the fifties, youngsters throughout time have been swept away while dancing. The only thing unique, therefore, is that this painting captures that giddiness, but the subject is street kids in New York City at the turn of the century. One 1915 journal offered the following review: "It is a joyous canvas, a picture to live with. For all their ragged attire, the two little maidens, locking their hands together, are as happy as princesses. Beneath their rags, their young bodies are responding . . . to a single emotion, to the unswerving, unalterable law of rhythm which acknowledges neither poverty nor wealth."[8]

The key to understanding what the Ashcan artists uniquely saw in the city comes out beautifully in *The Spielers*. The kids depicted here are typical of city youth: they don't know they're poor. They just know the world around them and make the most fun of it they can; there is no sense of envy or self-pity. They just love their life on the streets. That insight is something the reformers never quite understood.

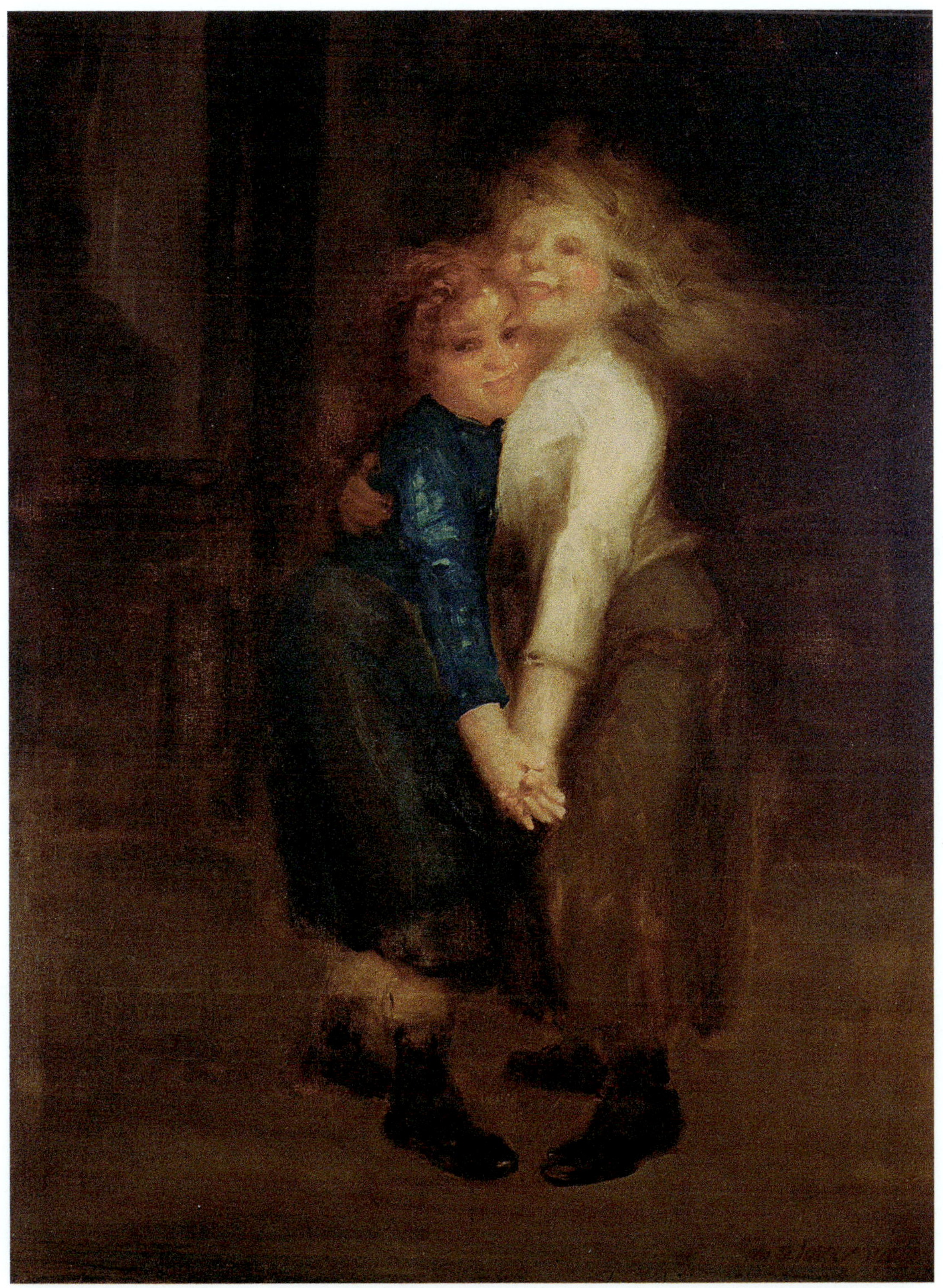

8.3 George Luks (1867–1933), *The Spielers*, 1905, oil on canvas, 36$\frac{1}{16}$ × 26$\frac{1}{4}$ inches; 91.6 × 66.68 cm. Addison Gallery of American Art, Phillips Academy, Andover, Massachusetts. Gift of anonymous donor. 1931.9. Photo credit: Addison Gallery of American Art, Phillips Academy, Andover, Massachusetts/Art Resource, New York.

Besides joy, the other great attribute of urban youth that the Ashcan artists captured was agency, the desire—and ability—of youngsters in the city to control their own destiny. In these art works, children were actors in the urban drama, with their own section of the script.

A number of scholars have discussed how children rejected the structured world of adult authority and instead created their own environment, where they decided the terms, mostly within the world of play. Howard Chudacoff, in his study of children at play, argued, "Dodging the control of parents has long been a part of growing up, but in the first half of the twentieth century resistance and the quest for autonomy flourished in ways that previously had not existed," primarily because of the new urban environment. Unlike the farm, where work and chores were constantly supervised, many urban youth, with parents toiling horrendous hours and school for just a short spell each day, had increasing amounts of free time to spend with their peers. This group "created a social arena in which youngsters subscribed to ideals and assumptions influenced by, but distinct from, those of parents, teachers, police, and clergy."[9]

This meant they rejected the adult world in favor of one of their own devising. As one youngster explained, "I can't go to the playgrounds now. They get on my nerves with so many men and women around telling you what to do." Instead, the child entered a world of adolescent structure where all the rules—whether of games, turf, or conduct—were locally devised, taught to the next generation of newbies to arrive, either by birth or off the boats from Europe. This also meant that their values—which were taught on the playground and enforced—set out what was ethical and acceptable behavior in *their* world.[10] Young people in the city, marginalized by adults of all classes, managed to create an alternative world just as ably as any novelist writing a best-selling series. These kids defined the players and what role to assign to each one, laid our spatial boundaries and defined zones just as surely as any geographer or anthropologist. Above all they defined the rules of their community, the most important element of any society.

A child's life in the city, in other words, was excellent training for life in a modern, industrialized democracy. As I wrote in an earlier work, "play taught even the very young how to create their own social system and how to devise rules so that the system worked to the benefit of everyone involved. . . . [they] received their first training in stability and community while playing on the urban side streets." In addition, because the small group was in charge, "children's games taught them the basics of small group democracy."[11]

Two works by George Wesley Bellows capture this culture. The appropriately named 1906 painting *Kids* clearly takes place in an urban setting, albeit a private one (*fig. 8.4*). This is no public, supervised park but rather a getaway where youth can congregate on their own terms out of sight of their adult antagonists. The lad on the far right, for example, smokes a cigarette. Others stand individually, while some are in a group, chatting. On the left a pair of older ones are taking one of their juniors in hand, quite literally, applying the discipline of the peer group. This is a close, intimate portrait of a city kid's world, drawn with empathy and respect.

The other work relevant to this discussion is *Paddy Flannigan* (*fig. 8.5*, pg. 134). Judging from his attire (or lack thereof), this urban youth comes from modest circumstances and is already working as a newsboy. Yet, this is a study in defiance. The thrust-out hips, the direct gaze, all denote the sense that young Paddy will not accept guff from anyone, at least not without a fight; he is master of his own destiny. One study called this "a canvas that brims with humor, impertinence, and audacity."[12]

A woman's life in the city was another prime topic for Ashcan school artists. They saw women—working-class, urban women—as a beautiful subject unto themselves, and in capturing that beauty, they presented a unique critique of American society, separate from what appeared in *The Masses*, which depicted females solely as capitalism's victims. As Sloan noted, "I am more interested in the human beings themselves than in schemes for betterment." Patricia Hills, in

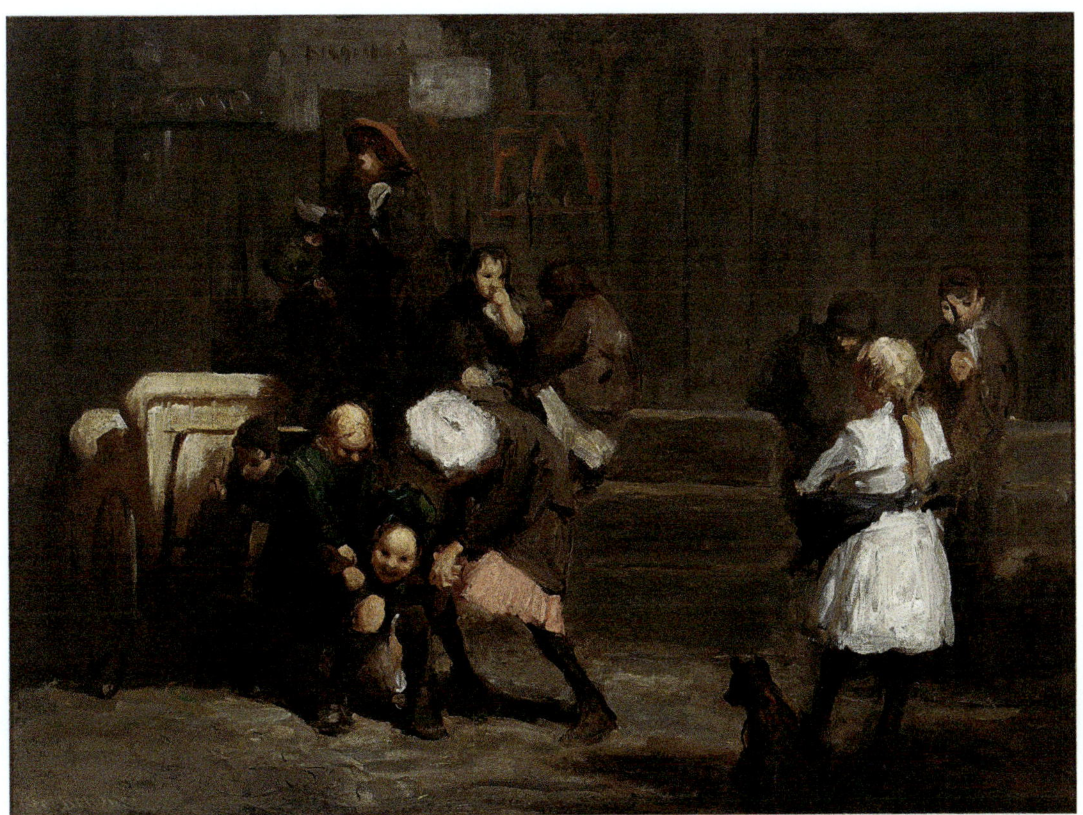

8.4 George Wesley Bellows (1882–1925), *Kids*, 1906, oil on canvas, 32.37 × 42.37 inches; 82.23 × 107.63 cm. Virginia Museum of Fine Arts, Richmond. The James W. and Frances Gibson McGlothlin Collection.

her pioneering article on that artist and working-class women, spoke of "his choice of women as subjects—those joyous, spontaneous women. . . . These women have been emancipated by the artist through his art, and they represent the smiling aspects of what everyday life might be." Sloan and his colleagues saw women as human, not ideal, but still beautiful. Their beauty lay not in their education or dress or bearing; instead, it emerged from their sheer humanity. Sloan defined art as "simple truth as felt by the painter."[13]

In truth, their focus on women was not unique. Portraits of elite women were *en vogue* for that class, and paintings of grand boulevards usually displayed elegant ladies strolling with their escorts. At the other end of the political spectrum, leftist artists drew women solely as the ultimate victims of capitalism, downtrodden and despairing. In neither case, however, were women seen as possessing autonomy, of controlling the terms of their own existence.

Two aspects of women's existence as captured by Ashcan artists at this time, therefore, became unique. There is no snobbism or class attitudes in their works. Women are women, regardless of their bank accounts or how much space they command; rather, they know how to adapt to their world in a way that granted them the most autonomy and pleasure.

First, these artists portrayed working-class women as enjoying parts of their life, as most people do in real life. On May 13, 1908, Sloan wrote in his diary about a walk up Eighth Avenue, how he

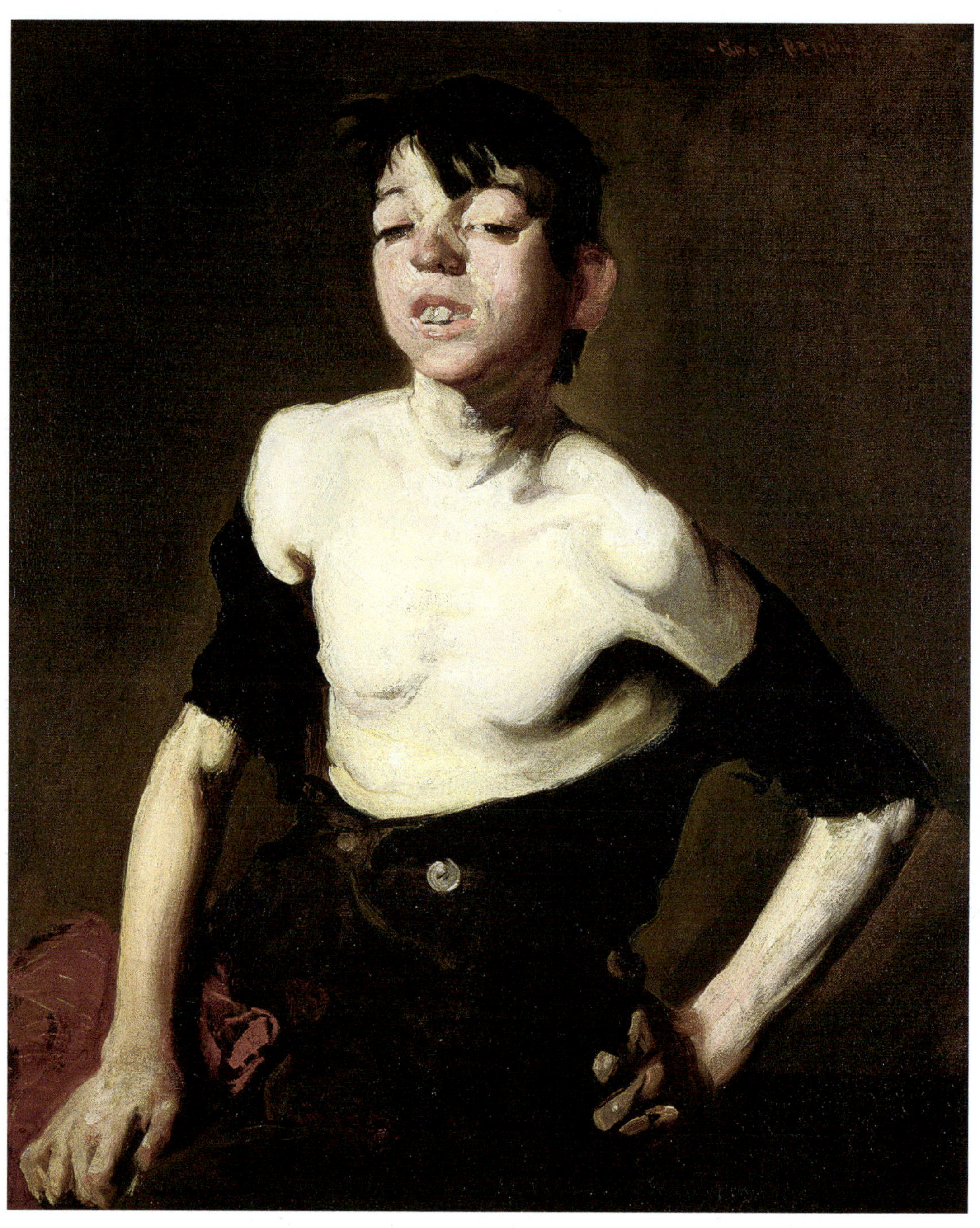

8.5 George Wesley Bellows (1882–1925), *Paddy Flannigan*, 1905, oil on canvas. Private collection/photo © Christies Images/Bridgeman Images.

"stopped and watched some tough working girls around a small lunch cart. Very amusing and fine with animal spirits." One critic of George Luks' art argued, "What really distinguishes Luks from the many other artists . . . was his singular attitude towards urban women. . . . At a time when female portraiture still meant images of aristocratic ladies . . . languid maidens . . . and pillars of virginity. . . . Luks' choices and approach seem remarkable, and still do. He . . . invested humble and unattractive subjects with a simple, unpretentious dignity."[14]

This sense, of working-class liveliness, best came through in Sloan's etching *Return from Toil* (*fig. 8.6*). In many ways, this could have been a classic depiction of the horrors of working-class capitalism. On their way home from a long day in the sweatshops, the women walk slowly, their shoulders slumped, their lives a torture.

While Sloan was well aware of such conditions and never denied this aspect of working-class life, he also recognized that other possibilities occurred, worthy of high art. As one biographer

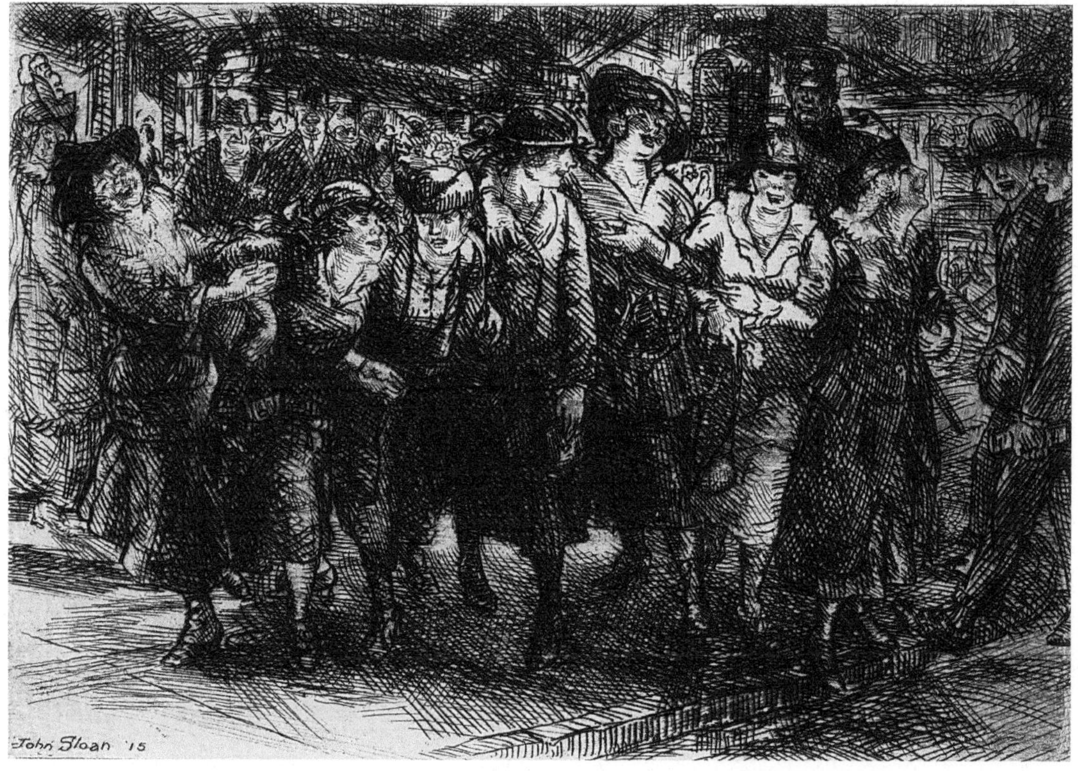

8.6 John Sloan (1871–1951), *Return from Toil*, 1915, etching, plate: 4¼ × 5⅞ inches, 10.8 × 14.9 cm; sheet: 5¹⁄₁₆ × 7⅞ inches, 12.9 × 20 cm. Gift of Mrs. Harry Payne Whitney, 1926. Metropolitan Museum of Art, New York. © 2016 Delaware Art Museum/Artists Rights Society (ARS), New York. Image © The Metropolitan Museum of Art. Image source: Art Resource, New York.

wrote, "Sloan perversely insists that not every young woman who works hard for a living goes home at the end of the day with her friends looking like a poster child for the IWW."[15]

Instead, these young women are happy. Clearly working class by their clothing, they are enjoying the end of a long, hard day, and of the freedom and relaxation they can now enjoy and use as they see fit. Also of importance is the group; one of the key aspects of working-class life that these artists drew was community, the sense of support and friendship available to these young women. Camaraderie, in other words, did not just emerge in paneled sanctums with restricted club membership; rather, it was just as likely to rise from a shop floor. The glue that cements these associations is clearly on display here: laughter, shared experiences, stories and secrets revealed, even gossip and comparisons of members of the opposite sex.

Even more unprecedented was the urban setting. In his diary, Sloan wrote about the city all around him, how he found "doorways of tenement houses. Grimy and greasy door frames looking as though huge hogs covered with filth had worn the paint away and replaced it with matted dirt. . . . Healthy-faced children, solid-legged, rich, full color to their hair. Happiness rather than misery in the whole life. Fifth Avenue faces are unhappy in comparison." The people he painted knew how to enjoy their lives, no small accomplishment given very real material limits. Their ability to recognize this represented another insight about urban life the Ashcan painters displayed in their art.[16]

Two of Sloan's works capture aspects of the urban, female lifestyle. His 1915 drawing *The Bachelor Girl* is a study in solitary tranquility (*fig. 8.7*). The setting is urban working class: a tight, narrow room, with a single lamp, and a coffee pot on a stand; a working girl's hat rests on the bed. She holds up a dress, possibly to wear tomorrow. Yet, there is a quietness here, no sense of turmoil, or even hardship. Her face is hard to read, but there is no sense of trouble, no furrowed brow. It is just a quiet night for a single woman in the city, with the same sense of peace as might be found in a scene of a farmer's cabin at eventide.

The importance of women's friendships, in an urban setting, are on display in John Sloan's *Sunday, Women Drying Their Hair* (*fig. 8.8*, pg. 138). This is an intensely urban scene. The only place many people in New York City had to get light and air was the rooftop, and this is where these women have congregated. It seems sooty and congested, framed by brick walls and clotheslines. Yet the women are happy; it is probably Sunday, their only day off, so they are enjoying a thorough cleanup, followed by a relaxing moment with friends. It is hardly a middle-class setting, yet these women are sharing a moment with friends, just as their later counterparts would do while relaxing in a beauty parlor.

Two aspects of city women's lives, in particular, defied the middle-class culture and morality of that era. In this view of life—which had prevailed for over a century—women were properly rural or else conventional middle class, in both cases limited to serving as custodians of the hearth and as guardians of the family. They watched over their domains like a jailer his charges, and made sure everything remained in order.

Now, as one scholar explained, there "was an acute awareness that rapid industrialization and urbanization had profoundly undermined the traditional role and status of women." Thus, their images of these females were particularly radical; showing them in settings that were vibrant, lively, and less than immaculate, was a shocking departure.[17]

Sloan renders this environment in *The Women's Page* (*fig. 8.9*, pg. 139). The scene is—to be blunt—messy. Clothes are strewn on the floor, hose are drying at the window, and the child is running amok. The woman lounges half-dressed, hardly prepared for the day. There is little of middle-class decorum here. And she does not seem to care in the slightest; this is her home, she has made it to fit her resources, tastes, and needs, and seems relaxed in it.

Yet, there is another vision here. The female at the center of things is reading the paper, usually the activity of men, who had to be aware of commerce and news. In the city, however,

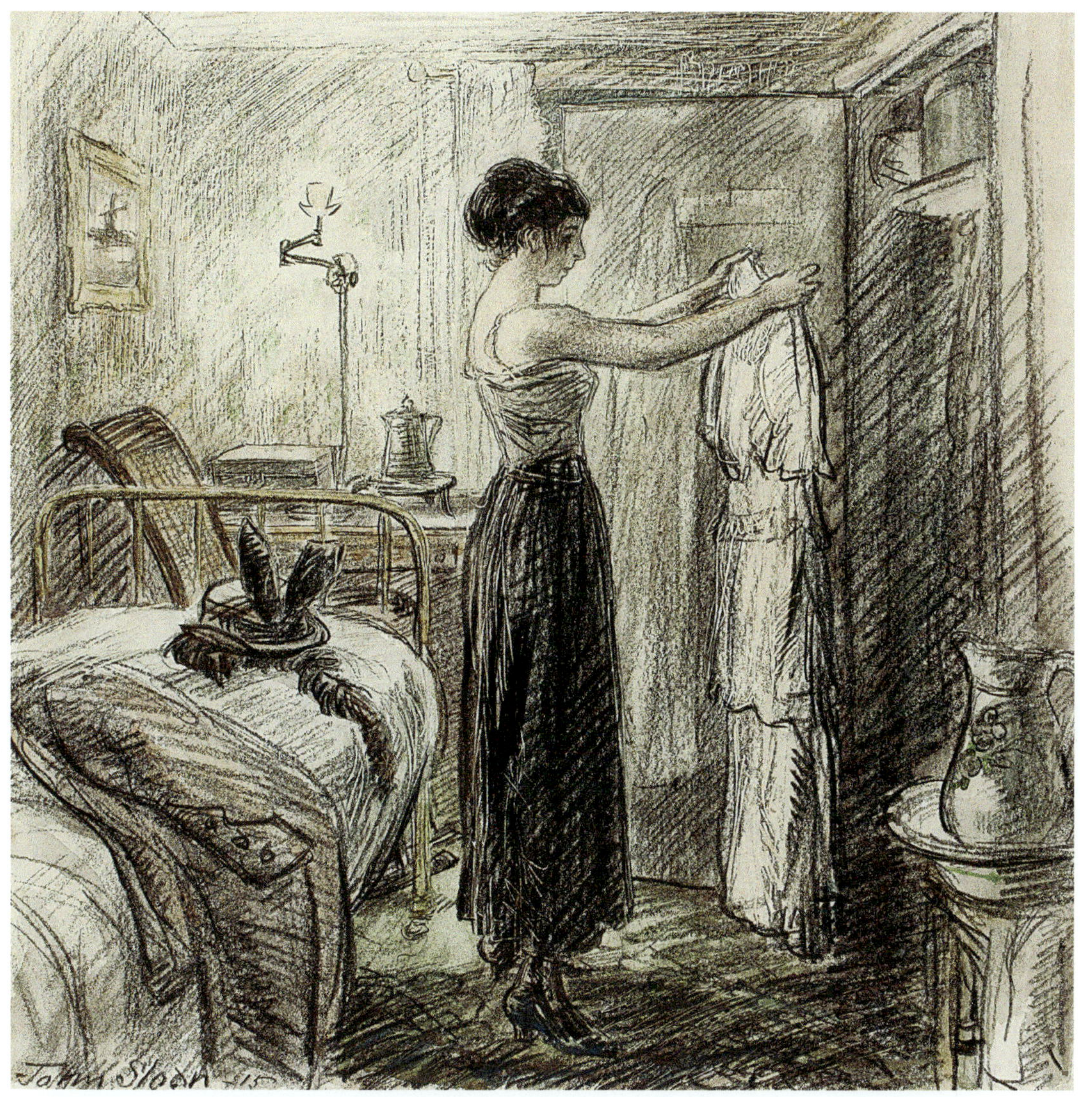

8.7 John Sloan (1871–1951), *The Bachelor Girl*, 1915, black crayon and watercolor, with scratching, over touches of graphite, on ivory wove paper, laid down on cream wove paper, 355 × 355 mm. *The Masses* 6 (February 1915): 6. Oliver Shaler Swan Memorial Collection, 1941. The Art Institute of Chicago.

women share this activity. She also seems to be reading ads for dresses; this is a depiction of a consumer as well. Women in the city defy convention in so many ways; for them the urban life is powerful, engaging, and highly unconventional.

An even greater challenge came in the form of women's sexuality. To the middle-class mind, any depiction—any mention—of this was taboo. As Mark Connelly, in his study of the oldest profession, accurately explained, "potentially all sexual activity unsanctioned by marriage could be characterized as prostitution."[18]

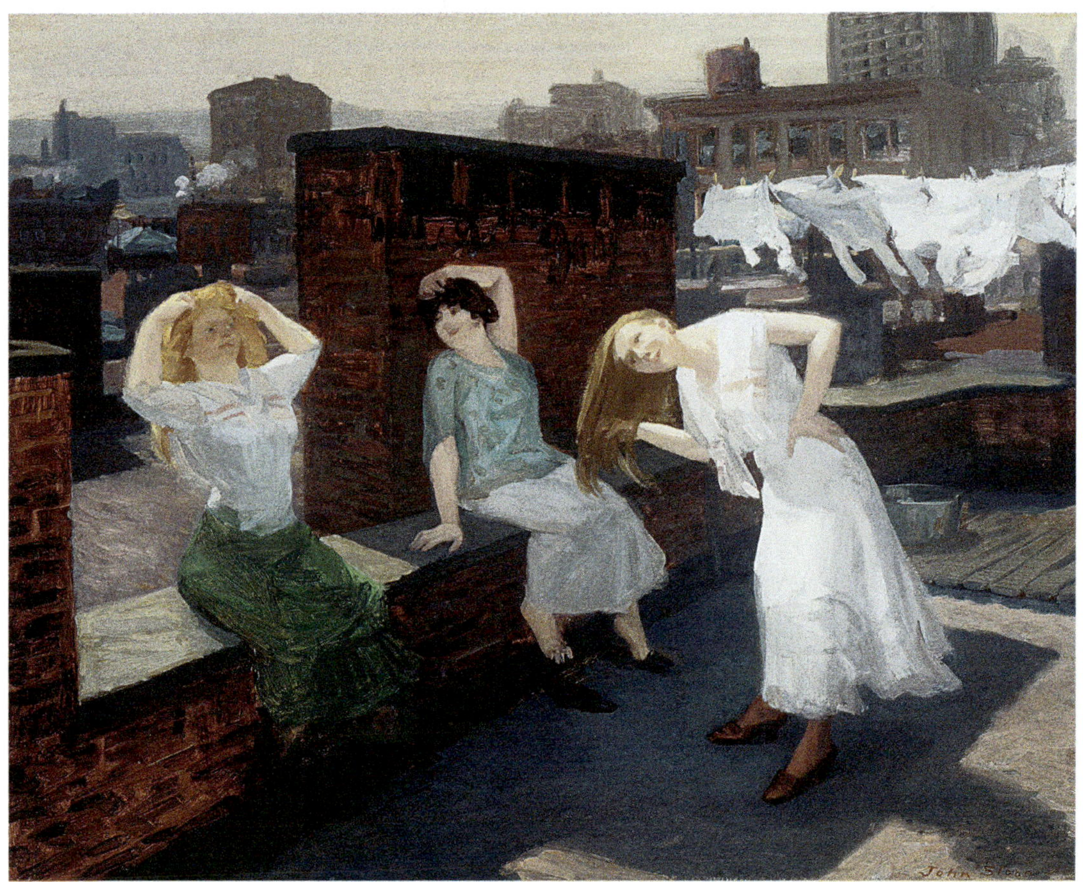

8.8 John Sloan (1871–1951), *Sunday, Women Drying Their Hair*, 1912, oil on canvas, 26⅛ × 32⅛ inches; 66.4 × 81.6 cm. Museum purchase (1938.67). Addison Gallery of American Art, Phillips Academy, Andover, Massachusetts. Photo credit: Addison Gallery of American Art, Phillips Academy, Andover, Massachusetts/Art Resource, New York.

In so many ways, urban life rejected this narrowness. Women also responded to the city by becoming, like men, flaneurs, strolling consumers of the urban spectacle. Other attractions included all the arcades selling things, and the bright lights of new entertainment forms. In 1915 the mother of Eugenia Kelly, scion of a banking family, had her daughter arrested to save her from a life of urban debauchery. Blaming the nightclub life for a debutante's decline, mama told how her offspring got home at three and four in the morning; when confronted, young Ms. Kelly replied, "Why, if I didn't go to at least six cabarets a night. . . . I would lose my social standing."[19]

A woman's role in the city had become a reversal of conventional wisdom. The females depicted in the Ashcan school artworks were frequently sexual, casual and careless about it. It was just part of everyday life, yet in a culture that had heretofore rejected the idea that women could share this need.

Sloan drew this attitude with his 1905 work *Turning Out the Light* (*fig. 8.10*). This is a New York apartment, cramped and cluttered. The woman on the bed is kneeling and about to turn

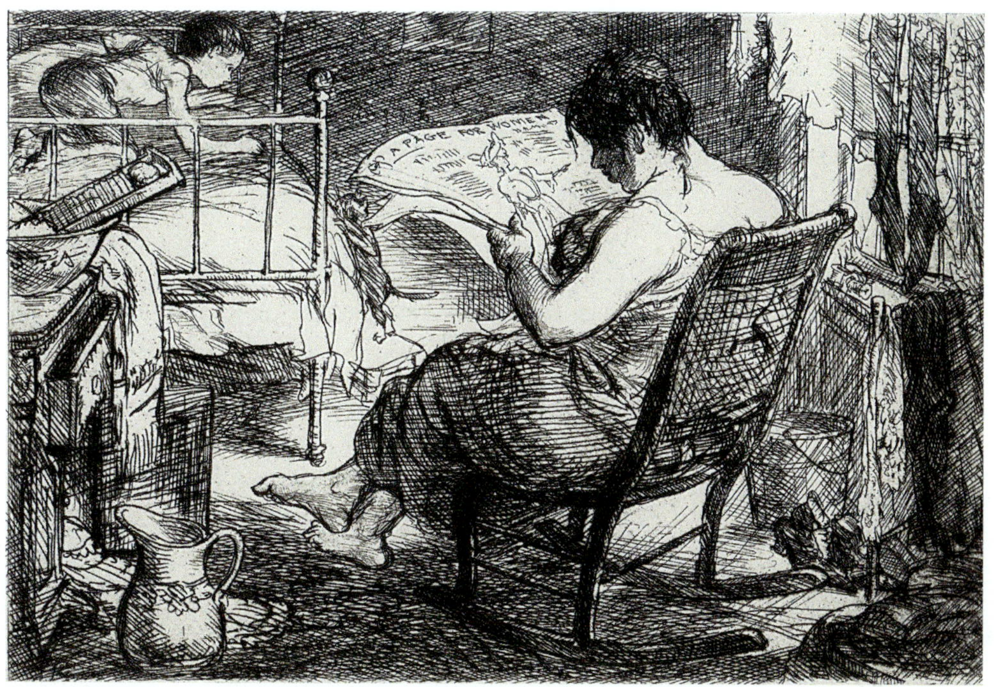

8.9 John Sloan (1871–1951), *The Women's Page*, 1905, etching. Detroit Institute of Arts, Detroit, Michigan/Gift of Mr. and Mrs. Bernard F. Walker. © 2016 Delaware Art Museum/ Artists Rights Society (ARS), New York.

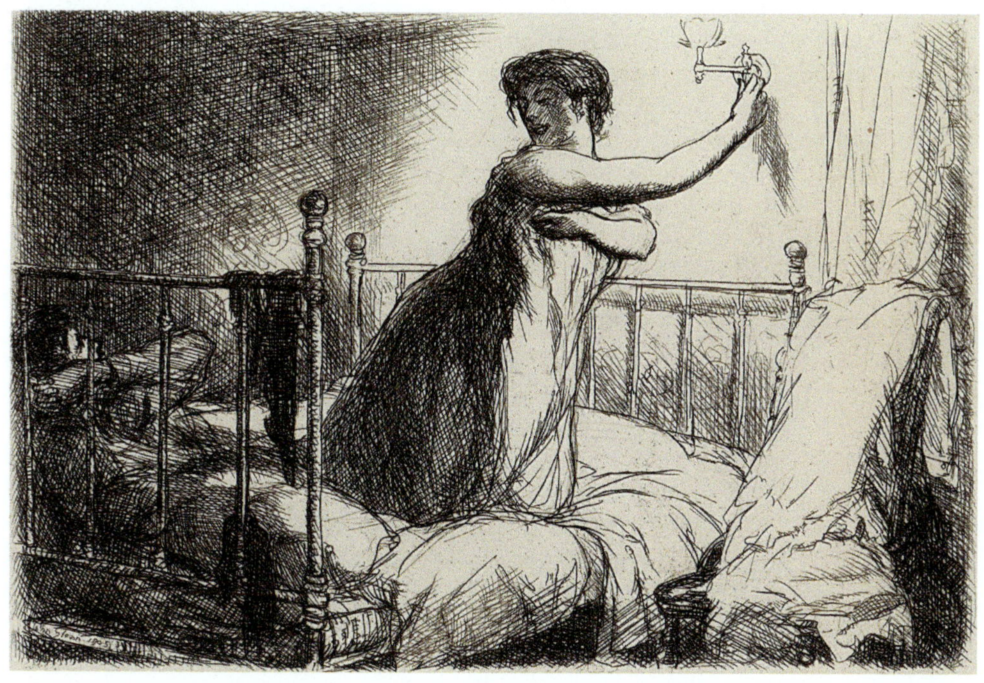

8.10 John Sloan (1871–1951), *Turning Out the Light*, 1905, print, 7 × 5 inches. Museum of the City of New York, New York. © 2016 Delaware Art Museum/Artists Rights Society (ARS), New York.

out the light; she holds her bedclothes loosely with her left hand and is about to drop these garments to disrobe. Her expression is one of affection, and her glance is to the foot of the bed, where a gentleman companion lounges. It is clear an assignation is about to begin, a scandalous subject for a painting, yet no one seems troubled in the slightest. The Ashcan depiction of women's life in the city was radical indeed.

The Ashcan approach to maleness can be summed up by explaining that they depicted the urban men's sporting environment, the bachelor subculture. This was a working-class environment that extolled competition in fields other than business, such as sport, gambling, drinking, wenching, and above all fisticuffs. The city was essential to its creation, since it provided the density in which, alone, such a development could arise, while also generating the market that formed the foundation for modern commercial sports. At the same time, it played off of broader American traditions; as Teddy Roosevelt explained it, from his youngest days, he "felt a great admiration for men who were fearless and who could hold their own in the world, and I had a great desire to be like them." The Ashcan artists picked up on this, and as Rebecca Zurier pointed out, they "defined art in terms of manliness."[20]

There were a range of formats they could explore. John Dos Passos wrote of the working man's lounge, the cheap restaurants that "smelled merrily of fried potatoes and cocktails and cigars and cocktails. It was hot and full of talking and sweaty faces." Or the saloon, where "a mottled beery smell came out through swinging doors. Inside the barkeep's face was like a russet apple on a snug mahogany shelf." Peter Baldwin bluntly declared, "The quintessential place of male leisure was the tavern."[21]

Sloan captured this world in *McSorley's Bar* (*fig. 8.11*). In later years this became a New York landmark, a historic watering hole that came to be frequented by artists, students, and yuppies. But in Sloan's time it was a classic men's tavern. Mementos of their exploits—of local teams and of the bar's heroes—crowd the walls in classic Victorian fashion. Males of all classes gather in a place like this—note the middle-class gent on the left, the workmen on the right— enjoying a world in which their gender, not their class is the prerequisite for admission to the club. Once a member, however, there are all kinds of rights. The folks on the right seem to have a mild disagreement—note the pointed finger—but no fight seems imminent. Once you're a local, one of the boys, it's all within the family, all handled by the comfortable male culture and its rules and ways.

Above all, the Ashcan artists adored the boxing scene and its place in the urban male world. As one chronicler of American boxing observed, "Prize fighting engendered a male aesthetic . . . displaying manliness, fair play, and finely developed physical skills." For the working-class world, in particular, abused by industrialization and monopoly capitalism, it permitted a display of "the old values of mutuality, reciprocity . . . bloodlust, prowess, and honor." It was manliness personified, a call of defiance in the face of economics, since "the ring elevates heroes and antiheroes who take their destinies in their own hands, who succeed through sheer will and ability, and whose struggles dramatize the humbler conflicts in all of us." Even better, in contradiction to Social Darwinism, this was an immigrant, urban, working-class phenomenon, with champions from every neighborhood, every ethnic group. The proper classes showed up as spectators, not as actors; one writer in *American Magazine* in 1909 gently described his titillation, at "such a contest as I was privileged to see the other night and not feel a thrill in the heart."[22] This was masculinity preserved in the face of a changing world—of anonymous factory jobs and backroom office tedium—that increasingly devalued it.

Though other Ashcan artists such as William Glackens tackled this subject,[23] the critical name was George Wesley Bellows. This should not surprise anyone, since he remains the greatest painter of boxing in the history of this country.

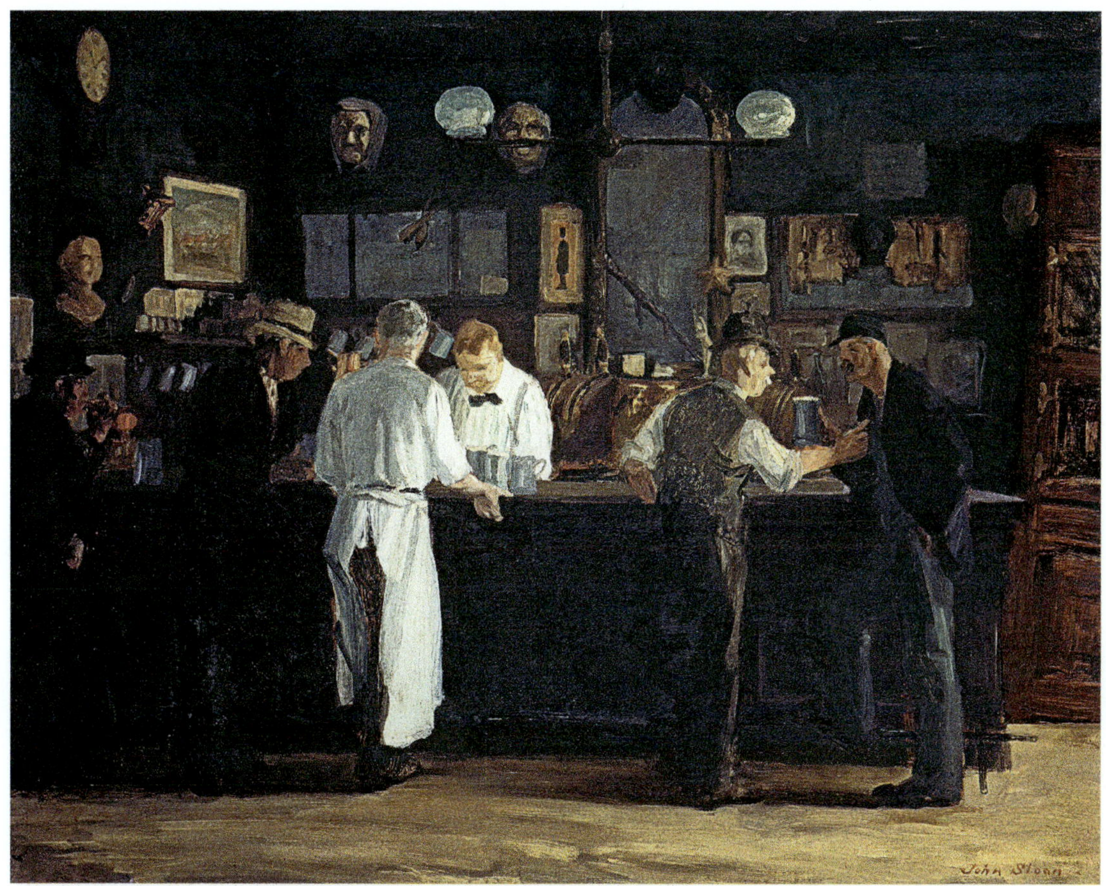

8.11 John Sloan (1871–1951), *McSorley's Bar*, 1912, oil on canvas. Detroit Institute of Arts, Detroit, Michigan/Founders Society purchase, General Membership Fund/Bridgeman Images.

Unlike his majestic pictures of industrial sites, Bellow's boxing images are up-close, personal, incredibly dynamic. The viewer can smell the sweat and the salts, hear the crowd and the grunts of protagonists. In these paintings, "Bellows' crowds press in with excitement and passion; his boxers clash in awkward and intense confrontation. Rather than the scientific approach of an anatomist and precarious draftsman, these paintings reveal the eye and hand of a journalist himself engaged in the heat of the moment." A 1912 critic observed, "It is brutal realism . . . in its strongest terms. The painter reminds one of the man who has learned all the forceful adjectives in a language and then hurls them out to express his opinion, regardless of the finished sentence." Bellows himself grunted, "I don't know anything about boxing. I am just painting two men trying to kill each other."[24] That rawness meant a great deal to men who were frantic, amid industry and offices, to reverse the trend away from masculine strength and individuality. The boxing ring served as a reassertion of traditional prowess, so often equated with muscles and the successful command of violence.

This drama grabs the viewer in *The Knock Out* (*fig. 8.12*). This is sheer violence, in so many ways. One fighter is defeated, senseless, and unable to get up, while the other still struggles to continue the beating, restrained by a struggling referee. Without him, this would be a murder. At the right spectators scream their encouragement, as bloodthirsty as anyone who cheered gladiatorial contests in the Roman coliseum. One catalog of Bellows' paintings claimed, "That Bellows captured on paper the heat and smell of the ring, the haze of cigar smoke, the noise and intensity of the event is a testament to this drawing's power." At the same time, it personifies the excesses of the male sporting culture at this time.[25]

Thus, in Bellows' boxing pictures, the context—the setting, the spectators—are as important as the fighters themselves. This quality is evident in the artist's masterpiece, *Stag at Sharkey's* (*fig. 8.13*). This picture could only have been conceived in a city. Tom Sharkey's athletic club was at Sixty-Fifth and Broadway, across the street from Bellows' studio. For a five-dollar monthly membership, one got in to see all the events going on there, fights both legal and otherwise. While the main arena seated three thousand, a smaller venue in the back provided for more intimate bouts.[26]

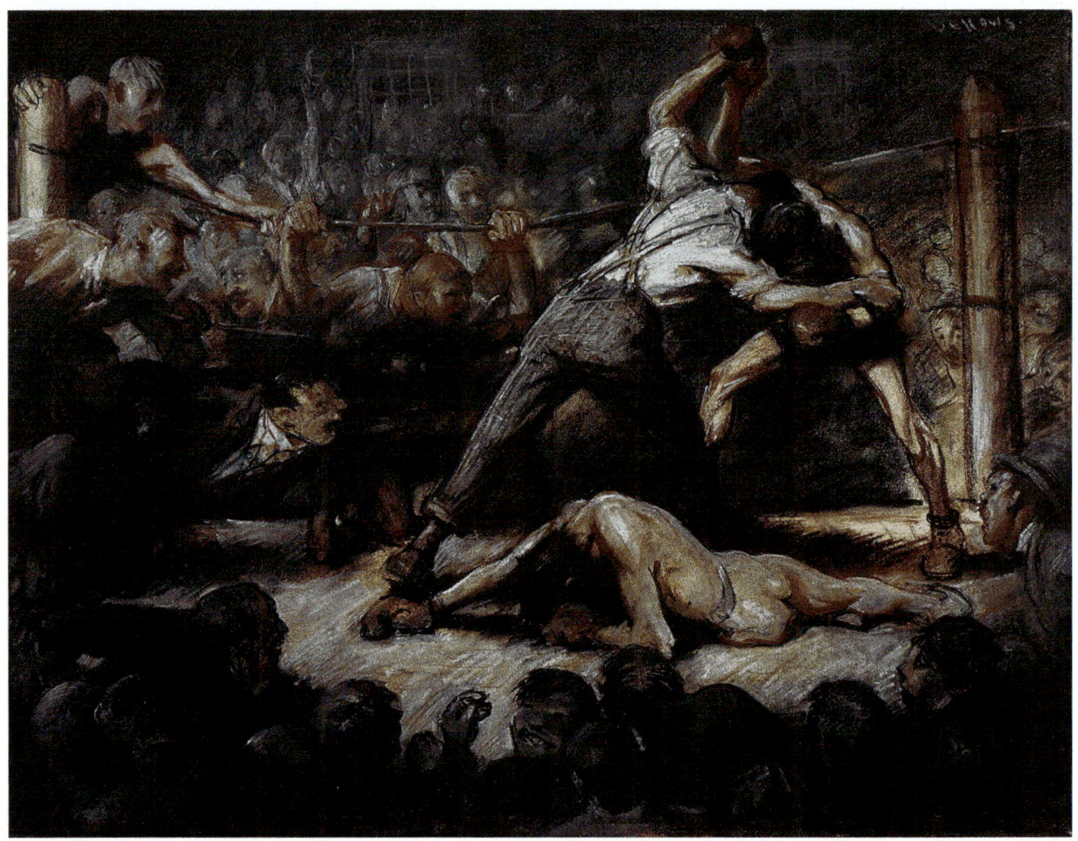

8.12 George Wesley Bellows (1882–1925), *The Knock Out*, 1907, pastel, ink, and graphite on paper, 53 × 70 cm; 21 × 27½ inches. Crystal Bridges Museum of American Art, Bentonville, Arkansas, 2010.82. Photography by Dwight Primiano.

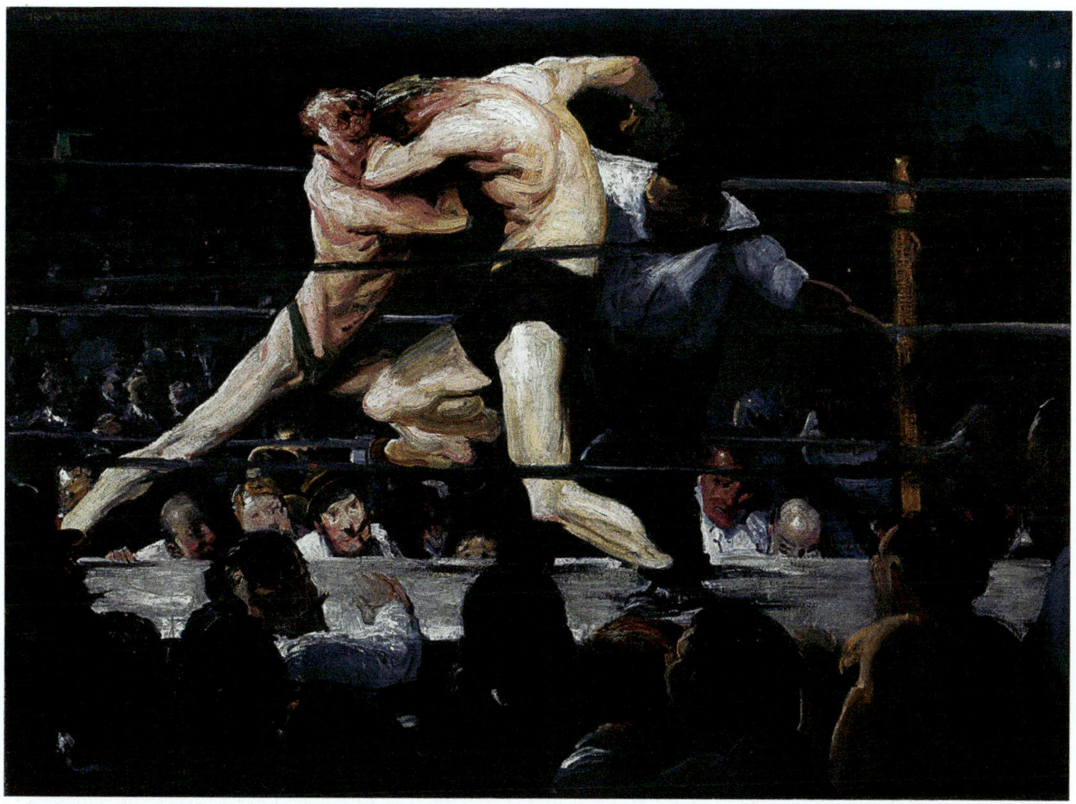

8.13 George Wesley Bellows (1882–1925), *Stag at Sharkey's*, 1909, oil on canvas, framed, 92 × 122.6 cm; 36¼ × 48¼ inches. Cleveland Museum of Art, Hinman B. Hurlbut Collection, 1133.1922. © Cleveland Museum of Art.

On the one hand, this is a private confrontation; two men hurl themselves at each other in combat, just like the animals cited in the title. This is an epic battle, all male ferocity; one can hear them roar as they lunge toward each other, fisted weapons pounding air and then flesh.

And yet, this is so much more. The crowd plays a major supporting role here. You not only see them; you hear them cheering for their respective champion. This is the all-male fraternity par excellence—there are no women in this picture, just men wrapped in the sheer joy of their own comradeship at being part of this event. This is not a passive activity; as the fight proceeds, they talk, argue, debate. Some of them may be nearly as close to blows as the two in the ring. As one of Bellows' biographers described the scene, "Around the ring is gathered as fine a collection of thugs and touts and hangers-on as Goya or Hogarth could have imagined." The world of urban working-class boxing, in other words.[27]

The Ashcan artists understood that the city was made up of its residents, all ages and genders. Armed with this knowledge, they drew the people who lived there, on the streets and in the apartments, on the job and at play. Above all, they grasped the beauty of working-class life, its vibrancy, and that this could naturally be the basis for great art. But by granting children, women, and men status—that they were fit subjects for painters—artists also realized, unconsciously, that they were drawing people with power. Working-class individuals had little wealth and controlled no railways, no giant corporations; they were not going to dinner with a Frick or a Morgan. Instead, with sheer creativity and buoyance, they had carved out parts of their lives where they could be in control, where they could determine their own fate and, in turn, enjoy it. Those moments were truly worthy of a painter's attention. The fact that the Ashcan artists uniquely grasped this fact, rather than dismissing it like the elites or ignoring it like the reformers, is what made this brief period of art worthy of being remembered.

CHAPTER NINE

LIFE IN THE ASHCAN CITY

THE ASHCAN SCHOOL INTRODUCED THE MODERN CITY TO THE ART WORLD—AND HELPED INTRODUCE it to America as well. They were the first artists to examine and detail modernism as it was breaking loose in the urban core and investigate its nuances. At a time when the country's— and even the industrialized world's—population was rapidly shifting from farms and villages to the urban centers, these painters were showing all of us what modern life, in all its complexity, not only looked like but what it *felt* like. In these documents you could not just *see* the city but almost *hear* it, *smell* it. And start to understand how these new Americans lived their lives.

Thus, the Ashcan artists recognized and understood the nature of the city, better than any creative force before them. Street corners and tenement rooms, the wide cast of characters, intimacy amid the din, they sensed all of this and put its essence into their art.

Above all, they realized that the key to the urban experience, its most unique feature, is *density*. People—*lots and lots of people* all around, in a limited space, is what makes the magic and the chaos that can simultaneously be a city. It provides the marketplace and, above all, the gallery of humanity that transform a rural zone into a metropolis.

This was a titanic change, a great leap into the modern world. The country was transforming from a rural to an urban society, one with masses of immigrants as well, both from overseas and from our own farmlands. The city was creating a new America, and density, the sense of having neighbors all around, was a key element of this. One 1911 article simply declared, "New York City is the example *par excellence* of concentration of population."[1]

Of course, too much density has the power to destroy life as well as invigorate it. As Jacob Riis noted, at the turn of the century parts of the Lower East Side had some of the highest occupancy rates in the world. According to the 1890 census, the Thirteenth Ward had a population per square mile of 274,432, while the Tenth Ward reached 334,080. Not all of Manhattan was like this. Overall, the island's density for that year was 73,299, an elevated but manageable figure. Thus, high but not insane density was the key to a successful urban environment.[2]

The writers caught on to the importance of this factor to creating a great city. John Dos Passos told about "hearing the yells of the children or the annihilating clatter of the L trains overhead or smelling the rancid sweet huddled smell of packed tenements," of "faces, hats, hands, newspapers jiggled in the fetid roaring subway car like corn in a popper." E. B. White, in his ode to the city, *Here Is New York*, explained how this tightness divides up in order to be personal and manageable, how "the city is literally a composite of tens and thousands of tiny neighborhood units." Each of these is a world unto itself, with friends and neighbors, a full range of retail services, no matter how compact the geography. He tells the story of a woman who moved to a new apartment, three blocks away. When she returns to her old grocer, "the proprietor was in ecstasy—almost in tears—at seeing her. 'I was afraid,' he said, 'now that you've moved away I wouldn't be seeing you any more.' To him, *away* was three blocks, or about seven hundred and fifty feet."[3]

This is what the artists drew on their easels. Art historian Rebecca Zurier wrote that Glackens "consistently drew crowds not as a vague mass viewed from a distance, but as something that could be seen—as a series of individual portraits that put faces on the thundering herd and gave viewers something to look at." An early critic dismissed George Wesley Bellows' work as "too much portrayed, too much literalism, too little left to the imagination, too harsh an insistence on the raw facts of a street scene." The emphasis is on exaggeration; there is "too much" of everything, the packed life that density provides. A biographer remarked, "Sloan created his own myth of New York—and by extension, all of modern urban life—as a place built to human scale, a magnet for human problems and new kinds of stimulation, a messy center of energy that affirmed life as inherently interesting and worthwhile through the very proximity of so many conflicting values and people." In 1919 an interviewer found that the view from John Sloan's studio "released to the artist's eyes as he gazed from roof to roof—old women were there hanging up clothes . . . young women sat on the coping washing their hair and drying it in the sunlight, children played games and lovers met in the moonlight. . . . early in the morning work-worn old folks came up with their knitting and sewing and gossiped happily for hours." As they looked out the window, Sloan told her he saw there "all the world. Work, play, love, sorrow, vanity, the schoolgirl, the old mother, the thief, the truant, the harlot. I see them all down there without disguise. These wonderful roofs of New York bring to me all of humanity." Their world was urban, and modern, and through their art was helping America adjust to this enormous change.[4]

A number of the Ashcan artists spoke to this quality. Moving to the back of a building, Ernest Lawson illustrates crowded life in *Harlem Flats (Back Lot Laundry)*; while the density is high in this image, it is still rendered with a humane eye (*fig. 9.1*). Clearly a great many people live here, judging by the amount of wash on the lines. Yet there is no sense of the despair captured in a similar scene in Riis' photographs; here the colors are bright, the sky is clear and blue, the few figures are not distressed.

By contrast, in William Glackens' *Patriots in the Making*, it is the density of a city street that is on display (*fig. 9.2*, pg. 148). A lot is going on here, and people are everywhere. America is learning about places new—and mysterious—to so many of its residents living on farms and in small towns. In this scene, the street is packed, with ambulances and fire trucks, with playgroups and mothers and a drunk in the lower right. But Glackens recognizes that city life is three dimensional; that is how crowded it is, how full of life. Several stories above the street, on the fire escapes, are the spectators and even some participants. While the family on the right seem to be just taking it all in, above them a man is agitated and letting everyone know. He appears to be waving a gun. No one knows how this will turn out. Cities are like that, both in Ashcan art and in real life.

If any picture captures this reality of density, it is John Sloan's *Roofs, Summer Night* (*fig. 9.3*, pg. 149). After my parents died, when I was going through the family pictures, the ones they took as young marrieds before the kids were born, I was struck by how many were shot on the roof. There were pictures with friends, in bathing suits, or all dressed up to go out on the town. When you lived in a small apartment in the Bronx, the roof was a great place to take

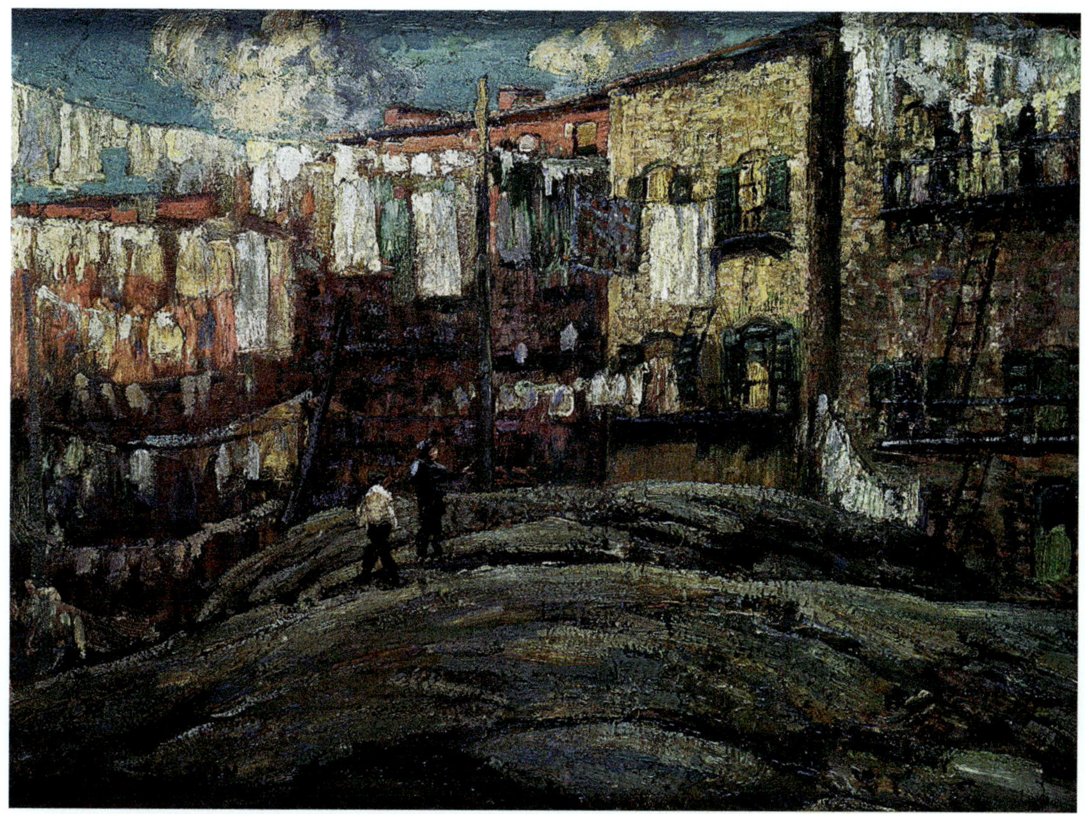

9.1 Ernest Lawson (1873–1939), *Harlem Flats (Back Lot Laundry)*, ca. 1907, oil on canvas, 18½ × 24⅛ inches; 47 × 61.3 cm. Huntington Library, Art Collections, and Botanical Gardens, gift of Kelvin Davis. © Courtesy of the Huntington Art Collections.

pictures. It provided space and light, with the sun as backdrop and as an essential ingredient for the film emulsion. As an article in the *New York Times* explained, roof tops are for "party-going, stargazing, baseball playing, nude sunbathing, pigeon keeping and kite flying."[5]

Or, in the case of this drawing, they provide air and maybe even a breeze on a hot night. The subjects are packed in here, and the circumstances are modest; bare bedding prevails. There are a lot of people on the tar-covered floor of the roof, whole families as well as single souls.

Yet, a serenity prevails. There is a warm, sleepy quality to this drawing, a feeling like your eyelids about to drop despite your best efforts otherwise. No sense of discord disturbs this tableau. The city is packed, yet restful.

This art also speaks to something else, the intimacy of high-density living. In some ways, only the very rich in the city can buy privacy; the immigrant novelist Anzia Yezierska, experiencing courtship in a tenement apartment full of borders, knew that "only millionaires can be alone in America." Or at least in New York.[6]

Even more, Sloan's work reveals something about this new society, makes an important observation. The people living here are developing new strategies wherein people with little private space are creating ways to still enjoy life, relax, achieve friendship, community, even intimacy.

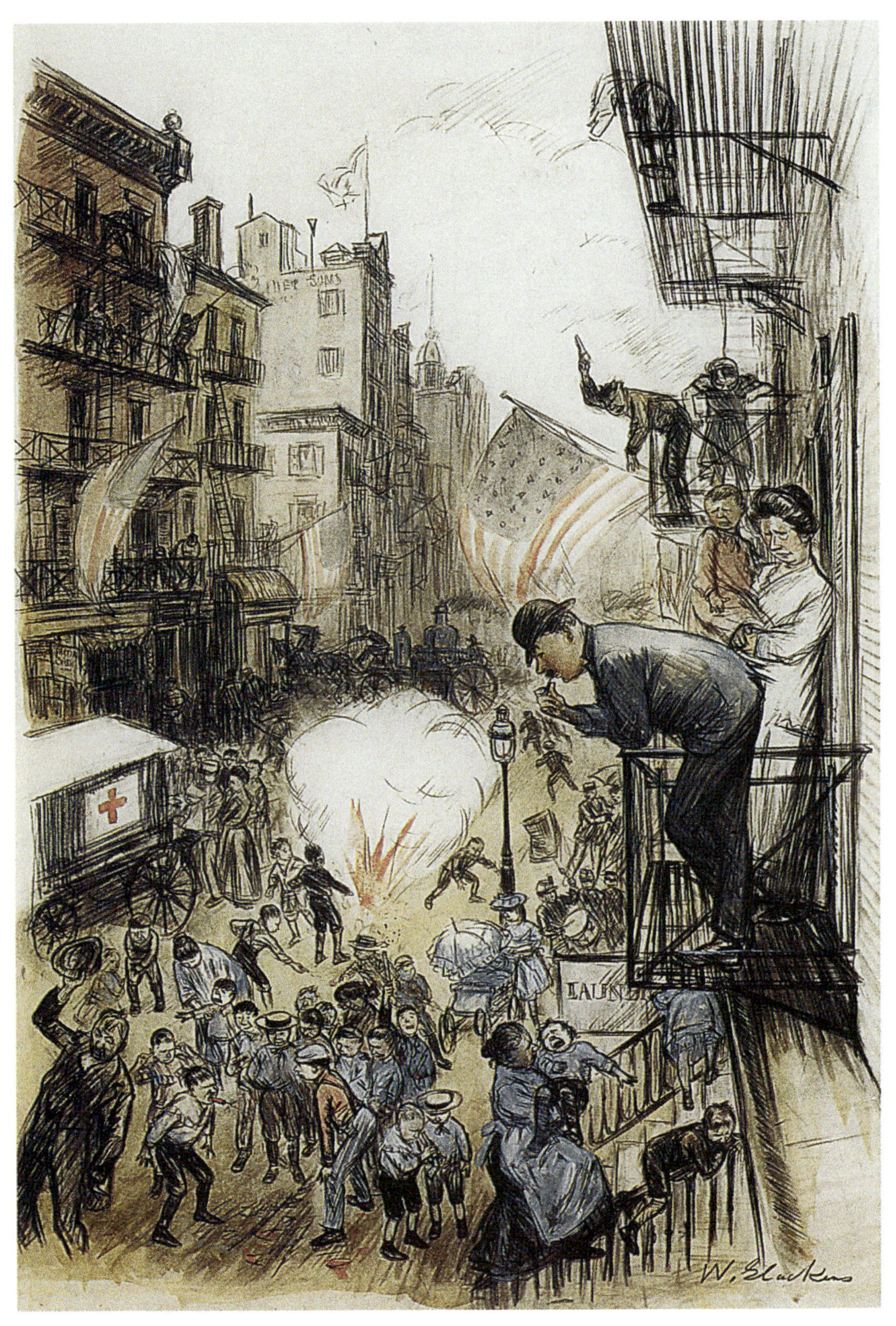

9.2 William Glackens (1870–1938), *Patriots in the Making*, 1907, charcoal and watercolor on paper, 81.28 × 63.82 cm; 32 × 25.13 inches. Originally on the cover of *Collier's*, July 4, 1907.

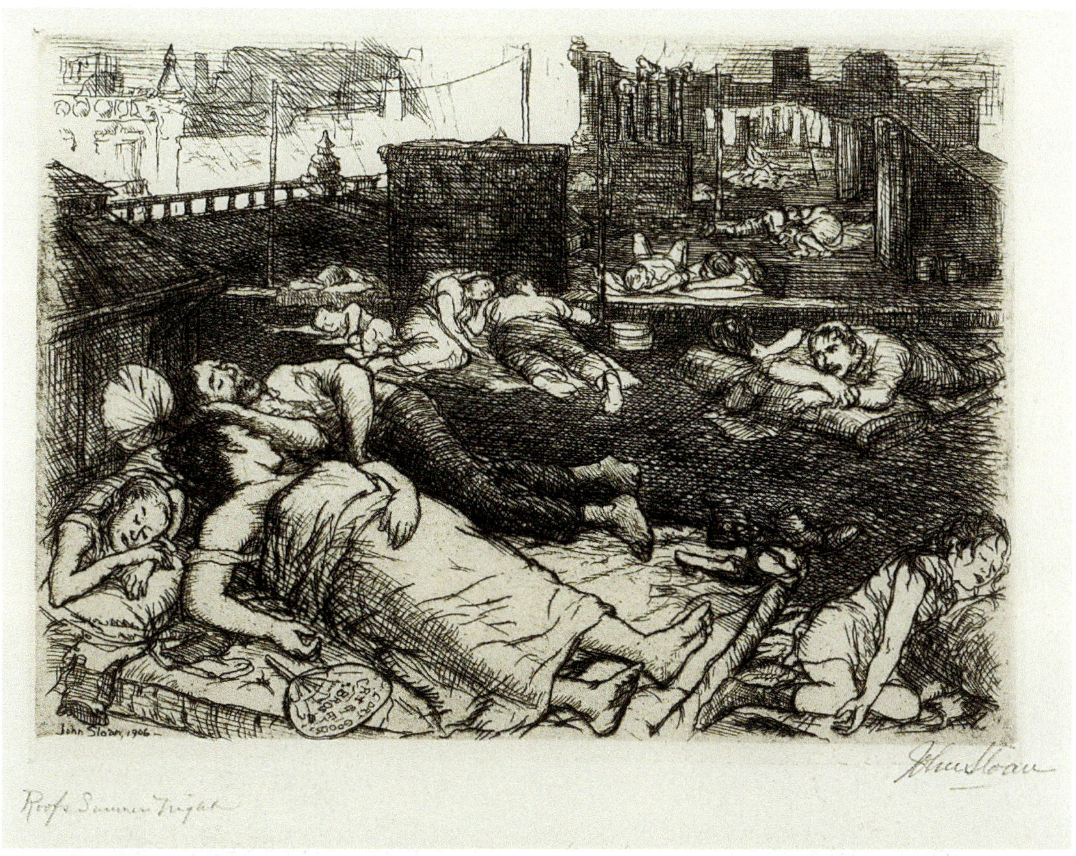

9.3 John Sloan (1871–1951), *Roofs, Summer Night*, 1906, etching on cream wove paper, 129 × 176 mm (image); 135 × 180 mm (plate); 252 × 318 mm (sheet). Gift of Mrs. Edward Porter, 1939.329, The Art Institute of Chicago. © 2016 Delaware Art Museum/ Artists Rights Society (ARS), New York.

Instead, the Ashcan artists celebrated the lack of middle-class virtues, made beautiful the enforced closeness. They recognized that the city forces people to do in public what in small towns or suburbs happens only behind closed doors. Whenever I'm in New York City I still see arguments, discussions, tears in public that I never expect to see in Los Angeles; when density is that high, everything is on display. There is just nowhere to go, other than the public sphere, especially for those impromptu, unguarded moments. Robert Snyder wrote about "the very public nature of life in the neighborhood. Socializing occurs not in the privacy of the parlor but on the sidewalk. Commerce draws people out of their apartments and into a wider community." Pène du Bois compared Ashcan art to the shocking novels of Theodore Dreiser, how "both have talked of formally forbidden subjects."[7]

In the urban world the private becomes public. To small-town proper society, this would denote economic and moral shortcoming, a display to one and all that these individuals were of a lesser sort. Ashcan artists, by drawing these scenes with sensitivity, taught that these environments were new but also civilized, and moral. You could live close by your neighbors yet still lead a decent existence. Something important was happening, and these artists pioneered in interpreting it.

Thus, lack of privacy creates multiple phenomena. On the one hand is a class issue—lack of income means lack of space, including personal space. But it is also an urban issue, in that one benefit is that it also facilitates people watching, the greatest attraction of the city. In many ways, high density is what makes all great cities so fascinating. If you live close to other people, you can see a lot, often a better drama than has appeared on any formal stage. Dense living means a loss of some qualities, but it provides a new array, often compulsively fascinating. In the city, people accustom themselves to the lack of space, figure out strategies to make life not only endurable but pleasurable.

No one understood this truth better than John Sloan. An "incorrigible window watcher," Sloan had access to "an array of roofs where tenement women hung out their wash and sometimes made love or slept on summer nights, there were back yards where stray cats took part in human dramas and there were animated windows, a dozen or a score."[8]

Three of Sloan's drawings capture this aspect of urban living. *Night Windows* celebrates the voyeuristic nature of being in Gotham (*fig. 9.4*). The scene is very crowded; there is not much air, but a lot is going on here. At the left the viewer can see in a window to the lighted

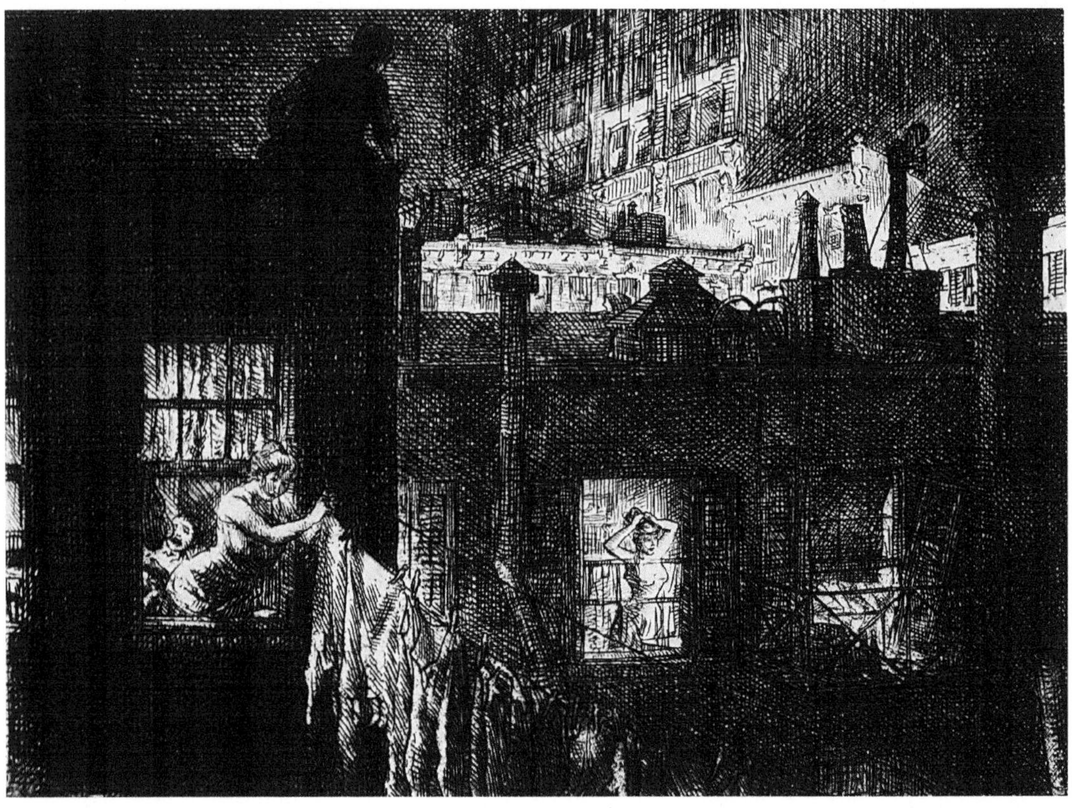

9.4 John Sloan (1871–1951), *Night Windows*, 1910 (etching), 5¼ × 7 inches. The Phillips Collection, Washington, DC, USA/Bridgeman Images. © 2016 Delaware Art Museum/ Artists Rights Society (ARS), New York.

apartment, the woman hanging clothes to dry, the man, further inside, grousing over some slight that only he may perceive. But just above, on the roof, is a shadowy figure, a watcher—and no stargazer, either; he is a voyeur. Instead, in the next building is a woman of modest attire, doing up her hair right in the window. Is this the only space she has? Does she covet a breeze, some fresh air? Or is she an exhibitionist? We have no idea, but know that she is the subject of the dark figure's curiosity, but what that interest is, is never clear. In the space of an alley, there is a multipart drama, a circus with many rings to peruse.

Moving inside, we learn about what life is like inside one of these apartments. There is not much space evident in *Man, Wife and Child* (fig. 9.5). Everything seems cramped here; kitchen goods are everywhere, there is no discernible space for dining, clothes spill on everything. Sloan himself described this as "a small family in scant quarters."[9]

The only thing in abundance, therefore, seems to be happiness. The couple are tripping the light fantastic (although their moves will be limited by space) and smiling merrily. Their daughter is enthralled by her parents' good cheer, happy as she offers comments. The message is clear; urban density does not automatically denote a dismal life. Quite the contrary.

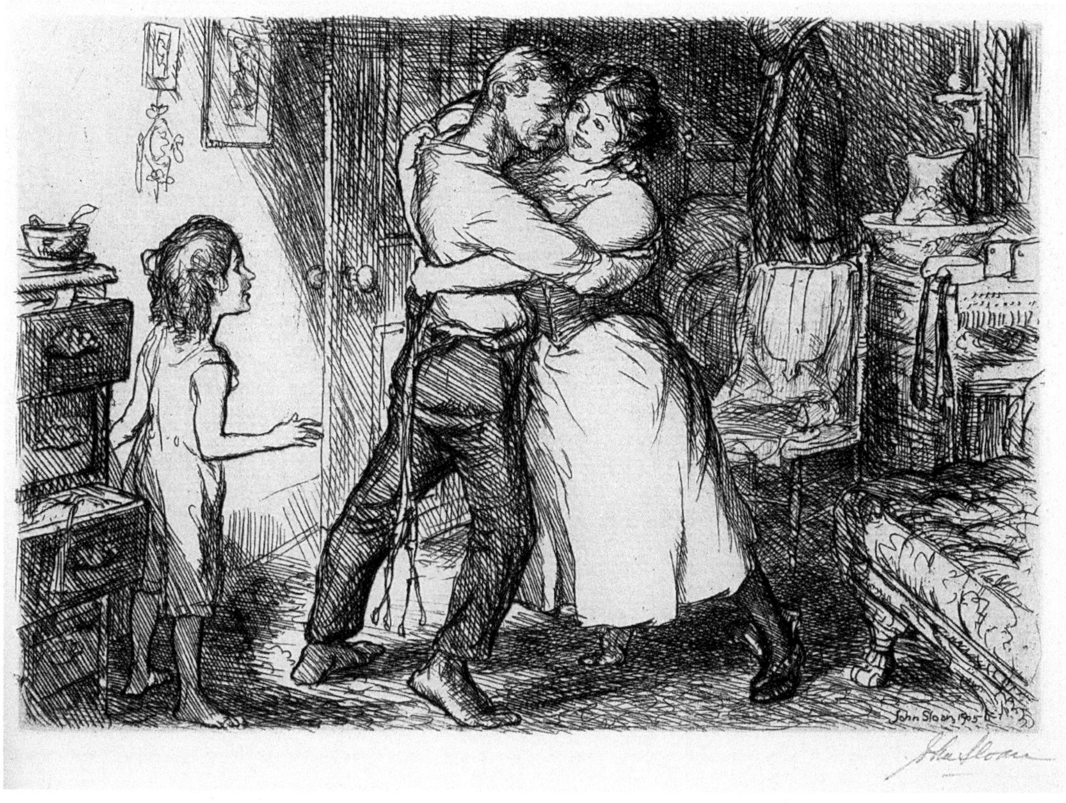

9.5 John Sloan (1871–1951), *Man, Wife and Child*, 1905, etching, sheet: 10 × 12¹³⁄₁₆ inches, 25.4 × 32.5 cm; platemark: 4⅞ × 6⅞ inches, 12.4 × 17.5 cm. Gift of Dr. and Mrs. Endre K. Brunner (Eleanor Carroll, Class of 1919). 1981.29. Davis Museum, Wellesley College. © 2016 Delaware Art Museum/Artists Rights Society (ARS), New York.

Finally, the most daring of them all, *Sunbathers on the Roof* (*fig. 9.6*). Although this work is decades later than the turn of the century, it has a timeless quality. Yet, to proper eyes, the scene is salacious. The two are clothed only in swimwear, perhaps undergarments. There is a sense that they might be lovers.

Because of the urban setting and the animal, however, this becomes a sweet moment. There is none of the abruptness of passion; they are chatting gamely with a cat, introducing themselves. While the city dominates the background, a retaining wall provides a measure of privacy. Life can go on with all the virtues of the parlor, amid brick and the din of the street. The great accomplishment of the Ashcan school was that it was able to overcome the prevailing middle-class culture to perceive and then render this important quality of the new urban lifestyle.

In so many ways, the Ashcan artists unpacked the multiple meanings of modern life in the metropolis. Another crucial aspect of everyday city living the Ashcan artists captured was diversity. High density pulls together in one place huge agglomerations of people; probability

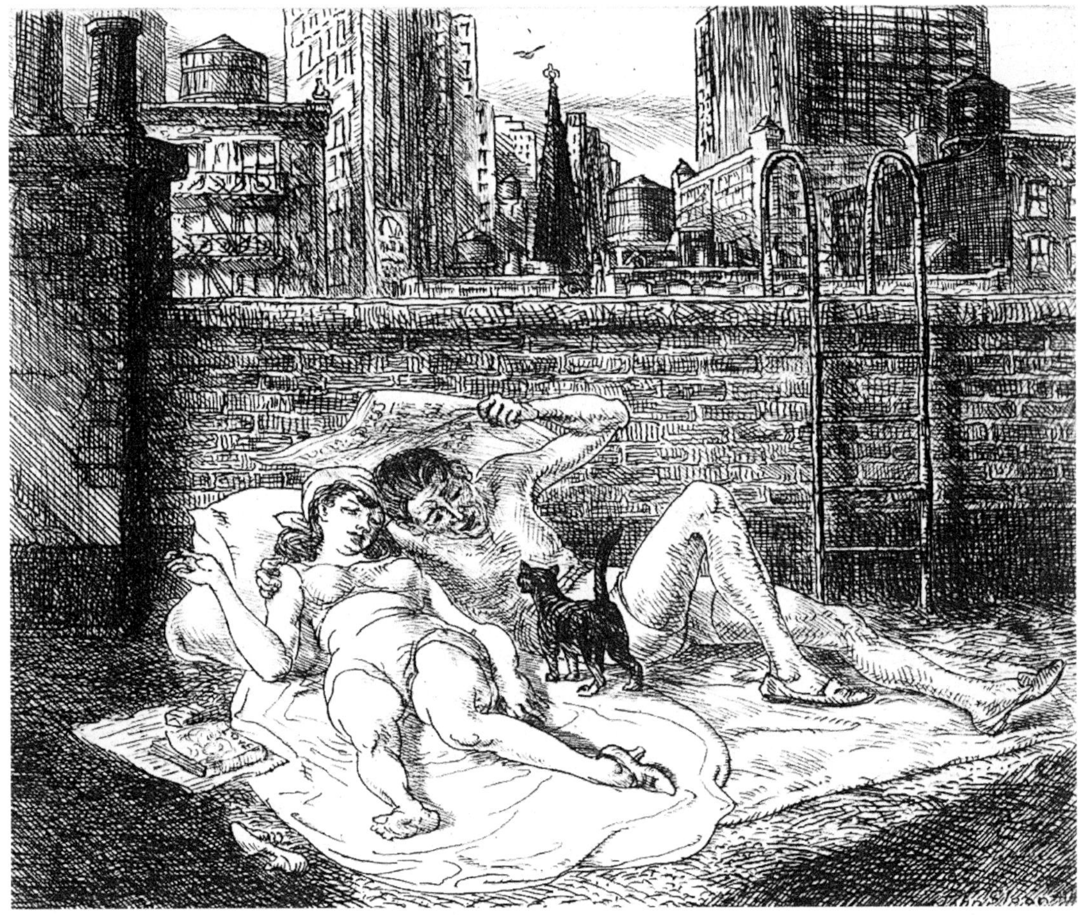

9.6 John Sloan (1871–1951), *Sunbathers on the Roof*, 1941, etching, plate: $5\frac{7}{8} \times 6\frac{15}{16}$ inches; 14.9 × 17.6 cm. Smithsonian American Art Museum. © 2016 Delaware Art Museum/Artists Rights Society (ARS), New York.

alone dictates that the different styles, approaches, ethnicities, races, religions, habits, and hobbies will all be present and probably on display, somewhere in Gotham. Theodore Dreiser pointed out, "The glory of the city is its variety. . . . On the streets of New York I have seen slipping here and there truly marvelous creatures." One team of academics argued, "In Sloan's New York, the parks, like the streets, were places where diverse individuals encountered one another every day. The city allowed male and female, old and young, affluent and impoverished, to observe and comment on each other." The artist himself penned in his diary on September 16, 1908, about a walk through McDougal and Sullivan Streets, how despite "their Celtic names, are principally inhabited by Italians." Thus, like anyone of his era, Sloan was extremely conscious of ethnicity but willing to accept differences as part of the mix in the city.[10]

This was a crucial step toward embracing the modern. Cities have lots of people; inherently they include a diverse population, even if one tries to shut them out. Instead, Sloan celebrates this reality, in opposition to those of his era who decried it, feared it. He appreciates that the city will be a bold world with lots of different characters, one of its most fascinating qualities at times.

But this engendered one other principle that makes big cities unique. Because of density, New York has to be tolerant. Not just of ethnicity and race, but of every oddball foible the human race can conjure up in its infinite imagination. In the small town, in the suburb, you can simply avoid those folks with whom you are not comfortable. But not in a city; here you have to encounter the awkward, the undesirable; they are on top of you. So you learn to put up with their eccentricity, their accent, their skin color. The only alternatives are moving out (for most an economic impossibility), getting violent and winding up in jail, or just going mad. You either are tolerant, or in Bellevue. The city forces that choice on you. E. B. White noted, "The citizens of New York are tolerant not only from disposition but from necessity. The city has to be tolerant, otherwise it would explode."[11]

Some perspective is relevant here. In order to make sense of such masses of humanity, and to guarantee reliability and safety among one's own, the city separates into neighborhoods, often where one group predominates. And the long history of urban race riots demonstrates that tolerance is often a lost virtue on the crowded boulevards.

Yet still, people get thrown together. Historical studies—and common sense—indicate that few spots have ever been truly exclusive to one group alone. With the exception of racial enclaves, there is usually some mixing of ethnic groups. Even more occurs in schools, on the shop floor and in the office, at the emporium or department store, on the subway platform. By the second immigrant generation, mixed marriages become more and more common.

Even more amazing, the Ashcan works included a racial perspective. National culture followed the court after the notorious *Plessy v. Ferguson* decision in 1896 permitting racial segregation, and images in the early film industry, in advertising and in graphic art, all portrayed blacks in the worst way possible, as "the nadir of human intelligence and beauty," the males especially obsessed with lust for white females.[12]

Instead, the Ashcan artists rejected this outlook, deciding to draw what actually happened on streets, how the great city looked and functioned. They knew of racial stereotypes, were informed by these visions, but moved past them. In 1910 Sloan described going to Harlem to see a baseball game between "colored" teams (his notation). Speaking of the crowd, he found "the people mostly black and well dressed and of splendid behavior." Clearly, there is a negative racial consciousness; he is too surprised by their middle-class manners. Yet still he is trying, making an effort to improve and see the positive in black society, which was far more than many others aspired to at that point and in this country. Thus, we do not find a great many depictions of black New Yorkers in these catalogs, but what is there are benign images; race is not a big part of the Ashcan artists' sense of the city, but it is not a source of fear or revulsion either.[13]

Two of their number, in particular, went the furthest in including images of blacks in the variety of their work. Robert Henri painted numerous canvases of black New Yorkers, the most famous of which is *Portrait of Willie Gee* (fig. 9.7). There is an arresting quality to this young man. No cowering, grinning minstrel, he is quiet and contemplative. Gee's family came from Virginia, and the young man delivered newspapers to Henri's building. One critic claimed that the youth was "portrayed with a mixture of dignity and an innocent sense of self-assurance," while social historian Joshua Brown believed that the painting was "startling in its quiet dignity. . . . his contemplative expression opens a vista of interpretive possibilities rather than pat conclusions." That was quite an accomplishment, a decade before *The Birth of a Nation* (1915) celebrated the Ku Klux Klan and only eight years after the Supreme Court enshrined segregation in *Plessy v. Ferguson.*[14]

Less well known but equally compelling was *The Laundress* (fig. 9.8, pg. 156). The subject of this work is a black woman who works, and likely works hard. Yet she has an open face and is unabashed, lively, and strong. There is no hint of condescension from the artist, no sense of any stereotype here.

Best of all is *Eva Green.* The young lady is a charmer. Upper working class or middle, she sports a dashing hat tied down with a pin and adorned with a red bow. Most of all, like the children in George Luks' *The Spielers*, she is just downright happy. This is no typecast image; eschewing the negative impressions of either racists or reformers, both of whom, for different reasons, claimed all blacks were downtrodden. This is just a child in the city who looks like she is enjoying herself. Who just happens to be black. That seems totally unimportant to Henri, especially compared to her charm.

George Wesley Bellows rates inclusion here, because he included black fighters in his boxing pictures. Not as demonic brutes but as champions, the peers of white athletes. *Both Members of This Club* personifies this (fig. 9.10, pg. 158).

In the small setting of Sharkey's, the fight is integrated. There is a lively crowd here, cheering the combatants on. Yet neither fighter seems favored, either by the artist or by the spectators; both are depicted in heroic posture and those around the ring seem not to be fixated on race. For those around the ring and for the one painting it, mixed-race activities in the city are exciting and even beautiful.

The Ashcan artists both recognized and celebrated the coming of a new—more modern, more complex, more diverse—world, one filled with love and happiness, pride and dignity, companionship and commerce. With remarkable sensitivity to small nuance, the Ashcan artists perceived and then drew the details that compose life in the great city. They understood the importance of density, diversity, and tolerance to the urban experience. Far better than contemporary sociologists or other scholars of city life, they looked at the bulk of Gotham's residents, the working classes, and captured their byways and their values, showing respect and insight rather than dismissing or denigrating these cultures, these environments—these people. That ability separates them from both the elites and the reformers, and it remains their great accomplishment.

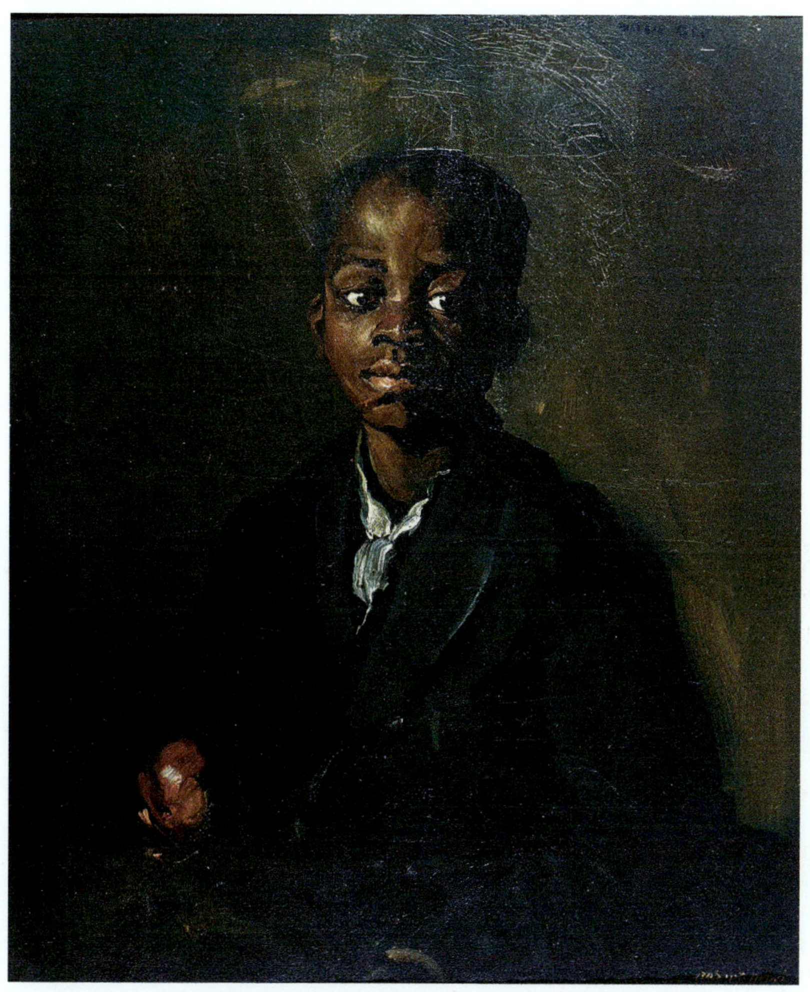

9.7 Robert Henri (1865–1929), *Portrait of Willie Gee*, 1904, oil on canvas, 79.4 × 66.7 cm; 31¼ × 26¼ inches. Purchase 1925. Collection of Newark Museum. 25.111. Photo credit: Newark Museum/Art Resource, New York.

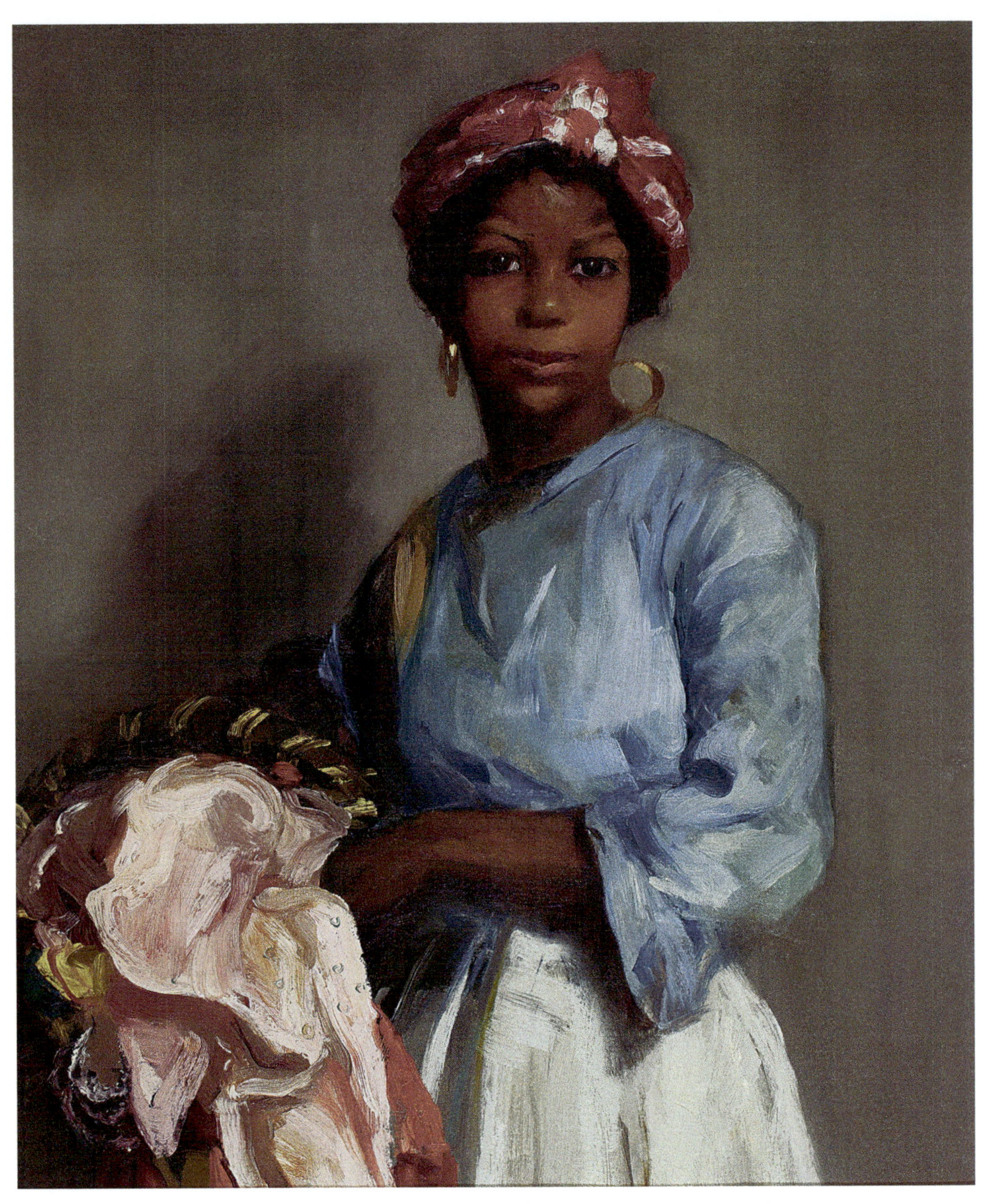

9.8 Robert Henri (1865–1929), *The Laundress*, 1916, oil on canvas, 89.54 × 74.3 cm; 35.25 × 29.25 inches. Collection of Phoenix Art Museum, Gift of Mr. and Mrs. Norman Hirschl.

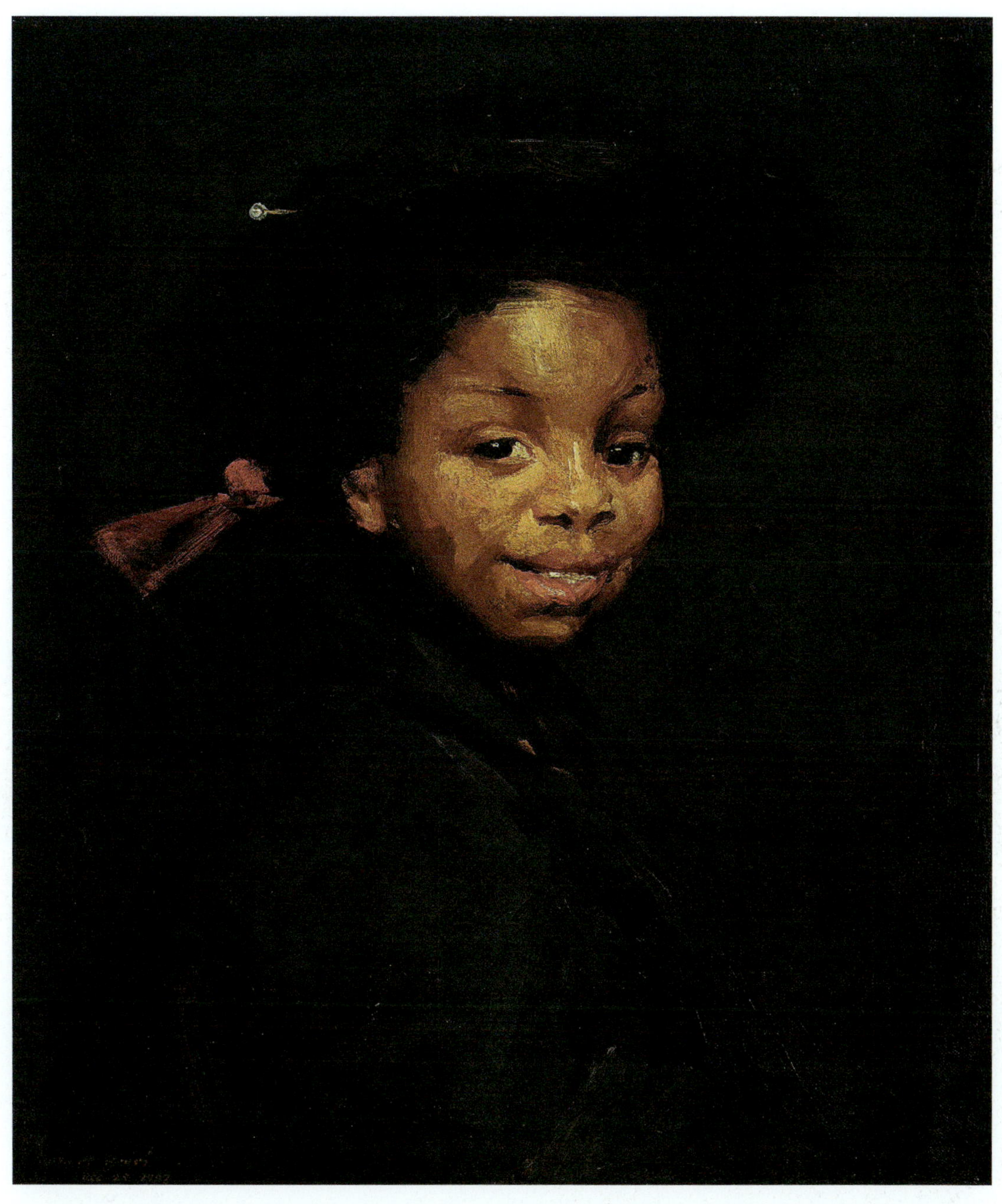

9.9 Robert Henri (1865–1929), *Eva Green*, 1907, oil on canvas, 24⅛ × 20¼ inches. Roland P. Murdock Collection, Wichita Art Museum, Wichita, Kansas.

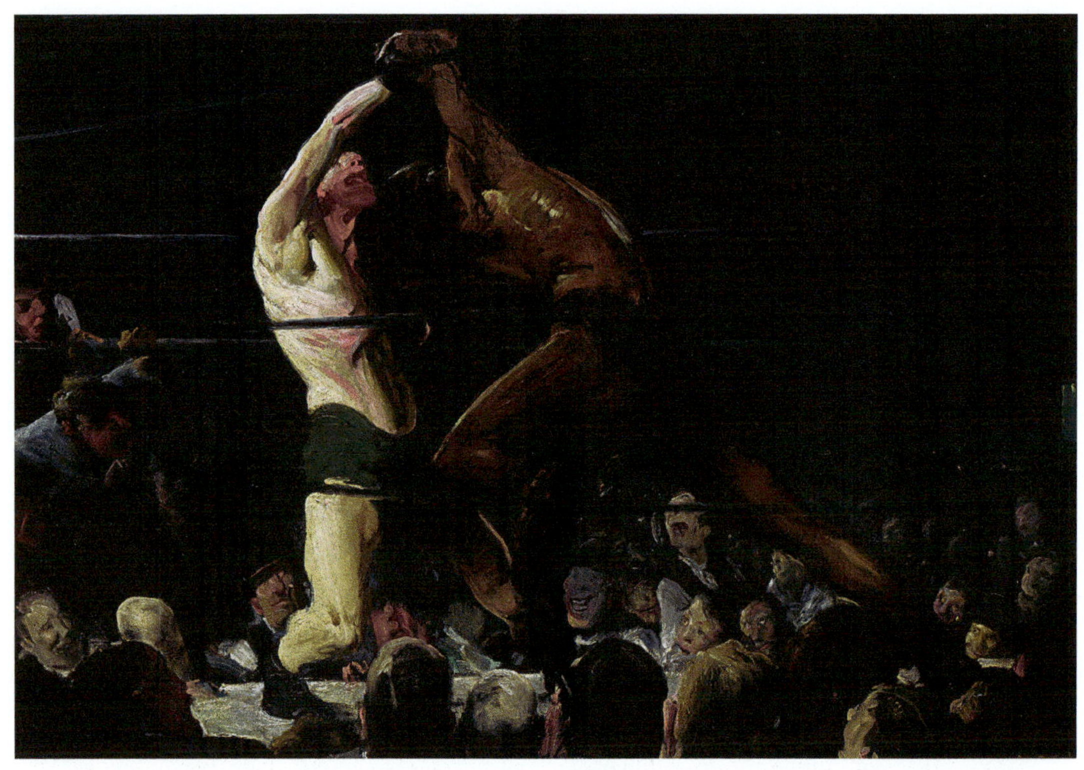

9.10 George Wesley Bellows (1882–1925), *Both Members of This Club*, 1909, oil on canvas, overall: 115 × 160.5 cm; 45¼ × 63³⁄₁₆ inches, framed: 133 × 177.8 cm; 52⅜ × 70 inches. 1944.13.1. Chester Dale Collection, National Gallery of Art, Washington, DC.

CHAPTER TEN

The Ashcan School and Its Critics

In some regards, the Ashcan school signaled the start of a truly American art form. Not because of a unique style, but as its subject matter offered a fuller range of the American experience at a crucial moment; the country was shifting from farm and small town to the up-and-coming dominant form, the dynamic city bursting with potent machines and self-reliant humanity.

Thus, what they did was vastly important. Sir Peter Hall wrote that "history shows that golden urban ages are rare and special windows of light, that briefly illuminate the world both within them and outside them." This, then, was the Ashcan artists' great achievement: at a time when it was so badly needed, they were able to take the new, powerful, and different metropolis and interpret it to America. The modern city was brought, in exquisitely sensitive detail, to an increasingly modern nation, and this helped the nation along the path to entering and accepting the twentieth century. In *Against Interpretation*, Susan Sontag wrote, "What we are witnessing is . . . the creation of a new . . . kind of sensibility. This new sensibility is rooted, as it must be, in our experience, experiences which are new in the history of humanity—in extreme social and physical mobility; in the crowdedness of the human scene."[1]

This service came at a crucial time for the country. Overwhelmed by massive alterations of industrialization, urbanization, and immigration, America during the Gilded Age and after, in the words of scholar Randall Griffin, "exemplifies anxiety over the loss of national identity." The frontier was closing, the city growing. There were new nationalities, and new business giantism. What really was America, and what was it becoming?[2]

Exacerbating these questions was our low status. Considered by many elites to be "a cultural backwater, American artists and critics faced the daunting challenge of finding native subjects. . . . 'American identity' was thus not easily pictured in the Gilded Age."[3]

The Ashcan artists provided a lasting answer, as American as the Statue of Liberty. At our core were the cities and their working people. This was what was worth drawing—and still is. If one sought the American experience, the search should take the questor to the streets and workshops of places like New York City. Theodore Roosevelt, a member of the elite yet a canny observer of the world around him, noticed how "the Bowery is one of the great highways of humanity, a highway of seething life, of varied interest, of fun, of work." In the introduction to Robert Henri's *The Art Spirit*, Forbes Watson wrote that the great mentor always "gave his followers complete respect for an American outlook." A critic of George Wesley Bellows noted how the artist, "while admitting the greatness of the old masters, . . . is determined to go his own gait. He wants America to be a self feeding nation in art." In various articles in the first decade of the twentieth century, George Luks' work was claimed to be "a reflection of American life as it is today, crude, vehement, inconsiderate though not without tenderness at times." Another analyst wrote, "Above all, Luks is an American."[4]

After creating a national art form, the Ashcan artists made other critical contributions. They were the first and best American painters to depict the power and wonderment of the city, when it enjoyed its most dynamic moment. They reveled in the power of an excavation site for a new building, understood the beauty of a subway thundering overhead.

They also moved beyond class boundaries, a remarkable ability given the social divisions of their era. They neither focused on the narrow segment of the very rich nor on the despairing poor of the underclass. Instead, they went for the larger crowd, depicting the life and communities of the urban working class.

Overall, this is not a bad list of achievements for folks who drew "ashcans."

Some critics take a different tack entirely, interpret this art in a very different way. The major criticism of the Ashcan school is that it was superficial. In an oft quoted article, Wanda Corn remarked that "these artists created vignettes of local color"; it was not a compliment. In a review of an Ashcan exhibit at the New-York Historical Society, *New York Times* critic Ken Johnson dismissed this genre: "The painters of the Ashcan School just wanted to have fun. . . . Robert Henri, George Luks, John Sloan . . . prided themselves on fielding a baseball team that regularly defeated those of the National Academy of Design and the Art Students League."[5]

Even worse, according to this depiction, they trod far too lightly and ignored reality. Richard Fitzpatrick felt "Sloan sentimentalized working and under class life," while another reviewer referred to them as "romantic journalists." Matthew Baigell commented, "how superficial were their social concerns." In another popular essay, Amy Goldin dismissed "the myth of the radical Eight" as "bad history and worse criticism."[6]

There are several problems with this line of thought, a number of points it overlooks.

First, the period of the Ashcan school was when the city was at its most dynamic stage in American history, whether measured by population growth or by the height or density of its buildings. This was the only time that the city was universally recognized as the coming life form, the most exciting place to be in the United States. No one recorded that critical moment—both literally and the spirit of things—better than these artists. No one better appreciated what was happening, unlike modern reform organizations that still feel the best thing you could do for city folk is to get them out of the city itself, as far away from the metropolis as possible.

Next, to the argument that the paintings lack social significance. In one sense that is true. The Ashcan artists never entered the lower depths, never painted the underclass with its very real—and very horrible—degradation and atmosphere of despair. On the other hand, however, they also went far beyond the downtown neighborhoods of rich swells, the grand boulevards of top hats and designer gowns.

Instead, they captured the vast bulk of the city's population, the working class. This is what made them different, and radical, in their day as well as our own. Even in the modern era, how few movies or television shows accomplish what these artists did, to focus on life in the urban neighborhoods with insight and sensitivity and even a little humor? Let alone depict how working people went about their lives, with respect? The subject matter of these paintings was—and remains—radical.

What is more, they endowed their working-class subjects with agency, the ability to shape their own lives and then enjoy them. This is hardly a given, among artists or anywhere else.

Among scholars, the work of David Nasaw stands out as unique for capturing and stressing this unrecognized feature of urban life. Even in an endeavor as far afield as municipal politics, Saul Alinsky is still read and quoted for advocating this same ideal, that working-class people in cities can exercise control. For the Ashcan artists, this is the most profound contribution of them all.

These artists knew working-class people were dominated by many large institutions, like the growing enterprises that employed them. But they also understood that urban residents were—at the same time—able to devise strategies to make the best use of their environment, to create lives with pleasure, worth living. If elites dismissed these folk altogether, reformers did not believe they could find these solutions without outside help. Only the Ashcan artists grasped the talents of the cities' working population, that remarkable ability to create a life for themselves.

What of later generations? In recent years there have been several different approaches to visually depicting New York. One route has been that of Richard Estes, a style usually referred to as photorealism. Estes' method is elegant, a technical feat of incredible virtuosity. The artist often states that his works are "not so much about what he paints as about how he paints." The critic Patterson Sims wrote of Estes, "his view of cities celebrates their formal structure." *The Candy Store* epitomizes this concept (*fig. 10.1*). Detail is astonishing. It makes one hungry just to look at the scene, and you yearn to walk in, to taste, and to buy.[7]

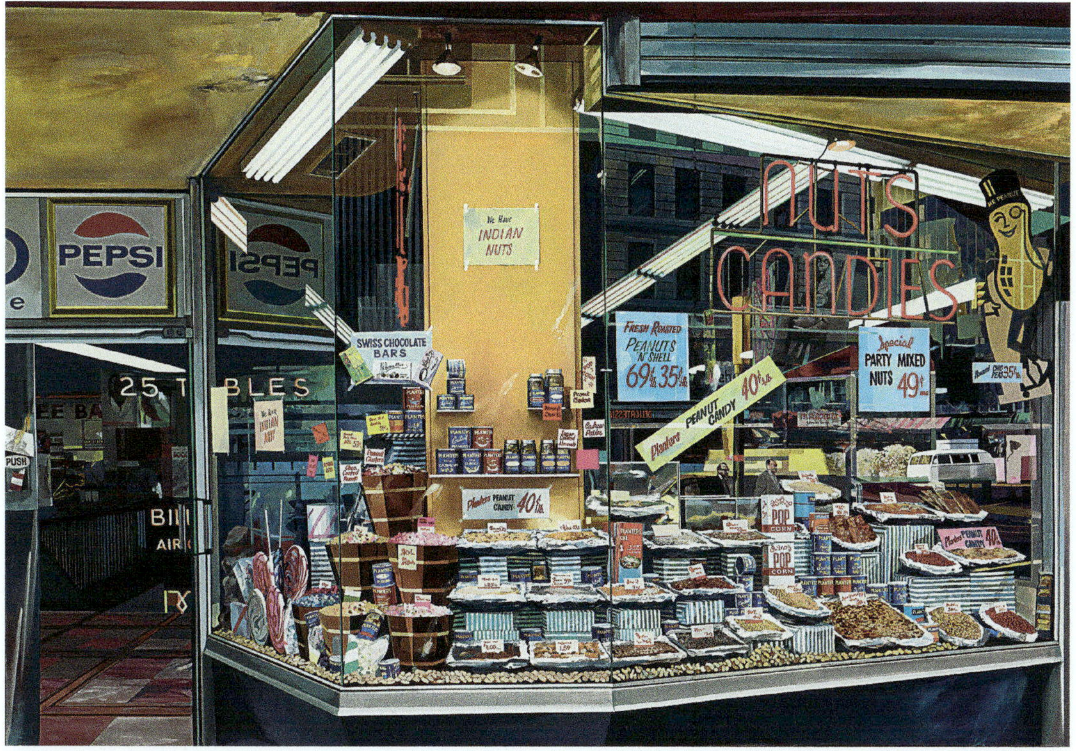

10.1 Richard Estes (1932–), *The Candy Store*, 1969, oil and acrylic on linen, 48 × 68⅞ inches; 121.9 × 174.9 cm. Whitney Museum of American Art, New York; purchase, with funds from the Friends of the Whitney Museum of American Art. 69.21. Digital image © Whitney Museum of American Art.

Yet, Estes' art is not a continuance of the Ashcan ethos. It reveals little of life—of people's lives—in the ongoing city. In fact, there are few individuals on display in his works, no sense of their interaction with each other.

One of his images, *Supreme Hardware*, personifies this approach (*fig. 10.2*). There is technical skill here of the highest order, but no people, no life. Compare this to another depiction of a commercial street, William Glackens' *Patrick Joseph Went and Bought Himself a Grocery Store in Monroe Street* in chapter 7 (*fig. 7.12*), where shops, pushcarts, sidewalks are all thronged with shoppers.

Yet another perspective of the city was adopted by Helen Levitt, the true successor to the Ashcan school. Just as Sloan's and Henri's and the others' paintings had done, Levitt's photographs captured the joy of living in the working-class city, for all ages, all genders, all races.

The most perceptive critic of this photographer was Adam Gopnik. Gopnik understood the difficulty of Levitt's assignment, writing, "New York is an easy city to paint in, and a hard city to picture." The problem is its duality: "Looking through a show of New York photographs, we are likely to be struck either by the buildings (lower Manhattan in twilight) or by the people (all those bathers at Coney Island) but rarely by the sublime unity of the two." Levitt managed to overcome this dichotomy by capturing Gotham's essence: "What she photographs instead is something simpler and more elusive—ordinary people going about the business of living in a city that is in no way ordinary." Capturing an ideal that was as much the Ashcan school's as Levitt's, Gopnik observed, "No greater theme exists than the real lives of the people who, against all odds and, increasingly common sense, clump in the shadows of its skyline." For her

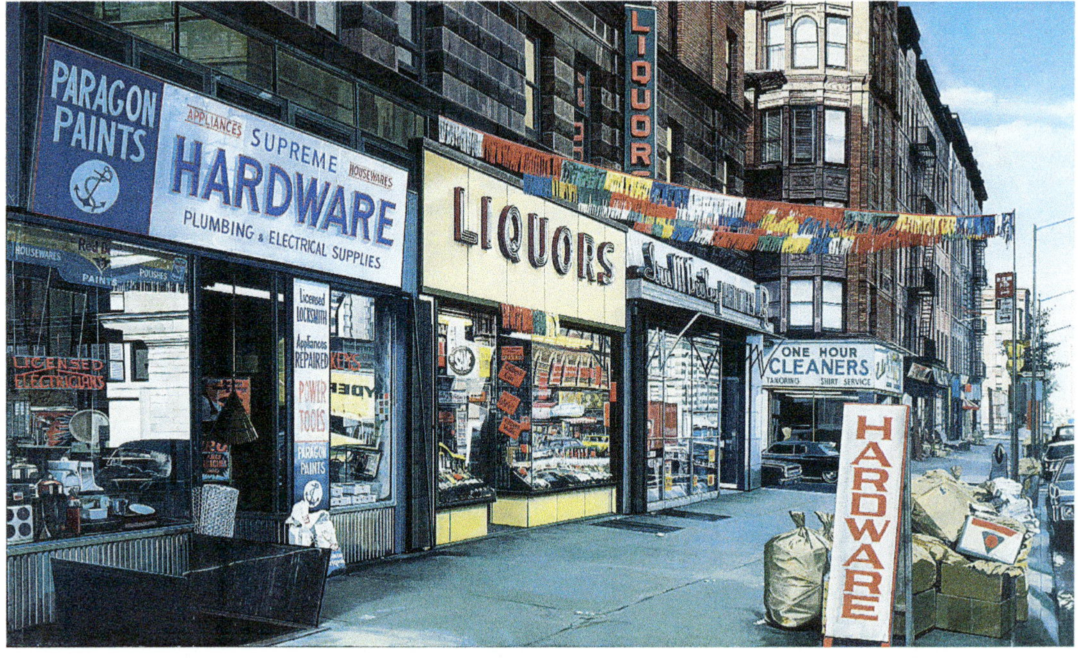

10.2 Richard Estes (1932–), *Supreme Hardware*, 1974, oil on canvas, 40 × 66¼ inches. Gift of Virginia Carroll Crawford. High Museum of Art, Atlanta, Georgia © Richard Estes, courtesy Marlborough Gallery, New York.

talent in capturing these lives, he dubbed Helen Levitt the "supreme poet-photographer of the streets and people of New York."[8]

Three of Levitt's pictures provide a sense of how she saw and what she saw in the city (*figs. 10.3, 10.4, and 10.5*).

Rarely has an image captured how much fun it is to be a child in New York. Color of skin, differing gender doesn't matter, just the dance. Though each have their own modes, their own

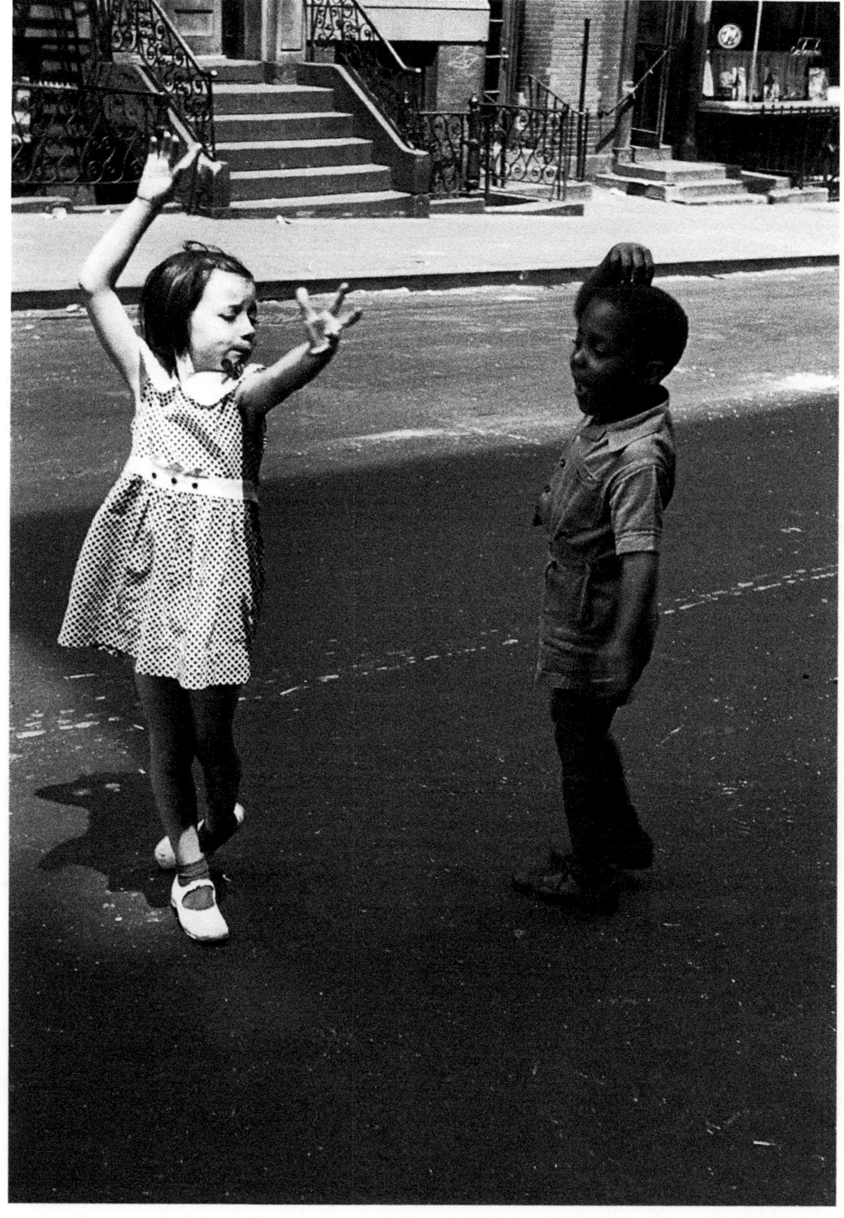

10.3 Helen Levitt (1913–2009), *Two Kids Dancing*, ca. 1940. © Film Documents LLC.

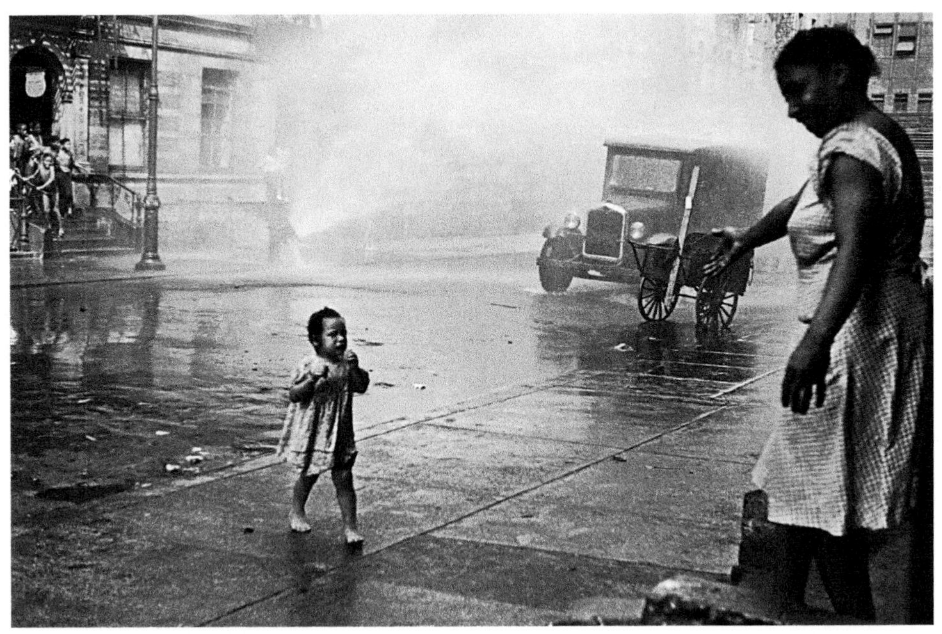

10.4 Helen Levitt (1913–2009), *New York, c. 1939 (child in hydrant spray)*.
© Film Documents LLC.

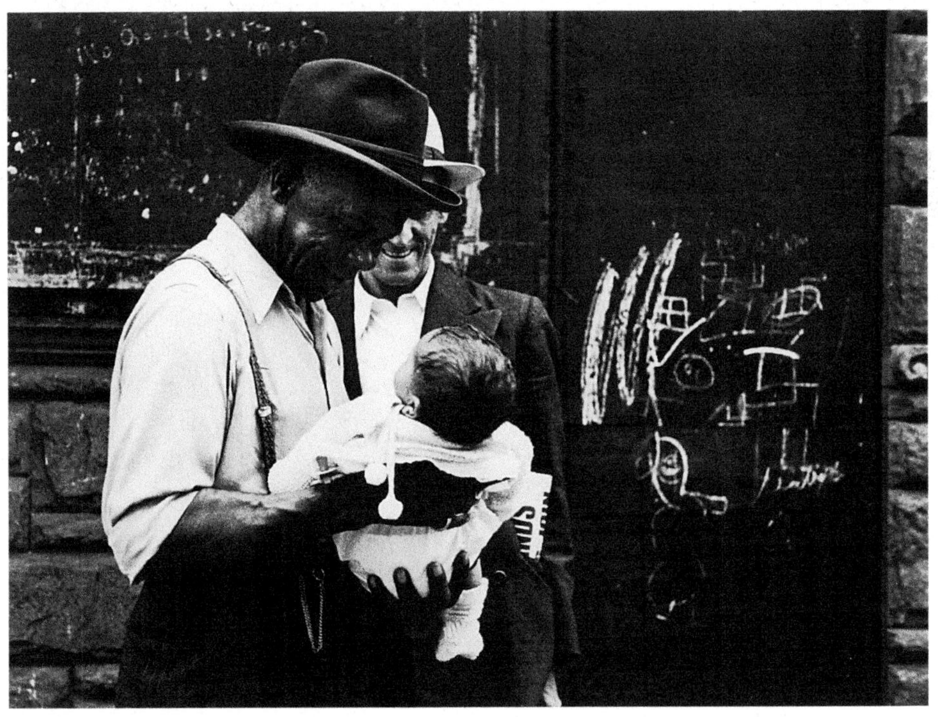

10.5 Helen Levitt (1913–2009), *New York, c. 1942 (man holding baby)*. ©
Film Documents LLC.

steps, this is a shared experience of joy. In the midst of one of the busiest, one of the densest metropolitan zones in the world, they have banished everything but their moment; the street is empty, the world is theirs to perform in.

Sometimes New York can be a scary place if you're little. The big kids open a hydrant; they may be having fun, but suddenly you're soaked and afraid. At a time like this, it is good that Mother is there, with an outstretched hand, a smile, and, safe bet, a hug as well. The city provides love and warmth amid its fury.

It is a cliché to say that a baby represents new life. To gentlemen getting on in years it means so much more. Look at the smiles on both their faces; the bundle makes them happy. Note the setting: the woodwork is frayed and the door is marred by graffiti. Their clothes indicate they are working class, and they are black as well as white. None of that seems to matter; they are united in pride over the infant.

Finally, in answer to charges that the scenes the Ashcan artists painted were not accurate impressions of New York City at all, but romanticized greeting card images, we turn to the New York City Municipal Archives Online Gallery, a collection of 870,000 photographs released in 2012. What is striking in the context of this discussion is how close some of these slices of reality were to the paintings and drawings discussed in this book.

Typical was this picture of a children's play yard at school (*fig. 10.6*). This image depicts children at play in a dense urban setting, just like many pictures by Ashcan school artists.

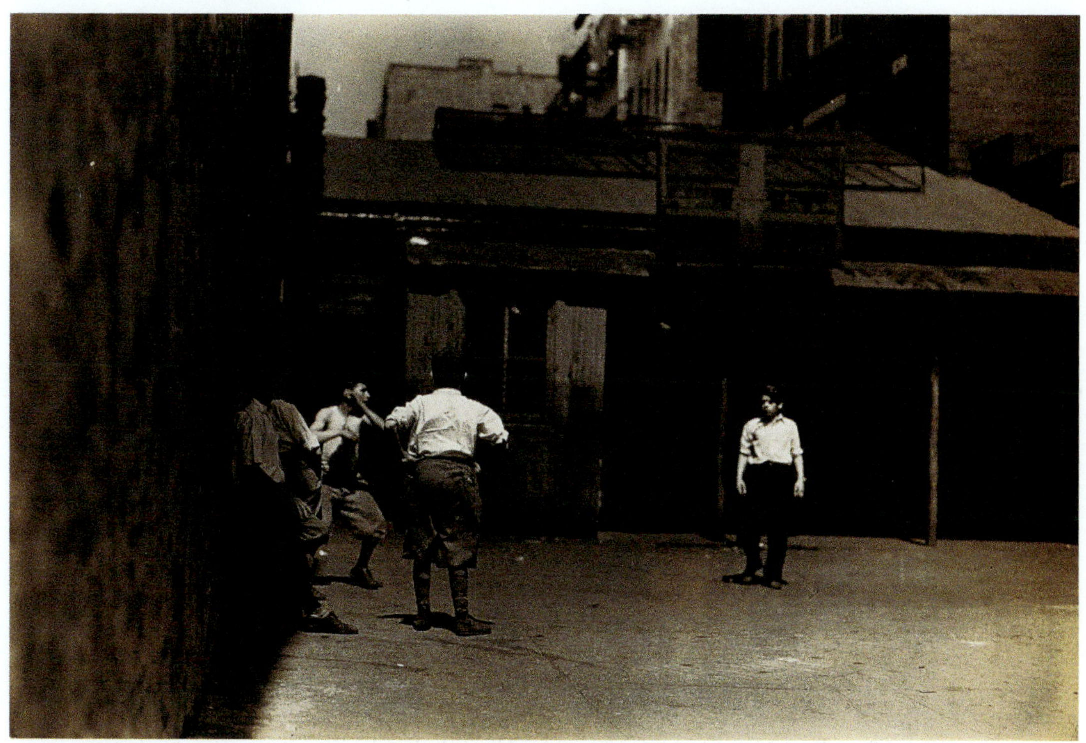

10.6 *Playground of P.S. 85, 1st Avenue & 117th Street Boys in back alley with basketball hoop,* June 1932, 4.5 × 6.5 inches. NYC Municipal Archives Collection. mac_2153. Courtesy NYC Municipal Archives.

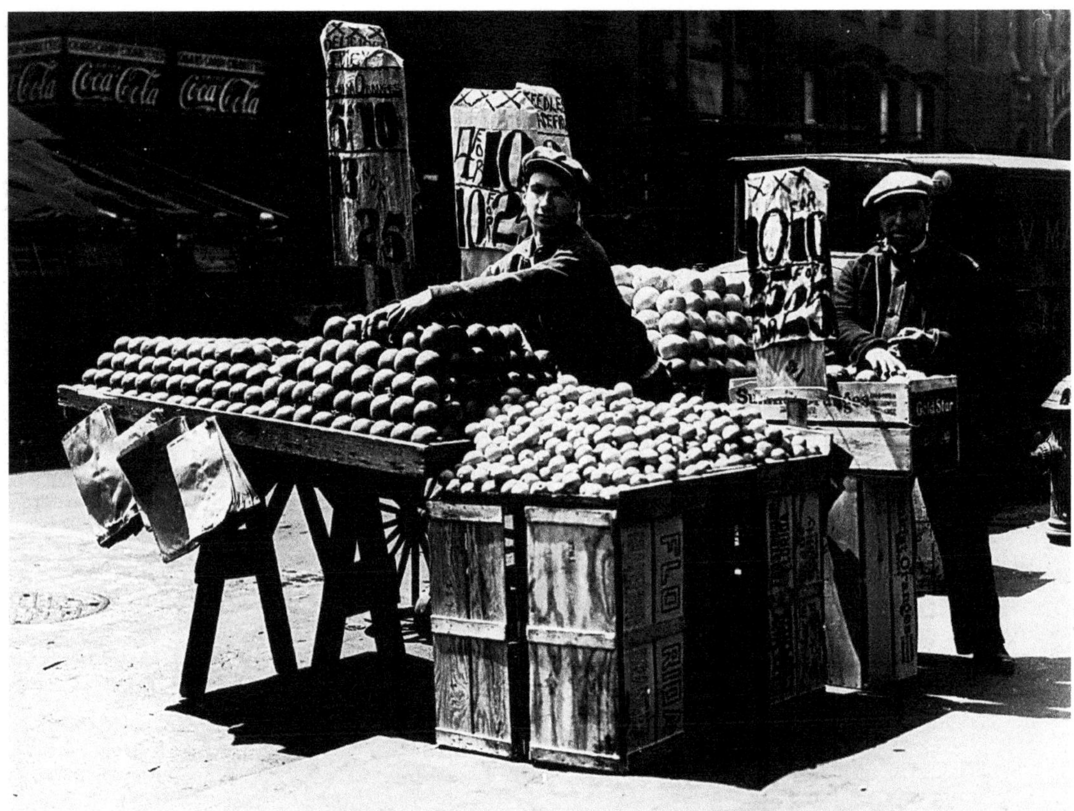

10.7 *Fruit stand, corner of 40th Street & 9th Avenue two vendors; oranges on crates (5 for 10 cents, 13 for 25)*, 1930–39, 8 × 10 inches. NYC Municipal Archives Collection. mac_1369. Courtesy NYC Municipal Archives.

This photo (*fig. 10.7*) looks like Luks' painting *Street Scene (Hester Street)* (see chapter 3, fig. 3.9).

The street scene in this photo (*fig. 10.8*) captures the same feel of New York as Glackens' *Patrick Joseph Went and Bought Himself a Grocery Store in Monroe Street* (chapter 7, fig. 7.12).

This image (*fig. 10.9*, pg. 168) is reminiscent of Glackens' *Far from the Fresh Air Farm* (chapter 7, fig. 7.4) or Luks' *Thompson and Bleecker Streets* (chapter 3, fig. 3.3).

Above all, we have one of the great vistas of the city, similar to those drawn by Sloan and Bellows (*fig. 10.10*, pg. 169). Compare this, more specifically, to Joseph Pennell's *Tenement Near Brooklyn Bridge*, in chapter 5 (*fig. 5.9*).

Note that this is a photograph of the Manhattan Bridge, the "unloved" span over the East River (compared to the Brooklyn Bridge). Part of this lessened affection came because its Manhattan terminus was in an immigrant district. Yet the photographer still made this a majestic scene. Just as the Ashcan artists did for working-class New York.

The streets, the people of New York City, really looked like this. The ability of the Ashcan artists to paint that reality, despite all the critical, cultural, and class obstacles, remains their greatest achievement.

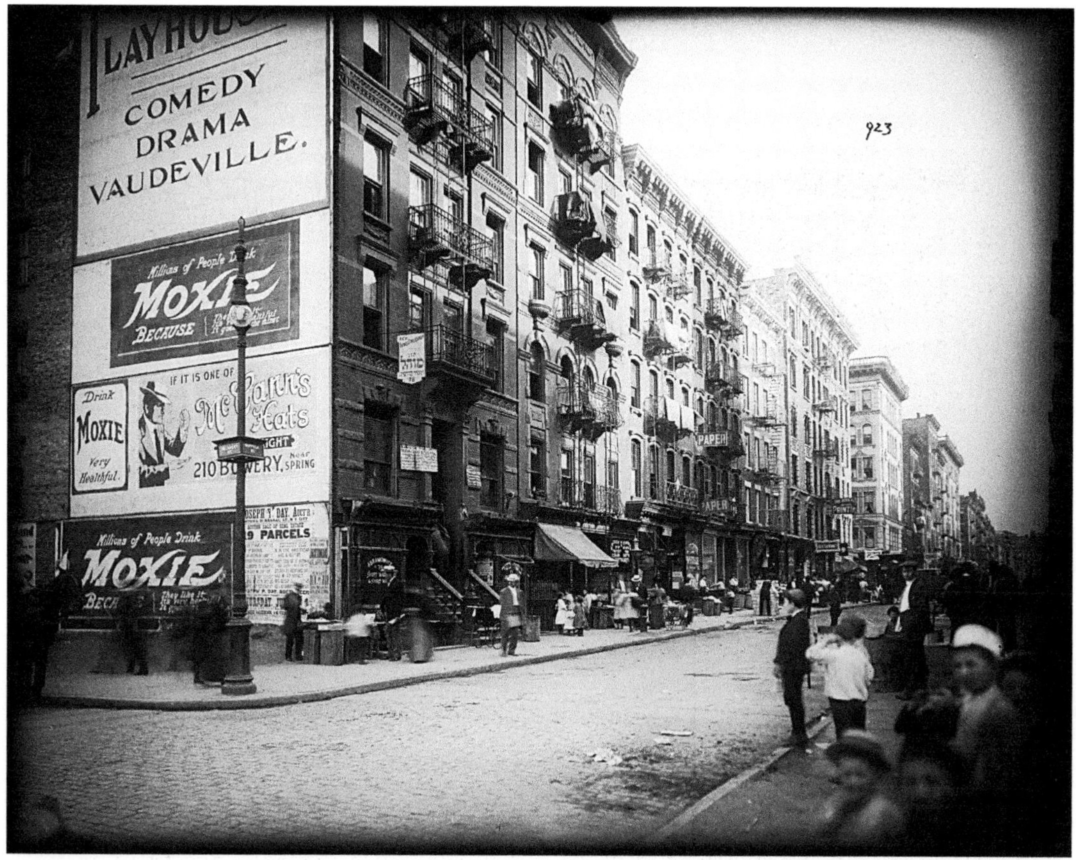

10.8 *Moxie billboards, playhouse advertisement, pedestrians*, June 12, 1906, 8-x-10-inch glass plate negative. NYC Municipal Archives Collection. bps_00923. Courtesy NYC Municipal Archives.

But in so doing, they transformed art. No longer was it just a matter for the middle and upper classes to encounter in downtown galleries, viewing images that depicted only their lives. Instead, this was a new interpretation, one that brought painting into the great social and industrial narrative of their era, the rise of the city. In unprecedented fashion, these artists believed it was important to capture the urban scene in all its dynamism and power, from el trains to ferry boats to construction sites, with different classes, ethnicities, races, and genders. This was new, and it remains one of their signal contributions, a rationale for our continued interest.

The Ashcan school of art did more than just paint pictures of the city, however, a great deal more. In fact, it did the country—that transforming entity, that radically shifting United States of America—a service, by helping it understand modernism, easing its way into the society it was about to become. Whoever viewed these images—whether the originals or in books or portfolios or even in postcards—learned so much about how we were developing, about what we were becoming.

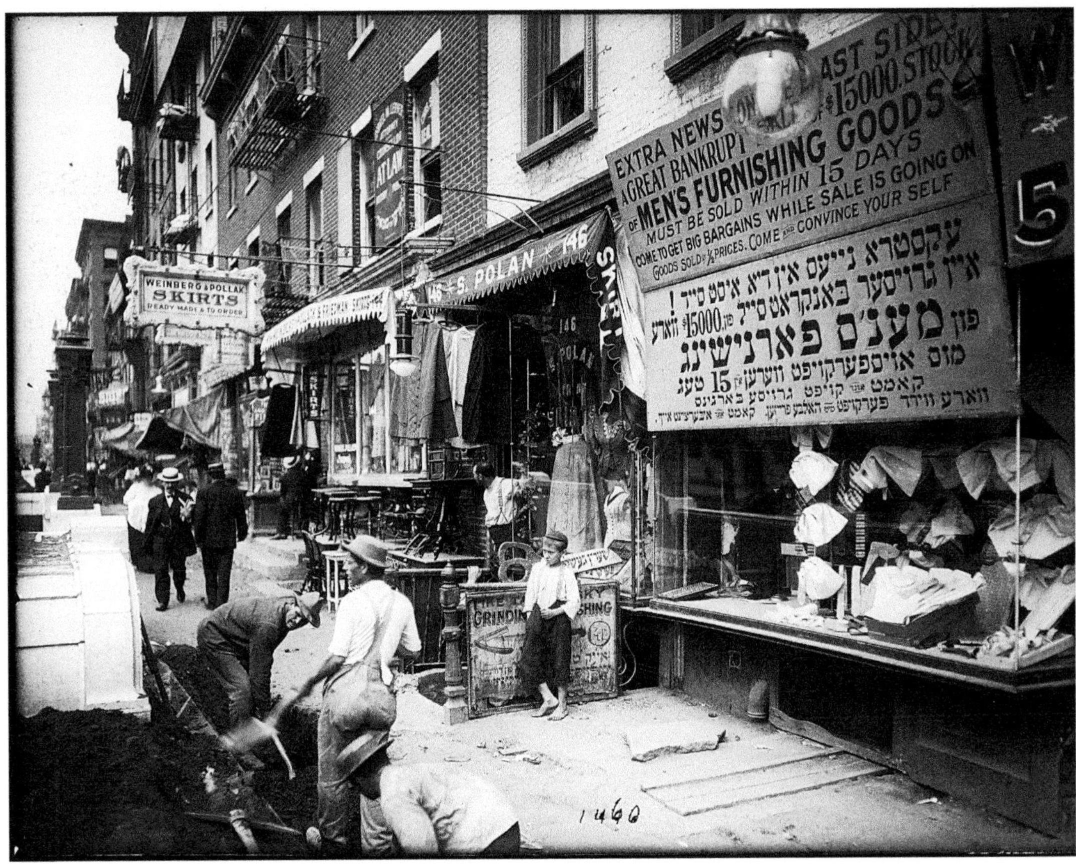

10.9 Eugene de Salignac (1861–1943), *Delancey Street, north side*, July 29, 1908. NYC Municipal Archives Collection bps_01460. Courtesy NYC Municipal Archives.

They learned about how to live in a crowded, dense environment, packed with all kinds of individuals, with everyone moving at a frantic pace. Despite this phantasmagoric, confounding sense, they also saw that people could thrive here, could enjoy the pride of work, the joy of friends and of lovers, relax and be at peace even in a narrow apartment. Even more, they were introduced to a new idea, that all these people had a sense of agency, that they strove to, and often achieved, control over significant parts of their lives.

Gallery visitors came to respect city folk in a way unprecedented at that time, in that America. Women were depicted as having full lives, with choices of their own making, in so many aspects. Even more radical, children, never granted adult status with rights and responsibilities, were seen as having the power to create and command their own world. Immigrants and workers were treated with dignity, people who lived full and rich lives rather than being marginalized as they were by both elites and reformers. People of all ethnicities and races, in a land of intense segregation, were instead drawn together in an urban setting, going about their lives. Above all, these artists introduced the city and its neighborhoods to America, with insight and sensitivity, showing that apartments and side streets, ferry boats and excavation sites, could all be scenes of beauty, filled with love and caring, power. By helping their country understand, or even to

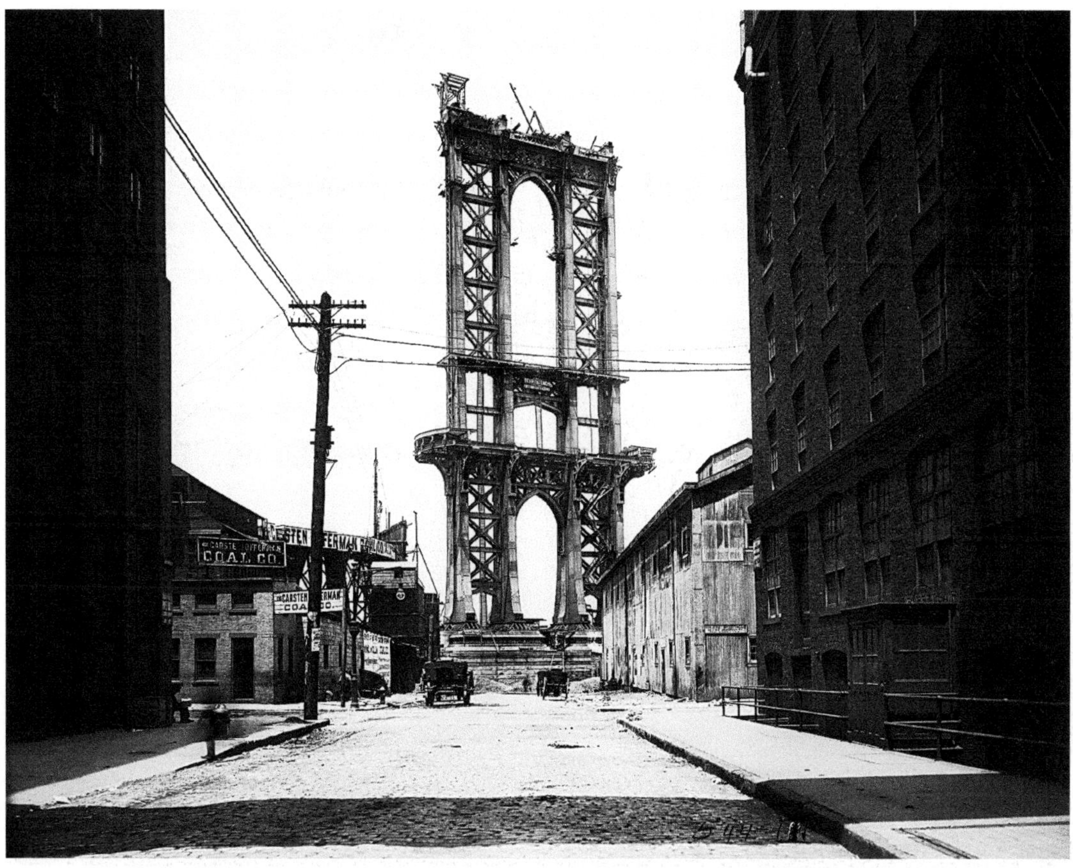

10.10 Eugene de Salignac (1861–1943), *From Washington Street looking west, Brooklyn*, June 5, 1908. NYC Municipal Archives Collection. bps_iii_0544. Courtesy NYC Municipal Archives.

just accept, these realities, this modern America that emerged in a new century, they made an enormous contribution to a growing nation.

As great as this was, the Ashcan artists achieved something far more important. In 1905, Sir Caspar Clarke had just taken over the reins of the Metropolitan Museum of Art, and he summed up the state of affairs: "America appears to be concerned with the art of every land save that of America." Galleries in cities across the national continent seemed like mausoleums with lavish, decorated coffins. Sloan saw that, how art in this country was at its lowest ebb, by its "pursuit of visual imitation."[9]

Robert Henri, the founder and philosopher of the Ashcan school, had the antidote. "Here in America we have a country filled with energetic people. We are a distinct people; we have tremendous ideas to express. And often it seems to me that I cannot wait to hear the voice of these people . . . the thing that we have to say as a people."[10]

This, then, became the most important contribution of the Ashcan school. Like Whitman and others before them, in periods where the canons had to be imported from across the Atlantic, Henri, Sloan, and the others created an American art style, urban, classless, and spontaneous.

One critic argued that "the Ashcan School . . . undoubtedly drew an attention to art in this country unexampled before in our history." Edward Hopper, successor to the Ashcan artists and one of the truly immense talents of his time, in a 1927 homage, simply yet powerfully insisted, "The story of John Sloan and his associates is the story of the first really vital movement in the development of a national art that this country has yet known."[11]

Notes

Chapter One. And Like That . . . They're Gone

1. Bennard Perlman, *Revolutionaries of Realism* (Princeton: Princeton University Press, 1997), xvii.

2. Theodore Dreiser, *The "Genius"* (New York: John Lane, 1915), 54.

3. John Baur, *Revolution and Tradition in Modern American Art* (Cambridge: Harvard University Press, 1951), 124.

4. Heather Coyle and Joyce Schiller, *John Sloan's New York* (Wilmington and New Haven: Delaware Art Museum and Yale University Press, 2007), 48.

5. Ibid., 48; Valerie Ann Leeds, "The Eight in Context," in Owen Gallery, *The Eight* (New York: Owen Gallery), Exhibition of Paintings, October 23–December 14, 2002; Elizabeth Milroy, *Painters of a New Century: The Eight* (Milwaukee: Milwaukee Art Museum, 1991), 22; Marianne Doezema, *George Bellows and Urban America* (New Haven: Yale University Press, 1992), 94–95.

6. Milroy, *Painters of a New Century*, 22; "The Henri Hurrah," *American Art News*, March 23, 1907; Doezema, *George Bellows and Urban America*, 95.

7. Bruce St. John, ed., *John Sloan's New York Scene* (New York: Harper and Row, 1965), 118; Aline Louchheim, "Last of 'The Eight' Looks Back," *New York Times*, November 2, 1952.

8. Milroy, *Painters of a New Century*, 61; *The Role of the Macbeth Gallery* (New York: American Federation of Arts, 1962).

9. Linda Henefeld Skalet, "The Market for American Painting in New York, 1870–1915," PhD dissertation, Johns Hopkins University, 1980, 201.

10. Skalet, "Market for American Painting," 206; Jerome Myers, *The Artist in Manhattan* (New York: American Artists Group, 1940), 26.

11. Bennard Perlman, *Painters of the Ashcan School* (New York: Dover, 1991), 118; Milroy, *Painters of a New Century*, 69; Charles Morgan, *George Bellows: Painter of America* (New York: Reynal, 1965), 72–73; Ira Glackens, *William Glackens and the Eight* (New York: Writers & Readers Publishing, 1957), 77; St. John, *John Sloan's New York Scene*, 126, 173; Robert Henri to William Macbeth, Correspondence, July 14, 1899, Macbeth Gallery Records, Smithsonian Institution, Washington, DC.

12. John Loughery, *John Sloan* (New York: Henry Holt, 1995), 115, 117; Bennard Perlman, *Robert Henri: His Life and Art* (New York: Dover, 1991), 81–82; William Innes Homer, *Robert Henri and His Circle* (Ithaca: Cornell University Press, 1969), 136; "Art Secessionists to Exhibit Work," *New York Herald*, December 19, 1907; Lloyd Goodrich, *John Sloan* (New York: Whitney Museum of American Art, 1952), 33–34.

13. Perlman, *Painters of the Ashcan School*, 178; St. John, *John Sloan's New York Scene*, 190; *New York Evening Post*, February 1, 1908; Scrapbook, Macbeth Gallery Records, Smithsonian Institution, Washington, DC.

14. *New York Tribune*, February 3, 1908; Loughery, *John Sloan*, 120.

15. Perlman, *Robert Henri*, 84; St. John, *John Sloan's New York Scene*, 194; *The Role of the Macbeth Gallery*.

16. Morgan, *George Bellows*, 81; Homer, *Robert Henri*, 138; St. John, *John Sloan's New York Scene*, 199.

17. *New York American*, February 4, 1908; *New York Herald*, February 4, 1908; *New York Sun*, May 15, 1907; *New York Evening Post*, February 7, 1908.

18. *New York Sun*, February 4, 1908.

19. *New York Tribune*, February 9, 1908; *New York American*, February 9, 1908.

20. Arnold Schwab, ed., *Americans in the Arts: Critiques by James Gibbons Huneker* (New York: A.M.S. Press, 1985), xxv–xxvi; John Loughery, "The New York Sun and Modern Art in America: Charles Fitzgerald, Frederick Gregg, James Gibbons Huneker, Henry McBride," *Arts Magazine* 59 (December 1984): 77; Arnold Schwab, *James Gibbons Huneker* (Stanford: Stanford University Press, 1963), 176.

21. Schwab, *Americans in the Arts*, liii; Schwab, *James Gibbons Huneker*, 179, 181.

22. Schwab, *Americans in the Arts*, 477–479.

23. James Huneker, "Growing Pains of American Art," *Current Literature* 44.4 (April 1908): 393, 296, 397.

24. Schwab, *James Gibbons Huneker*, 177; Walter Pach, *Queer Thing Painting* (New York: Harper and Brothers, 1938), 202.

25. *New York Tribune*, February 5, 1908; Royal Cortissoz, "Independent Art: Some Reflections on Its Claims and Obligations," *New York Tribune*, April 10, 1910.

26. Perlman, *Painters of the Ashcan School*, 97, 178; David Coleman, "The Social Commentary of John Sloan, 1900–1916, in the Context of American Progressivism," MA thesis, University of California, Berkeley, 1972, 2; Morgan, *George Bellows*, 83; undated and untitled article in Scrapbook, Macbeth Gallery Records, Smithsonian Institution, Washington, DC; Donald Braider, *George Bellows and the Ashcan School of Painting* (Garden City: Doubleday, 1971), 57; St. John, *John Sloan's New York Scene*, 193.

27. Glackens, *William Glackens and the Eight*, 88; Pach, *Queer Thing Painting*, 11.

28. Christopher Knight, "The Show That Shook the Art World," *Los Angeles Times*, February 15, 2013. Numerous art historians have referred to the Armory Show in this way. Most recently, on the one hundredth anniversary, the *Los Angeles Times* referred to it as "the most famous art exhibition of the 20th Century."

29. Walt Kuhn, *The Story of the Armory Show* (New York: Walt Kuhn, 1938), 4; Holland Cotter, "Rethinking the Armory Show," *New York Times*, Fine Arts and Exhibits Section, October 28, 2012.

30. Kuhn, *The Story of the Armory Show*, 5.

31. Meyer Schapiro, *Modern Art* (New York: George Braziller, 1979), 136; Myers, *Artist in Manhattan*, 36; Perlman, *Painters of the Ashcan School*, 210.

32. Perlman, *Robert Henri*, 109; Milton Brown, *The Story of the Armory Show* (New York: Abbeville Press, 1988), 41–42.

33. Perlman, *Robert Henri*, 109; Myers, *Artist in Manhattan*, 36; Kuhn, *The Story of the Armory Show*, 17; Brown, *The Story of the Armory Show*, 110.

34. Brown, *The Story of the Armory Show*, 136.

35. Mary Sayre Haverstock, *George Bellows: An Artist in Action* (London: Merrell, 2007), 85; Arthur Wesley Dow, "Modernism in Art," *The American Magazine of Art* 8 (January 1917): 113.

36. Lloyd Goodrich, *The Decade of the Armory Show* (New York: Whitney Museum of American Art), 30; Pach, *Queer Thing Painting*, 193; Brown, *The Story of the Armory Show*, 120, 131; Perlman, *Robert Henri*, 109; Holland Cotter, "Rethinking the Armory Show," *New York Times*, Fine Arts and Exhibits Section, October 28, 2012.

37. Brown, *The Story of the Armory Show*, 108; Christine Stansell, American *Moderns* (New York: Henry Holt, 2000), 102; Frank Seiberling Jr., "George Bellows, 1882–1925," PhD dissertation, University of Chicago, 1948, 59; Baur, *Revolution and Tradition in Modern American Art*, 6; Kuhn, *The Story of the Armory Show*, 21; Guy Pène du Bois, *Artists Say the Silliest Things* (New York: American Artists Group, 1940), 175; Christopher Knight, "The Show That Shook the Art World," *Los Angeles Times*, February 15, 2013.

38. Brown, *The Story of the Armory Show*, 145; Theodore Roosevelt, "A Layman's View of an Art Exhibition," *Outlook* 103 (March 29, 1913): 718–720.

39. Schapiro, *Modern Art*, 136; Pach, *Queer Thing Painting*, 52; Baur, *Revolution and Tradition in American Art*, 124; Goodrich, *The Story of the Armory Show*, 40; Kuhn, *The Story of the Armory Show*, 24–25; Peter Conn, *The Divided Mind* (New York: Cambridge University Press, 1983), 279; du Bois, *Artists Say the Silliest Things*, 166.

40. Steven Ross, *Working-Class Hollywood* (Princeton: Princeton University Press, 1999), 86.

41. *Helen Farr Sloan: An Artistic Vision* (Wilmington: Teleduction, 2000); Arthur Frank Wertheim, *The New York Little Renaissance* (New York: New York University Press, 1976), 142; Charles Hirschfeld, "'Ash Can' vs. 'Modern' Art in America," *The Western Humanities Review* 10 (Autumn 1956): 354; Andre Tridon, "America's First Aesthetician," *Forum* 55 (January 1916): 124; Ken Johnson, "Ashcan Views of New Yorkers, Warts, High Spirits and All," *New York Times*, December 28, 2007; Pach, *Queer Thing Painting*, 203.

42. Charles Brock, "George Bellows: An Unfinished Life," in Charles Brock et al., *George Bellows* (Washington, DC: National Gallery of Art, 2012), 11; John Loughery, "The Mysterious George Luks," *Arts Magazine* 64.4 (December 1987): 35.

43. Brown, *The Story of the Armory Show*, 88; Loughery, *John Sloan*, 188.

44. Mahonri Sharp Young, *The Eight* (New York: Watson-Guptill, 1973), 37; Perlman, *Robert Henri*, 109, 110.

45. E. C. Goosen, *Stuart Davis* (New York: George Braziller, 1959), 14.

46. Jean Bethke Elshtain, ed., *The Jane Addams Reader* (New York: Basic Books, 2002), 15, 17.

47. Lillian Wald, *The House on Henry Street* (New York: Henry Holt, 1915), 69–70.

Chapter Two. Top and Bottom

1. Samuel Lane Loomis, *Modern Cities and Their Religious Problems* (New York: Baker and Taylor, 1887), 5–6.

2. H. Barbara Weinberg, Doreen Bolger, and David Park Curry, *American Impressionism and Realism* (New York: Metropolitan Museum of Art, 1994), 138–139; Loomis, *Modern Cities and Their Religious Problems*, 27; Dominic Ricciotti, "The Urban Scene: Images of the City in American Painting, 1890–1930," PhD dissertation, Indiana University, 1977, 1; John Garraty, *The New Commonwealth* (New York: Harper and Row, 1968), 179; Carl Degler, *Out of Our Past* (New York: Harper and Row, 1959), 309.

3. Paul Boyer, *Urban Masses and Moral Order in America* (Cambridge: Harvard University Press, 1978), 123; H. Barbara Weinberg, "Cosmopolitan and Candid Stories, 1877–1915," in *American Stories*, ed. H. Barbara Weinberg and Carrie Rebora Barratt (New Haven: Yale University Press, 2009), 164.

4. "Workers Don't Suffer," http://www.populist.com/03.03.castagnera.html, accessed February 2, 2009; "George Frederick Baer," http://www.answers.com/topic/baer-george-frederick, accessed February 2, 2009.

5. Sven Beckert, *The Monied Metropolis* (New York: Cambridge University Press, 1993), 5, 215, 257; Thomas Bender, *The Unfinished City* (New York: New York University Press, 2002), 77; William Dean Howells, *A Hazard of New Fortunes* (New York: Harper and Brothers, 1890), 60; Edith Wharton, *The House of Mirth* (London: Virago Press Edition, 1990), 31; John Dos Passos, *Manhattan Transfer* (Boston: Houghton Mifflin, 1925), 262.

6. Beckert, *The Monied Metropolis*, 51, 164.

7. Ibid., 5–7, 12.

8. Beckert, *The Monied Metropolis*, 285; John Higham, *Strangers in the Land* (New York: Atheneum, 1972), 55; Michael McGerr, *A Fierce Discontent* (New York: Oxford University Press, 2003), 214; Richard Felton Outcault, *R. F. Outcault's The Yellow Kid* (Northampton: Kitchen Sink Press, 1995), 17; Arthur Schlesinger Jr., *The Crisis of the Old Order* (Boston: Houghton Mifflin, 1957), 126–127; Boyer, *Urban Masses and Moral Order in America*, 128, 129, 192; Higham, *Strangers in the Land*, 36; Bonnie Yochelson and Daniel Czitrom, *Rediscovering Jacob Riis* (New York: The New Press, 2007), 1.

9. John Van Dyke, *The New New York* (New York: Macmillan, 1909), 264.

10. Ibid., 241, 258, 261–262, 264, 266, 269.

11. Beckert, *The Monied Metropolis*, 218; Weinberg, "Cosmopolitan and Candid Stories, 1877–1915," 114; McGerr, *A Fierce Discontent*, 240.

12. I am not claiming that French artists faced the same social conditions as American artists. The class structure was very different, which was the most striking dissimilarity between the two. I am merely pointing out that French impressionism often depicted the upper classes. My thanks to Rebecca Zurier for bringing this to my attention.

13. David Shi, *Facing Facts* (New York: Oxford University Press, 1995), 149.

14. T. J. Clark, *The Painting of Modern Life* (Princeton: Princeton University Press, 1984), 189.

15. Ibid., 260.

16. Weinberg et al., *American Impressionism and Realism*, 8; William Gerdts, *Impressionist New York* (New York: Artabras, 1994), 34.

17. Gerdts, *Impressionist New York*, 45, 91, 149; Goodrich, *John Sloan*, 5.

18. Gerdts, *Impressionist New York*, 25.

19. Ronald Bukoff, "Childe Hassam: Cityscapes, 1885–1900," MA thesis, Indiana University, 1979, 3–7; H. Barbara Weinberg, *Childe Hassam* (New York: Metropolitan Museum of Art, 2004), 3; Jane Weaver, ed., *Sadakichi Hartmann: Critical Modernist* (Berkeley: University of California Press, 1991), 302.

20. Weinberg, "Director's Foreword," in *Childe Hassam*, 87; Myers, *The Artist in Manhattan*, 101–102; Elizabeth Broun, "Childe Hassam's America," *American Art* 13.3 (Autumn 1999): 33.

21. Broun, "Childe Hassam's America," 35, 44, 48.

22. Joshua Brown, " 'A Spectator of Life—A Reverential, Enthusiastic, Emotional Spectator,' " *American Quarterly* 49.2 (June 1997): 357; Weinberg, *Childe Hassam*, 93; Ulrich Hiesinger, *Childe Hassam* (Munich: Prestel, 1999), 76; William Taylor, "The Painter and the City," in *Painting the Town*, ed. Jan Ramirez (New York: Museum of the City of New York, 2000), 29.

23. Gerdts, *Impressionist New York*, 69.

24. Stansell, *American Moderns*, 39; Boyer, *Urban Masses and Moral Order in America*, 156; McGerr, *A Fierce Discontent*, xv.

25. Boyer, *Urban Masses and Moral Order in America*, 176; Angela Blake, *How New York Became American* (Baltimore: Johns Hopkins University Press, 2006), 16; William McAdoo, *Guarding a Great City* (New York: Harper & Brothers, 1906), 70; Mark Connelly, *The Response to Prostitution* (Chapel Hill: University of North Carolina Press, 1980), 12, 37; Michael Marks Davis Jr., *The Exploitation of Pleasure* (New York: Russell Sage Foundation, 1911), 3, 34, 59; Alison Isenberg, *Downtown America* (Chicago: University of Chicago Press, 2004), 3.

26. Robert Snyder and Rebecca Zurier, "Picturing the City," in *Metropolitan Lives*, ed. Rebecca Zurier, Robert Snyder, and Virginia Mecklenburg (New York: National Museum of American Art in Association with W.W. Norton, 1995), 116; Stansell, *American Moderns*, 127; Harold Faulkner, *Politics, Reform and Expansion* (New York: Harper and Row, 1959), 26.

27. "Foreign Immigration and the Tenement House in New York City," in *The Tenement House Problem*, ed. Robert De Forest and Lawrence Veiller (New York: Macmillan, 1903), 73, 75.

28. David Nasaw, *Children of the City* (New York: Oxford University Press, 1986).

29. Robert Hunter, *Poverty* (New York: Macmillan, 1904), v, viii, 58, 63–64, 66, 88, 192, 194, 198, 322; Edwin Markham, "A Book on Poverty," *New York Times*, January 7, 1905.

30. Blake, *How New York Became American*, 30–31.

31. Edith Patterson Meyer, *"Not Charity, but Justice": The Story of Jacob A. Riis* (New York: Vanguard Press, 1974), 67.

32. Yochelson and Czitrom, *Rediscovering Jacob Riis*, xvi, 105; Meyer, *"Not Charity, but Justice,"* xi–xii, 58–59.

33. Blake, *How New York Became American*, 24–25.

34. Cary Goodman, *Choosing Sides* (New York: Schocken Books, 1979), 6.

35. Yochelson and Czitrom, *Rediscovering Jacob Riis*, 23, 120; Maren Stange, *Symbols of Ideal Life* (Cambridge: Cambridge University Press, 1989), 4; Doezema, *George Bellows and Urban America*, 137; Samuel Freedman "Review of 'The Snakehead,' *New York Times*, August 16, 2009, *Sunday Book* Review, 9.

36. Mark Hellinger, *The Ten Million* (New York: Farrar and Rinehart, 1934), 157.

37. Marianne Doezema, "The "Real" New York," in Michael Quick, Jane Meyers, Marianne Doezema, and Franklin Kelly, *The Paintings of George Bellows* (New York: Harry N. Abrams, 1992), 103.

38. Rebecca Zurier and Robert Snyder, "Introduction," in *Metropolitan Lives*, 21; Blake, *How New York Became American*, 19, 29.

39. Kate Sampsell-Willmann, *Lewis Hine as Social Critic* (Jackson: University Press of Mississippi, 2009), 16, 17, 131, 149.

40. Ibid., 27–28.

41. Ibid., 32, 93.

Chapter Three. Vision from an Ashcan

1. Michael Owen, "Foreword," in *The Eight* (New York: Owen Gallery, 2002).

2. Loughery, *John Sloan*, 61.

3. Marianne Doezema, *American Realism and the Industrial Age* (Cleveland: Cleveland Museum of Art, 1981), 71; Myers, *Artist in Manhattan*, 48.

4. Dos Passos, *Manhattan Transfer*, 260.

5. "Introduction," in *American Impressionism and Realism*, ed. H. Barbara Weinberg, Doreen Bolger, and David Park Curry (New York: Metropolitan Museum of Art, 1994), 4.

6. Judith Zilczer, "The Eight on Tour, 1908–1909," *American Art Journal* 16.3 (Summer 1984): 35; Baur, *Revolution and Tradition in Modern American Art*, 5.

7. Conn, *The Divided Mind*, 259.

8. Theodore Dreiser, "'The Cliff Dwellers': A Painting by George Bellows," *Vanity Fair* (December 1925), 55.

9. William Taylor, *In Pursuit of Gotham* (New York: Oxford University Press, 1992), 2.

10. Doezema, *George Bellows and Urban America*, 41, 45; "The Big Idea: George Bellows Talks About Patriotism for Beauty," *The Touchstone* 1 (July 1917): 269.

11. Doezema, *George Bellows and Urban America*, 6; Louis Baury, "The Message of Manhattan," *The Bookman* 33 (August 1911): 592.

12. Dos Passos, *Manhattan Transfer*, 3.

13. Michael Lobel, "John Sloan: Figuring the Painter in the Crowd," *Art Bulletin* 93.3 (September 2011): 359–360; Sean Wilentz, "*Election Night, Times Square*: Spectacle, Politics, and the Young George Bellows," in *George Bellows*, ed. Charles Brock et al. (Washington, DC: National Gallery of Art, 2012), 37.

14. Rebecca Zurier, *Picturing the City* (Berkeley: University of California Press, 2006), 181; Deborah Fairman, "The Landscape of Display: The Ashcan School, Spectacle, and the Staging of Everyday Life," *Prospects* 18 (1993): 205.

15. Bruce Weber, *Ashcan Kids: Children in the Art of Henri, Luks, Glackens, Bellows & Sloan* (New York: Berry-Hill Galleries, 1999), 25.

16. Perlman, *Painters of the Ashcan School*, 12, 155; Zurier and Snyder, "Introduction," in *Metropolitan Lives*, 13.

17. Loughery, *John Sloan*, 93.

18. Brooks, *John Sloan*, 99; Homer, *Robert Henri and His Circle*, 84; Helen Farr Sloan, Introduction," in *John Sloan—Spectator of Life*, ed. Rowland Elzea and Elizabeth Hawkes (Wilmington: Delaware Art Museum, 1988), 9; David Coleman, "The Social Commentary of John Sloan, 1900–1916, in the Context of American Progressivism," MA thesis, University of California, Berkeley, 1972, 27.

19. Goodrich, *John Sloan*, 22; "The Big Idea," 275.

20. James Huneker, "George Luks, Versatile Painter of Humanity," *New York Times Magazine*, February 6, 1916, 13.

21. John Sloan, *The Gist of Art* (New York: American Artists Group, 1939), 5, 41; St. John, *John Sloan's New York Scene*, xx.

22. Patricia Hills and Roberta Tarbell, *The Figurative Tradition and the Whitney Museum of American Art* (London: Associated University Press, 1980), 59.

23. St. John, *John Sloan's New York Scene*, 308–309.

24. Suzanne Kinser, "Prostitutes in the Art of John Sloan," *Prospects* 9 (1985): 244.

25. Patricia Hills, "John Sloan's Images of Working-Class Women," *Prospects* 5 (1980): 174.

26. When I was growing up in the Bronx in the 1950s, the New York Central tracks were underground, occasionally breaking the surface, yet still they traveled below overpasses to carry the borough's traffic. If I was a good boy, my mother would take me to a particular perch, and we would wait for a train to wave to the engineer. Invariably, he would smile and wave back, a moment of recognition and intense delight for me.

27. Schapiro, *Modern Art*, 175.

28. Robert Henri, "A Practical Talk to Those Who Study Art," *The Press*, May 12, 1901.

29. Robert Henri, *The Art Spirit*, Icon Edition (Boulder: Westview Press, 1984), 17, 213.

30. *John Sloan/Robert Henri: Their Philadelphia Years (1866–1904)* (Philadelphia: Moore College of Art, 1976), 28; "The Big Idea," 275.

31. Wanda Corn, "The New New York," *Art in America* (July–August 1973), 58–65; Amy Goldin, "The Eight's Laissez Faire Revolution," *Art in America* (July–August 1973), 42–49; Louis Baury, "The Message of Proletaire," *The Bookman* 34 (December 1911): 409.

32. Emily Kies, "The City and the Machine: Urban and Industrial Illustration in America, 1880–1900," PhD dissertation, Columbia University, 1971, 75; Shi, *Facing Facts*, 264; Coleman, "The Social Commentary of John Sloan," 39.

33. Coleman, "The Social Commentary of John Sloan," 40.

34. Elzea and Hawkes, *John Sloan—Spectator of Life*, 11; Doezema, *George Bellows and Urban America*, 170–171, 173.

35. Brooks, *John Sloan*, 55.

36. Constance Schwartz, *The Shock of Modernism in America* (Roslyn Harbor:: Nassau County Museum of Fine Art, 1984), 11; Brooks, *John Sloan*, 1.

37. "Robert Henri, an Apostle of Artistic Individuality," *Current Literature* 52.4 (April 1912): 468.

38. George Moore, *Modern Painting*, enlarged new ed. (London: Walter Scott, 1906), 214; Henri, "Progress in Our National Art Must Spring from the Development of Individuality of Ideas and Freedom of Expression," *The Craftsman* 15.4 (January 1909): 387; Patricia Hills, "John Sloan's Images of Working-Class Women," *Prospects* 5 (1980): 158.

39. Perlman, *Painters of the Ashcan School*, 195; Shi, *Facing Facts*, 251–252; *Los Angeles Herald*, December 2, 1919.

Chapter Four. The Ashcan Artists

1. Rockwell Kent, *It's Me O Lord* (New York: Dodd, Mead, 1955), 81; Milroy, *Painters of a New Century*, 24; Perlman, *Robert Henri*, 9, 11, 79, 99; Everett Shinn, "Recollections of the Eight," in *The Eight* (New York: Brooklyn Museum, 1944), 22; for an example of Henri's handwriting, see samples in the Macbeth Gallery Records, Archives of American Art, Smithsonian Institution.

2. du Bois, *Artists Say the Silliest Things*, 86; Morgan, *George Bellows*, 39; Perlman, *Painters of the Ashcan School*, 89; Milroy, *Painters of a New Century*, 24; C. B. Ely, "The Modern Tendency in Henri, Sloan, and Bellows," *Art in America and Elsewhere* 10 (1922): 132.

3. Perlman, *Robert Henri*, 95; Henri, *The Art Spirit*, 5, 15.

4. Henri, *The Art Spirit*, 102–103, 104; Florence Barlow Ruthrauff, "Robert Henri—Master of Painters," *Fine Arts Journal* 27 (July 1912): 463.

5. du Bois, *Artists Say the Silliest Things*, 88; Brooks, *John Sloan*, 21.

6. Henri, *The Art Spirit*, 86, 138.

7. Kent, *It's Me O Lord*, 81–82; Henri, *The Art Spirit*, 127.

8. While Bennard Perlman claimed that a bout with pneumonia made Henri hesitant to paint outdoors, William Gerdts hypothesized that a 1902 show that had brought critical acclaim, but few sales, gave Henri cause to consider a new direction for his own art. No definitive answer to this quandary exists. Perlman, *Revolutionaries of Realism*, xvii; Gerdts, *Impressionist New York*, 35.

9. Perlman argued, "For some Henri will always remain a teacher first," and he quoted a newspaper reporter who remarked, "Robert Henri might have developed into America's greatest painter had he not chosen to become America's greatest art teacher." William Innes Homer, while admitting that Henri "is as important historically for his influence as for his painting," claimed that his "image has been badly

distorted" by "the myth that Henri merely painted on the side and was primarily a gifted and persuasive teacher." Perlman, *Revolutionaries of Realism*, 138; Homer, *Robert Henri and His Circle*, viii, 6.

10. du Bois, *Artists Say the Silliest Things*, 84; Perlman, *Robert Henri and His Circle*, 104; Betsy Fulman, "The Art Spirit in the Classroom," in *American Women Modernists*, ed. Marian Wardle (Salt Lake City: Brigham Young University Museum of Art, 2005), 113.

11. Erika Doss, "Complicating Modernism," in *American Women Modernists*, ed. Marian Wardle (Salt Lake City: Brigham Young University Museum of Art, 2005), 118; Perlman, *Robert Henri*, xv; *John Sloan/ Robert Henri: Their Philadelphia Years (1866–1904)*, 27; Homer, *Robert Henri and His Circle*, 159.

12. Homer, *Robert Henri and His Circle*, 269; Shi, *Facing Facts*, 258; Marian Wardle, "Thoroughly Modern, in *American Women Modernists*, ed. Marian Wardle (Salt Lake City: Brigham Young University Museum of Art, 2005), 6; Sadakichi Hartmann, "Studio-Talk," *The International Studio* 30 (December 1906): 183; Homer, *Robert Henri and His Circle*, vii; Morgan, *George Bellows*, 37; Joyce Carol Oates, *George Bellows* (Hopewell: Ecco Press, 1995), 13; Edward Hopper, "John Sloan and the Philadelphians," *The Arts* 11.4 (April 1927): 175; Gail Levin, *Edward Hopper: The Art and the Artist* (New York: W.W. Norton, 1980), 17; Stansell, *American Moderns*, 151; Guy Pène du Bois, "Robert Henri: The Man," *Arts and Decoration* 14 (November 1920): 36; Weaver, *Sadakichi Hartmann*, 270.

13. Schwartz, *The Shock of Modernism in America*, 17; St. John, *John Sloan's New York Scene*, 245, 280; Brooks, *John Sloan*, 16.

14. Material on Sloan's Philadelphia years from: Helen Farr Sloan, "Introduction," in *John Sloan: New York Etchings (1905–1949)*, ed. Helen Farr Sloan (New York: Dover, 1978), v–vi; Joyce Schiller and Heather Coyle, "John Sloan's Urban Encounters," in Heather Coyle and Joyce Schiller, *John Sloan's New York* (Wilmington and New Haven: Delaware Art Museum and Yale University Press, 2007), 24–26, 31; Brooks, *John Sloan*, 15; Avis Berman, "Artist as Rebel: John Sloan vs. the Status Quo," *Smithsonian* 19.1 (April 1988): 74.

15. Schiller and Coyle, *John Sloan's New York*, 31, 33, 57; Brooks, *John Sloan*, 188; Kent, *It's Me O Lord*, 219; Sloan, *John Sloan's Etchings*, ix.

16. Guy Pène du Bois, *John Sloan* (New York: Whitney Museum of American Art, 1931), 8, 9; Brooks, *John Sloan*, 69; Richard Fitzgerald, *Art and Politics* (Westport: Greenwood Press, 1973), 123.

17. St. John, *John Sloan's New York Scene*, 13; Brooks, *John Sloan*, 49; Berman, "Artist as Rebel," 74; Pach, *Queer Thing Painting*, 170.

18. David Scott and E. John Bullard, *John Sloan, 1871–1951* (Boston: Boston Book and Art, 1972), 20; Doezema, *American Realism and the Industrial Age*, 58; Rebecca Zurier, *Art for the Masses* (Philadelphia: Temple University Press, 1988), 56; Sarah Vare, "Sloan," in *The Eight and American Modernisms*, ed. Elizabeth Kennedy (Chicago: University of Chicago Press, 2009), 152.

19. Zurier, *Picturing the City*, 215; Estelle Ries, "The Relation of Art to Every-Day Things: An Interview with George Bellows," *Arts and Decoration* 15 (July 1921): 158.

20. Haverstock, *George Bellows*, 12; Zurier, *Picturing the City*, 215; Doezema, *George Bellows and Urban America*, 24.

21. Haverstock, *George Bellows*, 27, 30; Doezema, *George Bellows*, 183; Loughery, *John Sloan*, 77; Brooks, *John Sloan*, 95.

22. "The Spring Academy," *New York Sun*, March 17, 1911; *Addison Gallery of American Art, 65 Years* (Andover: Addison Gallery of American Art, 1996), 323; Ries, "The Relation of Art," 158; Oates, *George Bellows*, 7; Doezema, *George Bellows*, 198.

23. John Loughery, "The Mysterious George Luks," *Arts Magazine* 64.4 (December 1987): 34.

24. Perlman, *Painters of the Ashcan School*, 64; Outcault, *R. F. Outcault's The Yellow Kid*, 114; Robert Gambone, "George Luks, 'Hogan's Alley,' and Ashcan School Social Thought," *Aurora: The Journal of the History of Art* 6 (2005): 38.

25. Schiller and Coyle, *Sloan's New York*, 33; Glackens, *William Glackens and the Eight*, 97.

26. *The Eight*, Owen Gallery, New York, Exhibition of Paintings, October 23–December 14, 2002; Huneker, "George Luks," 13; Schwab, *Americans in the Arts*, 518, 524; Gambone, "George Luks," 39.

27. Perlman, *Painters of the Ashcan School*, 54, 55; Kent, *It's Me O Lord*, 229; du Bois, *Artists Say the Silliest Things*, 182.

28. Judith Hansen O'Toole, "Luks," in *The Eight and American Modernisms*, ed. Elizabeth Kennedy (Chicago: University of Chicago Press, 2009), 91.

29. Young, *The Eight*, 122; John Sloan to Dolly Sloan, August 18, 1908, John Sloan Papers, Helen Farr Sloan Library and Archives, Delaware Art Museum, Wilmington, Delaware; Henry Clifford, "Artists of the Philadelphia Press: William Glackens, George Luks, Everett Shinn, John Sloan, October 14–November 18, 1945," *Philadelphia Museum Bulletin* 11.207 (November 1945): 8; du Bois, *Artists Say the Silliest Things*, 180.

30. Young, *The Eight*, 125; Glackens, *William Glackens and the Eight*, 101; "George Luks, Lusty Proponent of American Individualism, Is Dead," *The Art Digest* 8.4 (November 15, 1933): 5; O'Toole, "Luks," 99.

31. Doezema, *American Realism*, 58; Brooks, *John Sloan*, 27; Clifford, "Artists of the Philadelphia Press," 7; Young, *The Eight*, 95.

32. Milroy, *Painters of a New Century*, 107; Zurier, *Picturing the City*, 184.

33. Homer, *Robert Henri and His Circle*, 81; Glackens, *William Glackens and the Eight*, 19.

34. Glackens, *William Glackens and the Eight*, 5; Zurier, *Picturing the City*, 184.

35. Rebecca Zurier, "The Making of Six New York Artists," in *Metropolitan Lives*, ed. Rebecca Zurier, Robert Snyder, and Virginia Mecklenburg (New York: National Museum of American Art in Association with W.W. Norton, 1995), 59; Letter from Edith Glackens to John Sloan, undated, John Sloan Papers, Helen Farr Sloan Library and Archives, Delaware Art Museum, Wilmington, Delaware.

36. Edith Deshazo, *Everett Shinn, 1876–1953* (New York: Clarkson N. Potter, 1974), xv; Aline Louchheim, "Last of 'The Eight' Looks Back," *New York Times*, November 2, 1952; Clifford, "Artists of the Philadelphia Press," 8.

37. Zurier, *Picturing the City*, 138–139.

38. Deshazo, *Everett Shinn*, 33, 34, 58; Perlman, *Painters of the Ashcan School*, 99.

39. Sylvia Yount, "Consuming Drama: Everett Shinn and the Spectacular City," *American Art* 6.4 (Autumn 1992): 90.

40. Zurier, *Picturing the City*, 179; Milroy, *Painters of a New Century*, 117; Young, *The Eight*, 143.

41. Homer, *Robert Henri and His Circle*, 129.

42. Baur, *Revolution and Tradition in Modern American Art*, 14; Myers, *Artist in Manhattan*, 49–50; St. John, *John Sloan's New York Scene*, 537; "Jerome Myers as an Etcher and a Student of Human Nature," *The Craftsman* 29.1 (October 1915): 32: Grant Holcomb III, *Jerome Myers* (New York: Kraushaar Galleries, 1970), introduction.

Chapter Five. The Art Scene

1. Ruth Bohan, *Looking into Walt Whitman* (University Park: Pennsylvania State University Press, 2006), 2, 170.

2. Kathleen Kennedy Townsend, "Walt Whitman and the Soul of Democracy," *The Atlantic*, July 8, 2011, http://www.theatlantic.com/national/archive/2011/07/walt-whitman-and-the-soul-of-democracy/241558/, accessed October 1, 2015; James Miller Jr., ed., *Complete Poetry and Selected Prose by Walt Whitman* (Boston: Houghton Mifflin, 1959), 12–13, 329–330.

3. Homer, *Robert Henri and His Circle*, 76; Robert Henri, "A Practical Talk to Those Who Study Art," *The Philadelphia Press*, May 12, 1901; Brooks, *John Sloan*, 19, 36; St. John, *John Sloan's New York Scene*, 428.

4. Lloyd Goodrich, *Thomas Eakins* (New York: Whitney Museum of American Art, 1933), 143, 144; Axel Von Saldern, *Triumph of Realism* (New York: Brooklyn Museum, 1967), 47; Bohan, *Walt Whitman*, 113.

5. Goodrich, *Thomas Eakins*, 3; Pach, *Queer Thing Painting*, 322; Henri, *The Art Spirit*, 91.

6. Goodrich, *Thomas Eakins*, 129; Alan Braddock, *Thomas Eakins and the Culture of Modernity* (Berkeley: University of California Press, 2009), 230.

7. Goodrich, *Thomas Eakins*, 139; Braddock, *Thomas Eakins and the Culture of Modernity*, 213.

8. Elizabeth Johns, *Thomas Eakins* (Princeton: Princeton University Press, 1983), 8–9, 11.

9. Johns, *Thomas Eakins*, 3, 47; Horace Traubel, "Thomas Eakins," *The Conservator* 28 (February 1918): 184; Shi, *Facing Facts*, 142.

10. Johns, *Thomas Eakins*, 49, 55; Goodrich, *Thomas Eakins*, 50–56.

11. Goodrich, *Thomas Eakins*, 51–54, 131–132; Randy Kennedy, "Shedding Darkness on an Eakins Painting," *New York Times*, July 18, 2010; Johns, *Thomas Eakins*, 76, 77; Von Saldern, *Triumph of Realism*, 48.

12. Randall Griffin, *Thomas Anshutz: Artist and Teacher* (Seattle: Heckscher Museum, 1994), 30–31; Shi, *Facing Facts*, 128.

13. Randall Griffin, "Thomas Anshutz's 'The Ironworkers' Noontime'": Remythologizing the Industrial Worker," *Smithsonian Studies in American Art* 4.¾ (Summer–Autumn 1990): 129.

14. Griffin, *Thomas Anshutz*, 51; Weinberg, "Cosmopolitan and Candid Stories, 1877–1915," 155.

15. Griffin, "Thomas Anshutz's 'The Ironworkers' Noontime,'" 129; Griffin, *Thomas Anshutz*, 52.

16. Thomas Pauly, "American Art and Labor: The Case of Anshutz's 'The Ironworkers' Noontime.'" *American Quarterly* 40.3 (September 1988): 334; Shi, *Facing Facts*, 252; Dolly Sloan to John Sloan, December 20, 1911, May 26, 1911, Thomas Anshutz to John Sloan, February 5, 1909, all in John Sloan Papers, Helen Farr Sloan Library and Archives, Delaware Art Museum; Loughery, *John Sloan*, 36.

17. Doezema, *American Realism and the Industrial Age*, 14; Joseph Pennell, *Joseph Pennell's Pictures of the Wonder of Work* (Philadelphia: J. B. Lippincott, 1916), 7; Joseph Pennell, "The World of Work in the Northwest," *Harper's Monthly Magazine* 132 (March 1916): 591.

18. Van Dyke, *The New New York*.

Chapter Six. Moving On

1. Zurier, "The Making of Six New York Artists," in *Metropolitan Lives*, 83; Katherine Manthorne, "John Sloan, Moving Pictures, and Celtic Spirits," in *John Sloan's New York*, ed. Heather Coyle and Joyce Schiller (Wilmington and New Haven: Delaware Art Museum and Yale University Press, 2007), 176.

2. Avis Berman, *Edward Hopper's New York* (San Francisco: Pomegranate, 2005), 7; Gail Levin, *Edward Hopper: The Art and the Artist* (New York: W.W. Norton, 1980), 19.

3. Frank Getelein, "The Legacy of Edward Hopper, Painter of Light and Loneliness," *Smithsonian* 2 (September 1971): 62.

4. Levin, *Edward Hopper*, 63; Jeremiah Moss, "Nighthawks State of Mind," *New York Times*, July 5, 2010.

5. Teresa Carbone, "Silent Pictures: Encounters with a Remade World," in *Youth and Beauty: Art of the American Twenties*, ed. Teresa Carbone (New York: Brooklyn Museum, 2011), 150.

6. Suzanne Burrey, "Edward Hopper: The Emptying Spaces," *Arts Digest* 1 (April 1955): 10.

7. Charles Burchfield, "Hopper: Career of Silent Poetry," *Art News* 49 (March 1950): 16; Peter Conrad, *The Art of the City* (New York: Oxford University Press, 1984), 102.

8. Conrad, *Art of the City*, 104; Getelein, "The Legacy of Edward Hopper," 66.

9. Levin, *Edward Hopper*, 45.

10. Conrad, *Art of the City*, 107, italics in original.

11. Scott and Rutkoff, *New York Modern*, 196; Goodrich, *Armory Show*, 64; Reginald Marsh, "What I See in Laning's Art," *Creative Art* 12 (March 1933): 187.

12. Hilton Kramer, "The Unhappy Fates of Hayes Miller," *New York Times*, March 11, 1979.

13. William Scott and Peter Rutkoff, *New York Modern* (Baltimore: Johns Hopkins University Press, 1999), 186–187.

14. Ann Wagner, *1934: A New Deal for Artists* (Washington, DC: Smithsonian American Art Museum, 2009), 6–7, 19–20, 27.

15. *City Life Illustrated* (Wilmington: Delaware Art Museum, 1980), 68; Lloyd Goodrich, *Reginald Marsh* (New York: Whitney Museum of American Art, 1955), 5; Samantha Baskind, *Raphael Soyer and the Search for Modern Jewish Art* (Chapel Hill: University of North Carolina Press, 2004), 89.

16. Baskind, *Raphael Soyer*, 54; Lloyd Goodrich, *Raphael Soyer* (New York: Whitney Museum of American Art, 1967), 5; Raphael Soyer to Mrs. John Sloan, March 17, 1941, John Sloan Papers, Helen Farr Sloan Library and Archives, Delaware Art Museum.

17. Baskind, *Raphael Soyer*, 1, 81; Matthew Baigell, "From Hester Street to Fifty-Seventh Street: Jewish-American Artists in New York," in *Painting a Place in America*, ed. Norman Kleeblatt and Susan Chevlowe (New York: The Jewish Museum, 1991), 62.

Chapter Seven. The City as Art

1. John Reed, "Almost Thirty," *New Republic*, April 29, 1936, 337; Henry Adams, *The Education of Henry Adams* (Boston: Houghton Mifflin, 1918), 499; "Silent Decade," *Art in America* (July–August 1973), 32; Doezema, *American Realism and the Industrial Age*, 75; Dreiser, *The "Genius,"* 108; Theodore Dreiser, *The Color of a Great City* (New York: Boni and Liveright, 1923), 3; Beckert, *The Monied Metropolis*, 111; David Peters Corbett, *An American Experiment* (New Haven: Yale University Press, 2011), 12.

2. Dreiser, *Color of a Great City*, 2; E. B. White, *Here Is New York* (New York: The Little Boardroom, 1949), 33.

3. Herbert Croly, "New York as the American Metropolis," *Architectural Record* (March 1903): 194; Howells, *A Hazard of New Fortunes*, 9; Blake, *How New York Became American*, 7.

4. St. John, *John Sloan's New York Scene*, 215, 419, 420, 434, 497; Ely, "The Modern Tendency in Henri, Sloan, and Bellows," 138.

5. Moe Foner, *Not for Bread Alone* (Ithaca: Cornell University Press, 2002), 7.

6. "Seeing America," last modified December 26, 2011, http://mag.rochester.edu/seeingAmerica/pdfs/35.pdf.

7. St. John, *John Sloan's New York Scene*, 240.

8. Betty Smith, *A Tree Grows in Brooklyn* (New York: Harper and Brothers, 1943), 135.

9. Leeds, "The Eight in Context," 30.

10. St. John, *John Sloan's New York Scene*, 4.

11. Ibid., 4.

12. Dreiser, *The Color of a Great City*, 74.

13. Smith, *A Tree Grows in Brooklyn*, 127.

14. Robert W. Snyder, "City in Transition," in *Metropolitan Lives*, ed. Rebecca Zurier, Robert Snyder, and Virginia Mecklenburg (New York: National Museum of American Art in Association with W.W. Norton, 1995), 33; Dos Passos, *Manhattan Transfer*, 156; John Foster Fraser, *America at Work* (London: Cassell, 1903), 7; Doezema, *George Bellows and Urban America*, 25.

15. Sampsell-Willmann, *Lewis Hine as Social Critic*, 22.

16. Doezema, *George Bellows and Urban America*, 31.

17. Dos Passos, *Manhattan Transfer*, 122.

18. Dreiser, *The Color of a Great City*, 112, 113.

19. Joseph Amato, *On Foot* (New York: New York University Press, 2004), 173; Snyder and Zurier, "Picturing the City," in *Metropolitan Lives*, 148; Snyder, "City in Transition," in *Metropolitan Lives*, 29.

20. Laural Weintraub, "Women as Urban Spectators in John Sloan's Early Work," *American Art* 15.2 (Summer 2001): 72.

21. Smith, *A Tree Grows in Brooklyn*, 11.

22. Deborah Fairman, "The Landscape of Display: The Ashcan School, Spectacle, and the Staging of Everyday Life," *Prospects* 18 (1993): 206.

23. John Sloan to Dolly Sloan, September 16, 1908, John Sloan Papers, Delaware Art Museum, Wilmington, DE.

24. Peter Baldwin, *In the Watches of the Night* (Chicago: University of Chicago Press, 2012), 155.

25. St. John, *John Sloan's New York Scene*, 133.

26. Zurier, *Picturing the City*, 14

27. Vanessa Schwartz, *Spectacular Realities* (Berkeley: University of California Press, 1998), 11, 20.

28. Joseph Yardley, "Joseph Yardley on 'The Lost Art of Walking,'" *Washington Post*, November 9, 2008; St. John, *John Sloan's New York Scene*, 428; Grace Paley, *Long Walks and Intimate Talks* (New York: City University of New York Feminist Press, 1991), 6.

29. John Sloan to Dolly Sloan, February 22, 1909, John Sloan Papers, Delaware Art Museum, Wilmington, DE.

30. Edward Martin, "Manhattan Lights," *Harper's Magazine* (February 1907): 365, 367.

31. John Sloan to Dolly Sloan, February 19, 1909, John Sloan Papers, Delaware Art Museum, Wilmington, DE.

32. Lewis Erenberg, *Steppin' Out* (Chicago: University of Chicago Press, 1981), 87.

33. Schwartz, *Spectacular Realities*, 18.

34. Dolly Sloan to John Sloan, March 22, 1909, and Robert Henri to John Sloan, January 24, 1908, both in John Sloan Papers, Delaware Art Museum, Wilmington, DE.

Chapter Eight. People of the City

1. William Whyte, *City* (New York: Doubleday, 1988), 2, 21; Michael Kimmelman, "Knickerbocker's Knicknacks," *New York Times*, September 22, 2000.

2. Outcault, *R. F. Outcault's The Yellow Kid*, 135; Weber, *Ashcan Kids*, 13.

3. Goodman, *Choosing Sides*, 3; St. John, *John Sloan's New York Scene*, 431; Michael Marks Davis Jr., *The Exploitation of Pleasure* (New York: Russell Sage Foundation, 1911), 4; "Jerome Myers as an Etcher and a Student of Human Nature," *The Craftsman* (October 1915): 25–26; Howard Chudacoff, *Children at Play* (New York: New York University Press, 2007), 130.

4. Ruth Gay, *Unfinished People* (New York: W. W. Norton, 1996), 53; Baury, "The Message of Proletaire," 405.

5. Michael Carlebach, *Bain's New York* (Mineola: Dover, 2011), 116.

6. Marianne Doezema, "Tenement Life: Cliff Dwellers, 1906–1913," in *George Bellows*, ed. Charles Brock et al. (Washington, DC: National Gallery of Art, 2012), 47.

7. Michael Quick, Jane Myers, Marianne Doezema, and Franklin Kelley, *The Paintings of George Bellows* (New York: Harry N. Abrams, 1992), 101, 102; "George Bellows, an Artist with 'Red Blood,'" *Current Literature* 5 (September 1912): 346.

8. John Cournos, "Three Painters of the New York School," *The International Studio* (1915): 241.

9. Chudacoff, *Children at Play*, 148, 151.

10. Ibid., 114.

11. Robert Slayton, *Back of the Yards* (Chicago: University of Chicago Press, 1986), 42–43.

12. Weber, *Ashcan Kids*, 20.

13. Hills, "John Sloan's Images of Working-Class Women," 163, 172, 180, 189.

14. St. John, *John Sloan's New York Scene*, 219; Loughery, "The Mysterious George Luks," 35.

15. Loughery, *John Sloan*, 183.

16. St. John, *John Sloan's New York Scene*, 13.

17. Connelly, *The Response to Prostitution*, 29.

18. *Ibid.*, 18.

19. Jim Cresswell, *The Tramp in America* (London: Reaktion Books, 2001), 89; Erenberg, *Steppin' Out*, 77–78.

20. Theodore Roosevelt, *An Autobiography* (New York: Macmillan, 1913), 29; Zurier, *Picturing the City*, 119.

21. Dos Passos, *Manhattan Transfer*, 39, 124, 148; Baldwin, *In the Watches of the Night*, 83.

22. Elliott Gorn, *The Manly Art* (Ithaca: Cornell University Press, 1986), 27, 69, 181; Doezema, *George Bellows and Urban America*, 68; "In Defense of Pugilism," *American Magazine* (August 1909): 414.

23. Doezema, *George Bellows and Urban America*, 81.

24. John Wilmerdling, "The Art of George Bellows and the Energies of Modern America," in *The Paintings of George Bellows*, ed. Michael Quick, Jane Myers, Marianne Doezema, and Franklin Kelley (New York: Harry N. Abrams, 1992), 2; "George Bellows, an Artist with 'Red Blood,'" 342; Morgan, *George Bellows*, 77.

25. E. A. Carmean Jr., John Wilmerding, Linda Ayres, and Deborah Chotner, *Bellows: The Boxing Pictures* (Washington, DC: National Gallery of Art, 1982), 51.

26. Snyder and Zurier, "Picturing the City," in *Metropolitan Lives*, fig. 179; Morgan, *George Bellows*, 69.

27. Morgan, *George Bellows*, 98.

Chapter Nine. Life in the Ashcan City

1. Sir Peter Hall, *Cities in Civilization* (New York: Pantheon Books, 1998), 747.

2. Jacob Riis, *How the Other Half Lives* (New York: Dover, 1971), 232.

3. Dos Passos, *Manhattan Transfer*, 9, 216; White, *Here Is New York*, 34–37.

4. Zurier, *Picturing the City*, 197; Sarah Newman, "George Bellows' 'New York' and the Spectacular Reality of the City," *American Art* (Autumn 2004): 92; Loughery, *John Sloan*, 101–102; Mary Fanton Roberts, "John Sloan: His Art and Its Inspiration," *The Touchstone and the American Art Student Magazine* 4 (February 1919): 362.

5. David Jay Lasky, "The Lure of the Roof Is More Than Just Tar Beach," *New York Times*, June 21, 2008.

6. Zurier, *Picturing the City*, 53.

7. Snyder, "The City in Transition," in *Metropolitan Lives*, 37; du Bois, *John Sloan*, 10.

8. Brooks, *John Sloan*, 49, 61–62.

9. Sloan, *John Sloan's Etchings*, plate 8.

10. Dreiser, *The Color of a Great City*, 154–155; Schiller and Coyle, "John Sloan's Urban Encounters," in *John Sloan's New York*, 47; St. John, *John Sloan's New York Scene*, 247.

11. White, *Here Is New York*, 47.

12. Nasaw, *Going Out*, 56, 167–168.

13. St. John, *John Sloan's New York Scene*, 441.

14. Weber, *Ashcan Kids*, 11; Brown, "A Spectator of Life," 378.

Chapter Ten. The Ashcan School and Its Critics

1. Hall, *Cities in Civilization*, 3–4; Sontag, *Against Interpretation*, 296.

2. Randall Griffin, *Homer, Eakins, and Anshutz* (University Park: University of Pennsylvania Press, 2004), xxii.

3. Ibid., xxi.

4. Theodore Roosevelt, "Dante and the Bowery," in *The Oxford Book of American Essays*, ed. Brander Matthews (New York: Oxford University Press, 1914), 480; Forbes Watson, "Introduction," in Robert Henri, *The Art Spirit* (New York: J. B. Lippincott, 1923. Icon Edition, Boulder: Westview Press, 1984), 5; Elizabeth Kennedy, ed., *The Eight and American Modernisms* (Chicago: University of Chicago Press, 2009), 92; Ely, "The Modern Tendency in Henri, Sloan, Bellows," 138; John Spargo, "George Luks, an American Painter of Great Originality and Force, Whose Art Relates to All the Experiences and Interests of Life," *The Craftsman* (September 1907): 601.

5. Corn, "The New New York," 62; Ken Johnson, "Ashcan Views of New Yorkers, Warts, High Spirits and All," *New York Times*, December 28, 2007.

6. Richard Fitzgerald, *Art and Politics* (Westport: Greenwood Press, 1973), 140; Brian O'Doherty, "The Silent Decade," *Art in America* (July–August 1973): 32; Matthew Baigell, "Notes on Realistic Painting and Photography, c. 1900–1910," *Arts Magazine* (November 1979): 141; Goldin, "The Eight's Laissez Faire Revolution," 42.

7. Patterson Sims, "Richard Estes' Realism," in *Richard Estes' Realism* (New Haven: Portland Museum of Art, 2014), 1.

8. Adam Gopnik, "Foreword," in Helen Levitt, *Here and There* (New York: Powerhouse Books, 2004).

9. Schwartz, *The Shock of Modernism in America* (Roslyn Harbor: Nassau County Museum of Fine Art, 1984), 11; Brooks, *John Sloan*, 1.

10. "Robert Henri, an Apostle of Artistic Individuality," *Current Literature* 52.4 (April 1912): 468.

11. Goosen, *Stuart Davis*, 14; Hopper, "John Sloan and the Philadelphians," 168.

Bibliography

Books

Adams, Henry. *The Education of Henry Adams.* Boston: Houghton Mifflin, 1918.
Addison Gallery of American Art, 65 Years. Andover: Addison Gallery of American Art, 1996.
Adelman, Melvin. *A Sporting Time.* Urbana: University of Illinois Press, 1986.
Alexiou, Alice. *The Flatiron.* New York: St. Martin's Press, 2010.
Altshuler, Bruce. *The Avant-Garde in Exhibition.* Berkeley: University of California Press, 1994.
Amato, Joseph. *On Foot.* New York: New York University Press, 2004.
American Stories. LACMA Exhibit Program. February 28–May 23, 2010.
Baldwin, Peter. *In the Watches of the Night.* Chicago: University of Chicago Press, 2012.
Baskind, Samantha. *Raphael Soyer and the Search for Modern Jewish Art.* Chapel Hill: University of North Carolina Press, 2004.
Baur, John. *Revolution and Tradition in Modern American Art.* Cambridge: Harvard University Press, 1951.
Beckert, Sven. *The Monied Metropolis.* New York: Cambridge University Press, 1993.
Bellamy, Edward. *Looking Backward.* New York: The Modern Library, 1954.
Bellows, George W. *The Vibrant Metropolis.* Mineola: Dover. 2002.
Bender, Thomas. *The Unfinished City.* New York: New York University Press, 2002.
Berman, Avis. *Edward Hopper's New York.* San Francisco: Pomegranate, 2005.
Blake, Angela. *How New York Became American.* Baltimore: Johns Hopkins University Press, 2006.
Bohan, Ruth. *Looking into Walt Whitman.* University Park: Pennsylvania State University Press, 2006.
Boswell, Peyton, Jr. *George Bellows.* New York: Crown, 1942.
Boyer, Paul. *Urban Masses and Moral Order in America.* Cambridge: Harvard University Press, 1978.
Brace, Charles Loring. *The Dangerous Classes of New York.* New York: Wynkoop and Hallenbeck, 1872.
Braddock, Alan. *Thomas Eakins and the Culture of Modernity.* Berkeley: University of California Press, 2009.
Braider, Donald. *George Bellows and the Ashcan School of Painting.* Garden City: Doubleday, 1971.
Brock, Charles, et al. *George Bellows.* Washington, DC: National Gallery of Art, 2012.
Brooks, Van Wyck. *John Sloan: A Painter's Life.* New York: E. P. Dutton, 1955.
Brown, Milton. *The Story of the Armory Show.* New York: Abbeville Press, 1988.
Burns, Sarah. *Inventing the Modern Artist.* New Haven: Yale University Press, 1996.
Byington, Margaret. *Homestead.* New York: Pittsburgh Survey and Charities Publication Committee, 1910.
Carlebach, Michael. *Bain's New York.* Mineola: Dover, 2011.
Carbone, Teresa, ed. *Youth and Beauty: Art of the American Twenties.* New York: Brooklyn Museum, 2011.

Carmean, E. A., Jr., John Wilmerding, Linda Ayres, and Deborah Chotner. *Bellows: The Boxing Pictures*. Washington, DC: National Gallery of Art, 1982.

Chudacoff, Howard. *Children at Play*. New York: New York University Press, 2007.

City Life Illustrated. Wilmington: Delaware Art Museum, 1980.

Clark, Eliot. *History of the National Academy of Design*. New York: Columbia University Press, 1954.

Clark, T. J. *The Painting of Modern Life*. Princeton: Princeton University Press, 1984.

Coco, Janice. *John Sloan's Women*. Newark: University of Delaware Press, 2004.

Cohen, Marilyn. *Reginald Marsh's New York*. New York: Dover, 1983.

Conn, Peter. *The Divided Mind*. New York: Cambridge University Press, 1983.

Conrad, Peter. *The Art of the City*. New York: Oxford University Press, 1984.

Conway, Robert. *The Powerful Hand of George Bellows*. Washington, DC: Trust for Museum Exhibitions, 2007.

Connelly, Mark. *The Response to Prostitution*. Chapel Hill: University of North Carolina Press, 1980.

Corbett, David Peters. *An American Experiment*. New Haven: Yale University Press, 2011.

Coyle, Heather, and Joyce Schiller. *John Sloan's New York*. Wilmington and New Haven: Delaware Art Museum and Yale University Press, 2007.

Cresswell, Jim. *The Tramp in America*. London: Reaktion Books, 2001.

Davis, Michael Marks, Jr. *The Exploitation of Pleasure*. New York: Russell Sage Foundation, 1911.

De Casseres, Benjamin. *James Gibbons Huneker*. New York: Joseph Lawrence, 1925.

Degler, Carl. *Out of Our Past*. New York: Harper and Row, 1959.

De Forest, Robert, and Lawrence Veiller, ed. *The Tenement House Problem*. New York: Macmillan, 1903.

Deshazo, Edith. *Everett Shinn, 1876–1953*. New York: Clarkson N. Potter, 1974.

Doezema, Marianne. *American Realism and the Industrial Age*. Cleveland: Cleveland Museum of Art, 1981.

———. *George Bellows and Urban America*. New Haven: Yale University Press, 1992.

Dos Passos, John. *Manhattan Transfer*. Boston: Houghton Mifflin, 1925.

Dreiser, Theodore. *Sister Carrie*. New York: Pocket Books, 2008.

———. *The Color of a Great City*. New York: Boni and Liveright, 1923.

———. *The "Genius."* New York: John Lane, 1915.

———. *Twelve Men*. New York: Boni and Liveright, 1919.

du Bois, Guy Pène. *Artists Say the Silliest Things*. New York: American Artists Group, 1940.

———. *John Sloan*. New York: Whitney Museum of American Art, 1931.

———. *William Glackens*. New York: Whitney Museum of American Art, 1931.

Eggers, George. *George Bellows*. New York: Whitney Museum of American Art, 1931.

Elshtain, Jean Bethke, ed. *The Jane Addams Reader*. New York: Basic Books, 2002.

Elzea, Rowland. *John Sloan's Oil Paintings: A Catalogue Raisonne, 2*. Newark: University of Delaware Press, 1991.

Erenberg, Lewis. *Steppin' Out*. Chicago: University of Chicago Press, 1981.

The Eight. Owen Gallery, New York, Exhibition of Paintings, October 23–December 14, 2002.

Elzea, Rowland, and Elizabeth Hawkes. *John Sloan—Spectator of Life*. Wilmington: Delaware Art Museum, 1988.

Faulkner, Harold. *Politics, Reform and Expansion*. New York: Harper and Row, 1959.

Fitzgerald, Richard. *Art and Politics*. Westport: Greenwood Press, 1973.

Flanagan, Maureen. *America Reformed*. New York: Oxford University Press, 2007.

Foner, Moe. *Not for Bread Alone*. Ithaca: Cornell University Press, 2002.

Fraser, John Foster. *America at Work*. London: Cassell, 1903.

Friedman, Isaac K., with eighteen illustrations by W. Glackens. *The Autobiography of a Beggar*. Boston: Small, Maynard, 1903.

Gallati, Barbara. *William Merritt Chase*. New York: Harry N. Abrams, 1995.

Garraty, John. *The New Commonwealth*. New York: Harper and Row, 1968.

Gay, Ruth. *Unfinished People*. New York: W. W. Norton, 1996.

Gerdts, William. *Impressionist New York*. New York: Artabras, 1994.

Glackens, Ira. *William Glackens and the Eight*. New York: Writers and Readers, 1957.

Goodman, Cary. *Choosing Sides*. New York: Schocken Books, 1979.

Goodrich, Lloyd. *The Decade of the Armory Show.* New York: Whitney Museum of American Art, 1963.

———. *John Sloan.* New York: Whitney Museum of American Art, 1952.

———. *Kenneth Hayes Miller.* New York: Zabriskie Gallery, 1979.

———. *Raphael Soyer.* New York: Whitney Museum of American Art, 1967.

———. *Reginald Marsh.* New York: Whitney Museum of American Art, 1955.

———. *Thomas Eakins.* New York: Whitney Museum of American Art, 1933.

Goosen, E. C. *Stuart Davis.* New York: George Braziller, 1959.

Gorn, Elliott. *The Manly Art.* Ithaca: Cornell University Press, 1986.

Grant, Madison. *The Passing of the Great Race.* New edition, revised. New York: Charles Scribner's Sons, 1918.

Griffin, Randall. *Homer, Eakins, and Anshutz.* University Park: University of Pennsylvania Press, 2004.

———. *Thomas Anshutz: Artist and Teacher.* Seattle: Heckscher Museum, 1994.

Hall, Sir Peter. *Cities in Civilization.* New York: Pantheon Books. 1998.

Hapgood, Hutchins. *Types from the City Streets.* New York: Funk and Wagnalls, 1910.

Haverstock, Mary Sayre. *George Bellows: An Artist in Action.* London: Merrell, 2007.

Henri, Robert. *The Art Spirit.* New York: J. B. Lippincott, 1923. Icon Edition, Boulder: Westview Press, 1984.

Herbert, Robert. *Impressionism.* New Haven: Yale University Press, 1988.

Hiesinger, Ulrich. *Childe Hassam.* Munich: Prestel, 1999.

Higham, John. *Strangers in the Land.* New York: Atheneum, 1972.

Hills, Patricia. *Raphael Soyer's New York People and Places.* New York: Cooper Union, 1984.

Hills, Patricia, and Roberta Tarbell. *The Figurative Tradition and the Whitney Museum of American Art.* London: Associated University Press, 1980.

Hofstadter, Richard. *Social Darwinism in American Thought.* Boston: Beacon Press, 1955.

Holcomb, Grant, III. *Jerome Myers.* New York: Kraushaar Galleries, 1970.

Homer, William Innes. *Robert Henri and His Circle.* Ithaca: Cornell University Press, 1969.

Howells, William Dean. *A Hazard of New Fortunes.* New York: Harper and Brothers, 1891.

Hughes, Rupert. *The Real New York.* London: Hutchinson, 1905.

Hunter, Robert. *Poverty.* New York: Macmillan, 1904.

Huthmacher, J. Joseph. *Massachusetts People and Politics.* New York: Atheneum Press, 1969.

John Sloan/Robert Henri: Their Philadelphia Years (1866–1904). Philadelphia: Moore College of Art, 1976.

Johns, Elizabeth. *Thomas Eakins.* Princeton: Princeton University Press, 1983.

Kaplan, Amy. *The Social Construction of American Realism.* Chicago: University of Chicago Press, 1988.

Kasson, John. *Amusing the Million.* New York: Hill and Wang, 1978.

Kennedy, Elizabeth, ed. *The Eight and American Modernisms.* Chicago: University of Chicago Press, 2009.

Kent, Rockwell. *It's Me O Lord.* New York: Dodd, Mead, 1955.

Kessner, Thomas. *Capital City.* New York: Simon and Schuster, 2003.

Kleeblatt, Norman, and Susan Chevlowe, eds. *Painting a Place in America.* New York: The Jewish Museum, 1991.

Kuhn, Walt. *The Story of the Armory Show.* New York: Walt Kuhn, 1938. (Note: Kuhn was executive secretary of the Armory Show exhibit.)

Kushner, Marilyn Satin, Kimberly Orcutt, and Casey Blake. *The Armory Show at 100.* New York: New-York Historical Society, 2013.

Lallemand, Henri. *Manet.* New York: Todtri, 1994.

Levin, Gail. *Edward Hopper: The Art and the Artist.* New York: W.W. Norton, 1980.

Levine, Lawrence. *Highbrow/Lowbrow.* Cambridge: Harvard University Press, 1988.

Loomis, Samuel Lane. *Modern Cities and Their Religious Problems.* New York: Baker and Taylor, 1887.

Loughery, John. *John Sloan.* New York: Henry Holt, 1995.

Lyons, Deborah, Adam Weinberg, and Julie Grau, eds. *Edward Hopper and the American Imagination.* New York: Whitney Museum, 1995.

Mathews, Nancy. *Moving Pictures.* Williamstown: Williams College Museum of Art, 2005.

Matthews, Brander. *The Oxford Book of American Essays.* New York: Oxford University Press, 1914.

May, Henry. *The End of American Innocence.* Chicago: Quadrangle Books, 1959.

McAdoo, William. *Guarding a Great City.* New York: Harper and Brothers, 1906.

McGerr, Michael. *A Fierce Discontent*. New York: Oxford University Press, 2003.

Meyer, Edith. *"Not Charity, But Justice": The Story of Jacob A. Riis*. New York: Vanguard Press, 1974.

Miles, William Sonntag. *William L. Sonntag 1882–1899; William L. Sonntag, Jr. 1869–1898*. Boston: Vose Galleries, 1970.

Miller, James, Jr., ed. *Complete Poetry and Selected Prose by Walt Whitman*. Boston: Houghton Mifflin, 1959.

Milroy, Elizabeth. *Painters of a New Century: The Eight*. Milwaukee: Milwaukee Art Museum, 1991.

Moore, George. *Modern Painting*. New edition, enlarged. London: Walter Scott, 1906.

Morgan, Charles. *George Bellows: Painter of America*. New York: Reynal, 1965.

Mowry, George. *The Era of Theodore Roosevelt*. New York: Harper and Row, 1958.

Mrozek, Donald. *Sport and American Mentality, 1880–1910*. Knoxville: University of Tennessee Press, 1983.

Myers, Jerome. *The Artist in Manhattan*. New York: American Artists Group, 1940.

Nasaw, David. *Children of the City*. Garden City: Doubleday, 1985.

———. *Going Out*. New York: Basic Books, 1993.

Neret, Giles. *Edouard Manet*. Paris: Taschen, 2008.

Nemerov, Alexander. *To Make a World: George Ault and 1940s America*. Washington, DC: Smithsonian American Art Museum, 2011.

Nochlin, Linda. *Realism and Tradition in Art, 1848–1900*. Englewood Cliffs: Prentice-Hall, 1966.

Novak, Barbara. *American Painting of the Nineteenth Century*. New York: Praeger, 1969.

Nugent, Frances. *George Bellows: American Painter*. Chicago: Rand-McNally, 1963.

Oates, Joyce Carol. *George Bellows*. Hopewell: Ecco Press, 1995.

Outcault, R. F. *R. F. Outcault's The Yellow Kid*. Northampton: Kitchen Sink Press, 1995.

Pach, Walter. *Queer Thing Painting*. New York: Harper and Brothers, 1938.

Paley, Grace. *Long Walks and Intimate Talks*. New York: City University of New York Feminist Press, 1991.

Pennell, Joseph. *Joseph Pennell's Pictures of the Wonder of Work*. Philadelphia: J. B. Lippincott, 1916.

Perlman, Bennard. *Painters of the Ashcan School*. New York: Dover, 1979.

———. *Robert Henri: His Life and Art*. New York: Dover, 1991.

———. *Revolutionaries of Realism*. Princeton: Princeton University Press, 1997.

Peterson, Brian. *The Cities, the Towns, the Crowds: The Paintings of Robert Spencer*. Philadelphia: University of Pennsylvania Press, 2004.

Philpott, Thomas. *The Slum and the Ghetto*. New York: Oxford University Press, 1978.

Quick, Michael, Jane Myers, Marianne Doezema, and Franklin Kelley. *The Paintings of George Bellows*. New York: Harry N. Abrams, 1992.

Ramirez, Jan Seidler, ed. *Painting the Town*. New York: Museum of the City of New York, 2000.

Riess, Steven. *City Games*. Urbana: University of Illinois Press, 1989.

Riis, Jacob. *How the Other Half Lives*. New York: Dover, 1971.

The Role of the Macbeth Gallery. New York: American Federation of Arts, 1962.

Roosevelt, Theodore. *An Autobiography*. New York: Macmillan, 1913.

Ross, Steven. *Working-Class Hollywood*. Princeton: Princeton University Press, 1999.

Rosenblum, Robert, Maryanne Stevens, and Ann Dumas. *1900: Art at the Crossroads*. New York: Harry N. Abrams, 2000.

St. John, Bruce, ed. *John Sloan's New York Scene*. New York: Harper and Row, 1965.

Sampsell-Willmann, Kate. *Lewis Hine as Social Critic*. Jackson: University Press of Mississippi, 2009.

Schapiro, Meyer. *Modern Art*. New York: George Braziller, 1979.

Schlesinger, Arthur, Jr. *The Crisis of the Old Order*. Boston: Houghton Mifflin, 1957.

Schreiber, Rachel. *Gender and Activism in a Little Magazine*. Burlington: Ashgate, 2011.

Schwab, Arnold. *James Gibbons Huneker*. Stanford: Stanford University Press, 1963.

Schwab, Arnold, ed. *Americans in the Arts: Critiques by James Gibbons Huneker*. New York: A.M.S. Press, 1985.

Schwartz, Constance. *The Shock of Modernism in America*. Roslyn Harbor: Nassau County Museum of Fine Art, 1984.

Schwartz, Vanessa. *Spectacular Realities*. Berkeley: University of California Press, 1998.

Scott, David, and E. John Bullard. *John Sloan, 1871–1951*. Boston: Boston Book and Art, 1972.

Scott, William, and Peter Rutkoff. *New York Modern*. Baltimore: Johns Hopkins University Press, 1999.

Shackleton, Robert. *The Book of New York*. Philadelphia: Penn, 1920.

Shi, David. *Facing Facts*. New York: Oxford University Press, 1995.

Sims, Lowery. *Stuart Davis: American Painter*. New York: Metropolitan Museum of Art, 1991.

Sinclair, Upton. *The Moneychangers*. New York: B. W. Dodge, 1908.

Sloan, Helen Farr, ed. *John Sloan: New York Etchings (1905–1949)*. New York: Dover, 1978.

Sloan, John. *The Gist of Drawing*. Wilmington: Delaware Art Museum, 1997.

———. *John Sloan on Drawing and Painting (Gist of Art)*. Mineola: Dover, 1944, 1977. Also: *The Gist of Art*. New York: American Artists Group, 1939.

Smith, Betty. *A Tree Grows in Brooklyn*. New York: Harper and Brothers, 1943.

Sontag, Susan. *Against Interpretation and Other Essays*. New York: Farrar, Straus and Giroux, 1966.

Stallman, Robert, ed. *Stephen Crane: Stories and Tales*. New York: Vintage Books, 1962.

Stansell, Christine. *American Moderns*. New York: Henry Holt, 2000.

Stange, Maren. *Symbols of Ideal Life*. Cambridge: Cambridge University Press, 1989.

Stary-Sheets, David. *California Style 1930s and 40s*. Sebastopol: Sebastopol Center for the Arts, 1997.

Strong, Josiah. *Our Country: Its Possible Future and Its Present Crisis*. New York: American Home Missionary Society, 1885.

Sussman, Elisabeth, with John Hanhardt. *City of Ambition*. New York: Whitney Museum of American Art, 1996.

Swados, Harvey, ed. *Years of Conscience*. Cleveland: World, 1962.

Swinth, Kirsten. *Painting Professionals*. Chapel Hill: University of North Carolina Press, 2001.

Taylor, William. *In Pursuit of Gotham*. New York: Oxford University Press, 1992.

Todd, Ellen Wiley. *The "New Woman" Revised*. Berkeley: University of California Press, 1993.

Tottis, James, Valerie Ann Leeds, Vincent DiGirolamo, Marianne Doezema, and Suzanne Smeaton, with contributions from Michael Cane and Kirsten Olds. *Life's Pleasures*. London: Merrell, 2007.

Van Dyke, John. *The New New York*. New York: Macmillan, 1909.

Von Saldern, Axel. *Triumph of Realism*. New York: Brooklyn Museum, 1967.

Wagner, Ann. *1934: A New Deal for Artists*. Washington, DC: Smithsonian American Art Museum, 2009.

Wald, Lillian. *The House on Henry Street*. New York: Henry Holt, 1915.

Wardle, Marian, ed. *American Women Modernists*. Salt Lake City: Brigham Young University Museum of Art, 2005.

Weaver, Jane, ed. *Sadakichi Hartmann: Critical Modernist*. Berkeley: University of California Press, 1991.

Weber, Bruce. *Ashcan Kids: Children in the Art of Henri, Luks, Glackens, Bellows and Sloan*. New York: Berry-Hill Galleries, 1999.

Weinberg, H. Barbara. *Childe Hassam*. New York: Metropolitan Museum of Art, 2004.

Weinberg, H. Barbara, Doreen Bolger, and David Park Curry. *American Impressionism and Realism*. New York: Metropolitan Museum of Art, 1994.

Weinberg, H. Barbara, and Carrie Rebora Barratt, eds. *American Stories*. New Haven: Yale University Press, 2009.

Wertheim, Arthur Frank. *The New York Little Renaissance*. New York: New York University Press, 1976.

Wharton, Edith. *The House of Mirth*. London: Virago Press, 1990.

White. E. B. *Here Is New York*. New York: The Little Bookroom, 1949.

White, William Allen. *The Autobiography of William Allen White*. New York: Macmillan, 1946.

Yochelson, Bonnie, and Daniel Czitrom. *Rediscovering Jacob Riis*. New York: The New Press, 2007.

Young, Mahonri Sharp. *The Eight*. New York: Watson-Guptill, 1973.

Zurier, Rebecca. *Art for the Masses*. Philadelphia: Temple University Press, 1988.

———. *Picturing the City*. Berkeley: University of California Press, 2006.

Zurier, Rebecca, Robert Snyder, and Virginia Mecklenburg. *Metropolitan Lives*. New York: National Museum of American Art in Association with W. W. Norton, 1995.

Articles

Alper, M. Victor. "American Mythologies in Painting, Part 2: City Life and Social Idealism." *Arts* 46 (December 1971–January 1972): 31–34.

Arnavon, Cyrille. "Theodore Dreiser and Painting." *American Literature* 17.2 (May 1945): 113–126.

Arts & Decoration. March 1913. (Special exhibition number on the Armory Show.)

Baigell, Matthew. "Notes on Realistic Painting and Photography, c. 1900–1910." *Arts Magazine* 54 (November 1979): 141–143.

Baker, John. "Voyeurism in the Art of John Sloan." *The Art Quarterly* 1 (1978): 379–396.

Baker, Kevin, "New York Was So Much Older Then." *New York Times*. Sunday Opinion Section. January 18, 2009.

Barrell, Charles Wisner. "The Real Drama of the Slums, as Told in John Sloan's Etchings." *The Craftsman* 15 (February 1909): 559–564.

Baury, Louis. "The Message of Manhattan." *The Bookman* 33 (August 1911): 603–612.

———. "The Message of Proletaire." *The Bookman* 34 (December 1911): 399–413.

Berman, Avis. "Artist as Rebel: John Sloan vs. the Status Quo." *Smithsonian* 19.1 (April 1988): 74–84.

"The Big Idea: George Bellows Talks about Patriotism for Beauty." *The Touchstone* 1 (July 1917): 269–275.

Blazier, Wendy. "Selections from the Bank of America Collection." *American Art Review* 20 (May–June 2008): 72–79.

Boyesen, Bayard. "The National Note in American Art." *Putnam's Monthly* 5.3 (May 1908): 130–140.

Boylan, Alexis. "Neither Tramp nor Hobo: Images of Unemployment in the Art of the Ashcan School." *Prospects* 20 (2005): 433–450.

Broun, Elizabeth. "Childe Hassam's America." *American Art* 13.3 (Autumn 1999): 32–57.

Brown, Joshua. "A Spectator of Life—A Reverential, Enthusiastic, Emotional Spectator." *American Quarterly* 49.2 (June 1997): 356–384.

Brown, Milton. "The Ash Can School." *American Quarterly* 1.2 (Summer 1949): 127–134.

———. "The Two John Sloans." *Art News* 50 (January 1952): 24–27, 56–57.

Burchfield, Charles. "Hopper: Career of Silent Poetry." *Art News* 49 (March 1950): 15–18.

Burrey, Suzanne. "Edward Hopper: The Emptying Spaces." *Arts Digest* 1 (April 1955): 8–10.

C.A.Z. "Henri and Manship." *The Little Review* II (October 1915): 38–39.

Canaday, John. "George Bellows and the End of a World Picasso Never Knew." *New York Times*. March 31, 1966.

Chambers, Bruce. "Robert Henri's Street Scene with Snow (57th Street, NYC): An Idea of City in 'Snow Effect.'" *Yale University Art Gallery Bulletin* 39 (Winter 1986): 30–39.

Clifford, Henry. "Artists of the Philadelphia Press: William Glackens, George Luks, Everett Shinn, John Sloan, October 14–November 18, 1945." *Philadelphia Museum Bulletin* 11.207 (November 1945): 1–32.

"Congregational Missions." *New York Times*. June 6, 1902.

Corbett, David. "Ashcan Perspectives." *Journal of American Studies* 39 (2009): 535–542.

Corbin, John. "The Twentieth Century City." *Scribner's Magazine* 33.3 (March 1903): 259–272.

Corn, Wanda. "The New New York." *Art in America* (July–August 1973): 58–65.

Cortissoz, Royal. "Art Exhibitions." *New York Tribune*, February 5, 1908.

———. "Independent Art: Some Reflections on Its Claims and Obligations." *New York Tribune*. April 10, 1910.

Cotter, Holland. "Rethinking the Armory Show." *New York Times*. Fine Arts and Exhibits Section. October 28, 2012.

Cournos, John. "Three Painters of the New York School." *The International Studio* 56 (1915): 239–246.

Craven, Thomas. "The Independent Exhibition." *The New Republic*. March 14, 1923. 70–71.

Croly, Herbert. "New York as the American Metropolis." *Architectural Record* 13.3 (March 1903): 193–206.

DeKay, Charles. "Eight-Man Show at Macbeth's." *New York Post*. February 7, 1908.

———. "Six Impressionists: Startling Works by Red-Hot American Painters." *New York Times*. January 20, 1904.

Dinnerstein, Harvey, and Bert Silverman. "New Look at Protest: The Eight since 1908." *Art News* 56 (February 1958): 36–39.

Dow, Arthur Wesley. "Modernism in Art." *The American Magazine of Art* 8 (January 1917): 113–116.

Dreiser, Theodore. "'The Cliff Dwellers': A Painting by George Bellows." *Vanity Fair* 55 (December 1925): 55, 118.

du Bois, Guy Pène. "Robert Henri: The Man." *Arts and Decoration* 14 (November 1920): 36, 76.

Edgerton, Giles. "The Younger American Painters: Are They Creating a National Art?" *The Craftsman* 13 (February 1908): 512–532.

"'The Eight' Exhibit New Art Realism." *New York American*. February 4, 1908.

"Eight Independent Painters." *New York Sun*. May 15, 1907.

Ely, C. B. "The Modern Tendency in Henri, Sloan, and Bellows." *Art in America and Elsewhere* 10 (1922): 132–143.

Engel, Charlene Stant. "The Realist's Eye: The Illustrations and Lithographs of George W. Bellows." *Print Review* 10 (1979): 70–86.

Fairman, Deborah. "The Landscape of Display: The Ashcan School, Spectacle, and the Staging of Everyday Life." *Prospects* 18 (1993): 205–235.

Gallatin, Albert. "The Art of William J. Glackens." *The International Studio* 15 (May 1910): lxviii.

Gambone, Robert. "George Luks, 'Hogan's Alley,' and Ashcan School Social Thought." *Aurora: The Journal of the History of Art* 6 (2005): 38–78.

"George Bellows, an Artist with 'Red Blood.'" *Current Literature* 53.3 (September 1912): 342–345.

"George Luks, Lusty Proponent of American Individualism, Is Dead." *The Art Digest* 8.4 (November 15, 1933): 5–6.

Getelein, Frank. "The Legacy of Edward Hopper, Painter of Light and Loneliness." *Smithsonian* 2 (September 1971): 60–67.

Gold, Susanna. "A Timely 'Look' at the Ashcan School." *Reviews in American History* 35.4 (December 2007): 606–613.

Goldin, Amy. "The Eight's Laissez Faire Revolution." *Art in America* (July–August 1973): 42–49.

Griffin, Randall. "Thomas Anshutz's 'The Ironworkers' Noontime': Remythologizing the Industrial Worker." *Smithsonian Studies in American Art* 4.¾ (Summer–Autumn 1990): 128–143.

Harris, James. "Nighthawks." *Archives of General Psychiatry* 63.7 (July 2006): 715–716.

Hartmann, Sadakichi. "Studio-Talk." *The International Studio* 30 (December 1906): 178–183.

Haywood, Robert. "George Bellows' 'Stag at Sharkey's': Boxing, Violence, and Male Identity." *Smithsonian Studies in American Art* 2.2 (Spring 1988): 2–15.

Henri, Robert. "My People." *The Craftsman* 27.5 (February 1915): 459–469.

———. "A Practical Talk to Those Who Study Art." *The Philadelphia Press*. May 12, 1901.

———. "Progress in Our National Art Must Spring from the Development of Individuality of Ideas and Freedom of Expression." *The Craftsman* 15.4 (January 1909): 387–401.

———. "What About Art in America?" *Arts and Decoration* 24.1 (November 1925): 35–37, 75.

Hills, Patricia. "John Sloan's Images of Working-Class Women." *Prospects* 5 (1980): 167–196.

Hirschfeld, Charles. "'Ash Can' vs. 'Modern' Art in America." *The Western Humanities Review* 10 (Autumn 1956): 353–373.

Hirshler, Erica. "The 'New New York' and the Park Row Building: American Artists View an Icon of the Modern Age." *American Art Journal* 21.4 (Winter 1989): 26–45.

Hoeber, Arthur. "Art and Artists." *The Globe and Commercial Advertiser* (New York). February 5, 1908.

Holcomb, Grant. "The Forgotten Legacy of Jerome Myers, (1867–1940)." *American Art Journal* 9 (May 1977): 78–91.

———. "John Sloan and 'McSorley's Wonderful Saloon.'" *American Art Journal* 15.2 (Spring 1983): 4–20.

Homer, William. "The Exhibition of 'The Eight': Its History and Significance." *American Art Journal* 1.1 (Spring 1969): 53–64.

———. "Stieglitz and 291." *Art in America* (July–August 1973): 50–57.

Hopper, Edward. "John Sloan and the Philadelphians." *The Arts* 11.4 (April 1927): 168–178.

Howells, William Dean. "Editor's Study." *Harper's New Monthly Magazine* 79 (August 1889): 476–481.

Huneker, James. "George Luks." *New York Sun*. March 21, 1907.

———. "George Luks, Versatile Painter of Humanity." *New York Times Magazine*. February 6, 1916, 13.

Huneker, James. "Growing Pains of American Art." *Current Literature* 44.4 (April 1908): 393–397.

Hunter, Sam. "'The Eight'—Insurgent Realists." *Art in America* 44 (Fall 1956): 20–22, 56–58.

"In Defense of Pugilism." *American Magazine* (August 1909): 414–416.

Ives, A. E. "Mr. Childe Hassam on Painting Street Scenes." *Art Amateur* 27.5 (October 1892): 116–117.

"Jerome Myers as an Etcher and a Student of Human Nature." *The Craftsman* 29.1 (October 1915): 25–32.

Johnson, Ken. "Ashcan Views of New Yorkers, Warts, High Spirits and All." *New York Times*. December 28, 2007.

Keny, James. "Brief Garland: A Life of George Bellows." *Timeline* 9 (October–December 1992): 2–39.

Kinser, Suzanne. "Prostitutes in the Art of John Sloan." *Prospects* 9 (1985): 231–254.

Kramer, Hilton. "The Unhappy Fate of Hayes Miller." *New York Times*. March 11, 1979.

Kuspit, Donald. "Individual and Mass Identity in Urban Arts: The New York Case." *Art in America* 65 (September–October 1977): 66–77.

Kwiat, Joseph. "John Sloan: An American Artist as Social Critic, 1900–1917." *Arizona Quarterly* 10 (Spring 1954): 52–64.

Lanes, Jerrold. "Edward Hopper: French Formalist, Ashcan School Realist, Neither or Both?" *Artforum* 7 (October 1968): 44–50.

Lasky, David Jay. "The Lure of the Roof Is More Than Just Tar Beach." *New York Times*. June 21, 2008.

"Latest Fad in Portraiture." *New York World American Magazine Section*. February 9, 1908.

Liasson, Mara. "The Eight and 291: Radical Art in the First Two Decades of the Twentieth Century." *American Art Review* 2 (July–August 1975): 91–102.

Lobel, Michael. "John Sloan: Figuring the Painter in the Crowd." *Art Bulletin* 93.3 (September 2011): 345–368.

Loomis, Samuel Lane. "Foreigners and American Churches." *The Chautauquan* 17 (April–September 1993): 180–184.

———. "The Magnetic Influence of Great Cities." *Andover Review*, reprinted in *Public Opinion* 3.1 (April 16, 1887), 36.

Louchheim, Aline. "Last of 'The Eight' Looks Back." *New York Times*. November 2, 1952.

Loughery, John. "The Mysterious George Luks." *Arts Magazine* 64.4 (December 1987): 34–35.

———. "The *New York Sun* and Modern Art in America: Charles Fitzgerald, Frederick Gregg, James Gibbons Huneker, Henry McBride." *Arts Magazine* 59 (December 1984): 77–82.

Low, Will. "National Art in a National Metropolis." *The International Quarterly* 6 (September–December 1902): 107–126.

Maciejunes, Nannette. "Master of the Stone: The Lithography of George Bellows." *Timeline* 9 (October–December 1992): 40–67.

Marquis, Albert Nelson. "Samuel Lane Loomis." *Who's Who in New England*. Chicago: A. N. Marquis, 1909. 601.

Marsh, Reginald. "What I See in Laning's Art." *Creative Art* 12 (March 1933): 187–188.

Martin, Edward. "Manhattan Lights." *Harper's Magazine* 114 (February 1907): 359–367.

McIntyre, Robert. "George Bellows—An Appreciation." *Art and Progress* 3 (August 1912): 679–682.

Mecklenburg, Virginia. "New York City and the Ashcan School." *Antiques Magazine*. November 1995, http://findarticles.com/p/articles/mi_m1026/is_n5_v148/ai_17743158. Accessed July 25, 2008.

Moss, Jeremiah. "Nighthawks State of Mind." *New York Times*. July 5, 2010.

Naves, Mario. "Glackens, Sloan and Friends: The Ashcan Artists' New York." *New Criterion* 14.10 (June 1996): 48.

"New York, the Beauty City." *The Sun*. February 23, 1913.

"New York Realists." *Time*. February 22, 1937. http://www.time.com/time/magazine/article/0,9171,770622,00.html. Accessed August 8, 2009.

Newman, Sarah. "George Bellows 'New York' and the Spectacular Reality of the City." *American Art* 18.3 (Autumn 2004): 92–99.

Pach, Walter. "Manet and Modern American Art." *The Craftsman* 17 (February 1910): 483–492.

Pauly, Thomas. "American Art and Labor: The Case of Anshutz's 'The Ironworkers' Noontime.'" *American Quarterly* 40.3 (September 1988): 333–358.

Pennell, Joseph. "The World of Work in the Northwest." *Harper's Monthly Magazine* 132 (March 1916): 591–600.

Pittenger, Mark. "A World of Difference: Constructing the 'Underclass' in Progressive America." *American Quarterly* 49.1 (March 1977): 26–65.

Plagens, Peter. "The Critics: Hartmann, Huneker, De Casseres." *Art in America* (July–August 1973): 66–71.

Read, Lolan C., Jr. "The New York School of Art." *The Sketch Book* 3.8 (April 1904): 219–223.

Reed, John. "Almost Thirty." *New Republic* 86 (April 29, 1936): 332–336.

Ries, Estelle. "The Relation of Art to Every-Day Things: An Interview with George Bellows." *Arts and Decoration* 15 (July 1921): 158–160, 202–203.

"Robert Henri, an Apostle of Artistic Individuality." *Current Literature* 52.4 (April 1912): 464–469.

Roberts, Mary Fanton. "John Sloan: His Art and Its Inspiration." *The Touchstone and the American Art Student Magazine* 4 (February 1919): 362–370.

Roosevelt, Theodore. "A Layman's View of an Art Exhibition." *Outlook* 103 (March 29, 1913): 718–720.

Rotundo, E. Anthony. "Body and Soul: Changing Ideals of American Middle Class Manhood." *Journal of Social History* 16.4 (Summer 1983): 23–38.

Ruthrauff, Florence Barlow. "Robert Henri—Master of Painters." *Fine Arts Journal* 27 (July 1912): 463–466.

Shinn, Everett. "Recollections of the Eight." *The Eight*. New York: Brooklyn Museum, 1944. 11–22.

Simons, David. "Hometown." *Timeline* 9 (October–December 1992): 68–78.

Singal, Daniel. "Towards a Definition of American Modernism." *American Quarterly* 39.1 (Spring 1987): 7–26.

Spargo, John. "George Luks, an American Painter of Great Originality and Force, Whose Art Relates to All the Experiences and Interests of Life." *The Craftsman* 12.6 (September 1907): 599–607.

"The Spring Academy." *New York Sun*. March 17, 1911.

Stalter, Sunny. "Picturing the City: Urban Vision and the Ashcan School (Review)." *Modernism/modernity* 15.1 (January 2008): 191–193.

"Striking Pictures by Eight 'Rebels.'" *New York Herald*. February 4, 1908.

Swift, Samuel. "Revolutionary Figures in American Art." *Harper's Weekly* 51 (April 13, 1907): 534–536.

Tonks, Oliver. "Robert Henri—An Appreciation." *The American Museum of Art* 7.12 (October 1916): 473–479.

Townsend, James. "'The Eight' Arrive." *American Art News* 6.17 (February 8, 1908): 6.

Townsend, Kathleen Kennedy. "The Henri Hurrah." *American Art News* 5.23 (March 23, 1907): 6.

———. "Walt Whitman and the Soul of Democracy." *The Atlantic*. July 8, 2011. http://www.theatlantic. com/national/archive/2011/07/walt-whitman-and-the-soul-of-democracy/241558/. Accessed October 1, 2015.

Traubel, Horace. "Thomas Eakins." *The Conservator* 28 (February 1918): 184–186.

Tridon, Andre. "America's First Aesthetician." *Forum* 55 (January 1916): 124–129.

Tyrrell, Henry. "The Battle of Artists." *New York World*. June 5, 1910.

Van Rensselaer, Mariana. "Fifth Avenue." *Century Illustrated Magazine* 47.1 (November 1893): 5–19.

Wall, James. "The Ashcan School: Transition in American Art." *The South Atlantic Quarterly* 69.3 (June 1970): 317–326.

Watson, Forbes. "John Sloan." *Magazine of Art* 45.2 (February 1952): 62–70.

———. "Realism Undefeated." *Parnassus* 9.3 (March 1937): 11–14, 37–38.

Weintraub, Laural. "Women as Urban Spectators in John Sloan's Early Work." *American Art* 15.2 (Summer 2001): 72–83.

Wilentz, Sean. "Low Life, High Art." *The New Republic* 207 (September 28, 1992): 41–44.

Williams, Jesse Lynch. "The Cross Streets of New York." *Scribner's Magazine* 28 (November 1900): 582–584.

Yablon, Nick. "John Sloan and 'the Roof Life of the Metropolis.'" *American Art* 25.2 (Summer 2011): 14–17.

Yardley, Joseph. "Joseph Yardley on 'The Lost Art of Walking.'" *Washington Post*. November 9, 2008.

Yount, Sylvia. "Consuming Drama: Everett Shinn and the Spectacular City." *American Art* 6.4 (Autumn 1992): 86–109.

Zilczer, Judith. "The Armory Show and the American Avant-Garde: A Re-Evaluation." *Arts Magazine* 53.1 (September 1978): 126–129.

———. "The Eight on Tour, 1908–1909." *American Art Journal* 16.3 (Summer 1984): 20–48.

Dissertations and Theses

Bukoff, Ronald. "Childe Hassam: Cityscapes, 1885–1900." MA thesis, Indiana University, 1979.

Bullard, Edgar John, III. "John Sloan and the Philadelphia Realists as Illustrators." MA thesis, University of California, 1968.

Coleman, David. "The Social Commentary of John Sloan, 1900–1916, in the Context of American Progressivism." MA thesis, University of California, Berkeley, 1972.

Kies, Emily. "The City and the Machine: Urban and Industrial Illustration in America, 1880–1900." PhD dissertation, Columbia University, 1971.

Ricciotti, Dominic. "The Urban Scene: Images of the City in American Painting, 1890–1930." PhD dissertation, Indiana University, 1977.

Seiberling, Frank, Jr. "George Bellows, 1882–1925." PhD dissertation, University of Chicago, 1948.

Skalet, Linda Henefeld. "The Market for American Painting in New York, 1870–1915." PhD Dissertation, Johns Hopkins University, 1980.

Manuscript Collections

Jerome Myers Papers, Helen Farr Sloan Library and Archives, Delaware Art Museum, Wilmington, Delaware.

John Sloan Papers, Helen Farr Sloan Library and Archives, Delaware Art Museum, Wilmington, Delaware.

Macbeth Gallery Records, Archives of American Art, Smithsonian Institution, Washington, DC.

New York City Municipal Archives Online Gallery, New York City Department of Records.

Robert Henri Papers, Archives of American Art, Smithsonian Institution, Washington, DC.

Film

Helen Farr Sloan: An Artistic Vision. Wilmington: Teleduction, 2000.

The Crowd. MGM, 1928.

Index